# FRACTURED
# REBELLION

# FRACTURED REBELLION

The Beijing Red Guard Movement

*Andrew G. Walder*

*Harvard University Press*

*Cambridge, Massachusetts*

*London, England*

First Harvard University Press paperback edition, 2012

*Library of Congress Cataloging-in-Publication Data*

Walder, Andrew G. (Andrew George), 1953–
Fractured rebellion : the Beijing Red Guard movement / Andrew G. Walder.
p.  cm.
Includes bibliographical references and index.
ISBN 978-0-674-03503-4 (cloth:alk. paper)
ISBN 978-0-674-06413-3 (pbk.)
1. China—History—Cultural Revolution, 1966–1976.
2. Hong wei bing—History—20th century. 3. Protest movements—China—
Beijing—History—20th century. 4. Student movements—China—Beijing—History—20th
century. 5. Political violence—China—Beijing—History—20th century.
6. Social conflict—China—Beijing—History—20th century.
7. Zhongguo gong chan dang—History—20th century. 8. Beijing (China)—
History—20th century. 9. Beijing (China)—Social conditions—20th century.
10. Beijing (China)—Politics and government—20th century. I. Title.
DS778.7.W33  2009
951.05'6—dc22      2009001689

*To Jean*

# CONTENTS

# TABLES

# ACKNOWLEDGMENTS

Several colleagues and friends were indispensable sources of documents, information, and advice. Among the most important are Michael Schoenhals, Song Yongyi, Yin Hongbiao, and Wang Youqin. Special thanks go to Michael Schoenhals, who combines a masterful command of Cultural Revolution history and documentation with a remarkable generosity toward students of the politics and history of the Mao era. Michael has provided so many documents, source citations, and other forms of intellectual guidance that it is impossible to specify them all in the endnotes, so I provide a blanket acknowledgment here. Song Yongyi has also provided more materials than I can name, in addition to his contributions as the editor of major documentary collections.

Many friends also provided inspiration. Years ago, when he was my senior colleague at Harvard, Rod MacFarquhar insisted on the value of new documentary sources on the Cultural Revolution and constantly reminded me that oral histories were not enough. Hong Yung Lee inspired my interest in this topic during my first year of graduate school at the University of Michigan, where he worked as a postdoctoral fellow on his pathbreaking interest-group interpretation of Cultural Revolution politics. Readers of this book will understand what an important influence his work has been in shaping the questions whose answers I pursue in these pages. I am also very grateful to Doug McAdam, Fred Teiwes, and Jeff Wasserstrom for sympathetic critical readings of a much longer earlier draft of this book. I have been only partially successful in responding to their many suggestions.

My first explorations of this subject were funded by fellowships from the John Simon Guggenheim Memorial Foundation and the Wang Institute for Chinese Studies. Subsequent funding was provided by the Henry

Luce Foundation in a grant to the Fairbank Center for East Asian Research at Harvard. A grant from the Chiang Ching-kuo Foundation provided time to begin writing. I have also received generous support from the Shorenstein Asia-Pacific Research Center, the Freeman-Spogli Institute for International Studies, and the School of Humanities and Sciences at Stanford University. None of these organizations is responsible for what I have written here.

Several libraries provided much-needed assistance. At Harvard, the Fairbank Center Library (Nancy Hearst) and Harvard-Yenching Library (Eugene Wu) were very generous, especially in the early stages of my work. The Universities Service Centre Library at the Chinese University of Hong Kong (especially Jean Hung) deserves special thanks. I have also enjoyed the assistance and resources of the Centre Chine Library in Paris, the Shanghai Municipal Library, and the Beijing National Library. Closer to home, the East Asian Collection of the Hoover Institution was also very helpful.

Passages from earlier publications of mine are used in the present volume, with my thanks to the original publishers: "Beijing Red Guard Factionalism: Social Interpretations Reconsidered," *Journal of Asian Studies* 61 (May 2002): 437–471, © 2002 by The Association for Asian Studies, Inc.; "Tan Lifu: A 'Reactionary' Red Guard in Historical Perspective," *China Quarterly* 180 (December 2004): 965–988, © 2004 by The China Quarterly; "Factional Conflict at Beijing University, 1966–1968," *China Quarterly* 188 (December 2006): 1023–1047, © 2006 by The China Quarterly; and "Ambiguity and Choice in Political Movements: The Origins of Beijing Red Guard Factionalism," *American Journal of Sociology* 112 (November 2006), 710–750, © 2006 by The University of Chicago.

Finally, I would like to thank Jean Oi for her long encouragement of my work on the Cultural Revolution. For many years she has wondered why I was writing about the impact of China's economic reforms when such an interesting research topic was put on the back burner. I am sorry that I did not listen to her earlier. For this and many other reasons I dedicate this book to her.

# A NOTE ON DOCUMENTATION

The narrative accounts in this book unavoidably refer to a large number of individuals, both famous and obscure. I realize that this will likely create confusion, especially for readers unfamiliar with Chinese names and the history of the period. To reduce confusion, I refer to individuals by name only when necessary. To help identify individuals who are referred to repeatedly, I include brief biographical descriptions in the Glossary of Names.

I use only four abbreviations in the text: "CCP" for Chinese Communist Party, "PLA" for People's Liberation Army, "CCRG" for the Central Cultural Revolution Group, and "Beida" for Beijing University. In the notes, "CCRM" is used to refer to the compilations of red guard materials published by the Center for Chinese Research Materials.

# FRACTURED
# REBELLION

1

## THE BEIJING RED GUARDS

### *An Introduction*

For more than two full years after the middle of 1966, the world's largest communist state was torn apart by mass protests and chaotic local rebellions that in some regions escalated into virtual civil war. Not until August 1968 were the flames of China's Cultural Revolution extinguished by the imposition of a harsh regime of martial law. These two chaotic years of political warfare were the defining moment of the Mao era and a traumatic watershed in the history of the People's Republic of China, but the mass movements of this period remain inadequately documented and poorly understood.

The most puzzling feature of these upheavals was their intense factionalism. Seemingly everywhere, organized militants divided into two factions that fought each other for control of schools, workplaces, and local governments. Both sides pledged loyalty to Mao and the Communist Party; both portrayed their fight as a defense of the revolution and an attack on leaders who had betrayed the cause. In the nation's capital, student red guards were divided from the very inception of the movement in August 1966. These divisions rapidly evolved into a conflict between two alliances that dominated the early politics of Beijing's Cultural Revolution. After one side was defeated and denounced as "conservative" at the end of 1966, the victorious coalition immediately split into two completely new factions. Despite the constant entreaties of their elite sponsors and repeated attempts to force them to unite, the two sides fought with increasingly violent intensity until August 1968, when Mao Zedong ordered the army to occupy the campuses, disband student organizations, and detain their leaders for reeducation. Paralyzing factional conflict had turned the red guards into a frustrating political liability.

These factional divisions have long been viewed as the key to unlocking the central puzzles of the red guard movement. Who were these rebels, and what were their motivations? Why did they divide into two opposing groups and engage in violent warfare despite sharing a professed loyalty to Mao? Why did they refuse to unite despite repeated urgings by their elite sponsors? Answers to these questions, important in themselves, also promise to reveal how the structures of the regime and society generated such a large and distinctive mass movement—something that Mao and his followers evidently failed to understand.

Many have sought to explain the features of the red guard movement by referring to the character of Mao-era social and political institutions. Some claim that the intense political indoctrination of China's youth into the cult of Mao and the doctrines of class struggle created dogmatic mentalities of unquestioning loyalty that fueled the violence and intolerance of mobilized students.[1] Others argue that the Chinese political system enclosed citizens in social institutions where they were closely monitored, labeled politically in ways that affected their welfare and futures, and periodically subjected to stressful mass campaigns that left aggrieved victims in their wake—circumstances that contributed to the subsequent tumult.[2] Still others emphasize the evident passion and emotion of the student activists, especially the devotion to Chairman Mao that was such a striking feature of red guard rhetoric, doctrine, and artistic expression.[3]

These arguments bear directly on questions about the political mentalities of red guards and their propensity for violence. However, they apply equally to both sides of the conflict and do not differentiate the views and aims of the contending groups. Arguments that refer to general social conditions or to mentalities and beliefs presumably shared by all red guards do not help us explain what turned students against one another.[4] To explain factional divisions, we need to understand what issues divided students and why they joined one faction or another. This requires an even closer look at the social and political circumstances of the Mao era.

The mass movements of the period revealed much that previously had been unknown about the political and social inequalities of Mao-era China, and this information lent a great deal of surface plausibility to social interpretations of factions. It appeared that factions could be distinguished as either "conservative" or "radical" on the basis of their orientation to the status quo. A conservative orientation would logically appeal to people tied to the political establishment and otherwise favored by the regime. A more radical orientation would appeal to groups less favored.[5] Although the evidence was often circumstantial at best, and documentation was scarce, it seemed obvious that factional conflict was somehow rooted in the social inequalities of postrevolution China, which pitted those with vested interests in the status quo against those who sought to change it.[6]

The red guard movement, of course, did not emerge spontaneously. It was initiated and encouraged by China's highest political authorities. The decision to mobilize popular attacks on the structures of party and state was Mao Zedong's unique reaction to political frustrations that had grown out of the failures of his Great Leap Forward of 1958–1960 and the subsequent Sino-Soviet split. By the mid-1960s Mao had declared the Soviet Union a "revisionist" regime that was on the road back to capitalism. Nikita Khrushchev had relaxed the Soviet Union's confrontational stance toward the United States and spoke openly about peaceful coexistence. In declaring the end of arbitrary campaigns of repression, Khrushchev announced that there were no antagonistic class struggles under socialism, and that the mass persecutions of the Stalin years, justified as a search for hidden enemies of the revolution, were a tragic deviation in the history of socialism. Henceforth the superiority of socialism would be demonstrated through peaceful evolution: the ability to stimulate economic development and enhance popular welfare by employing the most advanced scientific methods of management and organization.[7]

During the preceding decade Mao had taken China in a very different direction, and the growing gap between his policies and rhetoric and those of the Soviet Union was a source of increasing tension and, for Mao, defeat and frustration. Against the resistance of other Chinese leaders, he had forced through his Hundred Flowers policy that encouraged open criticism of the party's shortcomings in early 1957. When the criticisms gathered force and students and workers began to organize protests, he lashed back with an anti-rightist campaign that ruined the lives of hundreds of thousands of victims, many of them educated party members, with punishments that ranged from labor camps to ruined careers.[8]

Immediately afterward Mao launched his Great Leap Forward, a massive mobilization campaign that promised vast increases in output simply by working faster, putting in longer hours, and casting aside conventional methods of cropping and industrial production. Instead, agriculture and industry collapsed, and the crisis deepened into one of the largest famines in Chinese history, during which 20 to 30 million people died. Industry was thrown into a depression that lasted until 1963.[9]

Mao backed down and turned the administration of the country over to others, but only after unleashing a second anti-rightist campaign that targeted those who had expressed criticism of the Great Leap Forward. Rural communes were scaled back, and in many regions collective agriculture was abandoned; forms of management previously denounced as "bourgeois" were restored; and bridges were rebuilt to the educated elite both within and outside the party with a thaw in literature and arts and a more respectful stance toward experts.[10]

Mao soon began to insist once again on the pervasiveness of class struggle, the need to be vigilant against ideological backsliding, and a spirit of militant confrontation of enemies at home and imperialism abroad. The 1964 ouster of his nemesis Khrushchev may have reminded him—as had Khrushchev's earlier denunciation of Stalin—that his ability to shape his country's future course was limited. Mao also sensed that many of his colleagues did not share his vision of ceaseless political struggle and were inwardly attracted to many features of the more technocratic Soviet model. Khrushchev's colleagues, after all, removed him from power for blundering and erratic leadership in carrying out what they termed his "harebrained schemes"—a charge that applied to Mao with more tragic force. Mao drew around himself a small group of trusted loyalists who would help him direct a rolling series of purges and mass mobilizations. He moved with indirection and stealth to place loyalists in key positions of power as he laid plans for an unprecedented mass movement that would shake the regime to its foundations.[11]

Mao's actions were highly unusual, but his impulses were actually a return to some of the core themes of Stalinism during its prebureaucratic "revolutionary" phase from 1927 to 1934.[12] Mao, however, did not simply order the internal security services to purge the leadership and carry out mass arrests. He had in mind something much bigger, more disruptive, and potentially much more enduring. He intended to initiate a populist purge—a mass movement in which the people themselves would identify, criticize, drag out, and punish those whose actions and words had betrayed the revolution and "Mao Zedong thought." This rebellion would shock China's officialdom from top to bottom, and the chastened survivors would presumably conduct themselves differently in the future. Ordinary citizens, especially China's educated youth, would gain revolutionary experience that would ensure commitment to Maoist ideals for another generation. This mass movement—or more precisely an uncoordinated and violent array of disparate movements—eventually spread to the entire country, igniting local civil wars and the collapse of civilian governments and ending with martial law in 1968. How and why such intense social conflict originated and spread is one of the central puzzles of the Cultural Revolution. It all began with the student rebellion in Beijing in the late spring of 1966.

## The Problem of Factions

The most widely accepted explanation of the factional divisions that plagued the red guard movement is that they expressed the social and political inequalities of Mao-era China. This idea has two essential features. The first is that factions expressed different orientations toward the status quo. On one side, a conservative faction offered a relatively moderate critique of the status quo and, reluctant to attack the highest organs of political power, emphasized positive aspects of the regime and its accomplishments and even defended incumbent officials from extreme accusations and violent treatment. Opposing these conservatives, according to this view, was a radical faction that was much more critical of the status quo, emphasized the regime's failure to live up to revolutionary ideals, and launched daring attacks on the highest organs of power. In other words, factions expressed different orientations toward the status quo, and for this reason they were unable to make common cause.[13]

Why did these different political viewpoints arise? The second part of the explanation is essential: factions pursued the opposing interests of different social groups. Conservative and radical factions represented individuals from different social backgrounds. The varied interests of mass constituencies, in turn, explain both the factional divisions themselves and the intensity of their conflict. Surely such intense conflict could not spring from nowhere; fundamental social and economic interests must have been involved. Conservative factions, according to this view, expressed the interests of those who were closely tied to the Communist Party and who enjoyed better living standards and future prospects. Radical factions, on the other hand, expressed the interests of those whose ties to power structures were weaker or whose position and future prospects were less bright. In short, factions expressed the interests of different social constituencies, even though group interests were submerged in a Maoist rhetoric that masked self-interested aims. By suddenly immobilizing a well-organized and repressive political regime, it seemed, the Cultural Revolution inadvertently provided a political opportunity for these underlying social conflicts to find organized expression.[14]

One of the fascinating features of the Cultural Revolution was the way in which it exposed political and social inequalities and their attendant dissatisfactions. Temporary and contract workers protested their exclusion from secure state-sector jobs.[15] Urban youths sent to the countryside after failing university entrance exams returned to the cities to demand urban residence.[16] Demobilized soldiers assigned to remote state farms instead of to the urban jobs they expected formed brigades of skilled fighters to protest their plight.[17] These groups all lodged complaints that distinguished their interests from the interests of those who were more favored.

The Cultural Revolution also exposed divisions among students. High-school red guards openly debated the relevance of family political heritage as a qualification for leadership of the red guards. The debate revealed dimensions of political life that seemed directly relevant to student factions—powerfully expressed in a famous Beijing tract that denounced the entire system of political discrimination based on family heritage.[18] Certain red guards proclaimed that the movement should recruit members primarily from proletarian households, and that leadership rightfully belonged to the offspring of revolutionary veterans from the party and army. These red guards typically scorned "reactionary" households (capitalists, landlords, and Nationalists) and were reluctant to accept students from these families as full partners in the movement. This stance was strenuously opposed by students from other backgrounds, especially the offspring of the former professional and middle classes who were heavily represented in universities and academic high schools. Some argue that this was the decisive issue in defining high-school red guard factions, and that students from "red" and especially "revolutionary" families were much more likely to join conservative factions than students from other backgrounds.[19]

The debate about class origin revealed the importance of political status and activism in the allocation of educational and career opportunities. Competition for admission to universities and the best high schools was intense: a combination of standardized test scores, political evaluations, and judgments about family political loyalty decided students' futures. Students from "revolutionary" and "proletarian" households were to be shown favoritism, while students from "reactionary" households were penalized. The debate about class origin echoed an explicit party policy. The regime classified households according to the occupation and political affiliation of the male head of the household at the time the regime was established. It openly favored two types of "red" households: those classified as "revolutionary" (Communist Party member, Red Army soldier, or revolutionary martyr) and "proletarian" (manual wage earner, poor and lower-middle peasants). These labels were inherited through the male line and influenced educational attainment and recruitment into the party and leadership positions.[20]

Students had to decide how to allocate their time between the pursuit of academic excellence and the compilation of a strong record as a political activist.[21] Classroom counselors and political instructors regularly placed formal evaluations in political dossiers that were kept on every student and that would follow them throughout their careers. A record of active participation in the Communist Youth League could enhance one's educational opportunities and improve one's job assignment at the completion of schooling. Students who became classroom or youth league leaders, known as "student cadres," and eventually (in universities) party members were shown the strongest preference. China's schools bred a highly competitive environment in which politics played a singularly important role.

These considerations inspired a strong scholarly consensus. Whether defined by family background or political affiliations, the identity of students before the Cultural Revolution determined their interests and political orientations once the movement began.[22] As one summary of this consensus described the university red guards, the "conservative" faction

was composed mainly of people who, due to their family background, belonged to the privileged strata of Chinese society. Many persons among that faction were sons and daughters of high- or medium-ranking cadres. Many were already Party members or, alternatively, if they had not reached this stage—were youth league members—a stepping-stone towards Party membership . . . As their families represented the vested interests within society, they were not prepared to accept the destruction of the prevailing order through social upheaval.

Opposing this faction were "radicals":

They did not have a 'good' family background and enjoyed no particular privileges. Most of them were not members of the youth league or the Party—clearly a serious disadvantage in a society which had erected an invisible wall between those who were Party members and those who were not . . . Their response to Mao's call to the masses to liberate themselves . . . was different. They saw in it an unexpected opportunity to express their resentment against a social order which they considered repressive.[23]

## *Network Mobilization? In Search of an Explanation*

I began research for this book convinced of the accuracy of this interpretation. The only question in my mind was which version best fit the evidence for the red guards of Beijing. I chose Beijing because of the unusual prominence of its student movement and the remarkable lack of a book-length study of the subject in any language.[24] The capital's population of university students was more than twice as large as that of any other Chinese city, and as a consequence they played an unusually important and highly visible role. Beijing's students were the first to mobilize, their activities were widely publicized as a nationwide model, and they exercised considerable influence over the movement as it spread nationwide.

Equally important is a rich documentary record that makes Beijing's student movement highly accessible for research. Several decades ago, when documentary sources were largely unavailable, researchers relied primarily on the oral reminiscences of former red guards who managed to migrate to Hong Kong. As a result, the early studies focused on the nearby city of Guangzhou (Canton) and the experiences of the high-school students who dominated its student population. In the post-Mao era documentary sources gradually became more widely accessible, and by the late 1990s a remarkable array of new sources was at hand: near-complete runs of factional newspapers from dozens of universities, collections of wall posters, detailed chronicles of events written by students at the time, and transcripts of hundreds of speeches by officials at red guard rallies or in private meetings with students.[25] By far the largest of these collections are from the nation's capital.

When I began my research, the only question in my mind was which version of a social interpretation was valid. The primary candidate was political status as defined by family heritage and enforced by the regime's policy of household political labels. Past research on high-school red guards seemed to show that this was the crucial characteristic that defined the interest of students and divided them into opposing red guard factions.

But a different idea appealed to me. My previous research on Chinese industry in the Mao era convinced me that authority in factories was exercised through a vertical hierarchy of social ties that linked the party organization to a network of political loyalists among ordinary employees.[26] Loyal followers were rewarded preferentially and enjoyed the prospect of subsequent promotion. These networks tied together individuals of different rank and social status and created shared interests that encouraged mutual support and loyalty. My past research suggested that political cleavages among workers were created along these network lines— very few factory workers were from "revolutionary" households, and almost all of them came from "red" proletarian families.[27] The categories created by household political labels had little relevance on the shop floor. Much more salient were divisions between workers who had joined the party or who actively did its bidding and those who avoided these involvements.

In China's universities, I suspected, the party's networks were probably composed of individuals from a variety of "red," "ordinary," and in some cases even "reactionary" family heritage. Students from "revolutionary" households, after all, were a tiny minority of China's population—only some 4 percent of urban residents.[28] They were overrepresented on university campuses, but even if they were highly favored by party authorities, there were too few of them to fully populate its networks of party members and loyal political activists.[29] The party's networks in universities must have incorporated people from a variety of family backgrounds, and as a consequence these network ties, not status categories defined by family heritage, should have provided the social cleavages that generated factions.

I began with this idea: conservative factions grew out of networks of party members and political activists who instinctively defended their party organization from attack. A radical faction, based heavily on those previously excluded from these networks, led the attacks on university officials; the party's loyal, conservative followers fought back.[30] Red guard factions, so I thought, were probably a result of efforts by individuals tied to party networks to defend their vested interests in the preservation of the status quo.

### Shattered Networks: The Politics of Institutional Collapse

I quickly abandoned this idea soon after I started my research. I began by reading detailed accounts of events in individual schools in chronological order. I wanted to understand when factional cleavages first appeared, and I was looking for evidence about when and how factional identities formed. The attention to chronology unexpectedly revealed how student political allegiances and the factional identities depended on events that took place in schools during the first two months of the Cultural Revolution, when outside delegations of party officials known as "work teams" directed purges and mobilized students.

Given my preconceptions, it was remarkable how different the early politics of the Cultural Revolution looked as described in the writings and speeches of participants at the time the events occurred.[31] Very quickly I was forced to abandon the idea that members of party networks mobilized to defend them from attack. This expectation, I discovered, depended on a deeper assumption of which I was not initially conscious—that the work teams sent into schools during June and July tried to limit the attacks of militant students and preserve the party organization. Published scholarship had long portrayed the work teams as a bulwark of party authority in the universities: "Their mission was to bring the situation under control and to carry out the Cultural Revolution in an orderly manner. They tended to act in much the same way as the Party committees they had come to rescue, and suppressed students who had opposed these committees."[32] In line with this consensus, I had assumed that work teams encouraged party loyalists to mobilize in defense of their party organization. To my surprise, I found that this was very rare in Beijing. Power structures quickly disintegrated.

This was the first important assumption to fall. When I turned to the question of how work teams did divide students against one another, I found that the issues rarely involved an assessment of the status quo or one's position within it. Instead, the issues were more ambiguous and concerned the actions of the work team itself. How much authority should work teams exercise over students? Did they have the right to prevent violent struggle sessions? Who controlled the prisoners? Had the work teams targeted the right school officials? Had they overreacted in punishing defiant students? The controversies that rocked schools during this period were not about the status quo at all, but about the actions of the work teams.

Yet another assumption to fall was the idea that red guard factions had different views about the status quo. The red guards burst forth suddenly on university campuses in August 1966, immediately after the withdrawal of work teams. The issues that divided them, however, concerned the recent actions of the work teams rather than the status quo. A majority of student militants had avoided conflict with work teams and were left in charge of schools. A minority who had clashed with the work teams became the targets of a denunciation campaign. The majority wanted to continue the Cultural Revolution under student leadership, treating the work teams as a dead issue—a regrettable error of higher-level officials that should now be set aside. The minority demanded that the work teams be brought back to the schools to confess their errors and withdraw the charges against their student opponents, and they were willing to march to government offices to demand that incriminating materials be removed from their political files and that the work teams be surrendered. These different political orientations were based on the events of June and July and their impact on the students involved.

Who were the students who opposed the work teams and ended up in this more militant minority? Were they marginal to party networks and therefore more likely to challenge authority?[33] If so, prior network ties might still have defined factional cleavages. The evidence, however, pointed elsewhere. The very same party members and political activists whom I expected to defend party hierarchies and obey the work teams in fact led the militant minority. How did so many of them end up on the wrong side, according to my prior reasoning? Most work teams shattered existing hierarchies and sanctioned attacks on officials, immobilizing party networks and forcing those connected to them to react. Party members and political activists were expected to take a stand and were under pressure to react, and quickly. When a school's top officials were denounced and removed from office, many of their loyal followers concluded that they might be found guilty by association, and they hastened to repudiate rather than defend their erstwhile leaders.

However, work teams did not always make clear at first what kinds of behavior they expected or what their verdict on the party organization would be. In these ambiguous circumstances students tied to power structures made very different decisions. Abrupt shifts in work-team stances further complicated their political choices. Whether to challenge a work team had more to do with judgments about the work team's actions than with views about the status quo. Also, it often was not the students' political choices that created conflicts; work teams also attacked students who proved hard to control, turning them involuntarily into opponents. As a result, the social profiles of both factions were initially very similar, whether in terms of positions in school political networks or of social categories like household labels.

The cleavage between Beijing's "majority" and "minority" factions evolved by the fall of 1966 into a conflict between reputed conservatives and rebels. The more radical stance of the rebels, however, did not grow out of their prior exclusion from power and privilege. Their rebellion was a reaction to the anticipated consequences of their clashes with work teams. Maoist authorities openly embraced this rebel faction and ensured its victory at the end of 1966. Surprisingly, this alliance then promptly split into two new factions that fought each other until the end of the movement in 1968.[34] The divisions among former rebel allies did not originate in the earlier dispute over work teams, and the Beijing factions did not articulate different views of the status quo. Exploring this second wave of factional warfare led me to discover how interlocking alliances across schools cemented student rebels into two large blocs whose irresolvable antagonisms were rooted in deep splits among rebels on the two largest campuses—Beijing and Qinghua universities. The splits on these campuses were reactions against the authoritarian stances of leaders anointed by Maoist officials to lead the student movement. This new cleavage requires a separate analysis.

## The Genesis of Factional Identities

The explanation that fits the evidence differs from the group and network explanations that served as my starting point in one crucial respect. The political orientations and interests of movement activists were not given by their prior positions, whether these are conceived as common social status or network relationships. The Cultural Revolution did not activate preexisting interests and orientations simply by removing constraints and creating a political opportunity for existing groups to act. Prior identities were not relevant to the choices students faced at the outset of the Cultural Revolution. The analysis of prior, fixed group interests and allegiances in the context of shifting political opportunities would misrepresent what the Beijing red guard movement was about.

The alternative explanation is based on close attention to evidence about the formation and subsequent evolution of factions within schools. The shift from stable and repressive institutions to a situation where they are under challenge is not smooth or unproblematic. The process of institutional collapse is crucial. In China's schools during the summer of 1966, the institutions that stabilized expectations about authority and linked one's status and position to political responses were breaking down rapidly in novel and unpredictable ways. Those closely tied to power structures were pressured to take a stand. To take a stand put one in a position of opposition to those who took a different stand. Choice in this novel and ambiguous situation prevented those who were tied to power structures from acting in concert. The signals about expected behavior, very clear in stable circumstances, were suddenly scrambled. This divided those previously loyal to authority figures against one another in a conflict that generated new identities and urgent new interests. A person who could not successfully defend his or her earlier choice would suffer a sharp loss of status and bear the stigma of having committed a political error.

Another way of stating the argument is that factional identities and the common interests that define them are the product of political interactions rooted in specific contexts whose properties must be researched, not simply assumed. Individual decisions—to join factions, to oppose or support a work team—are not the product of prior socialization or social ties but are actively shaped by political encounters. The focus is on the interactions that generate choices and outcomes, not the prior statuses of individuals or their preexisting social and political ties. These processes determine when prior social statuses or network ties are activated in a conflict, and when they are not. This is the central puzzle of this book.

This is not, however, the central puzzle of contemporary political sociology, especially the branch that specializes in the study of social movements and contentious politics. For several decades that field has been preoccupied with the problem of mobilization, which treats the identities and motives of political groups as given. The central puzzle is why and how groups that have established identities and long-standing grievances are able to find common cause, organize, mobilize resources, exploit political opportunities, and achieve a collectively valued outcome.[35]

The pronounced emphasis on the problem of mobilization originated during the 1970s in the widespread recognition that societies with the most aggrieved populations are by no means the ones that are most likely to generate the largest political movements or the most frequent protest events. Why not? First, the relevant populations may not have the capacity to organize—they may lack means of communication, or they may lack regular contact with one another, or they may lack social solidarity because of weak community structure or ethnic and other status differences. Second, even if they have the capacity to organize, they may lack the resources or resourcefulness to be effective—leadership skills, strategy, supplies of material, equipment, or funds. Third, even with a strong organizational capacity, ample resources, and astute strategy, a movement may still be stymied by an inhospitable political opportunity structure—allies or coalition partners in other social groups may be absent at crucial points in time, or the authorities may be highly unified and have well-organized and effective strategies of repression. Some scholars have dissented from the analysis of organization and political opportunity and have sought to emphasize the cultural, symbolic, moral, and charismatic dimensions of popular mobilization by providing rich descriptions of the meanings that political actors attribute to their actions.[36] Even these attempts to forge a new approach remain focused on the problem of mobilization.[37]

However compelling the problem of mobilization is in many historical circumstances, it is not the enduring puzzle about China's red guards. All the structural and subjective circumstances essential for political mobilization were suddenly created for the student movement in 1966. After all, the movement was instigated at the apex of the political system and facilitated from the beginning by access to the mass media, funding, means of transportation and communication, and the support and advice of a powerful leadership faction. The nation's supreme leader openly supported it. The mass media celebrated the student rebels, developed an elaborate moral and political rationale for their actions, and applauded their activities. Classes were canceled along with entrance exams and job assignments. Dormitories were kept open, and meal services continued into the summer months and beyond. The security agencies and armed forces were ordered to support student radicals and not to interfere.[38] The puzzle is not how students mobilized but why they were so bitterly divided.

This does not mean that the familiar analysis of organization and political opportunity is of little use in understanding red guard factions. It is essential in understanding why factional divisions hardened after they first appeared and why they evolved the way that they did. Student factions responded to what they perceived as political opportunities as revealed by the mass media and Maoist officials at crucial points in the evolution of the movement. Throughout the two years of the movement these signals were frequently ambiguous and contradictory, and at key points they were reversed without warning. These ambiguous and shifting signals exacerbated divisions among students and deepened their mutual antagonisms. The evolution of Beijing's red guard factions was the product of intensive and repeated interactions between certain members of China's political elite and the leaders of the student movement.

The primary elite actors in this story were the members of a committee near the apex of national power that Mao appointed to help direct the student rebellion and ensure its growth and success. As they did so, they frequently shifted course and often worked at cross-purposes, influencing the course of the movement in both intended and unintended ways. This committee, the Central Cultural Revolution Group (CCRG), assumed increasing power in the course of the rebellion and played a key role in shaping Beijing's red guard factions.

*Elite Sponsorship: The Central Cultural Revolution Group*

Formed on May 28, 1966, at the Politburo meetings where the first wave of leadership purges was formalized, the Central Cultural Revolution Group initially played an informal, behind-the-scenes role in stimulating the insurgency. Its power grew steadily as China's top leadership was decimated in purges, and by February 1967 it replaced the Politburo and the Central Committee Secretariat and developed a large bureaucracy of its own.[39] The CCRG had nationwide concerns, but because it was very deeply involved in the capital's student movement, it had an enormous influence in Beijing.

Only a few of the members of this committee were ranking members of China's top leadership, and none of them were responsible for the management of the economy or the administration of the public sector. Virtually all of them were involved in propaganda, security work, and Marxist-Leninist ideology and were past advocates of Mao's more radical initiatives.

The two most important members were Kang Sheng and Jiang Qing. Kang was the group's "advisor," but he was deeply involved in its activities. Kang spent four years in the Soviet Union during the height of Stalin's Great Purges, and this experience honed his interests in counter-intelligence and security work.[40] In the wartime base area of Yan'an in the early 1940s, he led the party's first traumatic campaign to root out alleged traitors and fortify loyalty to Mao Zedong.[41] In the early 1960s Mao brought Kang into his effort to fight revisionism and ideological backsliding and put him in charge of a Central Committee department that developed the polemics against the Soviet Union. Kang personally arranged for the denunciation of officials at Beijing University (Beida) that served to ignite the student rebellion.[42]

Jiang Qing, Mao's wife since 1938, was a former Shanghai movie actress with leftist connections who made her way to Yan'an during the anti-Japanese war and formed a relationship with Mao. Jiang played no role in party politics until the early 1960s, when she became active in the fields of drama and the arts, promoting works with proper revolutionary content. She served as Mao's personal emissary in arranging publication of critical attacks on literary figures that presaged the launching of the Cultural Revolution.[43] Initially Jiang was named vice-chairman of the CCRG, but she effectively took over control from the nominal chairman Chen Boda in September 1966.[44]

Chen Boda, a specialist in propaganda and Marxism-Leninism, was vice-head of the party's Propaganda Department and editor of the theoretical journal *Red Flag*. As Mao's political secretary in Yan'an, he played a key role in developing the Mao cult and Mao Zedong Thought. He and Kang Sheng spearheaded the Yan'an rectification campaign in 1942–1943 that targeted errant intellectuals and alleged traitors in the party.[45] *Red Flag*, founded under his editorship in 1958, was the official mouthpiece of Mao's political line and the authoritative voice of the CCRG during the Cultural Revolution.[46]

The remaining members were younger propaganda officials. Zhang Chunqiao, 49, head of the Shanghai Municipal Propaganda Bureau, was a vice-chairman. He had earlier supported the publication of political attacks on authors and literary figures that led directly to the Cultural Revolution.[47] Several others held editorial posts under Chen Boda at *Red Flag*. Qi Benyu, 35, was a director of the History Editorial Group and became Mao's secretary in May 1966.[48] Wang Li, 45, had previously worked under Kang Sheng as vice-head of the Chinese Communist Party (CCP) International Liaison Department, where he had authored ideological polemics against the Soviet Union.[49] Guan Feng, 46, had worked his way up through the CCP Political Research Office, where he had extensive dealings with Chen Boda and Kang Sheng and briefly edited an internal theoretical bulletin read by Mao.[50] Mu Xin, 47, was editor-in-chief of the party's newspaper for intellectual affairs, *Guangming ribao* (Enlightenment Daily).[51] The younger members of the CCRG played an active role as liaisons with the student radicals.

The CCRG had little independent authority, and almost all its members were marginal political figures who depended entirely on Mao's backing. They often had to guess Mao's ambiguous and frequently shifting views. In addition, at crucial points members worked at cross-purposes and openly disagreed. Moreover, the membership of the committee shifted as individuals were purged after being judged insufficiently radical or were blamed for excesses that earned Mao's disapproval. The first major change occurred in August 1966, when the regional secretaries charged with coordinating the work teams were removed in disgrace. The second major change occurred at the end of 1966 when several more were purged for resisting the escalation of the movement (Tao Zhu, Wang Renzhong, and Liu Zhijian). Wang Li, Guan Feng, and Qi Benyu, strong advocates of radical students as the movement escalated, were blamed in late 1967 for the violence that resulted when mass factions were armed. Remarkably, by February 1968 only five of the original nineteen members and advisors of the CCRG survived (see Table 1.1).

The CCRG was deeply involved in the Beijing student movement from start to finish. Members met constantly with student leaders and spoke regularly at large rallies and small group meetings. Many of these sessions were recorded, transcribed, and published in student newspapers. Staff departments assisted the committee and grew in size as the Cultural Revolution proceeded. As its power grew with the decimation of the national bureaucracy, other officials regularly attended CCRG meetings in a nonvoting capacity. Reflecting the steady authoritarian drift of the Cultural Revolution, many of these participants had military and security posts.[52] Among those who served on the CCRG staff were Cao Yi'ou, Kang Sheng's wife, who was for a period the head of the staff office, and Lin Jie, a staff editor at *Red Flag* who played an active and visible role as a liaison with rebel students. At the outset of the Cultural Revolution the CCRG set up offices in the state guesthouse compound at Diaoyutai, on the western edge of Beijing near the Haidian university district.[53] The CCRG also built an intelligence network on the campuses. Reporters were transferred from the New China News Agency and *Liberation Army Daily* and stationed in universities, reporting daily on events and trends in the movement. In many cases student rebels viewed the reporters as direct channels to the top leadership and invited them to participate in their leadership meetings.[54]

The CCRG enacted the political initiatives of Mao Zedong, who worked behind the scenes through his proven loyalists. It ran the movement on Mao's behalf, encouraged, advised, and steered students in one direction or another, and often selected targets for attack. The CCRG

Table 1.1  The evolving membership of the Central Cultural Revolution Group, 1966–1968

| Position | May 1966 | October 1966 | February 1967 | February 1968 |
|---|---|---|---|---|
| *Head* | | | | |
| Politburo Standing Committee; editor-in-chief, *Red Flag* | Chen Boda | Chen Boda | Chen Boda | Chen Boda |
| *Vice-heads* | | | | |
| Wife of Mao Zedong, with interests in propaganda and culture | Jiang Qing | Jiang Qing | Jiang Qing | Jiang Qing |
| First secretary, Central-South Bureau of CCP; party secretary, Hubei Province | Wang Renzhong | Wang Renzhong | — | — |
| Lieutenant general; vice-head of PLA General Political Department, in charge of propaganda and culture | Liu Zhijian | Liu Zhijian | — | — |
| Secretariat, CCP East China Bureau and Shanghai Municipal Party Committee, in charge of propaganda and culture | Zhang Chunqiao | Zhang Chunqiao | Zhang Chunqiao | Zhang Chunqiao |
| *Advisors* | | | | |
| Politburo Standing Committee | Kang Sheng | Kang Sheng | Kang Sheng | Kang Sheng |
| Politburo Standing Committee; head, CCP Propaganda Department | Tao Zhu* | Tao Zhu | — | — |
| *Members* | | | | |
| Major general; head of Culture Division, PLA General Political Department | Xie Tangzhong | Xie Tangzhong | — | — |

| | | | | |
|---|---|---|---|---|
| Institute of History, Chinese Academy of Sciences; editor, *Historical Research* | Yin Da | — | — | — |
| Vice-editor, *Red Flag* | Wang Li | Wang Li | Wang Li | — |
| Vice-editor, *Red Flag* | Guan Feng | Guan Feng | Guan Feng | — |
| Vice-editor, *Red Flag* | Qi Benyu | Qi Benyu | Qi Benyu | — |
| Vice-editor, *Red Flag*; editor, *Guangming ribao* | Mu Xin | Mu Xin | — | — |
| Vice-head, Propaganda Bureau, Shanghai Municipal Party Committee; editor, *Jiefang ribao* | Yao Wenyuan | Yao Wenyuan | Yao Wenyuan | Yao Wenyuan |
| Vice-head, CCP Propaganda Department; Secretariat, Central-South Bureau, CCP | Zhang Pinghua | — | — | — |
| Secretariat, Beijing Municipal Party Committee | Guo Yingqiu | — | — | — |
| Secretariat, Northeast China Bureau, CCP; member, Jilin Province Party Committee | Zheng Jiqiao | — | — | — |
| Secretariat, Northwest China Bureau, CCP; first secretary, Qinghai Province Party Committee | Yang Zhilin | — | — | — |
| Vice-head, Propaganda Department, Southwest China Bureau, CCP | Liu Wenzhen | — | — | — |

*Sources:* Organization Department, CCP Central Committee (2000), 10: 61–62; and other reference works.
*Tao Zhu was promoted to these posts and added August 2.

decided which factions received resources and publicity, and it warned, criticized, and occasionally ordered the arrest of students who failed to heed its directives. Its efforts to manipulate the movement were only partially successful. It was unable to stem factional warfare among its followers and was briefly targeted by outspoken rebels who denounced its cynical manipulation of the movement for factional ends.

### Students and the Regime

The students who took part in Beijing's Cultural Revolution were at the apex of a steep educational pyramid, a select elite who could expect to enjoy favorable placement after completing their schooling. In 1965 China had a population of 750 million, but only 674,430 students were enrolled in 434 institutions of higher education. The competition to reach university was intense, and the odds of advancement to the top were very small. Of the 32.9 million students who entered primary school in 1965, only 9 percent could expect to enter junior high school. Only 15 percent of these junior high entrants, in turn, could expect to graduate and enter high school. Academic high school was already a rarefied atmosphere, but these graduates also faced steep odds: only 36 percent would make it to university. Overall, the odds of attending an academic high school for a student entering primary school in 1965 were 1.3 percent, and the odds of attending university less than 0.5 percent.[55]

Beijing had an unusually large concentration of university students. In addition to the largest and most prestigious liberal arts (Beijing University), science and engineering (Qinghua University), and teachers' colleges (Beijing Normal University), most of the more than forty national ministries and commissions operated university campuses devoted to training their future personnel. The largest of these were the Beijing Geology Institute (Ministry of Geology), the Beijing Aeronautics Institute (National Defense Science and Technology Commission), the Beijing Steel Institute (Ministry of Metallurgy), and the Beijing Mining Institute (Ministry of Coal). These schools were lodged in a bureaucratic hierarchy that tied them to the system of national ministries. Because of this concentrated bureaucratic presence, the capital's student population was remarkably top-heavy: there were 111,000 university students, one-sixth of the national total and double the number of local high-school students.[56]

High-school students in Beijing's Western, Eastern, and Haidian districts were also an elite group, but of a different variety. The universities drew students of all backgrounds from throughout the country. The elite high schools in the core urban districts of Beijing, which played a prominent early role in the Cultural Revolution, drew on a different population. National ministries and their housing compounds were concentrated in the Western District and to a somewhat lesser extent in the Eastern District. Haidian, at that time on the northwest edge of the city and still dotted with agricultural communities, was the site of the vast majority of the universities, most of which ran elite high schools that attracted students from throughout Beijing. The children of China's political elite were heavily overrepresented in these schools, as were the offspring of educated professionals and office staff.[57]

This was a highly closed system. All schools were government run and controlled by Communist Party committees and branches. There was virtually no option to study abroad: China had only 454 university students outside its borders in 1965.[58] Graduates were given mandatory job assignments by government agencies in consultation with school authorities. Assignments were heavily influenced by students' specialization and grades and also by household political label and individuals' records of political activism as recorded in their all-important political dossiers. A political error in this system could have costly and irreversible consequences for one's future, for the simple reason that behavior was carefully monitored, records were kept, and there was no exit from the system.

### The Organized Setting: School Power Structures

The national political hierarchy extended into the schools. The top party officials in universities were tied to a large network of politically active students who were destined for party membership and future career advancement. These power structures were extensive. They stretched from the university party committee in the central administration down through the general branches at the department level and the party branches at the basic level. The branch committees formed an interlocking pyramid in which the leaders at each level—party secretaries—sat on committees at the next higher level (see Table 1.2). Students, faculty, and staff participated in this network as members of party branches, which averaged twelve to fourteen members. Student party members attended regular branch meetings and were in constant contact with the party secretary of their branch and the occupants of other political posts, the most important of whom were Communist Youth League secretaries and political instructors. There

*Table 1.2* Party organization at Beijing and Qinghua universities, 1965–1966

| | Beijing University | | Qinghua University | |
|---|---|---|---|---|
| | Number of units | Members per unit | Number of units | Members per unit |
| Party secretaries | — | 5 | — | 7 |
| Party standing committee | 1 | 17 | 1 | 16 |
| Party committee | 1 | — | 1 | 40 |
| Party general branches | 20 | 109 | 18 | 183 |
| Party branches | 137 | 16 | 238 | 14 |
| Party members—total | — | 2,174 | — | 3,287 |

*Sources:* Fang Huijian and Zhang Sijing (2001), 1:809, 813, 818; Wang Xuezhen et al. (1998), 602–603, 640.

were 238 party branches at Qinghua University, Beijing's largest, in 1966. The school's power structure included well over 250 party secretaries at various levels and more than 400 party cadres overall (Table 1.2).

This network linked party officials with large numbers of student leaders who were not yet party members. Academic departments divided each year's incoming students into numbered "classrooms" (*banji*) of some twenty-five students. Each classroom was assigned a "classroom counselor" (*ban zhuren*), an instructor considered politically reliable by the party branch. Each classroom had its own Communist Youth League branch and selected its own youth league and classroom officers. These were "student cadres," destined eventually to join the party. Rates of student party membership ranged from 5 to 20 percent in the universities (see Table 1.3). At Qinghua, where there were 1,390 students in the party, two additional "student cadres" in each of the 425 classrooms would imply an additional 850 student leaders. The network therefore connected some 2,200 students to the party organization.

These arrangements explain why so many students mobilized so rapidly at the outset of the Cultural Revolution. Mao's call to criticize power holders reverberated through a hierarchy that directly linked large numbers of politically active students to the regime. Students were already formed into small groups with elected leaders accustomed to responding to regime-sponsored activities. Students who were closely connected to party leaders had a propensity for political activism and vested interests in their positions. A strong political record was an important criterion

*Table 1.3*  Student party membership at various universities, 1965–1966

| Institution | Students | Student party members | Percentage of students in the party |
|---|---|---|---|
| Beijing Aeronautics Institute | 4,787 | 1,013 | 21.2 |
| Qinghua University | 10,673 | 1,390 | 13.0 |
| Beijing Agricultural University | 2,959 | 310 | 10.5 |
| Beijing Industrial Institute | 4,153 | 414 | 10.0 |
| Beijing University | 8,917 | 693 | 7.8 |
| Beijing Steel Institute | 4,950 | 255 | 5.2 |
| Beijing Industrial University | 3,400 | 160 | 4.7 |

*Sources:* Beijing University of Science and Technology Archives Office (2006), 58, 530; Fang Huijian and Zhang Sijing (2001), 1:818; Li Rongfa (2000), 1, 532; Ni Fuqing and Pan Zhitian (1995), 507, 651; Shen Shituan (2000), 316–317, 433; Wang Buzheng (1995), 361, 618; Wang Xuezhen et al. (1998), 640.

for a favorable job assignment after graduation, especially in sensitive government posts. In addition, party membership was the first step on a career path toward positions that entailed power, prestige, and material privilege.[59] Student activists therefore had a great deal at stake in this kind of political campaign. It was important to display the proper level of loyalty and activism, but it was even more important not to commit a serious political error, because this could negate years of effort in both academics and politics.

In normal times these networks operated with a great deal of discipline. We should not overestimate their resilience, however, because their cohesion depended heavily on undivided authority and clear signals from the top. If authority was divided or uncertain, and the signals became scrambled, the cohesion of the network was lost, especially if the network itself was under attack. Ordinary party members, student cadres, and political activists had a propensity to respond to political campaigns, and they also faced considerable pressure, given their status, to be the first to take a stand. It was this feature of the political networks that made them so fragile when external work teams of ranking party officials entered the schools and initiated the purges of the Cultural Revolution.

## Overview of the Analysis

Each chapter explores a distinct dimension of the origins and evolution of red guard politics in Beijing. I try to achieve a balance between a focus on central questions about factional politics and a narrative account of a dramatic, complex, and poorly understood story. The student rebellion emerged suddenly and developed rapidly at the beginning of June 1966. On May 25, seven dissident party members from Beijing University's Philosophy Department put up a wall poster denouncing the university's president as an ally of municipal party officials who had recently been purged. Within days the poster was reprinted in the national newspaper, *People's Daily,* and lavished with praise; the university's president and two others named in the wall poster were removed from their posts, and a work team was sent to take control of the university and carry out a purge of its administration. As large numbers of individuals at other schools launched similar accusations against their own leaders, dozens more work teams took over from collapsing school administrations throughout the city.

In Chapter 2 I examine how work teams actually behaved toward the power structures of the universities. How did they treat top school officials and the rest of the party organization? Did they try to blunt attacks on the officials, or did they encourage them? Did they remove officials from power, or did they let them keep their posts? The answers to these questions will tell us what political choices actually faced student activists. A reconstruction of work-team actions in half of Beijing's universities reveals a confusing array of work-team actions, which varied widely across schools and often shifted abruptly, showing that work teams were often unsure how to proceed. These narratives illustrate the remarkable ambiguity and unpredictability of the political environment within which student activists had to take a stand during June and July 1966.

Chapter 3 describes how the work teams split university power structures into warring factions, with a focus on the issues that bred conflict between work teams and militant students. Only in rare and fleeting circumstances were the issues of contention about attacks on the incumbent power structure—a question that might distinguish "conservative" from "radical" political orientations. Instead, they were usually about the work team's authority over student actions and the physical control of officials held for interrogation, and about heavy-handed work-team punishment of students who proved hard to control. In many cases the work teams deliberately or inadvertently pitted officials and students against one another. As a result, the students who led the opposition to the work teams, and who were heavily represented among their victims, were political activists who previously had been connected to power structures—

a profile similar to that of the students who followed the work teams' lead.

Chapter 4 examines the divisions among university red guards that appeared in early August, immediately after the work teams' withdrawal. The factional struggle focused on the events of June and July and their consequences for the students involved. A vocal minority, led by those who had been punished by the work teams, demanded a campaign to force them to retract their charges. This "minority" faction's strategy undercut the authority of the students who had cooperated with the work teams and assumed control of the schools after they left. The majority faction, in turn, defended its earlier actions, minimized the work-team issue, and fought back against the minority's challenge. This conflict between "minority" and "majority" factions was actually about work teams, not the political status quo. The growing rebelliousness of the minority faction was rooted in grievances based on their clash with the work teams, not in a more critical stance toward the nation's political institutions.

Chapter 5 turns to events in the elite high schools of the Western, Eastern, and Haidian districts, which unfolded very differently than in universities and created different political cleavages. In the high schools opposition to work teams was led by politically active students from "revolutionary" family heritage, often the children of high officials. These early high-school militants were not left with the grievances of the university "minority" faction. Instead, Mao and the CCRG made them national celebrities, and the youth league officials who had sent work teams into the high schools were immediately purged. There was no split within high schools analogous to the minority-majority split in the universities. Two issues did divide high-school militants: family origin and red guard violence. These were arguments within the first wave of red guard militants from predominantly "red" households but they did not define clear factional identities. The students who took a strong stand against red guard violence—and who also took pride in their revolutionary and proletarian family origin—formed picket corps to rein in the violence and cruelty displayed by the early red guards and in so doing formed strong ties to the State Council apparatus under Premier Zhou Enlai. This stance put them on a collision course with their erstwhile sponsors on the CCRG.

Chapter 6 explores the path followed by the university minority as it gained CCRG support and became the dominant "rebel" faction. It achieved this status largely through daring attacks on national ministries that advanced the CCRG's objective of extending purges into higher levels of the party apparatus. These sit-ins, demonstrations, and building invasions did not express a more critical attitude toward China's political status quo than that of the minority's rivals in the majority faction. They were a product of the minority faction's attempt to confront the leaders of its work teams, extract confessions and apologies, and remove from members' records the negative political verdicts recorded by work teams. It just so happened that work-team leaders and their files were located in national ministries. The CCRG intervened to support the minority faction and undermine the university majority and the high-school picket corps, which confronted minority protesters when they attacked government offices and the homes of officials. During this period the CCRG's role in running the student movement and manipulating its outcomes became highly visible and, to many student militants, a cause of dissent.

Chapter 7 documents the rebellion of the university majority and the high-school pickets against their dismissal as "conservatives" by the CCRG. During November 1966 some of these students began a daring wall-poster campaign that offered a coherent critique of the CCRG's actions. They objected to their labeling as "conservatives" and to the increasingly heavy-handed manipulation of the student movement. In one of the clearest examples of rebellion against political authority during the Cultural Revolution, they openly challenged the arguments and actions of the CCRG and ridiculed some of its members. As their small movement developed, they began to charge that the CCRG contained anti-party conspirators. Some of the former leaders of the defunct high-school picket corps organized a citywide alliance, Liandong (United Action), to defend their position. This open challenge to the Maoist authorities provoked a harsh backlash. Openly violating its earlier prohibition against the use of security forces against students, the CCRG ordered a wave of arrests and unleashed a national propaganda campaign that vilified the dissidents and distorted their actions and motives in ways that have heavily influenced past scholarship. These dissidents are usually described as conservatives attempting to defend their privileged position in the status quo, but in fact these groups were responding to grievances that originated in the immediately preceding period and paralleled the minority faction's earlier grievances against the work teams.

Chapter 8 examines the puzzling disintegration of the rebel movement in January 1967, soon after the decisive victory over its opponents. Why did the victorious rebel coalition rapidly split into two opposing camps? In their earlier attacks on ministries and commissions, rebels stayed within separate bureaucratic hierarchies. Work teams were dispatched down these hierarchies to the schools under them, and the pursuit of work teams led rebels directly back up this hierarchy to the ministry or commission that sent them. When these rebels moved to seize power in national and municipal agencies, however, they crossed into different bureaucratic hierarchies. Rebel groups from different schools who went to the same organs of power turned quickly from allies into competitors. These competitive rivalries were exacerbated by deep splits that had earlier developed among rebel forces in the two largest and most important campuses, Beijing and Qinghua universities. The splits at Beida and Qinghua served as a wedge to divide rebel forces citywide, as factions in different schools aligned themselves with one or another faction at these two large campuses. The resulting split between "Heaven" and "Earth" factions crippled the student movement and frustrated the CCRG until the very end.

Chapter 9, finally, explains why it proved impossible for the two factions to unite despite repeated efforts to force them to do so. After the students' inept attempts at power seizures, Mao and the CCRG turned to an authoritarian solution and put the Ministry of Public Security and the Beijing Garrison Command in charge. This pushed students back into power struggles on their own campuses, and these struggles became increasingly violent and impervious to official mediation as 1967 turned into 1968. On almost all campuses two wings of the former rebel movement faced off, making extreme political charges against each other that were far more severe than the work-team verdicts that had originally inspired the rebel faction. The idea that students could unite to rule their campuses proved chimerical: antagonisms and mutual suspicion had so deepened that neither side could trust a political settlement that was not enforced by a neutral third party. As increasingly violent factional disputes developed into open warfare on some campuses in the spring of 1968, Mao and the CCRG abandoned all efforts to negotiate a settlement and, in obvious disgust, dispatched the armed forces to take over the campuses, shut down the student movement, and detain recalcitrant student rebels for reeducation.

# 2

## THE ASSAULT ON POWER STRUCTURES

### *Work Teams in the Universities*

The red guard movement exploded suddenly in August 1966, but only after a two-month period during which university power structures were torn apart by outside intervention. As public accusations against school authorities spread rapidly across Beijing in early June, work teams of party officials were hastily assigned to universities and high schools. Almost all of them came into conflict with students, teachers, and cadres. After their abrupt withdrawal two months later, universities were already divided into two nascent factions—a direct legacy of the work teams' interventions.

As work teams were withdrawn, Mao Zedong charged them with "suppressing the student movement." This was an "error of orientation and line," allegedly a deliberate effort to shield power holders in the schools. As the purges of the Cultural Revolution escalated, State Chairman Liu Shaoqi and Deng Xiaoping, general secretary of the CCP Central Committee, the second- and sixth-ranking members of the national leadership, were blamed for employing work teams to obstruct Mao's Cultural Revolution. Red guards echoed these charges, seemingly incensed that the work teams' suppression of the student movement was an effort to protect power holders in the schools.

The charge that the work teams "protected power holders" suggested a link between the behavior of work teams and the divisions among students. If work teams protected power holders, then student activists who cooperated with them must have had close ties to school power structures and vested interests in their preservation. These included party members, student cadres, and students from "red" family backgrounds favored by the party, especially families of officials and party and army veterans from the revolutionary era. These individuals had a strong stake in the status quo and would be a likely source of "conservative" students less critical of the status quo, who would tend to support work teams and be their natural allies. Students who clashed with work teams, according to this view, had weaker ties to school leaders and therefore fewer inhibitions in attacking them. They were less likely to be party members or student cadres or from families headed by officeholders or revolutionary veterans. To many early observers, this logic was compelling because it provided a direct link between red guard factionalism and the social and political structures of Mao's China.

This analysis assumes that we correctly understand the political contexts in which students decided whether to support or resist work teams. It hinges on a key factual question: whether work teams actually did try to preserve school power structures. If they did not, then students could not respond to them on the basis of their vested interests or lack thereof; their political choices would be different and more complicated. An explanation that links status before the Cultural Revolution to political orientation during the movement would have to be modified or replaced.

In this chapter I demonstrate that the work teams sent to universities did not consistently seek to preserve school power structures. Many tried briefly to do so but abandoned the attempt within two weeks and launched devastating attacks that immobilized and split school power structures. These actions split students from similar backgrounds into opposing factions. We therefore need a new explanation for the formation and perpetuation of factional struggle among red guards. But first we need to show that the explanation that has seemed so appealing for a generation does not withstand close scrutiny.

*Work-Team Interventions*

The speed and scale of the bureaucratic effort to send work teams to hundreds of schools and other organizations meant that hastily assembled and poorly briefed officials were sent into unfamiliar, conflict-ridden territory with ill-defined missions. Moreover, work teams were sent from a wide range of government agencies, and the rank of the officials who led them also differed. As a result, work teams behaved very differently and often shifted their strategies, sometimes abruptly.

On May 25, 1966, seven instructors of Marxism-Leninism in Beijing University's Philosophy Department, headed by the secretary of the department's general party branch, put up what later became known as the "first wall poster" of the Cultural Revolution. They denounced Lu Ping, the university's president and party secretary; Peng Peiyun, one of the vice-presidents; and Song Shuo, the deputy director of the university department of the Beijing Municipal Party Committee, as revisionists complicit with the Beijing party officials recently purged for blocking Mao's initial efforts to launch his new political campaign. Party members and activists in the university initially reacted in a predictable fashion—they rallied around the leadership. However, when on June 2 the wall poster was printed with editorial praise in the nation's leading newspapers and other mass media, defensive actions by those loyal to the leadership collapsed immediately.[1]

At this point the first work team was dispatched to Beijing University.[2] The decision was so abrupt that Zhang Chengxian, who led Beijing University's work team, was not informed of his assignment until shortly before the 8 p.m. broadcast of the wall poster on June 1. He was quickly briefed and sent to the campus in advance of the broadcast. He informed the school's party committee of the decision to suspend it, and shortly after midnight he gave a speech to all cadres, party and youth league members, and student cadres to announce that the work team was taking over.[3] On June 2 an official editorial condemned the officials denounced in the wall poster as an "anti-party clique," and the next day all three were publicly stripped of their posts and the wall poster's authors were praised.[4]

This had an immediate impact throughout Beijing. As the new municipal party secretary Li Xuefeng put it, "After June 1, the situation accelerated. As soon as the Beijing University wall poster appeared . . . it immediately affected all the schools and the leadership and activities of all work units. The broad masses and leaders stood face to face, exchanging fire."[5] A typical example was the Beijing Aeronautics Institute, where the first attack against the party secretary appeared on the same morning on which *People's Daily* published the Beijing University wall poster. Party leaders scrambled to head off its repercussions: "The Beijing University situation spread to our institute; many classes stopped meeting and the situation became tense." Six emergency meetings of the party committee and the entire party membership were held that day. At a mass meeting of the entire school, students demanded that party members speak out and expose the errors of the party committee. Wall posters denouncing the party committee went up all day.[6]

Events moved very quickly. Li Xuefeng testified, "At the time the new [Municipal] Party Committee had just been established. We were holding party work conferences, reshuffling the leadership of various agencies, leading the grassroots mass movement, all at the same time. Day and night, giving speeches here, giving speeches there . . . There was an awful lot going on."[7] At two separate meetings of the new Beijing Party Committee on June 2 and 3, university party secretaries were reassured that the movement would focus on academic authorities and scholars; "this does not include us here."[8] The officials were reassured that "the vast majority of party organizations at various levels are good," and "we have sent out a few work teams, but we cannot send out too many; mainly we have to rely on the leadership of party committees."[9]

Within days, however, these assurances were overtaken by events. Municipal officials were surprised at the way students and teachers eagerly denounced their leaders: "The masses had risen up, and the leadership of many units was paralyzed—what to do? We had no choice but to send in work teams."[10] The officials in charge of sending out work teams were later purged and accused of sending them intentionally to suppress the student rebellion, but the most urgent calls to send work teams initially came from Mao's followers on the CCRG. Guo Yingqiu, party secretary of Chinese People's University, was suddenly put in charge of the work-team effort in the capital. His predecessor as the municipal official in charge of the Cultural Revolution, Deng Tuo, had committed suicide two weeks before, shortly after he was labeled "anti-party" for mishandling Mao's earlier calls to launch the Cultural Revolution.[11] Kang Sheng and Chen Boda, two key figures on the recently formed CCRG, pressured Guo to get work teams into schools as soon as possible.[12]

The wave of officially sanctioned attacks on school officials created a chaotic, rapidly changing political environment into which the work teams rushed headlong. The nation's capital had by far the largest concentration of universities in the country. Most of the forty-nine ministries and commissions under the State Council ran at least one university or institute devoted to the training of their future personnel.[13] In little more than a week, thousands of party officials were selected, briefed, formed into more than 400 work teams, and sent with poorly defined missions to schools.[14] The capital's bureaucracy divided up the task: work teams for universities and institutes were organized by the state council commissions, national ministries, or municipal bureaus that supervised them, except for the most prestigious institutions under the Ministry of Higher Education, which were handled by the Central Party Secretariat itself. Some 3,800 individuals served on work teams sent to universities.[15]

Guo Yingqiu's efforts to coordinate the work-team effort were futile. Work teams were drawn from a large number of national and local agencies and reported to their superiors in these organizations. Leaders of these agencies maintained close contact with their work teams and, unlike the municipal government, often intervened directly in the schools, replacing work teams, providing instructions, and even making appearances at the schools. Coordination among them was haphazard at best.

### The Political Impact of Work Teams

The political impact of work teams depended, first of all, on whether they deposed the incumbent party committee and assumed command or permitted party leaders to carry out their own campaign. According to reports submitted by city officials at the time, the majority of university work teams took over from the party organization shortly after arriving at their schools. In some schools, however, work teams tried to defend party committees or a subset of officials in them. In these schools work teams temporarily kept incumbent leaders in their posts, and the party organization continued to operate. However, within two weeks almost all such efforts to defend party committees were abandoned.[16]

If a work team deposed the party leadership, it dealt a severe blow to any effort to rally party loyalists. When incumbent leaders were still in place, they were able to convene meetings at all levels. Members of the apparatus could coordinate resistance against those who attacked the power structure, and they could pressure student activists to defend their party superiors and counterattack against the critics. However, if a work team removed the party leadership and made leaders "stand aside" from their posts pending investigation, these leaders could no longer convene meetings or even communicate with their colleagues. For the duration of the campaign the work team decided what meetings to convene and who could attend. By depriving the party organization of its capacity to communicate and organize, a work team prevented the loyalist mobilization that was common where work teams were never sent.[17]

Even if a work team deposed school leaders, loyalist mobilization could still occur. If the work team supported university officials, considered their errors to be minor, and shielded them from extreme accusations, it could still mobilize loyal students to defend them. If the work team's sympathy clearly lay with the status quo, loyal individuals could draw appropriate conclusions. Such a work team would try to soften the impact of the campaign by directing the purge toward peripheral figures or rivals within the power structure and scapegoats outside.

When we look closely at the political impact of the work teams, we need to ask two things. First, how commonly, and how quickly, did work teams depose party committees and deprive them of a means of defense? Second, how thorough were attacks on the power structure, and to what extent were top officials permitted to participate in the process? The answers to these simple questions are far from straightforward. Work teams adopted different stances toward school power structures, and these stances often changed abruptly. Also, most work teams in the first wave were withdrawn within two weeks and replaced by ones that behaved very differently.

I have been able to reconstruct the events of June and July in half of the fifty-four tertiary institutions in Beijing in enough detail to characterize their work teams' behavior. The sample of twenty-seven schools includes nine of the largest ten and 76 percent of the city's university students in 1966 (see Table 2.1).[18] These accounts describe three different types of work-team behavior. The first was a "radical" strategy: the work team removed all party officials from their posts, declared the school's leaders and the entire power structure corrupt, and conducted an extensive investigation and purge of the vast majority of officials. These work teams welcomed severe political accusations against virtually any member of the university power structure. The second type was a "conservative" stance that is the opposite of the first: the work team declared the party leadership basically sound and either permitted it to conduct its own investigation and purges or absorbed top officials into the work team. These work teams reacted harshly against attempts to lodge serious political charges against trusted school officials. The third was a mixed type that contained elements of both the radical and conservative stances. These work teams declared that political problems at the school were severe because politically problematic individuals were undermining reliable "red" leaders. These work teams took over and shielded the officials they deemed reliably "red" while conducting a ferocious purge of the power structure to root out political suspects. This third approach resembled the radical one because large percentages of officials lost their posts; it resembled the conservative one in that a portion of the power structure was deemed reliable and defended stubbornly.

The picture is further complicated because work teams often changed strategies abruptly and without warning or were replaced by new work

*Table 2.1*  The sample of universities

| Institution | Student enrollment |
| --- | --- |
| Qinghua University | 10,673 |
| Beijing University | 8,917 |
| Beijing Steel Institute | 4,950 |
| Beijing Aeronautics Institute | 4,787 |
| Beijing Mining Institute | 4,121 |
| Beijing Geology Institute | 4,055 |
| Beijing Petroleum Institute | 3,920 |
| Beijing Normal University | 3,602 |
| Beijing Industrial University | 3,400 |
| Beijing Normal Institute | 3,400 |
| Beijing Post and Telecommunications Institute | 3,342 |
| Beijing Agricultural Machinery Institute | 3,340 |
| Chinese University of Science and Technology | 3,034 |
| Beijing Agricultural University | 2,959 |
| Beijing Railway Institute | 2,953 |
| Central Nationalities Institute | 2,647 |
| Chinese People's University | 2,519 |
| Beijing Forestry Institute | 2,200 |
| Beijing Foreign Languages Institute | 1,835 |
| Beijing Institute of Politics and Law | 1,628 |
| Beijing Light Industrial Institute | 1,228 |
| Beijing Foreign Languages Institute No. 2 | 1,131 |
| Beijing Sports Institute | 1,028 |
| Beijing Broadcasting Institute | 1,000 |
| Beijing Institute of Finance and Banking | 888 |
| Institute of Foreign Relations | 741 |
| Beijing Institute of Irrigation and Hydropower | 673 |
| Total student population in sample | 84,971 |
| Total student population in Beijing | 111,157 |

*Sources:* Beijing Normal University History Editorial Group (1982), 214; Beijing Statistical Bureau (1990), 481, 488; Beijing University of Science and Technology Archives Office (2006), 58; Chang Dianyuan (1994), 215; Chinese People's University (1992), 355; Fang Huijian and Zhang Sijing (2001), 1:818; Gao Yi (1982), 18, 45, 54, 642; Institute History Editorial Group (2001), 14; Jin Jichun (1994), 247; Li Rongfa (2000), 1; Li Xiaofeng (1992), 58, 99, 104, 109, 117; Northern Transportation University Annals Editorial Committee (1996), 278; Rong Shixing (2001), 6; Shen Shituan (2000), 433; Wang Buzheng (1995), 618; Wang Dechong and Lin Jintong (2005), 606; Wang Xuezhen et al. (1998), 640; Wu Peixu et al. (1992), 324; Xi Fuyun, et al. (1998), 69; Yu Shicheng (2003), 299; Zhao Pengda (2002), 177; Zhu Jinzhao (2002), 2.

teams with different strategies.[19] The conservative strategy was initially very common, but it was quickly abandoned in almost every school. If we suspect that work teams mobilized those with favorable positions in the status quo in an effort to protect their superiors, we are forced to confront some inconvenient facts. In the survey of the range of work-team experiences, there is one common theme: in virtually all schools, regardless of the work team's stance, power structures were fractured and their followers were divided against one another by the assaults of June and July.

### Radical Work Teams

There are six schools in our sample where one work team pursued a consistently radical course. Events at Beijing and Qinghua universities, the two largest and most important in the city, will be described here.[20] It was unusual for a work team to adopt a radical stance from the outset. The decisiveness of the work teams at the larger institutions—Beijing University, Qinghua University, Beijing Normal University, and the Beijing Institute of Politics and Law—was due to distinctive bureaucratic circumstances. These work teams were formed by units just below the Central Committee Secretariat and contained a variety of high officials from a range of ministries and commissions. These officials could not be personally implicated in any political problems uncovered in the schools and felt free to take a hard-line course.[21] In these cases, finally, the decision to depose the party committee and purge the school's party secretary for serious political transgressions was in fact made by higher officials even before the work team arrived.

### Beijing University

A survey of work teams in action must begin with Beijing University (commonly referred to as "Beida"). China's premier comprehensive university was the site of the "first Marxist-Leninist wall poster" that initiated these events. The work team immediately deposed the school's party leadership and conducted a purge that furthered the agenda of a small opposition group within the party organization. These party dissidents, based in the Philosophy Department, had been defeated and reprimanded after an earlier conflict with Lu Ping, the school President and party secretary, and his supporters during the Socialist Education Movement of 1964 and 1965.[22] The work team cooperated closely with this dissident faction, appointed its members to leading posts, and gave them free rein in attacking their enemies. This close cooperation between the work team and the university's indigenous "rebels" lasted until late July.

The May 25 wall poster is widely credited with inspiring the student rebellion that led to the red guard movement of August, and its authors later became prominent leaders of red guard factions. However, none of the authors were students. The first-named author, Nie Yuanzi, was general branch party secretary of the Philosophy Department, and her six coauthors were all instructors of Marxism-Leninism and senior party members.[23] Although Nie emerged as a famous rebel, she was clearly part of the party establishment. As a member of the Beida Party Committee and one of twenty-one general branch secretaries, she was among the top thirty officials in the school. When the wall poster appeared, she was forty-five years old and married to a high official in the central party apparatus twenty years her senior.[24]

Nie's rebellion against her party superiors was the culmination of two years of conflict with the university's top official, Lu Ping, and she initiated it only after prior assurances of backing from the highest levels of the national leadership.[25] The wall poster ignited a heated campus debate. Supporters of the party committee denounced Nie and her group as opportunists and accused them of an anti-party conspiracy.[26] The school's top leaders, however, split over the accusations. Two powerful figures—party First Vice-Secretary Ge Hua and standing committee member Cui Xiongkun—challenged Lu Ping to respond to the charges and resisted efforts to squelch the controversy. They argued that the wall poster raised basic political questions about the Socialist Education Movement and sent a letter to the Central Committee denouncing Lu Ping for attempting to "suppress revolution."[27]

The issue was settled when on June 1 Mao personally ordered that the wall poster be published nationwide. In instructions to Kang Sheng and Chen Boda, he wrote, "It is absolutely essential to circulate this in newspapers nationwide. Now we can start to smash the stronghold of reaction at Beijing University."[28] Zhang Chengxian arrived that evening and announced that Lu Ping was out, along with the entire party committee.[29] This was a complete victory for the school's dissidents. Cao Yi'ou, Kang Sheng's wife, who had instigated the wall poster on his behalf, became vice-head of the work team. She kept that post through the end of July and acted as liaison with the CCRG.[30] Several others who had helped instigate or write the wall poster or who had sided with the coauthors in past conflicts were given positions on the work team, which immediately implemented the agenda of the university dissidents.[31] Their original charge against Lu Ping in 1964 had been that he had permitted too many "politically impure elements" to assume prominent posts. In the ensuing weeks the work team directed a campaign to denounce the vast majority of administrators and faculty for reactionary political viewpoints and impure class origins or political histories. The purge targeted two groups: prominent intellectuals whose personal histories or political leanings were considered suspicious—the people the dissident party faction wanted to depose in the Socialist Education Movement—and Lu Ping loyalists who had defended him in the earlier struggle.[32]

By any standard the work team's purge was harsh. Accusations were made during public "struggle sessions": the accused were put on a stage and subjected to harrowing interrogations designed to extract confessions, usually with shouted denunciations, chanting crowds, and physical humiliation. According to the work team's records, by June 26, 230 cadres and teachers were targeted as enemies; 157 were dismissed from their posts, 192 had been put through struggle sessions, 94 had been beaten, and 107 had been paraded on campus in processions where they wore tall dunce hat and placards describing their crimes.[33] The work team classified all cadres into four categories according to the severity of their alleged errors. Category 1 consisted of those who had committed no errors and were entirely trustworthy; category 2 of those who had committed minor errors that could be remedied with sincere self-criticism; category 3 of those who had committed serious errors that required removal from their posts and a prolonged period of interrogation and self-examination. and category 4 of class enemies to be dismissed from the party and perhaps sent into a labor camp or internal exile.[34]

By July 10 the work team had almost finished, and its judgments were very severe. Only one out of twenty general branch secretaries (Nie Yuanzi) was judged reliable, and sixteen were placed in category 4 (see Table 2.2). Fewer than 8 percent of all the cadres were judged to be without error, and two-thirds were in categories 3 and 4. In sum, the work team vindicated the dissident group's accusations, dating back to 1964, that the school's party committee was a "revisionist black nest" and "rotten to the core."

The close cooperation between the work team and the school's dissidents lasted until late July. Prominent members of the dissident group played a leading role on the work team, making important speeches and

*Table 2.2* Work-team verdicts on party cadres at Beijing University, July 1966

| Unit | Category 1 | Category 2 | Category 3 | Category 4 | Total |
|------|-----------|-----------|-----------|-----------|-------|
| General branches | 1 (5%) | 0 | 3 (15%) | 16 (80%) | 20 |
| Party branches | 5 (3.3%) | 46 (30.1%) | 56 (36.6%) | 46 (30.1%) | 153 |
| Party-administrative cadres | 47 (9%) | 136 (26.1%) | 219 (42%) | 119 (22.8%) | 521 |
| Total | 53 (7.6%) | 182 (26.2%) | 278 (40.1%) | 181 (26.1%) | 694 |

*Source:* Wang Xuezhen et al. (1998), 647–648. Statistics were compiled on July 10 and exclude the History Department.

expressing support for the work team's conduct. Not until July 19 did Nie Yuanzi criticize the work team and its leader, Zhang Chengxian.[35] This was her response to information that Mao had grown disenchanted with the actions of work teams and was about to order their withdrawal.[36]

## Qinghua University

Qinghua was China's premier scientific and engineering university, and its president and party secretary, Jiang Nanxiang, was the highest-ranking academic administrator in the country, serving simultaneously as minister of higher education.[37] He was an obvious target for any purge of academic circles. For more than a week after the publication of the Beida wall poster, Jiang attempted to fend off similar accusations by relying on loyal members of Qinghua's party organization. These efforts ended abruptly after the work team's arrival on June 8 and Jiang's purge two days later.[38]

In the wake of Jiang's purge, a large work team headed by a vice-chairman of the State Economic Commission and two vice-ministers took over leadership of the school. Unlike Beida's work team, this one acknowledged no genuine "leftists" among the dissidents in the school hierarchy. It immediately suspended all school officials from their posts and had them stand aside for investigation and criticism.[39] Even the ordinary members of party branch committees were suspended.

The impact of the work team's assault on the power structure can be gauged from the treatment of those suspended from their posts. The work team organized two "labor reform brigades." In the first (type 1 in Table 2.3), the accused performed manual labor all day under the supervision of guards, with a signboard hanging from their necks labeling them members of the "black gang," and every day or two the victim would have to turn in a labor diary. The second was a lighter version (type 2 in Table 2.3) in which the victim worked without supervision or signboard for half a day and gave an oral report every few days. The top school authorities were treated the most harshly: only 14 of 206 top officials escaped labor reform, and 162 were type 1 "black gang." All but 2 of the 31 members of the university's party committee were subjected to the harsher type of labor reform (Table 2.3). Qinghua's work team conducted the most militant purge of any university I can document. Unlike Beida's work team, it did not acknowledge the revolutionary credentials of a dissident party group.

### Conservative Work Teams

Conservative work teams took a diametrically opposed approach. They insisted that the school's leadership was basically reliable, and they refused to depose the party secretary. Instead of orchestrating devastating purges of the entire party apparatus, they spent much of their time defending party officials. This was a common strategy among the first wave of work teams in early June. In almost all these cases the ministry directly responsible for administering these schools sent the work team. In some cases the individual personally responsible for supervising the school was put in charge. Conservatism appears to have been one response to a potential conflict of interest: if severe political problems were uncovered in the school, this would implicate officials in the ministry responsible for the school. A conservative work-team strategy was clearly an effort to minimize the political damage.

A conservative strategy usually encountered strong internal opposition and was difficult to sustain. At only four of the twenty-seven schools in my sample did the work teams maintain a conservative stance until the end of July. Another eleven work teams quickly shifted to a more radical course or were replaced by a second, more radical work team. The impact of the four conservative work teams was far from straightforward and was very different from what one might have imagined. Despite shielding top officials, conservative work teams conducted extensive purges that decimated the middle and lower reaches of the school's power structure.

Table 2.3  Labor reform brigades under the Qinghua University work team, June–July 1966

| Administrative level | Top decision makers | Type 1 labor reform | Type 2 labor reform | Percent | Other leading cadres | Type 1 labor reform | Type 2 labor reform | Percent | Others in labor reform | Total in labor reform |
|---|---|---|---|---|---|---|---|---|---|---|
| University party committee | 31 | 29 | 0 | 94% | 15 | 1 | 14 | 100% | 0 | 44 |
| Administrative offices | 33 | 23 | 4 | 82% | 55 | 32 | 12 | 80% | 8 | 79 |
| Academic departments | 142 | 110 | 26 | 96% | 141 | 18 | 66 | 87% | 88 | 308 |
| Total | 206 | 162 | 30 | 93% | 189 | 51 | 92 | 86% | 74 | 431 |

*Source:* Qinghua University Jinggangshan United General Headquarters (1967a), 4–5. Figures are from survey results reported in a wall poster dated November 7, 1966, and were taken from records of the former Cultural Revolution committee.

*Notes:* "Top decision makers" refers to members of party general branch committees in academic departments, general branch and division-level cadres in administrative offices, and ministry-level cadres in the university party committee office. "Others in labor reform" refers primarily to members of party branch committees or ordinary political instructors who were party members, and to "bourgeois academic authorities, hooligans, and bad elements."

By inviting criticism of top officials and then retaliating against those who did so, they created deep and irrevocable splits within the power structure itself. This is illustrated by events at the Beijing Mining Institute and the Central Nationalities Institute.[40]

## Beijing Mining Institute

The work team at the Beijing Mining Institute refused to depose the party leadership because the Ministry of Coal had already purged the party committee several months before.[41] The institute's president was removed from office for errors similar to those later lodged against Lu Ping at Beida, and its party committee was reorganized. When the Cultural Revolution began, ministry officials felt that they had already cleaned house in the Mining Institute. They were convinced that the new party secretary, Zhang Xuewen, was politically reliable.

The new school party committee began its purge campaign in mid-May, well before the appearance of the Beida wall poster. Party Secretary Zhang deflected criticism by claiming that he was already a proven leftist. He asserted that those who had studied in the Soviet Union were leftist, while cadres from bourgeois backgrounds or with questionable political histories were no good. Charging that the entire school, under the influence of his predecessor, had been infected with a "black line," Zhang proceeded to purge the apparatus under him of loyal followers of the previous party committee. He drew up a blacklist that included nineteen of twenty-three department chairmen and vice-chairmen.

The work team sent by the ministry in mid-June simply intensified the purge campaign that was already under way. Party Secretary Zhang left for the beach resort at Beidaihe and stayed until mid-July. In his absence the work team escalated the campaign against alleged followers of the old party committee, and cadres who protested were attacked and their houses searched. After the work team finished its purge and silenced dissenting voices, Zhang returned to the school and joined the leading group of the work team. When the work team was withdrawn at the end of July, it transferred power back to him, and he resumed his role as the tormentor of cadres loyal to the old party committee. The purge at the Mining Institute was extensive, but it was conduced by the existing school leadership with the firm backing of the ministry's work team.

## Central Nationalities Institute

The impact of the work team at the Central Nationalities Institute, sent by the Central Committee's Nationalities Affairs Commission, was especially complicated. It shows how even a conservative work team could split university power structures and present students with confusing political choices. The work team arrived on June 2, the same day the Beida wall poster was celebrated in the mass media. It was led by an official who was vice-head of the CCP United Front Work Department, vice-chairman of the CCP Nationalities Affairs Commission, and concurrently president of the Nationalities Institute itself.[42] Not surprisingly, this work team, led by officials directly responsible for the school, reacted with harsh defensiveness to all efforts to lodge accusations against the school's leadership. It appointed the institute's party secretary to head the school's Cultural Revolution committee and conducted a campaign that evaluated the political loyalty of all students and faculty and classified them as "leftist," "middle-of-the-road," or "rightist." In one department 80 percent of the faculty and staff were classified as "beyond redemption." Throughout the work team's stay, students and others put up wall posters demanding that the work team change course or withdraw, but they were attacked in turn.

Political alignments in the institute were scrambled when the vice-head of the Cultural Revolution committee, a teacher from a "revolutionary cadre" household named Zheng Zhongbing, defected to the opposition. Zheng had been loyal to the work team and actively defended it for more than six weeks, but suddenly on July 17 he and four others put up a wall poster that denounced the work team for sabotaging the Cultural Revolution and charged that "the work team did not come to the institute to foment revolution, but to hatch conspiracies." Zheng became a leader of the budding opposition, and on July 28, just as work teams were about to be ordered out of all schools, he authored a wall poster signed by more than 100 others that demanded the work team's withdrawal. Zheng subsequently claimed the mantle of the "anti-work-team" camp and eventually became the leader of one of the two main red guard factions in the school. However, he was opposed by large numbers of students who had opposed the work team from the beginning. They saw his late July about-face as an opportunist act by someone who had long cooperated with the work team. This was the origin of the split between rebel forces at the Nationalities Institute that lasted until the end of the Cultural Revolution.

## Mixed Strategies

Some work teams adopted a strategy that contained elements of both radical and conservative approaches. Its defining feature was that the work team found serious political problems at the school but identified a reliable "red" line within the leadership and defended it from criticism. This strategy was easily the most divisive of all. By identifying a "red" line in the school and turning its adherents against colleagues said to follow a "black" line, this stance divided the school's power structure in two and turned one side against the other. It shattered the power structure into two large and sharply opposing groups: victims and their tormentors. Work teams at six schools in my sample pursued it consistently through June and July. The examples of Chinese People's University, Beijing Agricultural University, and the Beijing Steel Institute will be described here.[43]

## Chinese People's University

The work team at Chinese People's University arrived late—June 14—and suffered from a severe conflict of interest that prevented it from acknowledging serious criticisms of the school's party secretary, Guo Yingqiu, who had been promoted three weeks earlier to direct work teams for the new Municipal Party Committee.[44] This put the work team in an impossible situation: if it resisted accusations against Guo, it would be seen as protecting him, but if it accepted the accusations, it would be crossing its superior.

Within the limits of its position, the work team adopted a militant stance from the outset. It seized power from the party committee and had all cadres in the power structure stand aside from their posts pending investigation, even political instructors and student cadres in the party and youth league. In a speech on the first day he arrived, the work team's head announced that anyone or anything could be exposed—there would be no limits. Cultural Revolution committees in all departments held accusation meetings against department leaders. In some departments almost all leading cadres were denounced.

When this process threatened to touch upon Guo Yingqiu, however, the work team backpedaled from its stated position. Shortly after the work team arrived, the vice-chairman of the Philosophy Department, who was also a member of the school's party committee, denounced one of Guo's deputies in connection with "the party committee problem." The next day the work team's head called an all-school mass meeting to declare that Guo Yingqiu was a genuine leftist. The work team refused to permit his deputies to be put through struggle sessions, and soon the vice-chairman of the Philosophy Department himself was accused of political crimes. Critics argued that in a school where so many in the power structure were found to have committed errors, those ultimately in charge could not be absolved of blame. Accusations persisted, and many of the critics were labeled anti-party and were subjected to struggle sessions. Within two weeks the work team decreed that all struggle sessions had to be cleared in advance. In the meantime, the work team's purge proceeded, and 538 individuals were designated "rightists"—12 percent of the entire school community. The purge hit the cadre ranks the hardest: 145 out of the 257 cadres in the school, more than half, fell in the campaign.

No matter how militant its purge, the work team was dogged by charges that it was protecting the leaders ultimately responsible for the school. As critics of the party committee continued to suffer from counterattacks, suspicion grew that the critics were victims of a conspiracy to cover up and protect Guo and his two associates. The more militant the work team's purge, the more it seemed that it was trying to protect Guo. The identification of the work team with the school's party secretary divided the school's power structure and the student community long after the work team's withdrawal.

### Beijing Agricultural University

The work team sent to Beijing Agricultural University refused to purge its power structure because this had already been done. In the first days of June, the Ministry of Agriculture acted to preempt student rebellion by unilaterally purging the party standing committee.[45] Claiming to have rooted out all political problems in the school, the ministry put the party committee in charge of the coming campaign. This left the original party secretary and one of the party vice-secretaries in control during the entire first half of June. Initially they shielded the party apparatus from attack. On June 3, the day after the publication of the Beida wall poster, the party secretary gave a speech and declared that his party committee was revolutionary. He formed an investigation group that would focus on bourgeois professors, health clinic workers, and the school's post office. He called on all political activists to expose and criticize people in these units.

After the work team arrived on June 14, it left the new party commit-tee in place, but it pushed for a more radical attack on the power struc-ture. It declared that its task was to distinguish the "red line" within the school from the "black line." The party secretary and a few of his close associates represented that "red line," while the "black line" had deeply influenced the rest of the power structure. The work team charged that the general branch secretaries were particularly problematic. It waged an extensive campaign against the power structure. Almost all officeholders were temporarily suspended. General branch secretaries, basic-level cadres, class counselors, and even ordinary party members were investi-gated and forced to make self-criticisms before a final verdict would be reached. In the end, only seven of the twenty-five members of the school's party committee kept their posts. Eighty percent of the cadres at the division-head level were forced to stand aside, and 90 percent of those at the general branch secretary level. Almost all of the nineteen department heads and general branch secretaries lost their posts, as did large num-bers of branch secretaries and classroom counselors. When the work team withdrew at the end of July, it left the original party secretary in charge of a thoroughly purged power structure made up of fortunate sur-vivors and activists who had been promoted for cooperating with the work team's assault. It also left behind a large number of victims who felt that top officials had sacrificed them in a cynical strategy of survival.

### Beijing Steel Institute

The Beijing Steel Institute's party secretary, Gao Yunsheng, initiated a campaign against politically backward elements in his school well before the work team arrived.[46] Unlike his colleague at Beijing Agricultural Uni-versity, however, his superiors in the ministry sold him out. In April 1966 Gao charged that one of his deputies, Vice-Secretary Zhang Wenqi, and two other members of the party committee had advanced a "bourgeois line" in education. He orchestrated a criticism campaign against them and their followers. Gao's preemptive show of leftist rectitude did little to prevent the appearance of wall posters denouncing him after the pub-lication of the Beida wall poster on June 2, nor did it win him the sup-port of his superiors in the ministry. In fact, his harsh purge campaign motivated many of the accusations against him. The work team arrived on June 4, having already been told by ministry officials that the school had serious political problems that centered on Gao himself. As wall-poster attacks on Gao escalated, the work team finally announced on June 10 that Gao was out, the work team would take control, and all cadres would stand aside for investigation.

Gao's downfall meant that the verdicts on his recent victims, Zhang Wenqi and two other party committee members, would be reversed. The ensuing campaign turned into an attack on the followers of "the Gao Yunsheng line," while the work team defended Gao's former victims and their reputed followers. In a manner typical of a mixed strategy, the school's power structure was turned against itself. Those who had earlier been threatened by Gao's campaign denounced him and his followers. Also typical of a mixed strategy, the purges hit roughly half the power structure. Out of the school's sixty-seven middle-level cadres, thirty were subjected to struggle sessions and paraded around the campus grounds with dunce caps, and forty-seven were placed in categories 3 and 4. The splits in the school were intensified by Gao Yunsheng's dramatic suicide on July 3. The divisions endured long after the work team's withdrawal, expressed as a debate over Gao's innocence or guilt.

## Work Teams That Reversed Course

Work teams sent by agencies directly responsible for a school faced a profound conflict of interest. Serious political problems in the school might implicate them as well. These work teams faced a strategic dilemma: should they try to shore up the school's party committee and deny serious political problems in the school, or should they adopt a radical stance and prove their rectitude with a militant purge? Some work teams adopted the first strategy but suddenly abandoned it for the second in the face of mounting student opposition. This sequence was observed at six schools where work teams, after an initial delay, suddenly shifted to a radical or mixed stance. Two of them—Beijing Aeronautics Institute and Beijing Geology Institute—had large student bodies and played a crucial role in the subsequent red guard movement.[47]

## Beijing Aeronautics Institute

The Beijing Aeronautics Institute, a college of aeronautical engineering, was directly under the National Defense Science and Technology Commission, which in turn was directly under the Ministry of Defense.[48] On May 23 Zhao Ruzhang, the official in the commission who was in charge of the institute, arrived with a liaison group that was sent to help the school carry out the Cultural Revolution.[49] After the Beida wall poster was publicized on June 2, posters critical of the school's party committee began to appear, and over the next few days new wall posters accused the commission of political errors. Soon afterward the liaison group was reorganized as a work team. Zhao Ruzhang remained in the school and attended all meetings of the party committee. He stated that his work team was there simply to assist the school party committee, and that the criticisms of it were overblown, cases of "leftists attacking leftists." He repeatedly counseled people to calm down, and he minimized the political problems in the school.

The work team was welcomed at a mass meeting on June 8, with Zhao Ruzhang as its head. Zhao proclaimed that the school's leaders would stay in power and the work team would work under their direction. The institute's party secretary gave a self-critical speech and invited criticisms of the party committee. The conciliatory attitude did not appease critics. The accusations escalated, and the party committee was increasingly put on the defensive. The work team did not intervene to halt the criticisms but eventually concluded that the party secretary would not be able to withstand the escalating attacks. Finally, on June 16 orders came down from the commission to remove the party secretary from his post.[50]

At this point the work team seized control and declared that the school's party organization had serious political problems. It initiated a campaign in which all officials stood aside for investigation. Of the eight top school officials, five were judged to have serious political problems, six were removed from their posts, four were subjected to struggle sessions, and all had their homes searched and performed manual labor on campus (see Table 2.4). Out of thirty-three cadres at the next two departmental levels, only four were judged to be free of serious political problems. Even political instructors were made to stand aside (88 percent), although few were found to have committed serious errors (10 percent) and fewer still were subjected to struggle sessions. The work team at the Aeronautics Institute therefore took fundamentally different positions before and after June 16. It was as if two different work teams had been sent to the school.

### Beijing Geology Institute

Anticipating the forthcoming campaign, the Ministry of Geology sent a small work group to the Geology Institute on May 20. The work group

Table 2.4  Work-team verdicts at Beijing Aeronautics Institute, June–July 1966

| Rank of cadre | Total number of cadres in rank | Put in categories 3 and 4 (percent) | Suspended from duty (percent) | In labor reform brigade (percent)* | Homes searched (percent)* | Target of struggle session (percent) |
|---|---|---|---|---|---|---|
| Party secretaries, president, vice-presidents | 8 | 5 (63%) | 6 (75%) | 8 (100%) | 8 (100%) | 4 (50%) |
| Middle-level political department cadres | 18 | 14 (78%) | 16 (89%) | 14 (78%) | 14 (78%) | 4 (22%) |
| General branch secretaries and department heads | 15 | 15 (100%) | 15 (100%) | 15 (100%) | 15 (100%) | 14 (93%) |
| Middle-level cadres in academic departments | 45 | 31 (69%) | 41 (91%) | 34 (76%) | 23 (51%) | 15 (33%) |
| Political instructors in various departments | 78 | 8 (10%) | 69 (88%) | — | — | 3 (4%) |
| Total | 164 | 73 (45%) | 147 (90%) | 71 (83%) | 60 (70%) | 40 (24%) |

*Source:* Beijing Aeronautics Institute Red Flag (1967), 7.
*Totals and percentages in this column exclude missing data for political instructors.

observed the uproar that followed the June 2 publication of the Beida wall poster. Wall posters denouncing the school's party committee went up the same day. One of the institute's party vice-secretaries gave a speech to students that day offering a self-criticism on behalf of the party committee. He then announced that the party committee would begin a rectification campaign that would start at the top of the party hierarchy. The next day the party secretary and ranking vice-minister of geology, He Changgong,[51] personally visited the institute and made a speech intended to avert extreme accusations. The school's party committee, he assured everyone, was revolutionary; it was not the same as Beida or the old Beijing Party Committee. This later proved to be a fateful act because it inserted the vice-minister personally into the internal politics of the school. Wall posters defending the school's party committee appeared shortly after He's visit. The critics later complained that they were on the defensive for the next week. Political instructors and party branch secretaries were ordered to hold study sessions to "absorb the lessons of the 1957 anti-rightist campaign," when critics of the party committees were accused of political crimes and sent to labor camps.[52]

Despite these warnings, critics persisted. On June 13 the full work team finally arrived. Led by Vice-Minister Zou Jiayou,[53] it included more than 200 members who were prepared to run investigations in all departments and offices. Inspired by the work team's arrival and by news of developments at nearby Qinghua University (where President Jiang Nanxiang's purge was announced on June 10), students and teachers organized struggle sessions against members of the party committee. The work team initially did not intervene and permitted the struggle sessions to take place.[54]

However, many students had not forgotten Vice-Minister He Changgong's June 3 speech, in which he asserted that there were no serious political problems in the school. In the course of struggle sessions, school officials confessed that their actions had the prior approval of the ministry—they were "just carrying out orders." Students drew the obvious conclusion: the school's "black line" extended into the ministry, just as Beida's problems were rooted in the Beijing Party Committee. Had not the vice-minister himself tried to cover things up?

This was a conclusion that the work team clearly wanted to avoid. The day the work team arrived at the school, Vice-Minister Xu Guangyi made a speech emphasizing that the political problems in the institute were not the fault of the ministry.[55] The institute's party committee, however, should be looked into. The next day the work team ordered the institute's party secretary and president, Gao Yuangui, to make a self-criticism before the whole school. Struggle sessions and interrogations of one of the institute's party vice-secretaries, however, turned up evidence implicating top ministry officials. At this point the work team intervened, canceled plans for further interrogation of the vice-secretary, and instead scheduled a mass criticism assembly against Gao Yuangui. On June 21 a member of the work team told students that the school's party secretary no longer had the support of the ministry and was fair game. Gao Yuangui had "failed to accept the correct leadership of the ministry."[56]

The work team's increasingly militant stance toward school officials was clearly intended to avoid implicating ministry officials in the escalating accusations. The work team had not tried to prevent student attacks against top school officials, but when their confessions began to implicate the ministry, it moved quickly against the school's party secretary. The Geology Institute work team, in the end, did not attempt to protect school officials but sought to blame them for all errors and in so doing shield the ministry. As we shall see in the next chapter, this maneuver split the school's power structure and student body into supporters and opponents of the work team's maneuver.

### Two Work Teams

Although some of the conservative work teams were able to reverse course and survive, others faced such serious opposition that they withdrew and had to be replaced. This occurred in five of the schools in my sample, and in every case the second work team adopted a radical stance. Two of these cases—Beijing Industrial University and the Beijing Post and Telecommunications Institute—had important implications outside their campuses and will be described here.[57]

### Beijing Industrial University

Perhaps the clearest example of successive work teams that adopted diametrically opposed stances is Beijing Industrial University. This obscure polytechnic under the municipal government had admitted its first class of students only in 1960. Its party secretary, however, was anything but obscure. He was Song Shuo, who was also vice-head of the Municipal Party Committee's University and Science Work Department and one of the three officials denounced in Nie Yuanzi's famous Beida wall poster, and whose June 3 purge was announced in *People's Daily*.[58] Fang Zhixi, vice-chairman of the Economics Department and member of the party committee of Chinese People's University, headed the first work team.[59] Fang's low rank attested to the low prestige of a new technical college run by the city government.

Despite the school's direct connection through Song Shuo to the anti-party conspiracy recently exposed in Beijing, the first work team took a remarkably soft line after arriving on June 2. It announced that it would "assist in revolutionizing the party committee" and left it in charge. Incumbent officials at each level would lead a movement of criticism and self-criticism; party and youth league members were to criticize their own errors and encourage others to do the same. Not surprisingly, this approach led to strong resistance from students and teachers who asserted that a party committee led by Song Shuo must have committed serious errors and could not be left in charge. The work team was unable to handle the growing opposition and was replaced on June 16 by a new work team that had an entirely different attitude.[60]

A cadre of much higher rank and more impressive political credentials led the second work team. Du Wanrong was vice-director of the Political Department of the People's Liberation Army General Staff Headquarters and had been a political commissar in the Eighth Route Army in North China during the 1940s.[61] He declared a radical agenda immediately after entering the school: every cadre in the school would step down from his or her post, be put in isolation, and write a self-examination. The work team suspended the entire party organization and took over the school, and the power structure was decimated by the campaign.

Figures later compiled by the opponents of the work teams reveal a purge that was as drastic as any in the city (see Table 2.5). Only 20 percent of the school's cadres were judged to be "good" or "relatively good," while 36 percent were "anti-party." The purge hit high-level cadres the hardest: none of the top officials and only four section and department heads were deemed at least "relatively good"—fewer than 10 percent. Lower-ranking cadres were treated more leniently—26 percent were at least "relatively good." Over half the middle-level cadres were subjected to struggle sessions, along with 20 percent of the basic-level cadres. The purge was so severe that even ordinary party members were often found to be lacking: in one department only four out of twenty party members were considered good enough to be nominated for a new

Table 2.5  Work-team verdicts at Beijing Industrial University, June–July 1966

| Rank of cadre | Total number of cadres in rank | Categories 1, 2 (good, relatively good) | Category 3 (major errors) | Category 4 (anti-party) |
|---|---|---|---|---|
| Top university officials | 5 | 0 | 1 (20%) | 4 (80%) |
| Department/section heads | 36 | 4 (11%) | 18 (50%) | 14 (39%) |
| Teaching section heads | 29 | 12 (41%) | 9 (31%) | 8 (28%) |
| Ordinary cadres at above three levels | 17 | 2 (12%) | 7 (41%) | 8 (47%) |
| Teaching office cadres | 31 | 6 (19%) | 16 (52%) | 9 (29%) |
| Total | 118 (100%) | 24 (20%) | 51 (43%) | 43 (36%) |

Source: Dongfanghong, 13 April 1967, 1–2 (CCRM 1999, 2:673–674).

party branch committee, and work-team cadres expressed the view that ordinary students and teachers were often more politically reliable than most party members in the school.

Industrial University's two work teams represented opposite extremes. A low-ranking cadre led the first one and followed a timid course, permitting incumbent leaders to run their own movement and restricting criticism to the lower levels of the power structure. The leader of the second one was a senior military officer and Red Army veteran who decimated the party organization in a purge that spared no one. As we shall see in the next chapter, the sudden and drastic shift in strategy from the first work team to the second created political divisions in the school and inspired a speech in defense of the *second* work team by one of the school's student leaders, Tan Lifu, that sparked one of the red guard movement's most famous controversies.

### Beijing Post and Telecommunications Institute

The Beijing Post and Telecommunications Institute was the capital's most tumultuous campus before August 1966. The Ministry of Post and Telecommunications was so deeply involved in the work team's actions in this institute that it is difficult to draw a distinction between the politics of the ministry and the internal politics of the school. Instructors in the school's Marxism-Leninism Teaching Office lodged the first serious accusations against the school's leaders. The school's "first Marxist-Leninist wall poster" was put up on May 24—a day before the more celebrated one at Beida—and was followed on June 3 and 4 by several others denouncing an "anti–Mao Thought clique" led by the school's party secretary.[62] Several party vice-secretaries rallied loyal party members in their defense, and militant students attacked the critics. The first work team, led by the head of the ministry's Education Department, arrived in the midst of this debate on June 4. It did not take a stand on the critical wall posters, but it left the party committee in charge and permitted the attacks on the critics from the Marxism-Leninism Teaching Office to continue.

The critics, like Nie Yuanzi's group at Beida, were all instructors of Marxism-Leninism, but the work team, instead of following the Beida scenario by deposing the party committee and elevating the critics, kept the party committee in power and left the critics vulnerable to retribution. The obvious violation of the Beida script led to increased support for the critics until on June 8 opposition to the work team became so intense that the work team retreated to the ministry's downtown offices.

On that same day the ministry sent a new work team led by the head of the ministry's Political Department. He announced on June 10 that there was a "black gang" in the party committee. All cadres would stand aside for investigation. This ended the orchestrated attacks on the party committee's critics. The work team announced that the school's president was stripped of all posts on June 18, and later that month the work team orchestrated criticism of the party secretary.

Despite this newly militant stand, the work team became entangled in an escalating dispute with students who had been victimized earlier in the month by the first work team. The conflict began on June 11, when 200 to 300 students marched to the ministry's offices to put up wall posters denouncing the head of the first work team, and they demanded that he be brought back to the campus to answer for his errors. The next day another group of students went to the ministry and raised the stakes of the struggle when they denounced the work team's superiors on the ministry's party committee. This set off a series of maneuvers by the ministry's top officials that drew the second work team into the middle of an escalating dispute. Increasingly under attack in the school, despite its militant stance toward the institute's party leadership, the work team was ordered to counterattack, and its purge of the party apparatus was diverted into a campaign against a large opposition movement that will be described in the next chapter.

The remarkably diverse work-team histories in the twenty-seven schools in my sample, summarized in Table 2.6, defy simple characterization. In the sixteen cases where a single work team pursued the same strategy to the end of July, the mixed strategy was as common as the radical one, while the conservative strategy was somewhat less common. In the other eleven cases an initially conservative strategy was quickly abandoned. In all but two of these cases the work team either reversed course and adopted a more radical stance or was replaced by a second, radical work team. When the cases are classified in this manner, there is no clear pattern.

If we classify cases differently, however, a clear pattern does emerge. Table 2.7 sorts universities according to the strategies adopted by their work teams over time. The table contrasts the stances of the first wave of work teams during early June with those of the second wave that followed in the middle of the month. The first wave classifies schools according to the initial strategies of work teams, whether or not they were

Table 2.6  A typology of university work-team histories

| Work-team orientation | University |
|---|---|
| Radical | Beijing Broadcasting Institute |
| | Beijing Institute of Politics and Law |
| | Beijing Normal University |
| | Beijing University |
| | Institute of Foreign Relations |
| | Qinghua University |
| Conservative | Beijing Institute of Irrigation and Hydropower |
| | Beijing Mining Institute |
| | Beijing Sports Institute |
| | Central Nationalities Institute |
| Mixed radical-conservative | Beijing Agricultural University |
| | Beijing Institute of Finance and Banking |
| | Beijing Normal Institute |
| | Beijing Steel Institute |
| | Chinese People's University |
| | Chinese University of Science and Technology |
| Shifted from conservative to radical | Beijing Aeronautics Institute |
| | Beijing Agricultural Machinery Institute |
| | Beijing Foreign Languages Institute No. 2 |
| | Beijing Geology Institute |
| Shifted from conservative to mixed | Beijing Petroleum Institute |
| | Beijing Railway Institute |
| Conservative replaced by radical | Beijing Foreign Languages Institute |
| | Beijing Forestry Institute |
| | Beijing Industrial University |
| | Beijing Light Industrial Institute |
| | Beijing Post and Telecommunications Institute |

replaced. The second wave classifies schools according to the strategy adopted after mid-June by either the initial work team or its replacement.

Now a dramatic shift in work-team behavior becomes obvious. During the first wave the most common stance by far was conservative. During the second wave the radical stance suddenly became the most common and the conservative stance became very rare. In other words, after the first two weeks of June the power structures of almost all the

*Table 2.7*  The shift in work-team strategies

| Orientation | First wave | Second wave |
|---|---|---|
| Conservative | Beijing Aeronautics Institute<br>Beijing Agricultural Machinery<br>   Institute<br>Beijing Foreign Languages Institute<br>Beijing Foreign Languages<br>   Institute No. 2<br>Beijing Forestry Institute<br>Beijing Geology Institute<br>Beijing Industrial University<br>Beijing Institute of Irrigation<br>   and Hydropower<br>Beijing Light Industrial Institute<br>Beijing Mining Institute<br>Beijing Petroleum Institute<br>Beijing Post and Telecommuni-<br>   cations Institute<br>Beijing Railway Institute<br>Beijing Sports Institute<br>Central Nationalities Institute | Beijing Institute of Irrigation<br>   and Hydropower<br>Beijing Mining Institute<br>Beijing Sports Institute<br>Central Nationalities Institute |
| Radical | Beijing Broadcasting Institute<br>Beijing Institute of Politics and Law<br>Beijing Normal University<br>Beijing University<br>Institute of Foreign Relations<br>Qinghua University | Beijing Aeronautics Institute<br>Beijing Agricultural Machinery<br>   Institute<br>Beijing Broadcasting Institute<br>Beijing Foreign Languages Institute<br>Beijing Foreign Languages<br>   Institute No. 2<br>Beijing Forestry Institute<br>Beijing Geology Institute<br>Beijing Industrial University<br>Beijing Institute of Politics and Law<br>Beijing Light Industrial Institute<br>Beijing Normal University<br>Beijing Post and Telecommunications<br>   Institute<br>Beijing University<br>Institute of Foreign Relations<br>Qinghua University |
| Mixed | Beijing Agricultural University<br>Beijing Institute of Finance<br>   and Banking<br>Beijing Normal Institute | Beijing Agricultural University<br>Beijing Institute of Finance<br>   and Banking<br>Beijing Normal Institute |

*Table 2.7 (continued)*

| Orientation | First wave | Second wave |
|---|---|---|
| | Beijing Steel Institute | Beijing Petroleum Institute |
| | Chinese People's University | Beijing Railway Institute |
| | Chinese University of Science and Technology | Beijing Steel Institute |
| | | Chinese People's University |
| | | Chinese University of Science and Technology |

universities in my sample were under severe assault. Either a radical work team attacked the entire power structure or a mixed strategy split it in two.

It should be apparent that university power structures were deeply altered, if not completely shattered, by the interventions of the work teams. According to incomplete statistics circulated in the Municipal Party Committee's internal bulletin at the time, by mid-July 55 percent of all university party first secretaries and 40 percent of all general branch secretaries had been labeled anti-party reactionaries and placed in category 4.[63] Work teams that launched a withering assault made it virtually impossible for those connected to the power structure to mobilize in its defense. Work teams that were radical from the outset decapitated school power structures and immobilized them. After a delay of a week or two, the same thing occurred at universities where conservative work teams changed course or were replaced. By the third week of June, party committees in all these schools were so thoroughly discredited that there was never any prospect for loyal students to mobilize in their defense. Where work teams pursued a mixed strategy and sought to shield trusted "red" elements in a school's leadership, the power structure splintered as those associated with one leadership group turned on the others.

When political hierarchies are shattered in this manner, they no longer provide a basis for predicting the political affiliations of those most closely associated with them. A favorable position in the status quo does not create uniform interests that distinguish the favored from the less favored. The status quo no longer exists. If work teams had never entered the universities, or if the brief interlude of work teams that supported party committees had not ended so abruptly, those closely tied to the power structure would likely have rallied around their party superiors—with their clear encouragement—to defend them against serious accusations.

This occurred in many of the universities in my sample when incumbent party officials were put in charge. But this stance did not survive past mid-June, and as school power structures were shattered, their once-formidable networks were paralyzed and fragmented. The next chapter documents how the abrupt and unpredictable breakdown of school power structures drew many students and others, including large numbers of those closely tied to school power structures, into harrowing confrontations with the work teams.

# 3

## THE GENESIS OF DIVISION

### Sources of Opposition and Conflict

Factions appeared soon after the abrupt withdrawal of work teams. Students who had actively or passively cooperated with the work team formed the dominant faction. In virtually every school, however, there was a smaller dissident group composed of two distinct kinds of people: those who had challenged the work team and were punished in response, and those who had not challenged the work team but were placed under political suspicion or otherwise marginalized. Understanding the origins of red guard factions requires a closer look at the conflicts that occurred within schools under the work teams.

We need to ask three questions about these conflicts. What *were* their origins, if they were not contests that pitted those with vested interests in the status quo against challengers formerly marginalized by it? Who challenged the work teams, and in particular, what is the evidence that the challengers commonly had strong ties to power structures? How did work teams create identifiable groups within the school who would sympathize with student challengers? Only by answering these questions can we explain the almost instantaneous emergence of two antagonistic factions in early August.

The first wave of work teams clashed with students immediately and often provoked harsh counterattacks. In his report to the Beijing Municipal Party Committee on July 3, Guo Yingqiu emphasized the need to curtail violence. Work teams struggled to control a rising tide of violence toward party officials. Of particular concern to Guo was a wave of violent struggle sessions at Beida on June 18 and on other campuses. Guo cited figures from nine leading institutions, where 138 leading cadres were beaten during spontaneous struggle sessions. The movement to drive work teams away from the universities reached a high point on June 17, and within a few days thirty-nine work teams had retreated from university campuses at least temporarily.[1] By early July the work teams were fully in control in only nine schools—Guo cited Beida as an example. In twenty-one schools the work teams had gained the upper hand after confronting their opponents—Guo cited Qinghua as an example. In ten schools, Guo said, the students were out of control.

Although the effort to curtail violence was indeed a major source of conflict, it was only part of a larger constellation of issues. Just as the political actions of work teams varied widely, so did the specific issues and motives that generated conflict. Work teams divided university communities no matter what stance they took, how severe the conflicts, or how widespread the opposition. This is clear if we examine the conflicts of the work-team period by their degree of severity. In the first category are "pacified" campuses, where the work team met no overt opposition or was able quickly to suppress it. The second category includes campuses where the work team confronted challenges from militant students and felt compelled to punish those who refused to back down. The third type consists of campuses where work teams faced major challenges and generated confrontations so severe that they had to call in higher authorities for help and mount an extensive campaign to punish and intimidate opponents.

### Pacified Campuses

After early June opposition on most of the campuses in my sample was either nonexistent or weak. These campuses experienced the entire range of work-team strategies. Two cases will be described in some detail because their factional divisions played an important role in the later development of the Beijing red guard movement: Beijing University and Beijing Industrial University. On six other campuses in my sample, conflicts initially generated by work teams were quickly suppressed, but in each case they left a lasting legacy. The example of Beijing Agricultural University will be described here.[2]

### Beijing University

Beida's work team was the first to be denounced and removed for suppressing the student movement, but it never faced serious opposition. It punished no more than a handful of students for violence during struggle sessions. Instead, conflict emerged from within the work team itself because of the factional maneuverings of politicians in the national leadership. The work team's defining act was its response to campus violence in mid-June. Its treatment of the perpetrators was remarkably mild, compared with what later transpired on other campuses, but its report to the Central Committee on the "June 18 incident" denounced student violence in no uncertain terms. The report was soon transmitted to party organizations nationwide as a model of how to restrain campus militants. It was this report that led to the work team's downfall.

During the second week of June violence on campus escalated sharply. Victims were fitted with tall dunce caps, placards were hung from their necks, they were shoved about violently on the stage, their hair was pulled, their arms were fixed behind them, big character posters were pasted on their bodies, and violence sometimes culminated in severe beatings. The vice-chairman of the History Department committed suicide on June 11 after this treatment. The work team counseled moderation, but with little effect. By June 17 it calculated that 178 cadres, teachers, and students had been indiscriminately beaten and humiliated.[3]

Zhang Chengxian later blamed this on the head of his staff office, Nie Yuanzi, who had contacts all over campus and was the main point of communication between the work team's leading group and other parts of the university.[4] Nie, he recalled, was motivated by personal revenge, freely accused people of serious political crimes, and let students drag out and beat whomever they pleased. Zhang felt that the work team needed to assert control: accusations and struggle sessions should come only after careful investigation to determine guilt.[5] At a mass meeting on June 15 he warned, "We must present the facts and reason things out. To just let yourself go, vent your anger, beat people, put tall hats on people does not solve anything."[6]

Despite these efforts, violent struggle sessions broke out across campus on June 18. Platforms were erected in several locations, and close to seventy prominent cadres and teachers were dragged onto them wearing tall hats and placards, their faces covered with black ink, and they were beaten and kicked while accusations were screamed at them. The victims included the university's top officials, most of whom had already been denounced by the work team. Six were members of the party standing committee, forty-one were members of the university's party committee or general branch committees, and seven were secretaries or members of youth league general branch committees. Members of the work team fanned out across campus, shut down the struggle sessions, and arranged first aid for the victims.[7]

The work team decided to make a negative example of the incident. Zhang Chengxian knew that there was wide participation in these activities, but in order to convince students that such tactics were illegitimate, he focused on a few scapegoats.[8] Zhang addressed the university over the public address system and described four "bad elements" caught redhanded. One was a "hooligan" who had beaten people and behaved in a licentious manner toward female students, and a second was a descendant of a Nationalist Army commander on the campus workforce who had beaten people severely. A third claimed falsely to be a student at Beida High School, and a fourth had torn the clothes of female party secretaries during a struggle session during which he fondled their breasts and groped inside their pants. The university security department detained all four.[9] Zhang charged that "bad elements" were infiltrating the campus to lead students astray and blacken the reputation of the Cultural Revolution. He called for greater discipline and vigilance; intruders should be kept off campus, and the work team should organize all future struggle sessions. The work team would conduct further investigations.[10]

The next day the work team submitted a report to the Central Committee about the "June 18 incident." It was necessary to "expose and condemn the counterrevolutionary conspiratorial behavior of such bad people," which served to "blacken the reputation of the work team and throw the movement into chaos." On June 20 the report was transmitted to party committees nationwide as a central party document, with the Central Secretariat's comment that the work team's actions in this case were "correct and timely."[11]

Other leaders wanted to take a stronger stand and place a more sinister interpretation on the event. Cao Yi'ou, Kang Sheng's wife, submitted a second report on behalf of the work team on June 21, charging that "this entire incident was an ambush carried out against us jointly by enemies within the school and outside to create chaos and disrupt our battle plan." Chen Boda, head of the CCRG, met with the Beida work team on June 27 and charged that an "underground headquarters" of Lu Ping loyalists was behind the event, trying to save themselves by discrediting the Cultural Revolution.[12] Because of Chen's pressure further investigations were pursued, and eventually twenty-four persons were censured for beating people. The next work-team report called the struggle sessions of June 18 a "counterrevolutionary attempt to divert the movement and create disorder, throwing the work team's battle plan into chaos."[13]

Work teams at other schools soon used this language in counterattacks against student activists who challenged them. Counterattacks were unnecessary at Beida, however, because the work team faced no serious challenge. The attacks against targeted officials continued, but struggle sessions were generally conducted under the supervision of the work team. On June 22 and 23 Lu Ping and Peng Peiyun, the top officials named in the May 25 wall poster, were put through two days of mass struggle sessions. By late June 230 cadres and teachers had been targeted; 153 were "dismissed from office by the masses," 192 were put through struggle sessions, 94 were beaten, and 107 were paraded with tall hats.[14]

With the backing of CCRG radicals and no dissent from the university "leftists" on the work-team staff, opposition was effectively squelched. This changed after Mao returned to Beijing on July 18 and expressed dissatisfaction with the way in which work teams had handled the movement. He convened a series of meetings with members of the CCRG and other officials over the next few days, complaining angrily that work teams had blocked student mobilization. It was obvious that they would soon be withdrawn, and Mao finally gave the order on July 21.[15]

Mao's lieutenants quickly backtracked, especially Chen Boda, Cao Yi'ou, and Kang Sheng, who had pushed for a harder line on the June 18 incident. As they rushed to reverse their positions, Zhang Chengxian was made a scapegoat for the "serious errors" of the work team. Once this change of course was made clear to individuals at Beida, opposition to the work team finally emerged, but from within, once again in the form of a denunciation by Nie Yuanzi. Zhang Chengxian could sense the shifting tide the week before. On July 16 he held a mass meeting to offer a self-criticism and correct the work team's earlier stance on the June 18 incident. On July 17 and 18 Zhang and other members of the work team gave additional speeches in which they emphasized that June 18 actually was a "revolutionary incident," and they encouraged students to write wall posters and criticize.[16] It was only then that Nie Yuanzi denounced her colleagues. In a speech on the evening of July 19 she accused the work team of "errors of orientation and line."[17]

Once again, members of the CCRG intervened directly in school politics. Jiang Qing and Chen Boda visited the campus on July 22 and 23, met with Nie, and expressed support for her stand. Jiang Qing declared that the work team did not stand with the revolutionary left and should stand aside. Chen Boda, completely reversing his earlier position, declared that "in his personal opinion," the June 18 incident was not counterrevolutionary, and that the work team's verdict was mistaken.[18] They returned on July 25 with Kang Sheng and other members of the CCRG and organized a mass debate about the work team. In his speech Kang Sheng said that students should organize their own leadership group. Most who spoke supported the claim that the verdict on June 18 was an error, although a vocal minority of students defended the work team and said that the earlier verdict was not wrong.[19]

A larger CCRG delegation returned on July 26.[20] The atmosphere was tense, the accusations were more extreme, and students who argued in Zhang's defense were emotional. After several hours, Chen Boda concluded the meeting by saying that the work team had obstructed the mass movement and should be withdrawn. Jiang Qing recommended that a Cultural Revolution committee lead the movement, and she nominated Nie Yuanzi to head the effort. Two days later a preparatory committee was elected with Nie as the chairman.[21] The work team was deposed and denounced by the same officials who had earlier urged a harsher stance on the June 18 incident.[22]

## Beijing Industrial University

The first work team at Beijing Industrial University left the party committee in charge, but it encountered strong resistance and had to be replaced. The second work team completely reversed political direction and led a harrowing purge of the school's leadership that even questioned the political reliability of many ordinary party members. Its militant stance and the military and revolutionary credentials of Du Wanrong, the head of the second work team, ensured that it faced no serious opposition, but its relations with some of the leading opponents of the first work team were strained. This did not create overt opposition, but it laid the groundwork for factions after the work team withdrew and transferred power to students in early August.

These tensions were muted during June and July. In the extensive documentation of the later debates about this second work team's activities, there is no mention of open opposition, nor were there any subsequent complaints that the work team failed to investigate the school power structure thoroughly, or that it retaliated against opponents. The political tensions did not surface until after the work team's withdrawal, when a group of students challenged classmates left in charge by the second work team.[23]

The most outspoken opponents of the first work team were party members and political activists from revolutionary cadre households. Despite favored positions in the power structure, they challenged the work team's soft line toward the school's party leadership. The first work team leveled charges of political disloyalty at this initial group of activists. When the second work team arrived, these activists apparently expected that the charges against them would be repudiated and that they would be recognized as the most politically advanced militants in the school. They were disappointed. Intent on resuming the stalled purge of the school leadership, the new work team deflected demands to investigate the first one. Resisting pressure from these early activists, the new work team turned to more responsive students, many of whom had not opposed the first work team or who had even cooperated with it.

Quietly appalled that the second work team ignored the risks they had taken in their early rebellion and instead recruited obedient activists regardless of their earlier stance, these militant students were passed over. Furthermore, because many of them had come from families with impeccable revolutionary backgrounds, they felt that the second work team was violating the party's class line and was instead recruiting obedient conformists regardless of political background. Months later they criticized the work team for ignoring their family heritage:

> As for Du Wanrong's class line . . . [the] standard was: whether or not you obeyed what the work team said. [At the June 21 speech to worker, peasant, and revolutionary cadre offspring, he said] if you do not listen to what the work team says, even if you are from a worker, peasant, or revolutionary cadre background, you will be attacked just the same, and be expelled . . . On the other hand, those from bad class background, the so-called "leftists" who obey what the work team says, will be relied on.[24]

This work team's militant purge of the power structure and its clear warnings against opposition from students regardless of their political credentials cowed these bypassed activists into sullen compliance. The resentments surfaced immediately after the work team's departure, however, when these students challenged the activists left in charge by the second work team. The struggle between the two nascent factions generated a famous but widely misinterpreted speech in defense of the second work team that will be examined in the next chapter.

## Beijing Agricultural University

The work team at Beijing Agricultural University pursued a mixed strategy that divided the school's power structure against itself. For almost two weeks before the work team's June 13 arrival, accusations against Party Secretary Wang Guanlan and his close associates on the party committee appeared in wall posters, and some of the most prominent critics were middle-level cadres in the school.[25] Before the work team arrived, Wang deflected criticism by announcing a campaign to investigate bourgeois professors, and he relied on loyal party branch secretaries to make counteraccusations against his critics.

The work team realized that this approach was insufficiently militant, and it initiated a thorough purge of the power structure. However, it decreed that Wang Guanlan and one of his deputies were politically reliable and would remain in their posts. The ensuing campaign took its heaviest toll on the party apparatus immediately below the party standing committee. Cadres who had earlier posted criticisms of Wang became a particular focus of the campaign and found themselves charged with antiparty activity. However, the purge was so extensive that many of those who had earlier defended the party secretary by making counteraccusations against his critics were also charged with following a "black line" in the school. This was widely interpreted as a cynical attempt by Wang Guanlan to save himself by sacrificing loyal subordinates. This created two distinct categories of cadres and party members who harbored strong grievances against the party secretary and the work team: loyal defenders who were sacrificed in the purge, and critics who had dared to expose his errors before the arrival of the work team.

The resentments did not find organized expression until after the work team left. There was little overt opposition during the work team's stay, and it responded rapidly and effectively against dissent. At a mass rally on June 18, for example, a group of students from one department criticized Party Secretary Wang. The department's general branch secretary was immediately stripped of his post, as was the class counselor in charge of the students who made the criticisms. When the students organized to resist, the minister of agriculture, Tan Zhenlin, went to the school and declared that Wang Guanlan was a revolutionary leftist and the work team would not be withdrawn.

The minister's intervention was effective: the work team kept the party secretary in power as it resumed its purge of the power structure.

Subsequent accounts written by victims do not describe significant opposition. Those who supported the work team and the party secretary and denounced their colleagues were promoted to replace them. When the work team withdrew at the end of July, Party Secretary Wang was still in office. He was soon challenged by two different categories of people who now found common cause: critics who had been purged in retaliation, and loyal defenders who had been sacrificed in the purge.

## Contested Control

Although pacified campuses represent a broad range of work-team types, all the schools where control was contested had radical work teams. Despite their militant stance, these work teams found it necessary to conduct a broad campaign against students who called for their removal. These conflicts were not about the targets of the purges or its scope, but about the work team's ability to control the process. Two of these schools, Qinghua University and Beijing Normal University, played a major role in the subsequent red guard movement and will be described here, along with the Beijing Foreign Languages Institute.[26]

## Qinghua University

Qinghua University's radical work team had firm control of the campus during its entire stay, but it encountered stubborn opposition from an outspoken group of students who chafed at restrictions on their activities. These tensions escalated in the third week of June, when the work team decided to counterattack. The conflict produced one of the most influential student leaders of the Cultural Revolution, Kuai Dafu, who played a key role in Beijing politics for the next two years.

Kuai Dafu was an entirely different kind of leader from Beida's Nie Yuanzi. Nie was a cadre in the party establishment, but Kuai, 20, was a third-year student of chemical engineering who had not yet joined the party.[27] Kuai was nonetheless closely associated with the regime and the university power structure. He was a youth league member, a political activist, and a student cadre in his class. He came from a "red" household: both parents were party members who had joined after 1949. Kuai had already earned a measure of political fame. When he was a freshman in the fall of 1963, his photograph was featured in the national magazine *People's Illustrated* as a model of the party's increasing emphasis on admitting students from a proletarian background to leading universities.[28] He took his political commitments very seriously. Shortly after his debut in the media, he wrote a letter to the Standing Committee of the National People's Congress exposing the extravagant lifestyles of cadres in his rural hometown.[29] At the outset of the Cultural Revolution, Kuai was head of his classroom's Cultural Revolution group, and it was from this position of leadership that he launched his challenge to the work team.

Qinghua's work team did not arrive until the evening of June 9, a full week after Nie Yuanzi's wall poster was publicized. In the interim, the university's party secretary, Jiang Nanxiang, tried to fend off mounting accusations that he was part of the same "black gang" that included Beida's leaders. Wall posters critical of Jiang appeared on June 2 and touched off counterattacks by students who denied the charges. Kuai Dafu put up his first wall poster critical of the party committee on June 3. A number of the authors of anti-Jiang posters were forced to make self-criticisms. The school was reportedly shocked on June 4 when Liu Tao, one of Liu Shaoqi's daughters, signed a "revolutionary" wall poster, and she and the son of Marshall He Long signed another wall poster the next day that criticized Jiang's defensiveness and passivity. On June 7 Kuai formed a "combat team" with twelve classmates and put up a wall poster that declared an anti-Jiang stand. Party committee loyalists counterattacked against the critics.[30] When the work team arrived, the entire party leadership was immediately deposed, and all cadres stood aside for investigation.

Kuai Dafu's initial stance was completely aligned with the work team. Why, then, did Kuai develop into an outspoken work-team opponent? Qinghua's work team was the most militant in the city, and its assault on the school power structure was uncompromising. Kuai's group did not accuse the work team of protecting power holders. Instead, its complaints were about how to conduct the assault, and whether the work team had authority over the student fighting groups that were forming in the classrooms. In less than two weeks Kuai moved from enthusiasm about the work team to strident opposition. This rapid evolution shows how factions formed out of a series of political interactions rather than from interests inherent in the positions of individuals before the Cultural Revolution, and so it is worth examining these interactions in some detail.

When the work team arrived on the evening of June 9 and announced the purge of Jiang Nanxiang and the overthrow of the party committee,

Kuai Dafu and his combat team were overjoyed. The next morning, however, Kuai began to have second thoughts. The first thing that bothered Kuai was the way in which erstwhile defenders of the party committee immediately changed their tune after the work team's arrival. "From the evening of June 9 to the morning of June 10, former hard-core conservatives suddenly 'mutinied' overnight, rising up everywhere to give speeches saying 'we were deceived.' On the 10th and 11th, 'dog-beating teams' came out of one department after another, and a lot of dogs were beaten until they were utterly routed and ran off with their tails between their legs."[31]

Although Kuai was suspicious, the about-face of the party committee's defenders was exactly what was expected of loyal party members and political activists. When a change in party line is pronounced, members are expected to fall in line without asking questions. This was what happened at Qinghua (and other universities), and the party views such behavior as a sign of loyalty, not duplicity. Those who had recently taken a stance now deemed incorrect in fact bore a special burden to show their loyalty to the new line through decisive action.

The day after the work team arrived, Kuai led an attempt to seize the control room of his dormitory's public address system and fought briefly with youth league leaders who arrived later to take over on behalf of the work team. Students in his classroom criticized his rash actions: "In seizing power we had lost the trust that our group had."[32] An even greater source of friction was the attempts of groups like Kuai's to organize their own struggle sessions. An early example was a certain student who put up "an extremely reactionary wall poster." Kuai complained, "When we tried to drag this active counterrevolutionary out of the dormitory to the classrooms for a struggle session, comrades from the work team stopped us . . . We want to ask the work team: why do you not permit us to struggle against a counterrevolutionary, while permitting his wall poster wide circulation? . . . We resolutely demand that the work team release [the author] for an all-school mass struggle session."[33]

Kuai observed that during its first week at Qinghua the work team had reined in mass action. First, it organized so many meetings that students had no time to conduct their own activities. When students demanded struggle sessions, they were accused of being "too subjective."

> We want to hold struggle sessions but you will not approve. We want to grab hold of a big black gang, put a hat on him and parade him around, you stop us . . . You say, talk about it here, discuss it there, what kind of struggle

is this? . . . Every department organizes dog-beating squads, looking every-where for dogs to beat. You say this is attacking on too broad a front . . . Previously we risked having our heads chopped off and carried out a strug-gle with the conservative party, and now we lift up our heads and curse the black gang, but our public address system and [work team head] Ye Lin's re-port repeatedly emphasize, "Do not curse people," and struggle sessions and parading people are not permitted; we cannot even curse people. We would like to ask the work team: is there an instruction of the Party Center against cursing people?[34]

Instead, the work team was always counseling the students to calm down, think things through, gather evidence, and investigate things thor-oughly, and this only served as a barrier to the revolutionary actions of the masses. The work team, Kuai argued, used the slogan "Everyone is equal before the truth" as a weapon against them.

The work team's leaders repeatedly say that the truth is in our hands, politi-cal power is in our hands. We should stress facts and reason things out, fully lay out our reasons, and they will naturally lose their arrogance. They use this to block us from holding struggle sessions, do not let us parade people, and even use this to block us from holding a mass struggle session against an active counterrevolutionary . . . Now we have lifted up our heads, but the work team is always saying we should stick to facts and be reasonable. But truth has a class nature. We are talking about proletarian truth. Can they get this through their skulls? If you do not strike at reactionaries, you cannot overthrow them. Toward class enemies you can only adopt dictatorship.[35]

Kuai was particularly angry about the attitudes of some of the work team's members toward militant students. One cadre, trying to persuade students to halt a struggle session, said, "The consciousness of you col-lege students is really low, you do not have any head for politics . . . You are considered high-level intellectuals, but your methods are not at all high level; you do not understand party policy." Even worse, he questioned whether Mao's classic essay "Report on the Peasant Movement in Hu-nan" should be taken by students as a guide to university politics in the 1960s: "Putting a tall hat on someone is the Nationalist's way of doing things; peasants can do it this way, but you should not; this just shows your incompetence . . . Doing things this way only shows how cruel you are, it shows you really have not studied the Chairman's works very well at all."[36]

Kuai was outraged. "We can hardly imagine that such talk came out of a work-team member, cursing the masses like this. We would like to tell this comrade, if you curse us, we do not mind; if you curse our poor and lower-middle class peasants, we will not respond. But if you curse our great leader Chairman Mao, we will defy you to the death!"[37] Kuai and his comrades expressed these complaints forcefully in a wall poster they put up on June 16, less than one week after the work team's arrival.[38]

Kuai was part of a vocal minority that posed no immediate threat to the Qinghua work team, but there was a danger that their arguments might attract support. This was happening on many other campuses, where the first wave of work teams had already been chased away from campus and a second wave was still struggling to quell strong opposition. Two days later the June 18 incident at Beida convinced many in the national leadership that it was time to take a stand. Unfortunately for Kuai, his forceful criticisms of the work team were viewed as part of a larger political threat, even though Kuai had little influence at Qinghua.

Kuai soon drew attention to himself in an inadvertently spectacular fashion. While he was reading campus wall posters on June 19, he ran into a senior official talking to a group of students. The cadre argued that the work team's actions were entirely correct. Kuai overheard this and could not restrain himself. He challenged the cadre and argued with him, showing no deference. He wondered aloud who "this old fat guy" was. Other students jumped in on the senior cadre's side, and after some forty minutes the official stalked off, clearly irritated. Four days later Kuai was informed that the "old fat guy" was in fact Party Vice-Chairman Bo Yibo, who was in charge of work teams in schools under the industry and transportation system.[39]

After this exchange the work team's attitude hardened. On June 22, as he was about to convene a meeting, Kuai was informed that Wang Guangmei, the wife of Liu Shaoqi, wanted to attend his group's meeting.[40] The students were excited, but in the end an unidentified middle-aged woman attended and said little. During the meeting Kuai and his comrades expressed further criticisms of the work team. At the end of the meeting they asked for the visitor's name, and it turned out she was not Wang Guangmei, but someone who would only identify herself as a staff member in the work-team office. Kuai and his comrades were outraged, and they ran to the work-team offices and demanded to know why Wang Guangmei had not shown up. They got few answers and waited most of the day. When they finally met with several officials, the exchanges were tense and disrespectful. Kuai and his comrades concluded that Wang Guangmei had sent her secretary to spy on them.[41]

The next day the atmosphere suddenly changed. Wall posters attacked Kuai, and another student who had made accusations against the work team was denounced for anti-party sentiments. On June 24 wall posters attacked Kuai, and he was forced to debate his critics. At a mass debate about his opposition to the work team on June 25, several speakers denounced him.[42] In a last-ditch attempt to prevent being framed as anti-party "rightists," Kuai Dafu and his comrades left campus for two days of fruitless attempts to lodge appeals at central party and government offices. When Kuai finally returned to campus, the campaign against him and "Kuai-type figures" was in full swing. The work team linked Kuai with the anti-work-team movement on other campuses and denounced Kuai and his supporters in its published collections of wall posters.[43] In long speeches at mass debates held on June 27, Kuai defended himself against accusations that he was anti-party and vigorously disputed distortions of his actions and ideas. He also continued to write wall posters and was free to walk on campus.[44]

On July 3 Kuai encountered Vice-Premier Bo Yibo on campus once again, and this time Bo heatedly lectured Kuai. Bo pointed out that the work team, not Kuai, had seized power from the party committee, but now Kuai wanted to seize power from the work team: "Kuai Dafu now is always thinking of seizing power, seizing power from the Communist Party . . . There is a bit of the diehard spirit of counterrevolution." Bo was still smarting from his earlier encounter with Kuai: "I will tell you something, that guy is arrogant. He said I was a fat old man. I admit I am old, but I do not like being fat." Bo said that the last time he had seen Kuai, he had told him that he should admit his errors, "but he just ignored it, the guy is arrogant." "Today I speak not on my qualifications as a fat old man, but as an ordinary person," Bo said. "Comrades, do not overestimate Kuai Dafu. If you overestimate him, you are being fooled. He is just a lackey frantically running around, he has no ability. We on the left must drag out the true black line; do not look on him as something special." As Bo was leaving, he turned to Kuai and said, "Kuai Dafu, I have done you a favor, I have treated you as a contradiction among the people. If we struggle with you, that is a real contradiction. But with class enemies we do things differently. We struggle with class enemies, exercise dictatorship, arrest people." Then, turning to the other students, he said, "In the future, when you struggle with him, do not give him a big label, and do not beat him. Learn from this teacher by negative example. This is a lesson in politics."[45]

The same day as his harrowing encounter with Bo Yibo, Kuai wrote a wall poster to protest the fact that he was now being restricted to campus, and that his letters were being intercepted and opened by the work team. On July 4 he put up a wall poster protesting these circumstances and declaring a hunger strike. For the next eighteen days he was confined to his dormitory, and his contacts with comrades were cut off. He was stripped of his youth league membership and leadership post. In the campaign against "Kuai-type figures," around 50 students were given damaging political labels, and another 700 students were forced to make self-criticisms for expressing views similar to, or in sympathy with, Kuai's.[46]

Kuai remained in isolation while the work team continued attacks against the Qinghua power structure, but after Mao ordered the withdrawal of work teams, Kuai was transformed from a counterrevolutionary to a victim of an erroneous political line. On the morning of July 22, two members of the CCRG visited Kuai and talked with him for three hours, and they told the work team's leaders that their treatment of Kuai was wrong.[47]

On July 28 work-team head Ye Lin announced at a mass meeting that the work team would soon leave and a preparatory committee would be formed to lead the school.[48] Between July 30 and August 3, as the preparatory committee was being formed, Zhou Enlai visited the campus several times to talk with the work team's leaders and visit Kuai. On August 4 Zhou chaired a mass meeting during which Ye Lin gave a self-criticism on behalf of the work team. Zhou questioned the conduct of the work team and stated that he had been sent by Chairman Mao and the Party Center to announce the rehabilitation of Kuai Dafu and others who had been similarly punished.[49]

## Beijing Normal University

Events at Beijing Normal University were influenced by a direct connection between a prominent activist in the school and radical figures close to Mao. This connection was through Tan Houlan, a fifth-year student in the Political Education Department who, like Nie Yuanzi and Kuai Dafu, later emerged as one of Beijing's key red guard leaders.[50] Tan was twenty-nine years old; she had previously worked in elementary schools and had established strong credentials as a model party member. As a reward for her strong political record she was admitted to Beijing Normal, the nation's leading teachers' college, as a "cadre transfer student." In January 1966 Tan was given a prestige assignment by her department's general branch secretary: she would work as an intern at the Central Committee's leading theoretical journal, *Red Flag*. The journal was a hotbed of radical Maoist activity and was a major force in the launching and subsequent direction of the Cultural Revolution. The journal's editor-in-chief was Chen Boda, who later became the chairman of the CCRG, and four *Red Flag* vice-editors—Guan Feng, Mu Xin, Qi Benyu, and Wang Li—became members. Tan Houlan worked directly under Lin Jie, a graduate of Beijing Normal who later played an important staff role on the CCRG.[51]

Tan's first act of rebellion was similar to Nie Yuanzi's: with higher-level backing she attacked the party secretary of her university. Late in the evening of June 1, a few hours after Nie Yuanzi's "first Marxist-Leninist wall poster" was praised in radio broadcasts, Tan left the *Red Flag* offices for the campus and put up a wall poster accusing her school's party secretary of similar political errors. More wall posters followed, and the campus was shortly in an uproar. On June 4 the school's party secretary was removed from all posts, and on June 6 a work team headed by Sun Youyu, vice-minister of the First Ministry of Machine Building, took over the school.

Also like Nie Yuanzi, Tan Houlan cooperated with the work team during much of its stay. The work team conducted a radical purge of the power structure, but it encountered vocal opposition that led to a June 19 wall poster calling for its departure. One of the main issues was that the former party secretary had left the school, and the work team refused to bring him back for interrogation and struggle sessions. Tan Houlan actively supported the work team after the initial challenges on June 20, writing a wall poster to praise the work team's militant performance and organizing a demonstration to express the loyal support of "revolutionary students." After this act Tan was recalled to the *Red Flag* offices for consultation, and she returned to campus on June 22 to reverse her earlier position, putting up a wall poster questioning the work team's harsh response to its critics. The work team then attacked Tan Houlan and her followers, putting work-team head Sun Youyu on a collision course with Maoist radicals on the CCRG.[52]

The work team's campaign against "fake leftists" was unusually harsh. The authors of the June 19 wall poster that touched off the furor were put through struggle sessions during which they were punched and kicked, as were many of the several hundred sympathizers they claimed in the school. The work team investigated the backgrounds and activities of the "fake leftists" and put materials into their personal files. The primary author of the critical wall poster was stripped of his position in his department's core leadership group and labeled a "rightist."[53] Sun Youyu was aware of the connection between Tan Houlan and Lin Jie, and through Lin Jie to Chen Boda and the CCRG, and protested the group's role in supporting what he considered anti-party activities in letters to Kang Sheng and others.[54]

Sun's complaints implied that radicals on the CCRG were engaged in underground factional activities that could be construed as anti-party, and there was a swift and severe response. Kang Sheng and members of the CCRG met with Sun on July 13, gave him a severe dressing-down, and ordered him to make a self-criticism in front of the entire school.[55] Sun refused, and as a result Beijing's party vice-secretary Wu De went to the school on July 16, criticized Sun Youyu, announced his replacement, called the stance of Tan Houlan and other critics of the work team "correct," and asked students to back the new work-team leader.[56]

After Sun Youyu's removal Tan Houlan's group quickly returned to its earlier stance of loyal support for the work team. Vindicated after their patrons on the CCRG retaliated against Sun, they felt secure in their positions. This was not true of the other victims of the work team, who did not have such close ties with national politicians. Tan Houlan argued for a relatively conservative course: loyalty to the work team and trust in the new Beijing Municipal Party Committee. Others who had been branded "fake leftists" were not mollified merely by the appointment of a new work-team leader. They called for criticism of the work team's errors over the previous weeks and for driving the work team off the campus.[57] By the time the withdrawal of all work teams was announced at the end of July, students at the university were split into three groups: those who had cooperated with the work team under Sun Youyu and two groups of Sun's opponents, one allied with Tan Houlan that supported the new work-team head, and another that had refused to be pacified by a mere leadership change.

### Beijing Foreign Languages Institute

Vice-Minister of Foreign Relations Liu Xinquan led a second work team to the Foreign Languages Institute on June 17. Liu abandoned the first work team's conservative effort to shore up the party committee and unleashed student activists on school officials.[58] Within a week, however, he was struggling to maintain control over the escalating attacks. Energized by the new work team's permissive attitude, students organized struggle sessions and decided that they should unilaterally determine which departmental cadres had a revolutionary standpoint and which were reactionary. Many departments proceeded to elect departmental revolutionary committees and circulated the slogan "All power to the revolutionary committees."

The work team launched a campaign to regain control on June 24. One work-team cadre asserted that the work team represented the Party Center, and to oppose it was mistaken. He argued that Mao's 1927 "Report on the Peasant Movement in Hunan"—the template for violent struggle sessions as a form of protest—was "passé." The students responsible for struggle sessions were criticized for recklessness and political confusion, and those who continued to challenge the work team's authority were subjected to criticism meetings and struggle sessions.

In the following weeks the work team pressured almost 900 students into self-criticisms. Figures compiled two months later revealed a common pattern: the work team's main challengers were politically active students closely associated with the power structure. Two-thirds of them were from "red" households, and over 80 percent were party or youth league members. Of those targeted for opposition, 35 percent were student cadres who lost leadership posts in their classrooms or on party and youth league branch committees.[59] During this period cadres who specialized in political investigations compiled dossiers on "persons of emphasis," interrogated them and their associates, analyzed their wall posters, read their diaries, and visited their families. The intense pressures brought to bear during interrogations and criticism meetings left many despondent and suicidal because they realized that their futures now appeared to be ruined. When the work team was abruptly withdrawn at the end of July, the victims seized the opportunity to reverse their misfortune and mobilized to overthrow students placed in positions of leadership on the school's preparatory committee.

### Major Confrontations

Major confrontations differ from the earlier ones in the scale of the opposition and the scope of the counterattack. These confrontations subsequently produced some of the most militant red guard factions. Especially important were events at the Beijing Aeronautics Institute and the Beijing Geology Institute. The confrontations at the Beijing Post and Telecommunications Institute and Chinese People's University were also severe.[60]

### Beijing Aeronautics Institute

Work-team head Zhao Ruzhang reversed his conservative course after it became clear that internal opposition was widespread.[61] Despite his radical assault on the party organization, he soon met resistance over how he was conducting the campaign. Zhao's first misstep was to designate middle-level cadres as the main force in the accusations against top school leaders, because they had inside information that students did not have. Student activists complained that they were being sidelined. The second problem was that political instructors and student cadres who had done the bidding of the party organization in the past were targets of the campaign, but many of these people were now leading the charge against the top party leadership. This led to accusations that the work team was "inciting students to struggle against students" to divert attention from the top officials. The third problem was over student-initiated struggle sessions. Work-team attempts to curtail them led to resentment. The final problem was insufficient student representation on the Cultural Revolution committee.[62]

These frictions bred opposition to the work team. Zhao was now fighting a political battle on two fronts. He tried to win support from the students by pushing a militant purge of the power structure while moving to silence those who challenged the work team's authority. Zhao's opponents were encouraged by news that work teams at many other schools had retreated in defeat, and they pushed their advantage. On June 20 several large delegations of students went separately to the State Council, the National Defense Science and Technology Commission, and the Municipal Party Committee to lodge complaints against the work team.[63] A provocative wall poster appeared on June 21, leveling an accusation directly at Zhao Ruzhang: if there was a "black line" in the school, did it really have no leader? Zhao, after all, was directly in charge of the institute. The implication was that he was trying to control the movement to protect himself.

On June 25 the work team began its counterattack, orchestrating criticism meetings against its most outspoken opponents. As its purge of the party hierarchy intensified, it pointedly excluded students critical of the work team from meetings of activists. On June 29 opponents of the work team were subjected to struggle sessions along with targeted officials. Lists of proscribed dissidents were drawn up that included over 200 authors of wall posters. Those accused of anti-party views countered that 95 percent of them were actually from reliably "red" family backgrounds.[64]

All these efforts unraveled after the work teams were withdrawn. Zhao Ruzhang announced that the work team would retreat to an "advisory" role, and the work team appointed a preparatory committee of twelve mass representatives, all from the Cultural Revolution committee elected the previous month. The committee was immediately challenged by the critics of the work team who had been silenced in the previous weeks, and this challenge led directly to the two opposing red guard factions that formed during the first days of August.

### Beijing Geology Institute

The work team at the Beijing Geology Institute also shifted from a conservative to a radical stance, but this failed to quell a strong opposition movement.[65] During struggle sessions organized by students, members of the school's party committee defended themselves by saying that they had acted on orders of the Ministry of Geology. Students saw this as evidence that there was a "black gang" in the ministry itself. Members of the work team argued that political problems in the school were limited to the campus, and they tried to redirect the students' attention to Gao Yuangui, the institute's president and party secretary. These students already had suspicions about the ministry's party secretary, He Changgong, who had earlier tried to dampen criticisms of the institute's leaders. Now they felt that the work team was diverting their attack onto Gao Yuangui in order to prevent them from fully investigating political problems in the ministry. During the next several days wall posters criticized the work team.

Matters came to a head on June 20. Early that morning several school officials delivered a written complaint to the State Council, criticizing the work team's conduct and calling for its withdrawal. The group was led by Li Gui, a preliberation party member, formerly head of campus security. Li Gui's stand was applauded by students critical of the work team. After Li and his group returned to campus, he delivered a speech that described the contents of his complaint. Students cheered his stand, put up wall posters supporting "Li Gui's revolutionary act," and organized a large demonstration the next day. They called for returning power over the school's movement to genuine leftists in the institute.[66]

Li Gui did not leave a written record of his motives, but he had a history of conflict with party vice-secretaries of the school who were cooperating with the work team's plan to lay the blame for all the institute's political problems on Gao Yuangui.[67] Gao had joined the party in the late 1930s as a student radical in the anti-Japanese movement at China University in Beijing. He later joined the Communist Party and served in guerilla base areas during the Japanese occupation. His revolutionary credentials were well known in the school.[68] In the course of the movement students learned that Gao had not always followed He Changgong's directives, and that the latter resented his headstrong subordinate. He Changgong had an even more distinguished record as a guerilla fighter beginning in the 1920s, when he served with Mao in his first base area in Jinggangshan.[69] Li Gui's rebellion and the controversy over Gao Yuangui drew the school into the ministry's internal politics.

Events at the school threatened to spin out of control just as the Party Center was reacting to Beida's June 18 incident. The ministry decided to intervene. On June 21 He Changgong returned to the campus with Vice-Minister Xu Guangyi and an even higher-ranking official, Li Renlin, vice-head of the political department of the State Council Industry and Transportation Department.[70] He Changgong certified that the work team was "revolutionary," and Li Renlin backed him up. Vice-Minister Xu Guangyi referred to the student opposition as "a disturbance created by a small minority."[71] On June 22 Li Renlin relayed an instruction he had received from his direct superior, Bo Yibo, who repeated the same points he had made orally to Kuai Dafu at Qinghua University on June 19: the work team represented the Central Committee and Chairman Mao, and seizing power from the work team was therefore anti-party.[72]

Bo Yibo's attempt to shore up the work team served only to split the campus further. Students opposed to the work team now put up wall posters directly critical of the officials who had come to campus to silence them. During the next three days hundreds of wall posters criticized the leaders' actions and questioned their motives. Some called for turning over control to the Cultural Revolution committees established in the departments and permitting them to independently run the school's campaign.[73]

On June 25 the counterattack began. The school's public address system broadcast Bo Yibo's directive against opposing work teams, and the work team rallied its supporters for an "anti-interference campaign." He Changgong and Xu Guangyi returned to the campus to give speeches. For the next three weeks the work team, with broad participation by politically active students, led a campaign to prevent "anti-party elements" from obstructing the work team. Li Gui and the group of cadres who had demanded the withdrawal of the work team were designated an "underground anti-party headquarters" and became the primary targets of mass struggle sessions. "Special case groups" built case files against more than ninety cadres and teachers who had sympathized with calls for the work team's withdrawal. In departments where opposition to the work team was strong, party and youth league branches were reorganized, and many student cadres were stripped of their posts.[74]

One of the focal points of the campaign was the Survey Department, whose Cultural Revolution committee openly opposed the work team. The committee was disbanded, and five out of seven members of the party general branch committee were removed from their posts; all ten party branch secretaries were replaced, as were large numbers of student cadres. Out of 494 students in the department, 352 were compelled to make a self-criticism, 50 were criticized by name in wall posters, and 39 were labeled participants in a "black gang." Of 93 teachers and cadres, 44 were criticized in wall posters, and 10 were subjected to struggle sessions. Opposition to the work team ran deep in the power structure itself: 34 of the 44 teachers and cadres who were criticized in wall posters were party members, and of the 10 opponents of the work team subjected to struggle sessions, 9 were party members and 7 were cadres.[75]

Figures for the Geology Institute as a whole are similar. The campaign struck hard against people who were predominantly part of or close to the power structure. A total of 435 people were forced to make self-criticisms, and materials documenting their political errors were compiled and placed in the files of 125 of them. The majority of the work team's opponents were from groups previously favored by the power structure. More than half of them were from "red" family backgrounds, and two-thirds were party or youth league members. Almost all of the 66 people who lost positions of authority in the campaign were from a "red" household (80 percent) or were members of the party or youth league (88 percent).[76] The campaign against the work team's opponents laid the foundation for a vigorous movement to overthrow the preparatory committee left in charge after the work team left. Because they had already clashed directly with ministry officials, these activists harbored unusually clear grievances against higher authorities. The faction that grew from this foundation played a crucial role in the radicalization of the red guard movement in its first stages and in Beijing's politics for the next two years.

### Beijing Post and Telecommunications Institute

Ministry officials were drawn even more directly into conflicts in the Beijing Post and Telecommunications Institute. The institute's first work team, led by the head of the Education Department of the Ministry of Post and Telecommunications, lasted only four days. It left the party committee in charge, and its members orchestrated counterattacks against critics of top school officials that began before the work team arrived. The second work team, led by the head of the ministry's Political Department, arrived on June 8, quickly deposed the party committee, and made all leading cadres stand aside for investigation.[77] Accusations against critics of the party committee were halted.

The second work team's radical stance failed to satisfy those who had been criticized the previous week. On June 11 students went to the ministry's offices and put up a wall poster demanding that the first work team's head return to the school to reply to their charges about the conduct of his work team. The next morning more than fifty students marched to the ministry, put up another wall poster, this time denouncing a vice-minister as well, and demanded that he return to the school along with the first work team's head to answer to charges. On June 13 students began to call openly for the withdrawal of the second work team in favor of teachers and students running their school's own Cultural Revolution without supervision. The ministry's party secretary, Wang Zigang, called a hasty meeting of the party committee and decided to send the first work team's head back to the school to give a self-criticism. On June 14 Secretary Wang returned to the institute with Tao Lujia, vice-chairman of the State Economic Commission, to observe the movement.[78] Tao declared his confidence that the second work team was revolutionary, and for that matter, so was the leadership of the ministry's party committee.

Apparently concluding that the disturbances at the institute would not be quelled until student demands were met, the ministry's party committee sacrificed Zhao Zhigang, the fourth-ranking vice-minister, already denounced by students in connection with the first work team. On June

18 a wall poster appeared in the offices of the ministry's party committee declaring that Zhao was revisionist. On June 19 Secretary Wang Zigang and First Vice-Secretary Zhong Fuxiang went personally to the institute to put up a wall poster denouncing Zhao.

The ministry's leaders caved in so quickly that the militant students became suspicious. On June 20 a group of forty marched back to the ministry and put up wall posters questioning the motives behind the denunciation of Zhao Zhigang by his superiors. Were the top officials only seeking to sacrifice Zhao to protect themselves? On June 21 the ministry's party committee announced that the institute's president would be dismissed from all posts, but this served only to multiply the number of wall posters targeting the ministry's party secretary, Wang Zigang. On June 23 more than 200 students marched to the ministry's offices to call out Secretary Wang Zigang for a debate. They were told that he was in a meeting, which they refused to believe. They staked out the ministry, chanting for him to come out. One hour later Wang emerged from hiding to face them. He argued that problems in the institute were the responsibility of Vice-Minister Zhao Zhigang and the former Beijing Municipal Party Committee. Problems in educational practices, he said, were the responsibility of the Ministry of Higher Education; his own ministry only supplied financing and maintained the physical plant. In the end, according to one red guard account, Wang Zigang cowered in front of the students, tongue-tied in the face of shouted accusations and slogans, "his authority and prestige completely gone."[79]

This direct challenge to top national officials—unprecedented at the time—spurred a counterattack, and the "anti-interference" campaign under way on other campuses was used against the opponents of the work team, who were now accused of "rightist" attacks against national ministries. Concerned about the attack on the ministry, Tao Lujia visited the campus on June 24 to kick off the campaign against opposition at the school. Wall posters appeared in support of the second work team, and others attacked the "rightists" who had protested at the ministry. On June 26, after Tao Lujia decreed that the attack on the ministry was counterrevolutionary, a broad attack on its participants began. In several mass meetings held over the next two weeks, 52 cadres were labeled "rightists," and 799 students and student cadres in the classes were subjected to struggle sessions and faced similar charges. More than 800 individuals on a campus of around 5,000 were punished. On July 27, after the order to withdraw work teams, the work team's leader gave a summary report. He did not apologize for the campaign against anti-party elements and was applauded by the students who had followed his lead.

## Chinese People's University

The work team at Chinese People's University labored under an unusual restriction: the school's party secretary, Guo Yingqiu, was in charge of supervising work teams for the Municipal Party Committee. The work team insisted on a thorough purge of the entire power structure, but it fought to prevent the accusations from focusing on Guo and Sun Huan, his deputy on the party committee.[80] The work team did not arrive until June 14, after almost two weeks of wall-poster criticism and attacks on top officials. By this time prominent members of the school power structure, in imitation of Nie Yuanzi and her celebrated comrades at Beida, had already denounced the school's top officials. To assert control and steer attention away from Guo, the work team had to roll back political initiatives that had already been taken by school militants over the preceding two weeks. Not surprisingly, this stimulated resentment, resistance, and opposition.

The university's Research Institute was an early source of rebellion against Sun Huan and Guo Yingqiu. Its first wall poster on June 8 criticized the party committee and gained widespread attention. Over the next week many more wall posters directly attacked Sun, Guo, and other top school officials, and a militant opposition group formed. In the course of these events two vice-directors of the institute went over to the rebels in their campaign to overthrow the party branch secretary, who was trying to fend off the opposition. On June 14, the day the work team arrived, the two vice-directors and seven others were elected to a Cultural Revolution committee to take over leadership of the campaign from the party branch. The work team dispatched a group to rectify the institute and roll back the earlier rebellion. It initiated a criticism campaign against "fake leftists," disbanded the institute's Cultural Revolution committee, and trumped up political charges against the two vice-directors who had sided with the rebels. A number of students and teachers resisted these actions and were in turn attacked.[81]

To reassert control, the work team concentrated on units that had bred the most outspoken and best-organized challenges to Guo and Sun. More than thirty people who had signed wall posters attacking Guo Yingqiu were labeled counterrevolutionaries and subjected to struggle sessions. In its effort to root out Guo's critics, the work team ignored political credentials and reportedly attacked revolutionary cadres and large numbers of teachers and students from proletarian households. By mid-July over 130 cadres and teachers below the rank of department vice-chairman were given political labels and attacked by name for denouncing Secretary Guo: 111 of them were party members, 102 were ordinary teachers or cadres, 17 were heads or vice-heads of teaching offices, and 7 were department vice-chairmen. Thirty-five of them were subjected to struggle sessions and home searches.[82]

The work team generated widespread opposition as it tried to roll back these independent opposition movements and created large numbers of victims. At the same time it mobilized large numbers of political activists in its campaign against the rest of the power structure. Many student activists were attracted by the work team's policy of permitting accusations against virtually any cadre in the departments, and they were willing to abide by the work team's condition that struggle sessions be cleared in advance. On July 29, shortly after work teams were withdrawn, Guo Yingqiu was dragged back to the campus to answer for his errors. This created an opportunity for the victims of the work team—cadres and students alike—to press their cases, and it forced militants who had collaborated with the work team to defend their decision.[83]

In the previous chapter we saw that work teams did not present clear choices to political activists between support for and opposition to the status quo. In this chapter we have seen the consequences: power structures and the students tied to them were deeply divided. Repeatedly, party officials denounced their own superiors or protested the actions of the work team. Repeatedly, large percentages of the students attacked by the work team for challenging its authority were from the same groups that had the strongest vested interests in the status quo: party members, student cadres, youth league activists, and students from "red" and even revolutionary cadre households.

This chapter has also shown why this was so. There were repeated examples of prominent party officials who denounced their superiors in the party organization at the beginning of June in imitation of Nie Yuanzi at Beida. Nie herself was a party general branch secretary and a member of the university's party committee, and her coauthors were all political instructors and relatively senior party members. Her act encouraged imitators from similar backgrounds across the city. There were repeated cases of ranking party members, especially political instructors, who lodged accusations against their school's top officials before the work team arrived. These critics, moreover, quickly developed a following among students.

If the work teams had followed the Beida scenario, they would have praised the early rebels, given them prominent positions on the work team, and immediately deposed the party committee. This almost never happened. Conservative work teams decided to support the officials whom these rebels had already denounced, and the critics were then punished in retaliation. Radical work teams refused to acknowledge the revolutionary credentials of cadre rebels and forced the early critics to stand aside for investigation along with the people they had earlier denounced. In casting doubt on the entire party organization, radical work teams often forced student cadres and party members to undergo criticism and examination as tools of a corrupt power structure—even those who had earlier rebelled against their superiors. Work teams that pursued a mixed strategy created opponents in both ways: they targeted the critics of the officials said to represent the school's "red line" while forcing large numbers of cadres, party members, and student cadres to stand aside as followers of a "black line."

No matter what strategy they pursued, work teams created four distinct categories of individuals who were pitted against one another. The first category, relatively large, consisted of all those who sided with the work team. In the case of conservative work teams, this meant that they accepted the claim that the school's political problems were not severe. In the case of radical work teams, it meant that they accepted the work team's charge that their school's political problems were very severe. Under work teams that pursued a mixed strategy, it meant that they accepted the work team's decision about whom to protect and whom to purge—if they were lucky enough to escape suspicion themselves. To demonstrate one's allegiance to the work team required one to participate actively in the denunciation of the movement's political targets and to take a stand against the work team's opponents, denouncing them in rallies or in wall posters. The work team's most active supporters were elevated to positions of leadership as part of a new power structure. After the work team left, members of this group were forced to defend their cooperative stance.

The second category was much smaller—those punished for opposition to the work team. These people received punishments ranging from small-group criticism to a harrowing and violent denunciation in a mass struggle session. At best, their political error would be noted in their dossiers and could potentially haunt them at some future point in their lives. At worst, they would be labeled a "rightist" or even "counterrevolutionary"—a political charge that would ruin their career opportunities and potentially lead to incarceration. At the end of July this group was a distinct minority. It was of negligible size in those schools where there was no significant opposition to the work team, but it was much larger in schools where there were major confrontations. These people were militant activists who for various reasons ran afoul of their work teams and ended up unexpectedly as some of the earliest victims of the campaign. After the withdrawal of the work teams, this group had the most urgent interest in reversing the outcomes of the work-team period.

In the third category were party members and student cadres who had been politically active before the Cultural Revolution, but who were sidelined by the work team's assault on school power structures. This group was relatively large under radical work teams that required all party members and student cadres to undergo investigation. Those certified as reliable and permitted to become loyal activists under the work team, and those who adopted an oppositional stance toward the work team, moved into the first or second categories. All others, however, remained in a kind of political limbo—forced to step down temporarily from their posts purely because of their association with a discredited party leadership, not fully trusted but at the same time not formally charged with any specific wrongdoing. They were sidelined or, as they put it, "left hanging" (guaqilaile) without clear verdicts. This group was smaller under work teams that pursued a conservative or mixed strategy, although even in these cases many student cadres and party members were sidelined by the work team's campaign. These people were almost invisible under the work teams. They previously had been trusted activists who enjoyed high status and promising futures, but now they were in a marginalized and tenuous position, unsure of what the future might bring. The withdrawal of the work teams provided an opportunity to dispel this uncertainty, and members of this group became vocal and active in August.

The fourth category included those who became victims of the purge campaign for reasons other than opposition to the work team. Primarily composed of cadres and teachers, these were people who were denounced as followers of a "black line" in the party apparatus. The more extensive the work team's purge, the larger this group. People in this category obviously harbored very strong grievances about their treatment during June and July, but they did not become politically active until mid-1967, when Maoist officials called for new school power structures that included significant numbers of "revolutionary cadres."

For the rest of 1966 these new cleavages defined the interests and identities that drove factional conflicts. These categories were not defined by status in relation to school power structures before the work teams entered the schools. Instead, they were defined by one's immediate experience in the political interactions of June and July and the likely future consequences. In other words, students were not divided by prior social or political status, but by changes in status that resulted from the dramatic events of June and July. As we shall see in the next chapter, the most militant rebels in August and September came from the second and third categories—those who had experienced sharp status reversals. The radical vanguard of the movement initially came out of universities where major confrontations had occurred.

# 4

## DIVIDED AT BIRTH

### The University Red Guards

Freed from work-team authority, university students organized to continue the Cultural Revolution on their own. Red guard organizations proliferated during the first two weeks of August. From the outset they disagreed fundamentally about the direction the movement should take, and dramatic debates polarized university campuses. By September groups that articulated parallel arguments on their respective campuses sought support in cross-campus alliances. These alliances developed relatively coherent political identities and articulated sharply opposed positions about the next stage of the Cultural Revolution.

These factional differences, the emotional debates of August, and the sharpening factional struggles of September were not about the status quo. They were not about the features of school power structures or the policies they had pursued. These conflicts were about the events of June and July and their implications for students who had had different experiences under the work teams. They expressed divisions created by work teams when they shattered existing power structures and divided their members and followers against one another.

Two groups instigated the conflict and spearheaded a rebel insurgency. Among the most active and vocal were those who had been punished for challenging their work team. This group was especially large on campuses where major confrontations had occurred. Joining them was a second group: party members, student cadres, and others who had been political activists before the Cultural Revolution but had been sidelined politically as work teams assaulted school power structures. Both these groups suffered losses of status during June and July and were strongly motivated to reverse these losses and to achieve political vindication.

Arrayed against these insurgents were the majority of students who had cooperated with work teams, led by those appointed to chair Cultural

Revolution preparatory committees. The most committed of them were students who had actively supported work teams in their confrontations with opponents. These student leaders were now on the defensive: the insurgents charged that they were implicated in an erroneous political line. Should their opponents succeed in unseating them, the majority would be saddled with political errors.

In the campus debates of August and the factional mobilization of September, these two sides fought for leadership of their schools and the ability to define the objectives of the next stage of the Cultural Revolution. They competed for the allegiance of the majority of students who had passively complied with the work teams. These students now faced a choice between two starkly opposed visions of the next stage. Should they set aside the events of June and July, dutifully criticize the errors of the work teams, and then continue the Cultural Revolution in their schools as if the work teams had never intervened? Or should they take the fight off the campuses, locate and detain the work teams' leaders, bring them back for interrogation and struggle sessions, and then identify and attack the higher officials who had supported them?

The first position was the one adopted by the "majority" faction, the second by the insurgent "minority." The position taken by the latter had much more explosive implications for the direction of the Cultural Revolution because it led student militants directly up the chain of command that had dispatched work teams and into confrontations with national leaders who headed the functional ministries in charge of the earlier campaign. For obvious reasons, the "minority" position was viewed as more radical and subversive of the status quo, a fact eventually recognized by the CCRG and Mao, who had not foreseen this development but who quickly exploited it by openly supporting the minority faction in its struggle against their majority faction opponents, whom they eventually dismissed as "conservatives."

The radicalism of the minority faction, however, was not a product of its members' position within university power structures before the Cultural Revolution. It was a product of the changes in status that their encounters with work teams had brought about. They did not have fundamentally different points of view about the status quo, but they did have fundamentally different points of view about the actions of the work teams. It was this issue and these interests, rooted in the dramatic university events of June and July, that divided student rebels and set the minority faction on a political course that radicalized the Cultural Revolution in the fall of 1966.

## The Official Apology

These divisions crystallized within three weeks. On July 29, 1966, the Beijing Municipal Party Committee summoned hundreds of activists from schools across the city to attend a mass meeting in the Great Hall of the People. Beijing party secretary Li Xuefeng read the order withdrawing all work teams, and then the officials responsible for the policy proceeded to explain the reversal and provide guidance on what the next stage would bring.[1] Deng Xiaoping, general secretary of the Communist Party, spoke first, explaining that Chairman Mao had ordered the withdrawal of work teams because "practice has shown that the work-team format is unsuited to the requirements of the Cultural Revolution in universities and high schools and must be changed."[2] Deng emphasized two points. First, the errors committed by the work teams were due to organizational confusion, haste, and lack of experience: "Some comrades have said, old revolutionaries have run into new problems, and indeed this is so. And in sending work teams to every school we were also extremely hasty because they did not undergo thorough study and discussion. We comrades working at the Party Center and the Municipal Party Committee did not have any experience with this kind of historically unprecedented movement." Although the work teams had not worked out well, Deng argued, not all of them had committed errors, and the errors that had been committed were not uniformly severe: "Some work teams were good, some relatively good, but some also committed various errors; some very serious errors, they suppressed the masses, attacked the revolutionary left . . . obstructing the development of the Cultural Revolution . . . The vast majority of comrades on the work teams were willing to do their jobs well, but the leadership did not give them enough help."

Premier Zhou Enlai elaborated these themes, emphasizing that officials had sent work teams only after activists in the schools had demanded them, having lost confidence in their party committees after the purge of the Beijing Municipal Party Committee.[3] He also emphasized that the work teams' errors were due to haste and insufficient preparation. Even so, some of the work teams had done a good job, and the vast majority of their members had honestly attempted to do the job properly: "Of course, as Comrade Xiaoping has just said, some of the work teams were good, but the majority of the work-team comrades were good . . . Subjectively they did not mean to do this, but they worked according to the old methods; as everyone says, 'Old revolutionaries have run into new problems.'"

State Chairman Liu Shaoqi spoke last and elaborated on the theme "Old revolutionaries have encountered new problems."[4]

> How to carry out the Cultural Revolution? You are not too clear, do not really know, so you ask us 'How to carry out revolution?' I will answer you honestly and sincerely: I do not know either. And I think that a lot of other comrades at the Party Center also do not know. We have to rely on you to carry it out, to learn from the practical revolutionary experience of the teachers, students, and staff of various schools in carrying out revolution.

Liu acknowledged that the desire of some students to criticize the work teams was understandable, and that this should occur, but he also emphasized that their actions were at the behest of the Party Center. So what to do about the work teams? "Now that the work-team format is no longer suitable to the present needs of the Cultural Revolution, the Party Center has decided to withdraw them. If you let them leave, then they will leave. If you do not let them leave, and if you still have contrary views, then raise them; if you have criticisms, then criticize them to the full until you have had enough."

Unknown to the participants, Mao Zedong listened to the proceedings offstage, incensed by the way that his colleagues were minimizing the errors of the work teams and especially by the slogan "Old revolutionaries have encountered new problems."[5] Just as Liu's speech ended, Mao suddenly walked through the curtains onto the stage, setting off thunderous applause and prolonged chanting of "Long live Chairman Mao!" from the ecstatic student activists. He walked slowly back and forth across the stage, saying nothing and looking impassive. After a few minutes he walked back off stage, followed by Zhou Enlai, having ignored completely both Liu Shaoqi and Deng Xiaoping, who remained standing awkwardly on the stage.[6]

### Mixed Messages

As officials fanned out to speak to students, they carried with them very different messages. Deng Xiaoping, Zhou Enlai, and Liu Shaoqi carried their conciliatory message to several universities in an attempt to deflect anger from the work teams and persuade students to unite and continue the movement within the schools.[7] Members of the CCRG, however, emphasized the perfidy of the work teams and the necessity to make them answer for their crimes—a message that resonated strongly with students who had clashed with them. As early as July 24 Kang Sheng, Jiang Qing, and Chen Boda gave speeches at the Beijing Broadcasting Institute, where in early July students had demanded their own Cultural Revolution committee to replace the work team and had been attacked in response. Kang Sheng set the tone:

> The work team's errors were very serious . . . Have you not taken charge? Do you not have the power to dismiss the work team? Are you too afraid? Have you any guts? They said you were anti-party, anti-socialist, a black gang, are you afraid? Some students say, "All power to the Cultural Revolution committee"—is this slogan right or not? . . . The entire membership of the CCRG approves of this slogan, supports this slogan. But others—Comrade [name crossed out] from the State Broadcasting Agency and others, the head and vice-head of its political department, the head and vice-head of the work team—all think the slogan is wrong. They are mistaken, you must call them to account! They must answer! Write wall posters accusing them! They must publicly confess their errors![8]

Jiang Qing then stepped to the microphone and attacked the head of the work team at the Beijing Foreign Languages Institute No. 2, Zhang Yan, who had been removed from his post weeks before. Jiang was not entirely coherent, but she was clear about her political accusations:

> Zhang Yan committed errors. Comrade Chen Boda went to read wall posters, with twenty-nine people accompanying him; Zhang followed Chen Boda right to his doorstep, and then called him on the phone. Chen Boda did not even have the freedom to read wall posters. Two days later, Zhang Yan gave a report and said that those twenty-nine people were counterrevolutionary "backbone elements." He had them attacked repeatedly, one had a mental breakdown, eyes all bulging out. Comrade Kang Sheng went to see him, he cried his heart out, after Zhang Yan pulled out. This is a serious counterrevolutionary incident!

Chen Boda continued the attack on Zhang Yan, making clear that the dispute was personal and not merely political:

> Some comrades say, "Did not Zhang Yan himself suggest the Cultural Revolution committees?" Zhang Yan did not think this up, he just heard that this was being considered so he opportunistically brought it up. In fact he was

scared to death of the idea. As soon as he heard in the Commission on Foreign Cultural Relations that someone wanted to set one up, he treated these
comrades as counterrevolutionaries and labeled the vast majority counterrevolutionaries, with twenty-nine people as counterrevolutionary backbone elements, not just ordinary counterrevolutionaries. Moreover, he said that their
backstage boss was Chen Boda. Because I had supported them in establishing
a Cultural Revolution committee, I became a counterrevolutionary backstage
boss. Do you people here consider me a counterrevolutionary backstage boss?
Do you trust me or not?[9]

The anti-work-team rhetoric escalated further when the entire CCRG
visited Beijing Normal University for a mass rally on July 27. In denouncing the school's work-team head, Sun Youyu, for suppressing the student
movement, Kang Sheng suddenly accused him of trying to cover up an alleged coup attempt that student radicals at the school had exposed in a
wall poster:

Peng Zhen [former Beijing party secretary] actually did plot a coup, he actually did want to seize power . . . But Sun Youyu said this was a false rumor:
look at the stand that Sun Youyu took—he took an anti-party, anti-socialist
stand . . . Students, think about this, should not someone who argued on behalf of Peng Zhen be removed from his post? (Audience: YES!) . . . As Sun
Youyu carried out his anti-party activities, they no longer opposed this
black gang but instead turned to attack the Party Center, *Red Flag* magazine, and attacked our leftist comrade Lin Jie. Look, I have brought Lin Jie
with me here today, what about him? Comrades, Lin Jie is a graduate of Beijing Normal University, he was a good student, your good classmate. But
Sun Youyu said, with ulterior motives, that Lin Jie wanted to persecute leftist students, that Lin Jie's backstage supporter was Guan Feng, Guan Feng's
backstage supporter was Chen Boda, that behind Guan Feng was a black
line, and who was the backstage boss? We want you comrades to examine this
question: are we up here a black gang, are we a black line? (Audience: Red
Line!) . . . Sun Youyu violated the directives of the Party Center and Chairman Mao. They attacked revolutionary students and argued on behalf of
the Peng Zhen black gang. This is class struggle inside the party, among
the people, reflected inside the party, and reflected in relations between the
enemy and the people.[10]

The CCRG's effort to vilify the work teams reached a climax on August 4, when Kang Sheng and Jiang Qing led a mass rally at Beida to denounce the head and vice-head of its work team. Kang and Jiang fed

the emotions of the crowd with their strident accusations, which were remarkably extreme in light of the fact that very few students had been punished for their role in the violent events of June 18. Kang Sheng nonetheless charged that the work team's report on the incident was "counterrevolutionary":

> We have been through a severe and pointed episode of class struggle. This struggle was with Zhang Chengxian's anti-party, anti-socialist line . . . He used his powers of office, used the name of the work team, used the task given him by the upper levels, to come to Beida to suppress revolution. This right-wing opportunist line represents the road of the capitalist class coming to suppress the proletariat. At Beida, after "June 18," he carried out White Terror.[11]

Jiang Qing's rhetoric was equally inflammatory:

> As for those who resolutely carried out Zhang Chengxian and Zhang Dehua's unrepentant right-wing opportunist line, they should be resolutely struggled against and overthrown, struggled against till they stink, criticized and overthrown, criticized until they stink. The overwhelming weight of the facts shows that they did not come here to make revolution, they came to suppress your revolution, and to this very day they have remained very dishonest.[12]

The mass rally turned into a struggle session, with university militants yelling accusations at the victims, who were forced to stand on the stage, bent over at the waist. At one point red guards from Beida High School jumped onto the stage and whipped the two officials with leather belts. When the students were finished, Jiang Qing gave one of them a warm embrace.[13]

China's top officials were therefore signaling two starkly opposed interpretations of the work teams' errors just as student militants were taking power in their schools. The official position was that the work teams' errors were inadvertent and due to haste, poor preparation, and the novelty of the movement. These were well-meaning comrades, "old revolutionaries who encountered new problems," and they should be treated with sympathy and respect. Kang Sheng, Jiang Qing, and other members of the increasingly active CCRG, however, openly incited students, charging that many work teams carried out anti-party activities amounting to counterrevolution and were part of a deeper, more threatening conspiracy against Chairman Mao.

## The Ambiguous "Sixteen Points"

In the midst of all this campus activity Mao ordered a plenary session of the Eighth Central Committee. After several days of preliminary meetings to relay the contents of Mao's recent criticisms of the work teams, Central Committee members and forty-seven "responsible persons and revolutionary teachers and students" (including Nie Yuanzi) convened on August 1 for the opening session of the Eleventh Plenum.[14] The plenum decisively altered the political situation in the capital and shaped the environment for the student movement that was about to explode. First, Mao issued several letters in which he praised the fighting spirit expressed in the wall posters of the first red guard organizations, and he reprinted and circulated the student wall posters to all in attendance. Mao's sentiments were relayed to the students in private meetings. Second, Mao gave an August 4 speech that contained serious political charges against the actions of the Central Committee on the work-team question, and he made sarcastic and dismissive comments about Party Vice-Chairman Liu Shaoqi. In that speech he praised Nie Yuanzi's May 25 wall poster, likening its political significance to "the Paris Commune of the twentieth century." Third, he had Nie's Beida wall poster reprinted and circulated to the participants with an appended "wall poster" of his own, "Bombard the Headquarters."[15] Finally, Liu Shaoqi and Deng Xiaoping were demoted in the leadership hierarchy, while Marshall Lin Biao and several members of the CCRG—Kang Sheng, Chen Boda, and Tao Zhu—were promoted.

The most important document to emerge from the Eleventh Plenum was the "Decision Concerning the Great Proletarian Cultural Revolution," or the "Sixteen Points," released on August 9. It gave the official verdict on the work teams and laid down guidelines for the subsequent student movement. It reportedly went through more than thirty drafts and ended up as a compromise between those who wanted to mobilize a mass movement and those who wanted to limit its disruptive effects.[16] The document's ambiguities and contradictions enabled students with fundamentally different views to claim support for their actions.

A clear example of these ambiguities is the way the document mixed conciliatory and incendiary language when describing cadres, and especially the behavior of cadres on work teams. The "vast majority" of cadres in schools, according to point 8, belonged in categories 1 and 2—"good" and "relatively good."[17] Although most work teams had gone much further in attacking school power structures, the document was silent on this point and did not criticize them for excessive zeal. Point 3 contained an even more mixed message about cadres: although there were indeed good cadres who had dared to mobilize the masses, welcomed wall posters, and criticized their own errors, there were also "power holders who had taken the capitalist road after infiltrating our party" who, when faced with exposure, "engaged in further conspiracies, launched hidden attacks, created rumors, spared no effort to confuse the distinction between revolution and counterrevolution, and attacked the revolutionary faction." The document clearly stated that students who had been attacked and labeled by the work teams had been wronged. The labels given to them were the primary example of the "errors in orientation and line" of the work teams. "In the midst of the movement," point 7 declared, no student should be punished for any reason, "unless they committed such counterrevolutionary acts as murder, arson, poisoning, sabotage, or seizing state secrets."

Finally, the document articulated a vision of lively campus debate carried out in an atmosphere of mutual respect and democracy. Point 6 admonished students to "correctly handle contradictions among the people" by not suppressing the minority that had a divergent viewpoint. "Protect the minority, because sometimes the minority has truth on their side. Even if the opinions of the minority are mistaken, permit them to argue, permit them to hold to their own opinions," and in carrying out debates, "use reason, not force." The new Cultural Revolution committees that were springing up in the schools, point 9 explained, had "great historical significance." They were by no means temporary expedients but "long-term, permanent new mass organizations." They should be elected "according to the principles of the Paris Commune . . . The nomination lists must be thoroughly discussed by the masses before the elections." Once elected, the members of the committees "can be criticized at any time, and if they turn out not to be suitable for the post, after discussion among the masses, new elections can be held and they can be replaced."

As a guide for student radicals, the "Sixteen Points" was inadequate in several respects. First, it did not say anything about what students should actually do with their newly established organs of power. It was silent about what the new objectives of the movement, if any, should be, or if the students should now simply carry on the work team's job without the work team. Second, although it acknowledged that work teams had wrongly attacked many students, it also implied that some of these students might have committed serious errors and might have been actual rightists. It was silent about what remedies such students had, and how they might go about clearing their names. Third, although it acknowledged that cadres ranged from "good" to reactionary, it did not provide any guidelines for drawing distinctions, or who would decide.

Students could draw two very different conclusions from this document. Those who had cooperated with the work team and now controlled school Cultural Revolution committees could take heart that they were "permanent" new organs of power and had the imprimatur of the Central Committee. Because these students had cooperated with the work team, they were pleased to read that not all of them had committed serious errors. They could also conclude that students who were upset about their treatment by the work team should be satisfied with official acknowledgment that they had been unjustly attacked and should stop harping on the work-team issue.

Students who had borne the brunt of the work team's attacks, however, could draw a very different message from the "Sixteen Points." Their persecution showed that they were indeed "revolutionary," certainly more so than those who had cooperated with work teams. Moreover, the work-team cadres who had attacked them were evidently "anti-party, anti-socialist elements who infiltrated the party"—exactly the kind of targets that the Cultural Revolution was meant to expose. Therefore, the main task of the Cultural Revolution should now be to focus on the errors of the work teams and to examine the higher officials who had led them into such serious political errors. The "Sixteen Points" said that although their opinions were in the minority, they should be respected, and the document also said that the truth might be on their side. It also said that nomination lists had to be "thoroughly discussed by the masses" beforehand, and if those who were elected turned out not to be suitable, they could be criticized and new elections held. Therefore, these students felt encouraged to challenge the new Cultural Revolution committees and shift the direction of the movement against the work teams and those who had sent them.

## The Process of Campus Polarization

Despite the denunciation of the work teams and assurances that their attacks on "revolutionary" students were erroneous, university campuses were immediately polarized over the work teams' political legacy. The fundamental problem was that students who had cooperated with the work teams were left in charge of schools and had clear majority support. In schools where there had been serious challenges to work-team authority, many of these students participated in the counterattacks against opponents, and a large number of victims were on the losing end. They immediately challenged the new organs of power and put the student militants who staffed them on the defensive.

The first documented factional divide was at the Beijing Construction Institute. This institute's work team labeled a number of its opponents "counterrevolutionary" in mid-July. On July 31, after the Municipal Party Committee decreed that these opponents were now considered "left-wing," more than 100 of those who had cooperated marched to the Municipal Party Committee to protest the decision. In response, some 200 students and teachers who supported the decision formed the August 1 Combat Team to defend their view. On August 2, a much larger group of 1,100 established the Revolution Corps to defend their prior cooperation with the work team.[18] This was the first clear split between a "minority" and a "majority" faction. On August 2 and 3 Liu Shaoqi visited the campus to try to mediate, advising the two sides to be tolerant of each other and trying to lessen animus against the work team.[19]

Similar splits occurred at universities throughout Beijing, most notably at three that later generated strong rebel movements and famous red guard leaders—Qinghua University, the Geology Institute, and the Aeronautics Institute.

### Qinghua University

When the Qinghua work team withdrew, it left behind a network of departmental Cultural Revolution committees composed of student activists who cooperated actively in the work team's campaigns against both the old party apparatus and opponents of the work team like Kuai Dafu. The school's first red guard organization was established on August 5 by Liu Tao, one of Liu Shaoqi's daughters and coauthor of an early wall poster attacking Party Secretary Jiang Nanxiang.[20] The Qinghua Red Guards were established on August 19. It emphasized family revolutionary heritage as a criterion for membership—initially, only children of revolutionary cadres and soldiers were admitted. This alienated student cadres and party members who were from other kinds of "red" households (peasants and workers), and it also alienated students from revolutionary households who opposed this "closed-door" strategy.[21]

As the work team was preparing to leave, a campus debate broke out. One group of students denounced the work team for "serious errors of orientation and line," while another argued that despite its errors, the work team's radical orientation was basically correct. During his campus visit on August 4, Zhou Enlai had tried to smooth over the disagreements. He acknowledged the work team's errors and announced the rehabilitation of Kuai Dafu and others, but he told the students to forget about the work teams, unite under the preparatory committee, and continue the struggle against the school's "black gang."[22] On August 7 the preparatory committee issued a call for all students to unite under its leadership and continue the struggle within the school. It was immediately challenged by students who organized the August 8 Alliance in favor of intensified criticism of the work team. In response, the preparatory committee established the August 9 Alliance, which argued that students should not get entangled in the work-team question but should instead push the offensive against the school's revisionists. As its first step in this program, it held a mass struggle session against one of the school's party vice-secretaries.[23]

The leaders of the "minority" August 8 Alliance were student activists with "red" family heritage and strong party ties who had been marginalized under the work team, along with some of the students who had been attacked with Kuai Dafu for challenging the work team. They included Tang Wei, who was the son of a revolutionary martyr, and Chen Yuting, whose father was a party cadre. Liu Quan, like Kuai Dafu, was one of the boldest critics of the work team and one of the best-known victims of its campaign against opponents and had been publicly exonerated by Zhou Enlai in his August 4 speech. Liu was a student cadre—the youth league branch secretary of his classroom—and his father was a provincial vice-governor. In June he had called for the replacement of the work team's leader in a wall poster. The work team had attacked him as a counterrevolutionary in retaliation.[24]

Shen Ruhuai, from a poor peasant household, was a youth league branch secretary, but he was also a party member and head of his party cell.[25] Even before the arrival of the work team, Shen put up a wall poster attacking Party Secretary Jiang Nanxiang, but he also argued that the party organization was still basically Marxist. After the work team arrived, it denounced the entire organization as rotten. His classroom's youth league and party organizations ceased to function, and he was forced to stand down from his post and undergo examination along with the rest of the party apparatus. New leaders appointed by the work team ran the classroom, and Shen watched passively as students freely targeted cadres.[26]

Shen was eventually cleared of political charges and was invited by the work team to help it run the campaign in his department, but he harbored strong doubts about the work team's behavior. Shen felt that the work team's attack on loyal and well-meaning party members, some of whom were his friends and comrades, was far too harsh. When students encouraged by the work team's radical stance went too far in their rebellion and eventually chafed at its authority, the work team cracked down on them.

> Although we all expressed our support for the work team, we were really bothered by their behavior. First, they came in and dragged out all manner of black gang elements among the leaders, but now, all of a sudden, why are they grabbing all kinds of counterrevolutionaries among the students? How can there be so many class enemies at Qinghua? I could not figure this out and felt that the work team's methods were problematic. First, the work team kicked all 500 cadres out of power and called them a black gang, inciting the students to put them through struggle sessions and parade them around. Then, when as a result of this policy the students went too far, they tried to rein them in, causing students to resist. Then they turned around and attacked all these students as counterrevolutionaries. The work team should have objectively assessed the reasons for the students' behavior and corrected it, but instead they considered them rightist students who were plotting to seize power.[27]

These August 8 activists established their own political organization, the Maoism Red Guards, on August 22. A few days earlier, two of the organizers, Tang Wei and Chen Yuting, put up a wall poster calling Liu Shaoqi's wife, Wang Guangmei, a "political crook" for her actions while advising the Qinghua work team. They were surprised when in response leading supporters of August 9 put up their own wall posters critical of Wang Guangmei. Of particular note were a wall poster by He Pengfei, the son of Marshall He Long, and six other high officials' children, and a separate wall poster by Liu Shaoqi's daughter (Wang Guangmei's stepdaughter), Liu Tao. The attacks on the state chairman's wife by these high officials' children signaled to the others that Liu Shaoqi must be in serious political trouble. In response, the August 8 group went further and put up a wall poster that described Liu Shaoqi's speech at the July 29 mass meeting of student activists at the Great Hall of the People as a violation of Mao Zedong thought.[28]

Zhou Enlai once again tried to calm the controversy in a trip to Qinghua on August 22, bringing the former work-team head Ye Lin along with him. Ye Lin read out an extended self-criticism, and Zhou Enlai denounced the work team's errors and the "white terror" it had imposed on revolutionary students. However, he instructed students to unite and strengthen Qinghua's new organs of political power. Students associated with August 8 nonetheless continued to put up wall posters critical of Liu Shaoqi, and some of them criticized Zhou Enlai's weak political stand, demanding instead that recordings of more militant speeches by Jiang Qing and Kang Sheng be broadcast over the school's loudspeaker system.[29]

On August 24 the Qinghua Red Guards met on campus with representatives of majority factions from twelve other universities and agreed on a coordinated response. He Pengfei, who chaired the meeting, accused the Maoism Red Guards of attacking the party center and Chairman Mao. That evening some 2,000 red guards from twelve schools entered the Qinghua campus, took over the auditorium, and disrupted a meeting of the Maoism Red Guards. They closed off the wall-poster area, took over the school's broadcasting system, and issued an ultimatum charging that the Maoism Red Guards were composed of rightists who were trying to overthrow the Communist Party. They took photos of offending wall posters and recorded the authors' names. They chased away readers, searched their book bags, and tore down offending wall posters. Afterward they tore down the historic university gate. That evening they marched across campus, calling for suppression of "rightists" in the minority faction. They also intensified the attacks on Qinghua's middle-level cadres, invading their homes, searching through their belongings, and beating and imprisoning them. From this point until mid-September the August 9 faction controlled the school.[30] Not until late September did it face a serious challenge.

## Beijing Geology Institute

At the Geology Institute a well-organized opposition movement had mounted a major challenge to the work team. The minority faction was organized and led by veterans of that struggle, almost all of whom were Communist Youth League cadres, and one of whom was a party member. One of the organizers of the opposition was Mei Jianming, who was from a revolutionary cadre household: his father was Mei Gongbin, who joined the party in the 1930s and was the secretary general of both the Central Committee's United Front Work Department and the Chinese

People's Political Consultative Conference.[31] Only a first-year student, Mei Jianming was already a political activist and student cadre. Before the arrival of the work team, he nonetheless joined in the criticism of departmental cadres and was immediately at odds with his party superiors. After the work team arrived, he felt vindicated and became a leading Cultural Revolution activist, but he opposed the work team's harsh attacks against student critics: "Before the work team came, we were an oppressed minority, but now we were supported, we were movement activists. But the work team started to criticize the masses and collect materials on them, and this bothered me more and more, so I eventually raised criticisms of the work team. In an instant I became an opponent of the work team. I became an object of criticism and struggle overnight, from an activist to a reactionary student."[32] Emboldened by his father's prestige, Mei Jianming wrote a wall poster attacking the work team. Despite the work team's efforts to isolate Mei, he still had many sympathizers on campus and refused to be intimidated. He suddenly realized the seriousness of the situation when the work team persisted and labeled him a counterrevolutionary: "This woke me up—the label was real."[33]

After the work team's departure the students who had cooperated with the work team controlled the preparatory committee. Veterans of the anti-work-team movement immediately challenged them and established the Mao Zedong Thought Red Guards, which merged with other anti-work-team groups to form the East Is Red Commune on August 17.[34] The leaders of East Is Red were youth league activists, and many of them were youth league cadres. Among them were Zhu Chengzhao, a 25-year-old "cadre transfer student" and son of a bureau-level official who was a fourth-year student in the Hydrology Department, and Jiang Lianpu, a fifth-year student in Mei Jianming's own Survey Department. Also prominent was Wang Dabin, a party member who later assumed leadership of the group in early 1967.[35] East Is Red called for criticism of the work team's actions and for its leader to return to campus for interrogation and public apologies. It also refused to continue the work team's campaign against top school officials because the work team had targeted its prominent allies in the school leadership—especially party standing committee member Li Gui—and had attacked Party Secretary Gao Yuangui as a scapegoat for errors committed by other school officials.

The preparatory committee responded by pulling together the student groups who supported it into the Geology Institute Red Guards on August 22.[36] It had the backing of officials in the Ministry of Geology, who had already clashed with opponents of the work team during June and July.[37] The debate about the work team therefore had a special intensity. East Is Red's attack on the work team and its accusations against ministry officials directly undermined the majority faction's position and implicated its members in alleged political errors.

## Beijing Aeronautics Institute

Student opposition at the Aeronautics Institute had forced a major confrontation with the work team similar in scope to the one at the Geology Institute. News of the denunciation of Beida's work team led immediately to calls to reverse the verdicts against the student opponents branded "reactionary" and to replace departmental Cultural Revolution committees staffed by work-team loyalists. On July 29 work-team head Zhao Ruzhang held a mass meeting to announce the work team's withdrawal and the appointment of twelve students to a preparatory committee that would organize elections for a Cultural Revolution committee.[38]

This announcement touched off a debate over the preparatory committee and the status of students branded "reactionary" by the work team. Opponents renewed their accusations against the work team, arguing that the preparatory committee was illegal, and that the political charges against them should be overturned. Supporters argued that despite the work team's errors, its radical stance was basically correct, and that some of the wall posters did express reactionary views. In response to charges that it was illegal, the preparatory committee called for early elections.

During this period the preparatory committee began setting up red guard organizations, and these plans became controversial. On August 1 it announced that the criterion for membership was the acceptance of the work team as revolutionary. The preparatory committee gave the work team a warm send-off when it departed on August 2. In protest, forty anti-work-team students marched downtown to the Central Committee offices and demanded an audience with the CCRG. The next day they met with Zhou Rongxin, secretary-general of the State Council, who agreed with them that the work team should return to the school for criticism.

In the meantime, the preparatory committee went ahead with its plans. On August 3 it announced the formation of the Aeronautics Institute Red Guards. Although its founding proclamation immediately touched off a campus debate, the preparatory committee continued plans for elections. The opposition argued that the elections must be postponed until after the debate about the work team. Ignoring these arguments, the preparatory committee held elections, and the victorious incumbents argued that their position was now ratified by the masses and no longer rested solely on the departing work team's final act.

In protest, on August 10 the opposition mobilized over 400 students to march to the Central Committee's offices to demand that work-team head Zhao Ruzhang return to the campus for criticism. Their demands were immediately granted. In an effort to placate the opposition, the preparatory committee announced that Zhao would return to the campus the next day for a mass meeting, after which he would leave immediately. Instead of helping reconcile the two factions, the August 11 mass meeting led to a confrontation that further widened the growing divide. Members of the work team entered the campus, escorted by members of the Aeronautics Institute Red Guards, who gave them a warm welcome. Along the way, some of the red guards tore down wall posters that denounced the work team, and others yelled "Long live the work team." Members of the work team gave brief self-criticisms and then immediately left the campus, escorted by the Red Guards. The opposition called the slogans in support of Zhao Ruzhang "reactionary" and intensified its accusations against his "crimes" in its wall posters.

The confrontations climaxed at a mass meeting on August 14 that was attended by several officials from the National Defense Science and Technology Commission. The event started with forty minutes of slogan chanting during which each side tried to shout down the other. After the uproar subsided, Zhao Ruzhang gave a more extended self-criticism, and representatives from both sides gave speeches. During the meeting a scuffle broke out in front of the stage, and several staff workers who supported the work team were injured. The work team's supporters labeled this a "counterrevolutionary incident," and the next day the Red Guards sent nine truckloads of delegates to the State Council offices to lodge an accusation. Family members of staff workers marched across campus to protest the "beating of workers," as did majority-faction red guards from the nearby Geology Institute, Forestry Institute, and Mining Institute. Student leaders on the preparatory committee adopted a more aggressive and accusatory tone, arguing that the opposition lacked proletarian class feelings.

Feeling that they were being framed by an incident that was being blown out of proportion, more than 500 students in the opposition set off for the CCRG offices on August 15 to plead their case. They returned to the campus the next day to announce an investigation into the alleged beatings. They held a series of meetings at which witnesses denied the allegations of the majority faction. In response, the preparatory committee organized a series of sessions at which campus workers testified about their oppression in the old society—meetings called to foster "proletarian class feelings." The preparatory committee also organized an official investigation that was boycotted by the opposition. Arrangements to hold a campuswide joint debate about the alleged incident broke down.

On August 19 the opposition set up its own red guard organizations, which soon merged into a campuswide minority faction, Aeronautics Institute Red Flag. That evening two of its representatives were selected to debate two students from the preparatory committee at a climactic mass meeting about the work team. Zhao Ruzhang read out a new self-criticism. As Zhao was escorted off campus the next day, he was cheered by some students, while others unsuccessfully attempted to block his exit, arguing that he should remain on campus to hear the criticism of the masses and continue the debate over the work team. That evening the minority faction formally inaugurated Aeronautics Institute Red Flag. On August 21 it held a mass meeting during which campus officials were pulled out for struggle sessions and paraded around the campus to humiliate them. In response, the preparatory committee organized an even larger mass meeting the next day and held struggle sessions against an even greater number of even higher-ranking "black-gang" elements, including the institute's party secretary and the leaders of all the academic departments.

The Aeronautics Institute now had two well-organized factions that were at loggerheads about the political legacy of the work team. Red Flag was convinced that the majority faction had prematurely closed off debate about the work team, and it still disputed the outcome of the "premature" elections of early August. Its grievances intensified on August 23 when it was revealed that Zhao Ruzhang had ordered the work team to draw up a blacklist containing the names of all those who had authored wall posters critical of the work team. The ambiguous outcome of the campus debate about Zhao Ruzhang, coupled with renewed fears about the documentation of the earlier political charges against the work team's opponents, spurred Red Flag to more daring attacks that shortly propelled it into the vanguard of the city's rebel movement.

## The Beida Exception

As campuses across Beijing split over the work-team question, Beida was a glaring exception. There was no majority-minority split over the legacy of the work team. Opposing factions appeared much later, in October, over different issues. The absence of a typical majority-minority division was due partly to the fact that Beida's work team faced no serious opposition and left almost no student victims, but the most important reason was the unique role of Nie Yuanzi. Celebrated in the mass media for her famous wall poster, praised effusively by Mao at the Eleventh Plenum, and working hand in hand with Beida's radical work team along with coauthors and supporters who staffed the work team's offices, Nie had nonetheless denounced the work team's leaders in late July and had been placed at the head of the school's preparatory committee by the CCRG. Nie therefore occupied a unique position. She was a senior official in the party apparatus and had strong elite ties, but she was also the university's most celebrated rebel. Despite her cooperation with the discredited work team, her prior ties with Maoist officials earned her their support and praise.

During the next six weeks Nie moved to consolidate her power at Beida. As Nie prepared for the elections, she established a regular working relationship with her elite sponsors. On August 10 she visited Cao Yi'ou at her home to plan struggle sessions. On August 14 Kang Sheng sent instructions about forthcoming struggle sessions, which she held at the Beida sports field on August 15 against former Party Secretary Lu Ping and other members of the party standing committee.[39] On August 18 she was invited onto the rostrum at a massive Tiananmen rally for the red guards, during which she had a personal audience with Mao in one of the reception rooms.

Beida's work team had done the bidding of Nie's dissidents all along, vindicating their actions in the Socialist Education Movement and persecuting those who had opposed her. The only difference now was that Nie and her Beida colleagues were in charge. Wall-poster collections formerly edited and published by the work team were issued in virtually identical format in the name of the preparatory committee and contained identical material.[40] In fact, the preparatory committee continued to issue wall-poster collections based on material collected under the work team, backdating several of its publications to mid-July.[41] This did not stop it from simultaneously publishing denunciations of the work team.[42] Beida cadres and instructors who had staffed the work team's offices continued to perform the same functions. The work team's operations simply continued under new management.

As confrontations between opposed factions grew on other campuses, Beida instead became a model unit, a revolutionary tourist site. During the first two weeks of August, 718,000 registered visitors flocked to the campus to view wall posters and exhibitions. Political suspects in the school were formed into "labor reform brigades." The preparatory committee issued an instruction manual, "How to Conduct People's War"—a guide to interrogations and extracting confessions from suspects—which was copied and reprinted throughout the country.[43] The number of struggle sessions increased, house searches intensified, and suicides were more frequent.[44] An official red guard organization was established at a mass rally on August 19 at which Nie Yuanzi presided. Red guards were to be organized at the department level and attached to the emerging new school power structure under Nie's direction. As was common with red guard organizations sponsored by preparatory committees, the organization was to be formed from descendants of the first generation of revolutionaries.[45]

On September 9 elections were held for the Beida Cultural Revolution Committee. Nie and her Philosophy Department comrades were elected to six of the forty-four seats; Nie became chairman and her longtime ally Kong Fan the first-ranking of four vice-chairmen.[46] Administrative posts were dominated by Nie's Philosophy Department allies: Yang Keming, a coauthor of the May 25 wall poster, was still head of propaganda and was the editor of the school's newspaper, *Xin Beida,* which put out its first issue on August 22, with masthead calligraphy supplied by Mao.[47]

With no real opposition to the Beida work team, there was no political basis for a minority faction. As the citywide struggle by "minority" factions challenged preparatory committees at other schools, Nie and her comrades stood to one side, quietly consolidating a new school power structure with backing from the highest levels of Maoist officialdom.

## The August Debates

By the third week of August clearly opposed majority and minority organizations had formed in the vast majority of the schools (see Table 4.1). The process accelerated after the first mass rally for red guards at Tiananmen Square on August 18. Majority factions frequently adopted a simple name, Red Guards, which signaled that they were the official

Table 4.1  August 1966 factions, majority and minority, by university

| School | Majority (date established) | Minority (date established) |
|---|---|---|
| Beijing Aeronautics Institute[1] | Aeronautics Institute Red Guards (August 3) | Red Flag Combat Brigade (August 19) |
| Beijing Agricultural Machinery Institute[2] | August 18 Red Guards<br>Struggle-Criticism-Transformation Corps | Mao Zedong Thought Red Guards (August 8) |
| Beijing Agricultural University[3] | Agricultural University Red Guards (August 21) | Maoism Red Guards (August 20) |
| Beijing Construction Institute[4] | Revolution Corps (August 2) | August 1 Combat Brigade (August 1)<br>Red Flag Brigade |
| Beijing Foreign Languages Institute[5] | Foreign Languages Institute Red Guards | Maoism Red Guards |
| Beijing Foreign Languages Institute No. 2[6] | Foreign Languages Institute No. 2 Red Guards (August 21)<br>August 18 Red Guards (August 19–24) | East Is Red Red Guards (August 22) |
| Beijing Forestry Institute[7] | Forestry Institute Red Guards (early August) | Maoism Red Guards (August 20)<br>East Is Red Commune (August 31) |
| Beijing Geology Institute[8] | Geology Institute Red Guards (August 22)<br>Struggle-Criticism-Transformation Corps (August 27) | East Is Red Combat Brigade (August 8)<br>East Is Red Commune (August 17) |
| Beijing Industrial University[9] | Industrial University Red Guards | East Is Red Commune |
| Beijing Machinery Institute[10] | Mao Zedong Red Guards (mid-August) | East Is Red Commune (August 23) |
| Beijing Mining Institute[11] | Maoism Red Guards | East Is Red Commune |
| Beijing Normal University[12] | Mao Zedong Thought Red Guards (August 23) | Jinggangshan Combat Brigade (August 23) |
| Beijing Petroleum Institute[13] | Petroleum Institute Red Guards (August 10) | August 18 Red Guards |
| | Maoism Red Guards (August 18) | May 25 Red Guards |
| Beijing Post and Telecommunications Institute[14] | — | Maoism Red Guards<br>August 18 Red Guards |

| | | |
|---|---|---|
| Beijing Railway Institute[15] | August 20 Red Guards (August 20) | Maoism Red Guards (August 23) |
| Beijing Steel Institute[16] | Steel Institute Red Guards (August 3) | — |
| Chinese People's University[17] | August 18 Red Guards (August 20) | Renda Red Guards (August 11) |
| Chinese University of Science and Technology[18] | Red Guard General Headquarters | Red Lantern<br>Revolutionary Rebel Brigade |
| Qinghua University[19] | Qinghua Red Guards (August 19) | Maoism Red Guards (August 22) |

1. Beijing Aeronautics Institute Red Flag (1966b), 10.
2. *Dongfanghong zhanbao*, 30 March 1967, 2 (CCRM 2001, 10:3892).
3. Wang Buzheng (1995, 368); *Xin nongda*, 10 June and 18 August 1967 (CCRM 2001, 34:13374, 13407).
4. Beijing Geology Institute East Is Red (1967b), 79–80.
5. *Hongweibao*, 19 October 1966 (CCRM 1999, 6:2703); *Wen'ge zhanbao*, 29 September 1966 (CCRM 2001, 34:12084).
6. *Hongweibing*, 20 September 1966, 1 January 1967 (CCRM 2001, 20:7633, 7650).
7. *Wen'ge zhanbao*, 29 September 1966 (CCRM 2001, 34:12081); Zhu Jinzhao (2002), 51.
8. Beijing Geology Institute East Is Red (1967b), 82; *Dongfangbong bao*, 17 February 1967, 2 (CCRM 2001, 9:3218); *Hongweibing*, 21 and 30 September 1966 (CCRM 2001, 20:7668, 7670).
9. Beijing Industrial University East Is Red Commune (1966c).
10. *Dongfanghong*, 13 August 1967 (CCRM 2001, 7:2663); *Hongweibing*, 20 September 1966 (CCRM 2001, 20:7633).
11. *Hongweibing zhanbao*, 13 and 17 September 1966 (CCRM 2001, 21:8257, 8262).
12. Beijing Geology Institute East Is Red (1967b), 98; *Jinggangshan*, 24 August 1967 (CCRM 2001, 24:9434).
13. *Hongse zaofanbao*, 17 March 1967 (CCRM 2001, 19:7303); Yu Shicheng (2003), 90.
14. *Bei You hongweibing*, 20 May 1967 (CCRM 2001, 3:1156).
15. Northern Transportation University Annals Editorial Committee (1996), 278.
16. *Hongweibing*, 12 September 1966 (CCRM 2001, 20:7686).
17. Chinese People's University Red Guards (1966a), 17–18; Chinese People's University Red Guards (1966b), 20–21.
18. *Dongfanghong*, 24 March 1967 (CCRM 2001, 8:3005).
19. Shen Ruhuai (2004), 21, 25–26; Tang Shaojie (2003), 5.

organization of their school's preparatory committee. Minority factions more commonly added a prefix to their title: "Maoism" or "Mao Zedong Thought." "Red Flag," and "East Is Red" were some of the more popular alternative names. The factional divisions were expressed in public debates, wall posters, and editorials published in newly established student newspapers. On virtually all campuses the "majority" was in the initially dominant position—people who had actively supported their work team and who ended up controlling the preparatory committees. Contesting their authority was a campus "minority" led by people who had clashed with the work team or who had been marginalized by its campaign.

The divergent points of view were already evident in early August, and positions hardened in the ensuing weeks. As animosities mounted, the debates took on an increasingly accusatory and threatening tone.[48] The issue that immediately drove a wedge between the two sides was the role that the work team had played in their school. The "Sixteen Points" stated that the work teams had committed serious errors of orientation and line because they had suppressed the student movement, thereby obstructing the Cultural Revolution. These pronouncements, however, failed to address key questions about university-level politics, because the students left in charge of the schools were activists who had cooperated with the work teams.

Students therefore disagreed about the severity of the work teams' errors. Majority factions drew on the speeches by Liu Shaoqi, Deng Xiaoping, and Zhou Enlai: the work teams had committed errors because they had "misunderstood" Mao's intentions. The leaders of the work teams were "veteran revolutionaries" who made great contributions in the past. The majority factions urged students to "criticize the work team but support the work team." The minority position was starkly different: the work teams had committed serious errors of orientation and line. Their errors were not inadvertent—they were trying to suppress student radicals and blunt Mao's Cultural Revolution.

The two sides also disagreed fundamentally about the next stage of the Cultural Revolution. The majority argued that it should continue the Cultural Revolution under student leadership and immediately hold elections to permanent organs of power, as the "Sixteen Points" stipulated. To this end, preparatory committees organized struggle sessions against major political targets and put large numbers of cadres and faculty under detention on campus in "labor reform brigades." The minority did not object to the further persecution of school officials, but it did object to

holding elections so soon. Elections should be postponed, it argued, because the work teams had biased the outcomes by putting their supporters in charge. Before any truly meaningful elections could be held, the
leaders of the work team must be brought back to the campus and made
to confess their crimes. In short, the movement should focus on the crimes
of the work team. Minority factions fought to postpone campus elections,
and after failing to do so, they objected that the results were unfair and
should be overturned.

Those in the majority faction understood that the attacks on the work
team were in fact aimed at them. Their claim to leadership, after all, was
based on their prior cooperation with the work team. After the elections,
however, they had a new claim to power—they were elected according to
official policy. They claimed that the minority was interested only in
narrow personal interests—its members sought personal "rehabilitation"
after their earlier clashes with the work team. This was why they per-
versely insisted on "turning veteran revolutionaries into counterrevolutionaries."

The minority countered that the elections were illegitimate because the
outcome reflected the influence of the work team. Most students still were
insufficiently conscious of the work team's crimes, and as long as these
crimes were covered up, the situation would not change. Second, the rehabilitation issue was not a narrow one but had broad political importance
because the suppression of the school's true revolutionary students was the
primary error of the work teams. Third, in response to the charge of "diverting the spearhead of the movement," they agreed that this was precisely what they were trying to do: the work teams had turned the spearhead of the movement against the revolutionary masses, but now they
were trying to turn the movement back onto the right track. Finally, concerning the idea that the minority was attacking "veteran revolutionaries,"
all who opposed Chairman Mao must be struggled against and could lose
their posts, no matter how high their position or how glorious their past
contributions.

### Tan Lifu: Majority Advocate

During these August debates the leader of the Beijing Industrial University Red Guards gave a powerful and passionate speech on his campus in
support of his majority faction's position. This speech was transcribed
and widely circulated and became highly influential. It strongly defended

the actions of his school's work team and praised the revolutionary credentials of its leader. Because the speaker, Tan Lifu, was the son of a veteran revolutionary who held a high post after 1949, and because he strongly defended the proposition that the children of revolutionaries had especially strong political loyalties, his speech was once considered key evidence for the idea that "conservative" red guards from elite backgrounds supported school power structures and the work teams that had defended them, and that red guard factions expressed the different interests of students from different family origins.[49] After the full text of the speech became available and details of the school's political history became known, it became clear that Tan's case instead illustrated how the work teams divided school power structures and split students from identical backgrounds over issues that had little to do with the status quo ante.[50]

Tan Lifu was a twenty-four-year-old student and already a member of the Communist Party. He had the most impeccable of family revolutionary credentials and had actually been born in the fabled revolutionary base area in Yan'an. His father, Tan Zhengwen, was an official in the Yan'an security apparatus and a close protégé of Kang Sheng. He was the first director of the Beijing Bureau of Public Security after the communist victory in 1949, and during the 1950s he served on the Beijing Municipal Party Committee and as deputy director of China's equivalent of the State Prosecutor's Office before his death in 1961 at the age of 51.[51] Tan Lifu's mother, Jiang Tao, was a section chief in the Beijing Bureau of Public Security.[52]

Despite these elite ties, Tan Lifu's political activism was motivated by real grievances against his school's party organization. Tan was far from a model student or party member, and his party superiors were so exasperated with him that, according to Tan, they "let everybody seize on my shortcomings" and "made me into an example of the way that high cadre kids were changing."[53] Although Tan knew that his party superiors thought little of him, he learned early in the Cultural Revolution that the party committee considered him to have a "revisionist viewpoint." It was then that Tan realized the full measure of his antagonism toward the "black gang" on the university party committee. This spurred him to get involved in Cultural Revolution politics in a big way.[54]

The first work team permitted the party committee to run its own campaign. However, the second one was completely different. Led by Du Wanrong, an official from the People's Liberation Army (PLA) General Staff Headquarters and a former political commissar with the Eighth Route Army, it proceeded with a radical purge. Because this radical work team, headed by a military cadre with genuine revolutionary credentials, was tormenting a party apparatus against which Tan harbored serious grievances, Tan became a leading activist and strong supporter. When the work team withdrew from the school on July 29, it appointed one of Tan Lifu's classmates, Liu Jing, to head the preparatory committee. Tan was put in charge of the red guards.[55]

The budding "minority" faction was led by students who had clashed with the first work team but who had been subsequently marginalized by the second, which refused to address the first work team's errors. The most outspoken opponents were also the children of revolutionaries, and all of them had been political activists before the Cultural Revolution.[56] These students now argued that the elections should be postponed. They immediately confronted Liu Jing and Tan Lifu, charging that the second work team had suppressed them as well, and that it was therefore no more revolutionary than the first one. In the face of mounting criticism, Tan's group proposed to move forward with elections, but the opposition objected. Its members argued that the situation at the university would not afford them a fair chance. The "lingering poison" of the work teams still tainted the university's political atmosphere, and the red guards and preparatory committee had unjustly benefited from their good relationship with the work team, which had earned them the support of a large student majority.

The opposition wanted to delay elections and hold a debate about the work teams' conduct, which it felt was necessary to strengthen its support. Tan and Liu Jing argued that this would only delay the movement by dragging in irrelevant side issues, but they agreed to one week of debates. The opposition, in turn, complained about the conduct of the debates, especially Tan's intimidating tone. After the debates were over, it objected to plans for elections because the debate had been unfair.

Tan's speech hammered at several key points. The first was that the prior school leadership had been dominated by members of the Peng Zhen "black gang" on the Beijing Party Committee that had been purged at the outset of the Cultural Revolution—specifically the school's party secretary, Song Shuo. Tan referred several times to "this rotten old nest of a university." The earlier leaders had promoted revisionism, using a "red millstone" to "force down the heads of the many students from worker, peasant, and cadre families."[57] Tan showed no trace of sympathy for the former leadership of the school. Revisionism had so dominated the school in recent years that there was a lot of cleaning up to do. "There are many enemies, and when we finish striking down one there is another to strike, and even though we are exhausted from sweeping them away, we still have not swept things clean."[58] Tan's starting point was the same position taken by Nie Yuanzi in her attacks against Beida's leaders in late May and early June: the school's leadership was rotten to the core and needed to be thoroughly cleansed.[59]

Tan's second point contained a barely concealed political threat against his opponents: they sounded like rightists who opposed the Cultural Revolution, they borrowed long-discredited arguments from the purged Beijing Party Secretary Peng Zhen, and in fact they were motivated by narrowly private interests. "Some say, 'The lingering poison of the work team has not been eliminated,' 'The work team's hidden remnants have not been scattered'; in my view it is the lingering poison of revisionism that has not been eliminated, the hidden remnants of Peng Zhen that have not been scattered!"[60] Tan argued that members of the opposition questioned the militant assertion of the party's class line because they were the same kind of revisionists as the previous school leaders, under whom they had flourished:

Some people do not hate the black gang; Peng Zhen's "emphasize performance" has left such a sweet taste in their mouths, how can they hate him? However, regarding the work teams, regarding these old revolutionary comrades, they hate them down to their very bones. They are still interested in the work team and struggling against the black gang. When they find out some cadre has made a mistake, they are happy as can be, they jump for joy. What are you happy about when a communist party cadre makes a mistake? Damn it! (someone yells, damn right! warm applause)[61]

Tan's third point was that the second work team had gotten it right. Whatever the errors of the first one or of work teams at other universities, the school's second one had pursued a consistently radical course and had been led by a genuine revolutionary cadre from the People's Liberation Army. Its members were not tools of any black gang; they were old revolutionary comrades who had done their jobs properly and who deserved respect and admiration:

When they saw that the work team headed by Du Wanrong supported us, and we "country bumpkins" had power in our hands, some people cursed us behind our backs. We knew this. We heard the sound of their teeth grinding behind our backs (laughter, applause). We know Du Wanrong . . . On the first day Old Du entered our school he gave us a very deep and lasting impression (applause). I will tell you all truthfully, that day a lot of comrades cried. How can those sons of bitches possibly understand? That day for the first time we heard at Industrial University the kind of talk that we can only hear at home, for the first time we felt like Industrial University was like home.[62]

Having defended the radical line taken by the second work team, Tan emphasized a fourth point, the one for which his speech later became so famous. He went on to defend the class line pushed at the outset of the Cultural Revolution: "As soon as you bring up the class line, we are people with 'vested interests.' Comrades, I will give you an example, a very simple one. How can the son of a poor peasant who has stood up, and the son of a landlord who has been the object of struggle, possibly have the same feelings about land reform? (warm applause). Comrades, this is what is called 'being branded by your class.' "

The real reasons for his opponents' criticisms, Tan argued, was that they were the ones with vested interests to defend:

Those people who have been overthrown, those who felt that from this point on they faced an uncertain future, those people who felt that from this point on their own younger brothers and sisters, their own families had no political future, how can they have the same feelings, how can they speak the same language as us? Some people make big speeches about "equality" and "fraternity." In a class society, where is there any "equality" or "fraternity"? We have a lot of brothers and sisters who are cruelly murdered by the enemies as soon as they are born; it is called cutting up the weeds and digging up the roots! (Silent hall: someone yells a slogan, "Always remember class bitterness! Do not forget the blood hatred!") Now, we exercise dictatorship over your parents, and exercise the policy of doing everything possible to remold them, giving them repeated opportunities to become an upright person. Their children can attend school, and if they perform well can enter the youth league, and the party. What else do they want? All this garbage about "equality" and "fraternity" that you are all parroting these days should all be sent straight to the toilet! . . . Here only 20 percent of us are children of workers, peasants, and revolutionary cadres; we get going for only a few days, and some people are already yelling we are too "left."[63]

Tan argued that those who opposed the party's class line had ulterior motives. They were trying to reverse the verdicts on their families, trying to restore the situation under the revisionists where the militant "left" class line was not being followed, trying to escape from the consequences of their opposition to the Left earlier in the Cultural Revolution, and trying to twist Mao Zedong thought to suit their own purposes. The real problem, Tan argued, was that these people did not really want revolution:

> As for reforming the system of university examinations, some people hide under their covers and cry, their beautiful dreams about job assignments smashed, and say, "If you carry out the class line, my future is finished, my family's future is finished!" After seventeen years of excessive lenience, your family is still not finished? You damn well should have been finished off long ago![64]

Instead, these students who now opposed the school's Cultural Revolution vacillated and whined and refused to get up on the stage to speak:

> If we have a debate, you do not want to debate. If we do not have a debate, you want to debate. To just send a few lackeys up here to tremble weakly . . . Some people do not speak, they say their materials are not fully prepared . . . There are people who are always looking through books searching for regulations, they all wait for instructions from the center; how are you going to be the "vanguard" of anything? I think it is only the children of workers, peasants, and revolutionary cadres who have that kind of guts, that kind of ability; who among all you others dare to? (warm applause) It seems that "the son of a hero is a real man" [laozi yingxionger haohan] (Masses: "The son of a reactionary is a bastard—it is basically like this!" [Laozi fandong er hundan, jiben ruci!] warm applause).[65]

Finally, Tan argued that his opponents were narrow-minded sectarians who were scouring official documents and Mao's works for quotations to demonstrate that the majority faction had committed doctrinal errors. Tan heaped scorn on the practice of wrenching quotes from Mao's works out of context to justify political positions. "Others say, we are all intellectuals, we are all petty bourgeois, and moreover quote from the classics and say that this is Chairman Mao's 'class analysis.' Take something that the Chairman said in the 1920s and apply it to the 1960s! How can this work? The living application of Mao Zedong Thought is in concrete matters, concrete analysis." Besides, Tan argued, Mao Zedong thought itself was not some dead classic but a guide to practical action: "Nowhere in the world is there anything that is 100 percent correct. Mao Zedong Thought itself is still developing continuously, and necessarily must still make new discoveries, inventions, creations, and advances! . . . These people taking Mao's book and simplifying it down into horseshit just does not make sense."[66]

Tan's speech carried the day and was reprinted and circulated throughout the city, winning strong approval from other majority factions and earning him the enduring enmity of the city's minority factions. Tan and Liu Jing won election to the school's Cultural Revolution committee and proceeded with a purge of the school's "black gang" that was, according to Tan's opponents, even more militant than the policies of the second work team.[67] Like majority factions at other schools, Tan's group was not about to leave itself open to charges that it was soft on the officials who had previously run the school.

Read out of context, Tan Lifu's speech is highly misleading. Because he coupled the defense of the party's standard class line with a defense of his school's second work team, one might be left with the impression that Tan was defending the vested interests of those tied to the regime by either party membership or birth against people from other backgrounds. Tan's leading opponents, in fact, were from a similar background. Tan's primary opponent at the time of the debate, Bai Zhiqi, was a full party member and the son of a revolutionary martyr. A young teacher in Tan's own department, he signed the first wall poster to attack the school's party committee, which went up on May 29, several days before the arrival of the first work team. When the first work team appeared bent on protecting the local power holders, he led the opposition. When the second work team chose to rely on other activists, he opposed them as well. A second prominent opponent, Zhang Jinmin, was a student from a revolutionary cadre background. He had also opposed the first work team and was eventually labeled "anti-party" by it—a verdict the second work team refused to reconsider.[68]

Tan's defense of the party's class line insinuated that his opponents were from less reliable political backgrounds, but this was a willful distortion, and Tan's opponents later fired back. Outraged that students from bad class backgrounds were being accepted as revolutionary activists while Tan supported his position by reference to the party's class line, his opponents replied: "We are from worker, peasant, and revolutionary cadre families; we have incomparably deep feelings of affection for the party and Chairman Mao."[69]

On August 29, shortly after the minority faction established its rival East Is Red organization, Tan Lifu expressed exasperation about the role of his "red" classmates in the opposition. "It is being said that some of the people in East Is Red are saying to people of bad class background, 'You do not dare to speak, we will speak on your behalf.' Scabs! In reality, ten or so worker peasant revolutionary cadre kids are acting as loudspeakers, with the phonograph in the back . . . We say our contradiction is not with this group of worker peasant revolutionary cadre kids; they do not represent us, but another group of people."[70] Was Tan's group composed primarily of students with revolutionary parentage? In a September 7 speech in which he acknowledged the growing strength of his opposition, he said, "Another group of people opposes those on the revolutionary committee, and they have made some gains in all-out mobilization. The revolutionary committee still has a certain amount of prestige because after all, it was elected. And it has the ironclad support of *a group of worker, peasant, and revolutionary cadre kids* [emphasis added]."[71]

Tan never argued that the revolutionary camp was restricted to students from red households. Although he saw that group as the natural leaders in a movement to rid the party of revisionism, others who exhibited revolutionary credentials in the course of the movement were welcomed into the fold. In their earliest wall poster Liu Jing and Tan Lifu wrote, "We must resolve to rely on the revolutionary Left to firmly unite with all forces that can be united, like the children of workers, poor and lower-middle peasants, revolutionary cadres, revolutionary martyrs, revolutionary intellectuals, and all revolutionary teachers and students." This emphasizes the "red" classes but explicitly excludes no one and specifically includes students from intellectual backgrounds. Near the end of his notorious August 20 speech, Tan declared, "We believe that the vast majority of the people in our school want revolution and can be revolutionary."[72]

The issue was not the party's class line—both sides agreed on its basic content—but its implications for the political circumstances at Industrial University in the wake of the work team. Tan used it to defend his position; his critics cited his use of it to illustrate that he was violating the party's policies regarding the conduct of the Cultural Revolution. The real issue was power in the school, disguised as a doctrinal argument over the correct interpretation of the party's class line and the "Sixteen Points." Despite outward appearances, Tan's speech did not express an underlying cleavage that divided the students in his school into camps that could be interpreted as "conservative" or "radical" with regard to the status quo; it was a typical majority-minority argument about the school's work team.

## Tactical Radicalism: Invading the Ministries

By late August the campus majority had the upper hand. The minority faction soon achieved a breakthrough with a tactical innovation that energized its movement and eventually brought it the support of the CCRG.[73] Minority factions that grew out of large confrontations with work teams and had strong grievances as a result pioneered this breakthrough. Two subsequently played a leading role in Beijing. The first was Aeronautics Institute Red Flag, which staged a daring and prolonged sit-in strike at the gates of the Ministry of Defense, behind which lay the offices of the National Defense Science and Technology Commission. The second was Geology Institute East Is Red, which demonstrated repeatedly at the offices of the Ministry of Geology and eventually invaded the building and occupied it.

At the Aeronautics Institute the Red Flag faction made little headway in its effort to push its criticisms of the work team. The majority red guards sheltered work-team head Zhao Ruzhang when he returned to the campus for a brief self-criticism and greeted him warmly. On August 24 the institute's red guards sealed off the school's wall-poster area, prevented Red Flag members from entering, and systematically removed all wall posters that criticized Zhao or other officials in the National Defense Science and Technology Commission. In response, Red Flag demanded a meeting with Zhao, who agreed to meet early the next morning at the commission's offices. The Red Flag delegation arrived at the gates of the Ministry of Defense, through which visitors gained access to the Technology Commission's offices, but at the appointed time the students were given a note explaining that Zhao was tied up in a meeting, and that the students should return to campus. The students refused to leave and decided instead to sit down and wait.[74]

Zhao never emerged, and the students stayed. Two days later the delegation was being referred to on campus as a "sit-down strike" and "hunger strike," although it appears that the latter description applied only because the school's cafeteria workers refused to deliver food to the participants. Back on campus, debates about the action broke out, with opponents labeling the sit-in at the headquarters of the Red Army "an insult to the nation." Representatives from the commission met with Red Flag leaders on campus to try to get them to call off the demonstration, but the school's red guards disrupted the meeting, and no agreement was reached. On August 28 military security guards forcibly removed the students from a small room they had occupied, and workers from the campus threatened to forcibly remove the protesters. A delegation from the Geology Institute's minority faction, East Is Red, arrived to express support.[75]

At around this time copies of Tan Lifu's speech were circulated on campus, inspiring the majority faction to take a more aggressive stance. On September 2 the head of the school's preparatory committee held a mass rally and called for dragging out "rightists" in Red Flag. In response, Red Flag held a rally of its entire membership, after which most of them marched downtown to join the sit-in. For the next week the majority faction continued to threaten Red Flag, while officials from the National Defense Science and Technology Commission tried unsuccessfully to hammer out an agreement to end the protest. On September 9 Zhou Enlai intervened to defuse the confrontation. He ordered Zhao Ruzhang and other commission officials to meet with the protesters at the gates, but red guards aligned with the school's preparatory committee intercepted Zhao, and the meeting never took place. On September 14 Zhou Enlai sent the secretary general of his State Council Office, Zhou Rongxin, to meet with the Red Flag protesters and express the premier's concern.[76]

The Aeronautics Red Flag protest occurred simultaneously with a much larger and more dramatic one by the Geology Institute's minority faction. Geology East Is Red grew rapidly during August and by the end of the month claimed close to 1,000 members, almost one-fourth of the school's students.[77] Up to this point the group had been frustrated in its efforts to get work-team head Zou Jiayou back to campus for criticism, so on August 23 most of the members marched to the Ministry of Geology to demonstrate, demanding that Zou come outside for a self-criticism and that he turn over to East Is Red all files containing information the work team had collected about students. Zou refused and instead bypassed the protesters and went directly to campus to give a self-criticism in front of the more congenial majority faction red guards.[78] Foiled in their attempt to confront Zou, East Is Red organized a second foray to the ministry on September 5. The Geology Institute protesters maintained their siege outside the ministry offices until September 19, when they invaded and occupied the building.

These attacks on the seats of national power changed the course of the red guard movement and eventually turned the tide in favor of minority factions across the city.[79] Aeronautics Red Flag and Geology East Is Red surged into the leadership of an emerging "rebel" coalition that quickly gained the unequivocal public support of the CCRG. The radicalism of this "rebel" faction, however, was tactical in nature and situational in its origins. It did not express an orientation toward the centers of national power that was inherent in the positions of minority activists in the status quo ante. Instead, it expressed a response by the minority faction to its members' experiences under the work teams. These activists were compelled to attack the leaders of work teams to reverse the political charges lodged against them and to discredit their rivals in the majority faction. Their invasions of ministries to capture the files of the work teams show their preoccupation with the potential consequences of damaging materials in their files. The minority factions that led these two attacks were from schools where major confrontations had occurred, and where large numbers of students had been attacked and labeled as a result.

Schools where major confrontations with work teams had not occurred did not organize similar attacks on national centers of power until much later, when it was clear that this was sanctioned and even encouraged by the CCRG. Student rebels from Beijing University, where the work team had never faced a serious challenge—and where former work-team collaborators were now in charge—had no reason to send protest delegations to central government offices. Also notably absent at this stage were rebels from Qinghua and Beijing Normal University, where the work teams had already been denounced by central-level officials who visited these campuses and absolved their opponents of all blame.[80]

These attacks on the seats of national power soon changed the tenor and direction of the capital's red guard movement. This shift was symbolized by the attacks staged by high-school red guard picket corps on both Aeronautics Red Flag at the Ministry of Defense and Geology East Is Red at the Ministry of Geology. These attacks were surprising because the militant students in these picket corps had been among the most active antagonists of the work teams in their own schools and had been pointedly praised by Mao weeks before for their rebellious spirit. As the CCRG threw its weight behind the new university rebels, it repudiated its former favorites among the high-school militants, driving the high-school radicals into an unexpected alliance with the university majority and eventually provoking some of them into a daring but ill-fated challenge to the CCRG itself. In order to understand these developments, however, we need to examine the impact of the work teams and the emergence of the red guard movement in Beijing's high schools, where events took a very different course.

# 5

# CLASS AND VIOLENCE

## The High-School Red Guards

University students dominated Beijing's red guard movement, but during a crucial early period high-school rebels played a highly visible role. The high-school movement, however, developed very differently than in the universities. The most striking difference was the absence of a division over the interventions of the work teams. High-school red guards were not divided by debates over the work teams, nor were they locked in rivalries over control of their schools. Instead, they took their militant activities into the city's neighborhoods. They vandalized temples, museums, and other public places and invaded the homes of vulnerable residents, often with fatal consequences. High-school students were the first to form independent political groups, and they invented a new name, *hongweibing*, for "red guards." For a brief period the high-school militants were praised by Mao and celebrated as national models.

These students were in the vanguard of the movement in August, but within two months they lost favor after they clashed with rebels from university minority factions and moved into a tacit alliance with the university majority. This political trajectory grew out of different encounters with work teams, which were shaped by the low rank of high schools in the city's bureaucratic hierarchy, combined with the decidedly elite character of many of the students.

The red guards who played this prominent role were, like Beijing's high schools, concentrated in three of the city's ten urban districts. There were 52,608 students enrolled in Beijing's urban high schools in the spring of 1966. Two-thirds of them attended the seventy-two schools in the core Western (Xicheng) and Eastern (Dongcheng) districts, where government offices and their residential blocks were concentrated, and the Haidian District, where most universities were located. The most politically active students were in the elite high schools that sent high percentages of graduates to universities. These included twenty high schools designated as "key points" for academic excellence by the city government, seventeen of which were in the Western and Eastern districts. A similar number of elite high schools were attached to major universities, almost all of which were in Haidian.[1] These were the breeding ground for the militant red guards who had a major impact on the early course of the Cultural Revolution in Beijing.

### Work Teams in the High Schools

Members of China's party, government, and military elite were concentrated in the same residential districts as Beijing's high schools. Children from these families attended the best primary and middle schools, were exposed to high parental expectations, and were given preference in a competitive admissions process.[2] They entered the best schools at high rates and made up much higher percentages of their student bodies than they did in the universities, which drew on a much larger national pool of applicants.

The contrast is evident if we compare Qinghua University with Qinghua High School. Most of the households headed by officials were labeled "revolutionary" on the basis of their membership in the Communist Party or the Red Army before its victory in 1949. They constituted a very small percentage of the population—only 2.4 percent nationwide, and 4.4 percent in urban areas.[3] At Qinghua University only 7 percent of the students came from these elite "revolutionary" households, but at Qinghua High School the figure was 25 percent.[4]

The elite backgrounds of these students contrasted sharply with the low rank of the cadres who led the work teams. High-school work teams were organized by the national Secretariat of the Communist Youth League, which dispatched them to each of the city districts. In turn, they sent "work groups" of ten to fifteen municipal- or district-level cadres to each of the high schools. The only exceptions were some high schools attached to universities. In such cases the university work team sent a work group to the affiliated high school, treating it as an entity parallel to a university academic department.

The confrontation between small numbers of low-ranking officials and student militants from elite families created a very different political dynamic than in the universities. Lower-ranking officials were more cautious about committing political errors and were wary of clashes with students whose parents outranked them. If they criticized recalcitrant students, they did so selectively and hesitated to lodge serious political charges. From the perspective of militant students from elite households, work-group cadres were far from intimidating.

Events in the high schools cannot be documented to the degree possible for universities. High-school students wrote much less about their experiences, and the work groups did not play an important role in defining their political viewpoints. It is nonetheless possible to characterize key events at several of the more influential high schools. Even in this limited sample it is clear that just as in universities, events unfolded in a variety of ways. The differences are evident in four case histories: "Western" High School, an elite school in the Western District; Beijing Normal Girls' High School; Beijing University High School; and Qinghua University High School. The last two spawned red guard organizations praised by Mao Zedong, and the last is widely credited as the birthplace of the red guard movement.

### "Western" High School

Events at the elite "Western" High School were described to me in an interview with the head of the school's work group.[5] This man (referred to by the pseudonym Gao) joined the party in 1949 and ended up as a cadre in the street affairs office of a city district. Like many other cadres suddenly mobilized for work-team service in early June, Gao had spent much of the preceding two years on a work team in the Beijing suburbs, conducting the Socialist Education Movement in rural villages. On June 9, 1966, along with several dozen colleagues, he was abruptly ordered to report to the Western District work team, headed by an official from the Communist Youth League Secretariat named Hu Qili.[6]

After the publication of Nie Yuanzi's wall poster on June 2 high-school students attacked their school officials both verbally and physically, and work groups were sent in an effort to keep order. Gao learned that he was to be assigned to Western High, which was a difficult assignment. The first work group had already retreated from the school after harrowing confrontations with violent students. Gao recognized clearly the dangers inherent in the assignment. First, handling students from elite backgrounds would be difficult:

> I did not want to go. The school was already in chaos, there were a lot of children of high officials and army officers—very complicated . . . Students

had criticized and struggled against the principal, party secretary, and the teachers in positions of authority, beat them, put them in struggle sessions. They had been beaten so badly that they had bruises all over their bodies . . . The students did not listen to anyone, not the teachers, not the leaders, not the work team, not anyone . . . Almost all the students took part, but the most active were the kind of people who later became red guards—children of cadres, good class background.

In addition, it was difficult to curtail violence and exercise authority without appearing to obstruct the Cultural Revolution: "Our task was to get students to rebel in an organized way. No beatings, no 'jet plane,'[7] use peaceful methods of criticism and struggle." Gao held a mass meeting and read out a document about how to conduct the movement properly.[8] He then organized small-group discussions led by work-group members and youth league leaders to get the students to "cool down." He also had to establish control over the imprisoned school officials, whom the students had already beaten badly by the time the work group arrived.

We allowed students to freely criticize the top party officials and teachers, we just would not let them beat them . . . The students had already set up a prison in the basement of one of the school buildings where they had imprisoned the "black gang" and beat them—the party secretary, principal, teachers. They had already put caps [political labels] on them. We did not release them from the prison . . . We could not because otherwise we would be opposing the mass movement and opposing the Cultural Revolution. We did not let them out of jail but we also did not let the students take them out to beat them.

By walking this political tightrope Gao's work group restored a semblance of order, but within a month he was forced to confront unruly students who continued to challenge the work group. "There was one group of students in the school, children of army officers . . . They were very fierce and did not listen to us at all." In late June work teams across the city began counterattacks against challengers, and Gao was pressured to act decisively at Western High:

The Youth League Central Committee criticized us for being too soft on this kind of student. They sent down a document ordering us to come down hard on saboteurs and extremists. They told us to hold a criticism and struggle session to declare them anti-party, make an example of them. But I did not think that was necessary. I called the upper levels and told them that if I did this, it would remain a contradiction among the people—I would declare no one to be a rightist.

After this Gao's work group held things together for several more weeks, until it became apparent that all the work teams would be withdrawn. The work group's authority evaporated, and two red guard groups formed, both of which criticized the work group's errors and called for its withdrawal. The more violent of the two seized and imprisoned the members of the work group and proceeded to torture them. Red guards also broke into the makeshift jail where the school leaders were held and beat two of them to death.[9] Later that night two other prisoners hanged themselves. In early August work teams were ordered out of the schools, but Gao and his two vice-heads were detained in the school's prison. His captors told him that they planned to execute him, but a phone call from the Municipal Party Committee secured his release.

The work group's experience at Western High was by no means extreme. Others found it even more difficult to establish authority. At Beijing Post and Telecommunications High School all ten members of the work group were imprisoned five days after they arrived. Students organized struggle sessions and forced work-group members to read confessions. On June 21 the students called the ministry to demand that it send a representative with a written order withdrawing the work team. The official who went to the school to negotiate was also imprisoned. The students sent out a second warning: "If the minister does not come personally, [the captives] will not be released, and you will bear responsibility for all consequences."[10]

### Beijing Normal Girls' High School

Located not far from Tiananmen Square and the Zhongnanhai leadership compound, Beijing Normal Girls' High School had a very elite clientele.[11] Close to half of its students were the offspring of high party officials. Both of Mao's daughters graduated from this school, and when the Cultural Revolution began, both Liu Shaoqi and Deng Xiaoping had daughters there (Liu Tingting and Deng Rong). On June 2, the day the Beida wall poster was publicized, the first wall poster attacking school authorities appeared. The first-named author was Song Binbin, whose father, Song Renqiong, was on the Central Committee.[12] The school's teachers warned students not to criticize school officials and reminded them of the fate of critics during the 1957 anti-rightist campaign. But students with highly placed parents had a clearer sense of the political winds. The work group arrived the next day, declared its support for Song Binbin's wall poster, removed the school's leaders, and invited students to criticize them. The work group formed a committee to take control of the school. The work group's head chaired the committee, and Song Binbin and the other authors of the school's first wall poster became vice-chairmen. Liu Tingting and Deng Rong were selected to represent their classes, and three of the other representatives were also daughters of high officials.

The entire school was swept up in a campaign against the school's top officials. The primary victim was Bian Zhongyun, party general branch secretary. Bian had joined the party in 1938 and had served in communist base areas, but with a college degree and a father who owned a small bank, she was vulnerable to suspicion. The work group held a series of denunciation meetings against her and printed a collection of wall-poster accusations. At one such meeting, on June 23, she was beaten severely. She wrote a letter of protest to the Party Center in which she did not refute the political charges but stated that veteran revolutionaries should not be beaten in this fashion.

On July 3 the work group submitted a report that labeled Bian an anti-party, anti-socialist element, and two days later it met with Deng Xiaoping, along with Song Binbin and several other students, and Hu Qili, who headed the Western District work team. During the meeting Deng brought up Bian Zhongyun's letter of complaint and asked whether she had in fact been beaten. He emphasized that such beatings were forbidden and suggested more lenient verdicts for many of the school's officials and teachers who had been charged with serious political errors.[13]

Accounts from the school mention no challenges to the work group, which carried out a purge with the cooperation of student rebels, many of whom were daughters of top national officials. Nonetheless, after Mao denounced the work teams, the school's work-group leaders were seized and subjected to struggle sessions, during which they were beaten and had their heads shaved. On July 31 students who had served under the work group formed a red guard unit and established a Cultural Revolution preparatory committee. On August 5 Bian Zhongyun was beaten to death at the school, the first recorded red guard murder in Beijing.

## Beijing University High School

The work group dispatched to Beida High School faced a stubborn group of students, led by children of high officials, who organized one of the first red guard organizations in the city, Beida High School Red Flag. The group was a headache for Shen Ning, who headed the school's work group.[14] Red Flag began by organizing struggle sessions against students from nonrevolutionary households who had penned wall posters critical of party leaders.[15] Its members also pressed for recognition of their organization and a "revolutionary committee" to lead the movement in their school. Neither was acceptable to the work group, which did not want students to attack one another and would not tolerate independent organizations.

Shen Ning tried to split the group and isolate its leaders. Work-group members visited parents to tell them that their children were flirting with trouble. They told the father of Niu Wanping, one of the founders of Red Flag, that his son was simply confused and was under the influence of Gong Xiaoji, who had a questionable character, and Peng Xiaomeng, whose father, despite revolutionary credentials, was politically unreliable.[16] Although the attempt to split Niu from Gong and Peng failed, most other Red Flag leaders were persuaded. Red Flag got the meeting it demanded with the work group, but when its members arrived, many former comrades now argued the work group's side. The membership of Red Flag shrank from 300 to around 100. The departing members, all from "revolutionary" families, aligned themselves with the work group's version of the correct course and eventually established a separate organization, the Beida High School Red Guards.[17]

The remaining leaders of Red Flag—Niu Wanping, Peng Xiaomeng, and Gong Xiaoji—persisted in their struggle. They were angered by the veiled threat that their organization was anti-party. They abandoned the plan for a revolutionary committee but resented Shen Ning's insinuation that their motives were impure. They were also upset that they were not selected to lead the school's picket corps. They appealed directly to Zhang Chengxian, head of the Beida work team, for affirmation that they still were considered revolutionary leftists. They demanded a meeting with Zhang, who stalled them and sent out vice-head Zhang Dehua instead. Red Flag staged an overnight sit-in on July 8 until it received a meeting, at which Zhang Chengxian brushed the group off with a fatherly admonition to stick to party policy.[18] Shortly thereafter the work team ordered Shen Ning to disband Red Flag.[19]

This relatively muted conflict nonetheless vaulted Red Flag into the vanguard of the anti-work-team forces once Zhang Chengxian was denounced at the end of July. Niu Wanping was selected as the sole high-school representative on the standing committee of the Beida Preparatory Committee.[20] Red Flag was rebuilt and grew to play a major role in the student movement. At mass rallies denouncing the work team, Red Flag's leaders criticized the work team's suppression of their group, and their members mounted the stage and whipped the work team's leaders with belts.[21]

## Qinghua University High School

The Qinghua High School Red Guards—even more prominent in subsequent events than Beida High Red Flag—emerged from similar conflicts with their school's work group. This group has the double distinction of inventing the new term for "red guard" used during the Cultural Revolution (*hongweibing*) and of forming the first independent student organization in the city. Many of its members were the children of officials who had joined the Communist Party before its victory in 1949.[22] Well before the Cultural Revolution school authorities clashed with politically enthusiastic and outspoken students who were influenced by transcripts of brief talks that Mao had given on the subject of education, and that were assigned and discussed by the party authorities in the school's political study classes.[23] In a discussion with his nephew Mao Yuanxin, Mao emphasized that in addition to the regular school curriculum, "class struggle" was also an important course.[24] Shortly afterward, in a talk with his grandniece Wang Hairong, a student of English at Beijing Normal Institute, Mao expressed irritation about all the rules and regulations in the educational system and encouraged her to rebel against them.[25] As early as the fall of 1964 the idealistic and ambitious Qinghua students soon tried to apply these lessons in ways that caused frictions with school leaders. They began to complain that the school's curriculum was too rigid and rule bound and its political content too watered down. They argued that there was an ongoing class struggle within their school, a claim the leaders denied. In October 1965 Luo Xiaohai put up a wall poster that called for rebellion against the school's rules and regulations, false "idols" fabricated by the school authorities.[26]

These long-simmering frictions came to a head in May 1966. On May 10 Luo Xiaohai put up another wall poster, this time accusing the school authorities of ignoring Mao Thought and trying to divert the Cultural Revolution into a meaningless academic exercise, and the next day a group of his classmates criticized the party secretary's report on the school's Cultural Revolution as too conservative and called for a campaign to criticize the school's leadership.[27] They demanded that students take action, stop listening meekly to school authorities, and attack the bourgeois line in education followed at the school.[28] On May 20, two other students accused school authorities of following a bourgeois educational line and of suppressing student criticism. They stressed that the students who clashed with the school authorities were student cadres and political activists. They addressed a copy to Chairman Mao and submitted it through the Central Committee's reporting system.[29]

These students were still an embattled minority, and during the last week of May they were under increasing pressure. Cadres in the school reminded them that critics of the party had been victimized in the 1957 anti-rightist campaign, and classmates who sided with school officials argued with them constantly. They met across the street on the grounds of the old Summer Palace (Yuanmingyuan) on May 29 and formally established an organization, giving it a new name, *hongweibing*, that translates as "red guard."[30] This is thought to be the first student organization of its type. On May 31 the group submitted a second report to Chairman Mao in which it listed twenty political errors committed by the school's party committee, including the denial of class struggle and the failure to implement Mao Thought. In a separate letter it told Mao of its struggles with school authorities.[31]

After Nie Yuanzi's wall poster was publicized, the group penned several wall posters with more serious accusations against its school's party committee.[32] Sensing a shift in the political winds, more than 100 students signed one of the group's wall posters to signal agreement, but the vast majority of students still supported the party committee.[33] After June 1 similar rebellions were brewing on nearby high-school campuses, and on the morning of June 8 more than 300 students from other high schools came to demonstrate their support. School authorities shut the school gates, but before the visitors were expelled, they put up wall posters in support, many of them adopting the name "red guard."[34]

Qinghua High therefore had a red guard organization with a history of conflict with school authorities even before the arrival of the work group. On June 8 the Haidian District work team dispatched a work group of fifteen youth league cadres to the school. In the wake of the purge of

Qinghua University's party secretary, the high school's work group sided with the red guards. The majority of students reversed their position and denounced school authorities. The work group convened a series of mass denunciation meetings against the party secretary and other officials. The red guards grew rapidly, from 101 to over 300 during June, by which point they constituted close to 25 percent of the student body.[35]

Despite this initial spirit of cooperation, frictions appeared over the red guards' plans to organize struggle sessions against "rightist" students, which the work group opposed, and then over the election of a new leadership body. The work group wanted a revolutionary committee broadly representative of all students and teachers. The red guards insisted that all the members be red guards. In the end, the red guards did not get their way, but one of them was selected as chairman and two others as vice-chairmen. The work group concluded that the red guards had an "incorrect attitude."[36]

The conflict came to a head on June 24 when the red guards put up wall posters criticizing the previous day's editorial in *China Youth News,* the youth league's national paper, that emphasized the "glorious responsibility of leftist students" to unite with the vast majority of their classmates. The wall poster denounced the article's "compromring" attitude.[37] On the same day they issued a wall poster that expressed support for Kuai Dafu and other students at Qinghua University who were under attack for criticizing the university's work team.[38] The work group considered these wall posters a direct challenge and reported the problem to its superiors on the Communist Youth League Secretariat, which ordered it to dismantle the red guards. In private meetings in mid-July the two sides argued for hours. The work group charged that the red guards undermined it behind its back and that some of their leaders had ulterior (that is, "anti-party") motives. The students responded that the work group only paid lip service to supporting them, but in fact acted behind their backs to isolate and split them, and that the work group's reports to its superiors fueled calls to disband red guards as illegal organizations.[39]

Despite these tensions, the red guards did not openly break with the work group until the end of the month. On July 27 their leaders attended a meeting of high-school activists at which Jiang Qing expressed her support for the student rebels and announced that the head of the Haidian District work team would be removed from his post. The red guards then openly split with the work group, returning to campus to put up a wall poster denouncing it.[40] On July 28 the CCRG held a reception for high-school leaders at the Beijing Exhibition Hall and announced the withdrawal of all high-school work groups. At the rally Luo Xiaohai and Kuang Taosheng read out the text of their two wall posters titled "Long Live the Proletarian Spirit of Revolutionary Rebellion." Before leaving the stage, they gave copies to Jiang Qing, along with a brief letter to Chairman Mao. The letter informed Mao that some people in their school had said that their wall posters were reactionary, and they asked Chairman Mao's opinion. Jiang Qing agreed to relay the material to her husband.[41]

## Political Celebrity

Unlike the minority faction in the universities, which ended the work-team period under a cloud, high-school students who challenged work groups became political celebrities, singled out by Mao for praise in the nation's mass media. The only university figure named by Mao in the August party plenum was Beida's Nie Yuanzi, whose "first Marxist-Leninist wall poster" received Mao's fulsome praise.[42] Mao met with Nie in the reception room atop Tiananmen during the August 18 red guard rally, a meeting publicized in the national media.[43] Mao conveniently ignored the fact that Nie had worked closely with the Beida work team for many weeks. Surprisingly, Mao did not single out any of the students who led large rebellions against work teams at the Geology, Aeronautics, and Post and Telecommunications institutes, and he took no notice of Kuai Dafu's challenge at Qinghua University. Instead, he singled out high-school rebels who had been the first to challenge school officials and at most engaged in relatively muted clashes with work groups.

Jiang Qing fulfilled her promise to pass on the Qinghua High Red Guards' wall posters and letters. Mao read them and responded enthusiastically. He wrote to the group on August 1, affirming that its wall posters were indeed "revolutionary," and he applauded its militant stand. He ordered the two posters, along with his letter, reprinted and circulated to all participants at the Eleventh Plenum.[44] Mao also took the opportunity to express his support for Beida High Red Flag and praised one of its leaders for her speech at one of the Beida mass rallies where Jiang Qing and other members of the CCRG were present.

Your two wall posters of June 24 and July 4 express anger and condemnation toward the oppression of workers, peasants, revolutionary intellectuals, and revolutionary parties and groups by landlords, capitalists, imperialists, revisionists, and their running dogs. This shows that it is right to rebel against reactionaries, and I express to you my enthusiastic support. At the same time, I also express my enthusiastic support for the wall poster by the Beida High School Red Flag Battle Group that showed that it was right to rebel against reactionaries, and for comrade Peng Xiaomeng's excellent revolutionary speech at the mass meeting at Beida on July 25 where she represented her Red Flag Battle Group. Here I want to say that I and all my revolutionary comrades-in-arms have the same attitude. We enthusiastically support anyone in Beijing or throughout the nation who adopts the same kind of revolutionary attitude.[45]

Mao's letter was not released for publication, but its contents were relayed directly to the Qinghua High Red Guards on August 3 by Wang Renzhong, vice-chairman of the CCRG in charge of liaison work with the Beijing student movement, who invited the group to the Diaoyutai State Guest House and read the text to it. The existence of the letter and its general contents became known nationwide.[46]

Mao followed up by inviting 1,500 student activists onto the reviewing stands for the first red guard rally in Tiananmen Square on August 18. More than twenty members of the Qinghua High Red Guards received invitations. Luo Xiaohai and two others slipped past security guards and entered the main reception building where Mao was standing. They got within earshot of Mao and got his attention. When Luo explained that they were from the Qinghua High Red Guards, Mao responded, "I resolutely support you!" The encounter was written up by the students and published a few days later in *People's Daily*.[47]

Peng Xiaomeng and her Red Flag comrades were also singled out for special attention. Peng was already well known to members of the CCRG. Mao's praise of her late July speech at Beida was based on a report by Jiang Qing, and she had also shared the stage with Jiang at a meeting of high-school red guards on July 28.[48] At a mass meeting on August 6, Kang Sheng praised Peng Xiaomeng personally and expressed his complete agreement with Beida High Red Flag and similar organizations.[49] At the August 18 Tiananmen rally, Peng chatted briefly with Mao and gave a speech to the crowd. The mass media identified her and Red Flag by name, earning them nationwide celebrity.[50] Also celebrated that day was Song Binbin, who led the red guards of Beijing Normal Girls' High. Song had penned the first wall poster to attack authorities at her school, and her father, Song Renqiong, had just been promoted to alternate membership in the Politburo. A famous photograph of her on the Tiananmen rostrum fitting a red guard armband onto a smiling Mao Zedong was carried on the front page of newspapers nationwide, along with a news report of her brief dialogue with Mao. In the following days the national media published excerpts from speeches by these high-school militants, along with copies of their wall posters.[51]

### The Political Context in High Schools

For high-school rebels the political consequences of the work-team period were very different than in universities. High-school work groups were small and staffed by ordinary cadres. The most successful of them maintained a fragile sense of order in their school. Even when they were challenged, they focused their critical attention on a handful of troublemakers and largely refrained from lodging serious political accusations. There is scant evidence of the kind of large confrontations seen at the Geology and Aeronautics institutes. High-school work groups therefore did not lay the groundwork for future splits. Even at Beida and Qinghua high schools, the work groups only sought to isolate the militant leaders, not to mobilize mass criticism.

In the aftermath of the work groups' withdrawal, students who had clashed with work groups had little reason to fear the consequences. On July 27 and 28 Jiang Qing chaired meetings of high-school students in the Haidian and Western districts and announced the removal of the work-team heads of these two districts, Zhou Jie and Hu Qili, who were each put on the stage for a struggle session.[52] On August 2 Guan Feng, representing the CCRG, met with students and told them that their red guard organizations were "completely legal," and he praised several of them and their leaders by name.[53]

Even more dramatic was the purge of the entire leadership of the Central Secretariat of the Communist Youth League. On August 5 Mao criticized the "three Hus" (Hu Yaobang, Hu Qili, and Hu Keshi) for mishandling the work teams, and the next day, at a meeting with red guards at the Tianqiao Theater, Jiang Qing and Kang Sheng criticized them and demanded that the national youth league organization be closed down.[54] At a mass meeting of high-school activists on August 13, Li Fuchun announced "on behalf of Chairman Mao and the Party Center" that the leaders of the Communist Youth League Central Committee would be purged.[55] Immediately afterward a wave of students rushed to the homes of Hu Yaobang and Hu Keshi and dragged them back to the Central Youth League offices for a struggle session. From this day forward rebellious students occupied the youth league's offices. Top officials were detained and forced to participate in daily mass criticism sessions.[56] On August 15 the youth league's leaders were officially removed from their posts and were forced to tour local high schools, denouncing the work groups' errors and praising the red guards.[57]

There was little reason for high-school militants to mount the kind of campaign pushed by the university minority against the higher officials who had sent their work teams—they had already been forced from power in disgrace. Unlike their university counterparts, high-school militants did not argue over control of their campuses. Instead, they competed to prove their revolutionary mettle by engaging in an array of "revolutionary actions" in the public places and neighborhoods of the city. Whatever differences they might have had under the work groups were quickly forgotten as the movement shifted to a new phase.

Other issues soon divided high-school students. The first was a debate about class origin as a qualification for membership in and leadership over the red guards. The second was a dispute about the proper conduct of red guards, especially the use of violence. A common misperception of the early high-school red guards is that they were uniformly chauvinistic students who were proud of their "revolutionary" family heritage, looked down on those from other backgrounds, and had a singular propensity for violence. The early high-school movement was indeed violent and dominated by students from "revolutionary" and other "red" family origins. However, the issue of class heritage and especially the question of violence served to divide student rebels from the favored "revolutionary" and "red" families.

### The Question of Class Origin

The debate about class origin was spurred by the appearance of a derogatory rhyme, a "couplet" *(duilian)* that praised students of revolutionary parentage and denigrated those from "bad" family origins. The debate was essentially about the relationship of the couplet to the party's "class line," which enshrined official discrimination against those from exploiting-class or "reactionary" political background and privileged those from "red" and especially "revolutionary" households.

The Cultural Revolution was launched as part of a militant reassertion of the party's class line. The first attacks against educational officials had labeled them "revisionist" because they gave too much prestige and authority to academics from bourgeois backgrounds and permitted students from reactionary backgrounds to advance at the expense of those from "red" classes. Emblematic of this revisionism was a policy attributed to Peng Zhen, the Beijing party secretary purged in May 1966: "emphasize performance" *(zhong zai biaoxian)* was said to express a neglect of the class line. This had been a central point of contention at Beida since the Socialist Education Movement, and it was at the core of Nie Yuanzi's critique of Beida authorities.

The offending couplet originated in early August at Aeronautics Institute High School. The controversial core was a two-line rhyme that praised the offspring of revolutionaries and insulted the offspring of "reactionaries."[58] The students defended it as an expression of the party's class line:

> Demons see this and worry [gui jian chou]
> It is basically like this [jiben ruci]:
> The son of a revolutionary is a hero [laozi geming er haohan]
> The son of a reactionary is a bastard [laozi fandong er hundan]

The couplet was actually a gross caricature of the party's class line, which claimed as a basic principle of class analysis that family class heritage influenced political loyalty. Those from families headed by former revolutionaries or exploited classes would tend to be more loyal because they benefited from the revolution. Those from families headed by members of exploiting social classes or reactionary political parties were hurt by the revolution and potentially subject to reactionary influences and had to work harder to develop the proper political consciousness. Those from households headed by former members of the middle classes fell somewhere in between—a wavering stratum that supported whichever side appeared to be winning.[59]

The couplet was provocative in several ways. First, it appeared to suggest that the children of revolutionaries were a hereditary political aristocracy, assumed to be "red" by birth. Second, it insulted students from less favored backgrounds by suggesting that they were damned at birth regardless of their actual loyalties. Third, it ignored those with "red" heritage in the working class and poor peasantry, who had benefited from the revolution but whose parents were not revolutionary "heroes." Students from these backgrounds—the working class and peasants, the middle class, and "bad" classes—were in the majority, even in elite high schools, and many were political activists and student cadres.[60] Not surprisingly, many students, including those from revolutionary households, began to criticize the couplet as discriminatory, politically self-defeating, and contrary to the party's class line.

Students at Aeronautics High School defended their creation in a way that exacerbated the controversy. "Most of those with good class origin, the vast majority, are revolutionary . . . but there is a small group of traitors among them. Those little sons of bitches with bad class origin are mostly not revolutionary, or stand alongside those with counterrevolutionary standpoints. Only a minority of them, after thoroughly betraying their families, are able to stand on the side of the revolution."[61] This was not likely to quell the critics.

Arguments over the issue escalated into violence among red guards on August 2. On that day students from Qinghua High and Beijing High School No. 47 went together to the Western District to hold a meeting on the athletic field of another high school. Soon after the meeting began, red guards began arguing over the microphone. Those from proletarian households claimed that they should go first because the "working class leads all." Those from revolutionary households argued that they deserved priority because their parents had actually shed blood to liberate the country. A student named Tang Wei spoke out and criticized the students' obsession with parentage. Tang Wei's late father, however, had been a "historical counterrevolutionary," and for this Tang was dragged off the stage to a rear courtyard for a struggle session and severe beating. His mother, who taught at the school, was dragged out for similar treatment. That evening Tang Wei got together with some friends and, armed with knives, tracked down and stabbed some of his tormentors outside the school.[62]

Apparently worried that arguments over the couplet would divide and weaken the movement, several members of the CCRG intervened. At an August 6 assembly Jiang Qing said:

I have heard that you are all facing one another down over this couplet. This is easy to resolve . . . I would like to talk about where this line "the son of a hero is a real man" comes from. There is a Beijing opera called *Lianhuan tao,* have you seen it? (The audience answers, no; Jiang Qing laughs) . . . If we get all tangled up in a question like this, we will never move forward . . . We think revising it like this is appropriate: The sons of revolutionaries should succeed them, the sons of reactionaries should betray them; this is the ideal.[63]

Jiang moved on to explain the correct version of the party's class line: "In thinking about a person, first you must look at their class standpoint, this is the basic question. Second, do not look only at class status; this refers to individuals from a certain class who betray their original class. Third, emphasize performance in terms of political thought, not just appearances."

Kang Sheng spoke next, but his advice must have seemed confusing. First, he strongly defended the party's class line as the essence of the Cultural Revolution. "In the past, under the Peng Zhen–Lu Dingyi black gang that opposed the proletarian line in education, in all the schools the vast majority of children of workers, peasants, and revolutionary cadres were discriminated against, persecuted, and you comrades suffered deeply from this persecution. It was very good that you comrades raised this question to express your resistance and resolute opposition to this persecution . . . and advocate rebellion." Kang then said that although it was absolutely correct to emphasize the class line, the "class-line policy" was to "unite with the vast majority." Without unity, Kang explained, the concept of proletarian leadership was empty.[64] Kang appeared to be warning the red guards against needlessly alienating the majority of students who did not come from favored revolutionary backgrounds. However, Kang did not address the central question of how important class origin should be in considering individuals for membership in the red guards.

The debate over the couplet ensnared other figures on the CCRG. When Qi Benyu reported the debate to Chen Boda, Chen offered a revision that was similar to Jiang Qing's: "The son of a hero will succeed him, the son of a reactionary will rebel against him; this is the ideal." Red guard delegations visited the joint State Council–CCRG reception center during August to ask officials to clarify their stance on the couplet. When a State Council official at the reception center (Xu Ming, a member of Zhou Enlai's State Council staff) offered Chen Boda's new version as an alternative, the red guards objected and asked on whose authority the weaker version was offered. When told that it was Chen Boda, the students angrily demanded that he retract it. Chen was alarmed when he heard of the episode, and he accused Xu Ming of deliberately goading red guards into attacking him.[65] Chen was therefore on his guard during an August 24 visit to Beida. When a student asked him point-blank whether the red guards should be "primarily" or "exclusively" made up of students from red family origin, Chen refused to answer, saying, "You talk it over."[66]

The members of the Qinghua High Red Guards were themselves predominantly from "red" classes, especially revolutionary cadres, and they became more so over time. Of the first 100 members on the eve of the work group's arrival, two-thirds were from "red"—primarily cadre—background.[67] In the wake of the work group's departure, the rapid expansion of the movement led the organization to be more attentive to the revolutionary purity of its new members as a means of enforcing unity and internal discipline: "What kind of organization are the red guards? The vast majority of them are children of cadres who come from good class backgrounds and have high political consciousness—this is a resolutely leftist proletarian force."[68] By mid-September this increased emphasis on class origin led to a membership composition that was 90 percent from "red" households.[69] This was a highly skewed membership profile because only 45 percent of the students at the school were from "red" households.[70] Clearly, this emphasis put "class origin" first, and also clearly, it did not put "sole emphasis" on class origin—one-third of the original membership and 10 percent of the greatly expanded membership were still from households that were not "red." Class discrimination was nonetheless obvious, and this caused controversy from the beginning.

The tenor of this debate is evident in the earliest programmatic statements about the party's class line. The strong claims to political leadership made by the offspring of revolutionary cadres at Qinghua and other high schools attracted spirited criticism from others. The critics responded, "What is so special about you worker-peasant-cadre kids?" "Workers and peasants are naturally stupid," and "Cadre kids enjoy high position and live in comfort; they are thoroughly corrupted!" The red guards' position, according to the critics, amounted to "not permitting others to make revolution" and "not uniting with others." "You use your status to bully people! Arrogant!" After all, "bad class background is just bad luck."[71]

Some red guards took great offense at these arguments, and their responses betrayed defensiveness about their elite status. Their first response was to charge that such comments expressed the ideology of defeated social classes who hoped for a comeback.

> We are materialists. We believe that being determines consciousness. Do you actually think that the reactionary consciousness of the exploiting classes will not have a profound influence on the sons and daughters who have

lived together with them for so long? And that we, the sons and daughters of the vast majority of workers, poor and lower-middle-class peasants, and revolutionary cadres, living together with our own families, being educated by our parents from the time we were small, do not have a simple class feeling toward the party and Chairman Mao that is diametrically opposed to the influences working on the sons and daughters of exploiting classes?[72]

The authors of this essay responded that they were the ones who had stood up and rebelled against the school's party branch even before the arrival of the work group: "During this Cultural Revolution, in the midst of this fierce class struggle, the children of workers, peasants and revolutionary cadres performed especially actively, especially bravely . . . But so many of the sons and daughters of the exploiting classes stood alongside the reactionary standpoints of their parents and were not of the same mind as us. In light of these facts, who can you rely on if not the children of workers, peasants, and revolutionary cadres?" After all, they argued, back when this all started, when the party branch was still in power, where were their critics? "At the outset when the black gang was in power and they suppressed us so badly we could not hold our heads up, how ferocious you were! Back then, why did you not let loose even a single fart?"[73]

The authors argued that their position was not a distortion of the party's class line but a correct application of it. "When we look at a person, first, we look at their class status; this is essential, the primary question. Second, we do not place sole emphasis on class status (you cannot reverse the order of the first and second). Third, emphasize performance. This refers to the various class elements betraying their own class."[74] The wording of this statement accurately reflects the standard interpretation of the party's class line. Whether the red guards' interpretation of the principles was fully in accord with their spirit, however, is as manifestly unclear as the inherently contradictory principles themselves, which essentially say, "Discriminate according to class origin, but do not overdo it."

The debate about class origin clearly touched a sensitive nerve among politically active students. The ambiguity of the basic policy and the contradictory pronouncements of officials who sought to clarify it did nothing to resolve the controversy. Many early red guards followed the practice at Beijing No. 1 High School, where students from "red" background were considered "leftists" and were permitted to join, while most students from middle-class households were steered into an affiliated "red auxiliary."[75] Although this debate flared during the late summer of 1966, it did not define factional alignments in the high schools. These early red guards had no organized rivals. The public praise showered upon them by the CCRG and Mao, and their political backing and elite connections, deterred other students from an organized challenge.

### The Issue of Red Guard Violence

A more serious division was over the issue of violence. This issue, even more than the issue of class origin, went to the very identity and aims of the red guard movement. This was a division among the original "old" red guards, the vast majority of whom were from "red" and especially "revolutionary" households. It did not develop into an open factional divide, but a vocal minority expressed strong criticisms of the chaos and violence of the month of August. This sentiment found organized expression in red guard "picket corps" (*jiucha dui*) in the Western, Eastern, and Haidian districts, whose initial purpose was to curtail random violence and provide discipline to an anarchic and rapidly growing movement. The picket corps failed in this mission, but in pursuing it they became entangled in the conflict between university factions at a crucial turning point in their struggle.

A wave of unrestrained violence swept over the city as soon as work groups were withdrawn. High-school students seized party secretaries, principals, teachers, and classmates and subjected them to violent beatings. Those who died as a direct result were a small percentage of those who suffered such mistreatment. At least eight high-school party secretaries, principals, or vice-principals were murdered or committed suicide during August.[76] Teachers and other administrators bore the brunt of the assault; suicide and beating deaths were common, and in some schools several died in a single day.[77]

High-school militants also charged off campus to attack targeted individuals. On August 19 red guards from Beijing High Schools Nos. 4, 6, and 8 held struggle sessions in the amusement hall of Zhongshan Park, next to Tiananmen. They targeted thirteen officials in the educational and youth league system and beat them severely.[78] On August 23 red guards took old theatrical costumes stored in the Cultural Bureau, piled them in the courtyard of the Confucian Temple, and set them ablaze. They conducted a struggle session against some thirty figures, including top officials from the Cultural Bureau, nationally prominent novelists and poets, and famous Beijing opera performers, during which the victims were whipped with belts. Noted author Lao She was beaten to the point that he bled from wounds to the head. His corpse was found floating in a nearby lake the next morning.[79]

Although the influence of family heritage on a student's political qualifications was controversial, attacks on the families of "reactionaries" were not. The last half of August saw a wave of attacks on residents with "bad" class backgrounds. Red guards roamed the city's residential streets, terrorized members of these households, invaded their homes, and subjected the occupants to violent struggle sessions. During this period red guards issued handbills that made two kinds of demands. The first was that the owners of courtyard homes in the old neighborhoods in the city center move into smaller quarters and stop charging rent to tenants. One typical handbill declared:

> Capitalist real estate owners (landlords), "respected" gentlemen and ladies, you are bastards, sons of bitches. The vast majority of you are s.o.b. black elements (landlord, rich peasant, counterrevolutionary, bad elements, rightists, etc.). Before liberation you sucked our blood and sweat, fed off our flesh and blood, acted like tyrants, committing every imaginable crime; you are truly maggots, leeches. After liberation you still have a strong little capitalist empire, taking rent, defying state regulations by raising rents, avoiding bankruptcy by oppressing your tenants (worker and peasant origins), truly despicable. Today, on behalf of the broad masses of workers, peasants, and soldiers, we open fire on you!

The notice demanded that all landlords in the neighborhood turn over their property to the government within ten days.[80]

Even more serious were red guard demands that all exploiting class and reactionary households be expelled from the city immediately. Red guards from Beijing High School No. 4, located in the core of the old Western District, demanded that all households headed by "four type elements" (landlords, rich peasants, counterrevolutionaries, and bad elements) leave the city by September 10. They declared that they would visit neighborhood police stations to check household registration records to ensure compliance with these "regulations."[81] The red guards of Beijing No. 2 High School were even more insistent. They ordered "all five black elements" to leave Beijing immediately. They asserted that members of these households threatened public order, created disturbances on the streets, and hung out in bars and teahouses all day. Their presence in the nation's capital was intolerable.[82]

The red guards also attacked hobbies and consumer habits that they associated with the capitalist class. One handbill notified all bookstores, hobby shops, post offices, and printing plants that they had seventy-two hours to "destroy all envelopes, stamps, book covers, paintings, posters, magazines, etc. that promote bourgeois consciousness." They called on "all red guard comrades" to help enforce these regulations and warned, "Those who fail to comply will be responsible for the consequences!"[83] Red guards from another school denounced stamp collecting as a bourgeois hobby and demanded that it be stopped, and that all materials left over from the old society be destroyed within forty-eight hours.[84] Red guards from Beijing High School No. 2 denounced bourgeois influences in clothing shops, used bookstores, barbershops, beauty shops, and photo galleries. They forbade foreign hair and clothing styles and demanded a halt to sales of denim cloth and foreign books. These items were all part of a plot by the bourgeoisie to restore capitalism, and "bourgeois bastards" must stop immediately.[85]

In identifying the homes of alien class elements, red guards were assisted by public security forces. At a meeting of the Beijing Bureau of Public Security in late August, Minister of Public Security Xie Fuzhi told officials, "We should not be restrained by existing regulations, whether they are national laws or public security bureau rules . . . The civilian police must stand alongside the red guards, get in touch with them, establish a close relationship, brief them on local conditions, and tell them about the local five bad elements." The speech served as a directive to help red guards identify the homes of "bad classes."[86] Members of these households assembled on high-school grounds and neighborhood parks for struggle sessions and beatings. Processions of victims being driven through the streets in the backs of trucks were a common sight.[87] In the month following the first Tiananmen rally on August 18, 114,000 homes were searched, and 44.8 million yuan of foreign currency, gold, and other valuables were confiscated, along with more than 2.3 million books and 3.3 million paintings, art objects, and pieces of furniture. In the Western District, the books, paintings, scrolls, and other items confiscated from 1,061 homes were set ablaze and burned for eight days and nights. During this period 77,000 people were expelled from their homes in the urban and inner suburban districts.[88] The violence crested during the last week of August, when an average of more than 200 people were dying every day. The official Beijing death toll for the month after August 18 was 1,772.[89]

## Red Guard Denunciations of Violence

Some red guards objected strongly to these events. One of the first protests came on August 6, well before the violence crested. A joint proclamation issued by red guards from Qinghua, People's University, and Beijing Aeronautics high schools was a direct response to the events at the August 2 rally where violence erupted and led to a revenge stabbing. The "Urgent Appeal" began:

> Very recently, a series of extremely serious erroneous incidents have appeared in the Cultural Revolution movement in Beijing's high schools. A small group of bastards and a bunch of incompetents who do not obey Chairman Mao have donned the revolutionary garb of such leftist organizations as Red Guards and Red Flag and, waving the banner of rebellion, have publicly defied Chairman Mao's instructions, publicly violated party policy, publicly violated the discipline of the dictatorship of the proletariat and communist moral character, and have suppressed and attacked revolutionary masses who have different opinions, going around everywhere beating people up, injuring a good many good people and children of workers, peasants, and revolutionary cadres, destroying offices and schools, carrying on like gangsters . . . You who wildly smash things without regard to right and wrong are gangsters, truly low-level; what kind of leftism is this? You are fake leftists, fake Red Guards, fake Red Flag![90]

The appeal stated that "genuine leftist organizations in the various schools must unite and take immediately effective action to strictly control indiscriminate beatings and gangster-like behavior that destroys state property." Those who committed such acts must be kicked out of all red guard organizations. "We children of workers, peasants, and revolutionary cadres absolutely must not damage the party's lifeblood."[91]

The Qinghua High School Red Guards, unhappy about the movement as it expanded during August, issued a series of criticisms and calls for greater discipline and restraint. Several days after its "Urgent Appeal" it issued a long critique of arrogant behavior among red guard leaders and called for red guards to "become a highly revolutionized, battle-hardened force like the People's Liberation Army." To achieve this unity and discipline, it was necessary to be selective in admitting members: "What kind of organization are the red guards? The great majority of its members are sons and daughters of revolutionary cadres with good class background and high consciousness."[92]

Mao initially welcomed the "Urgent Appeal" and had it printed and circulated to delegates to the Eleventh Plenum, which was still in session.[93] On August 13, with the support of the Municipal Party Committee, red guards staged a mass meeting at the Beijing Workers' Stadium to denounce violent "hooligans" among the red guards. Three high-school red guards who had been involved in the recent revenge stabbing were beaten during a struggle session, and similar incidents occurred sporadically at several schools in the following days.[94]

These efforts were ineffective, and the wave of violence crested in late August. Near the end of the month the Qinghua High Red Guards issued another criticism of the red guard movement titled "Ten-Point Assessment." The document began, "In the midst of such a tumultuous and historically unprecedented movement as the Great Proletarian Cultural Revolution, it is unavoidable that the red guards will exhibit some shortcomings and errors." Then it moved to the main point—violence.

> We must absolutely not beat people, and even if anti-party, anti-socialist rightists initiate the violence, we should not beat them . . . We red guards should be modest and prudent, stick to principles, respect comrades, and correctly resolve contradictions among the people. We absolutely must not be arrogant and domineering, impervious to reason, like a tiger whose backside you dare not touch, acting with utter disregard for human life, beating people to death, flying into a rage when contradicted and beating people. This is the behavior of Guomindang Fascists, of local tyrants, absolutely not the behavior of genuine red guards from the five red classes![95]

Red guard organizations should be disciplined and unified, "with five-red sons and daughters as the core," prevent individuals from becoming too powerful, regularly use criticism and self-criticism to correct errors, and guard against becoming arrogant and overbearing. Red guards should also strive to unite with the vast majority of students:

> With regard to those from non-five-red households, our own experience shows that after being tested in struggle and thoroughly remolding themselves we can unite with the vast majority of them. We cannot just call all of

them "sons of bitches." The purpose of uniting with them is to remold them. A minority of them, if their political performance is good, and if they are loyal to Mao Zedong Thought and the party's class line, can become red guards.

Even those who were unable to join the red guards could still be revolutionary and should be encouraged to participate in the movement. The document also warned against "deviations" in the campaign against remnants of the old society and culture.

> When some people see braids that are a little long, they cut them off and even shave the heads of female comrades. Some people indiscriminately search homes, no matter whose they are, and even create an uproar at the homes of revolutionary cadres, without any sense of class nature; this is a huge error, and we must pay serious attention to this. Some people will not let shops sell cakes, only steamed buns. And some gangster elements, using smashing the "four olds" as an excuse, engage in all kinds of gangster-like sabotage activities. These must be stopped![96]

The Qinghua High Red Guards and their allies were groping toward an alternative model for the red guards. The template for militant student activities was Mao's 1927 "Report on the Peasant Movement in Hunan." That essay described an upsurge of violent peasant retribution against landlords, including the tumultuous and spontaneous "struggle sessions" that students imitated as their primary public act of rebellion. Mao praised these outbursts as essential in advancing the revolutionary process, and he ridiculed party members who feared such spontaneity and claimed that this was "going too far." Mao argued that this should be welcomed, and that it was a test for party members to see which of them were truly revolutionary.[97]

These red guards offered a different revolutionary model, the People's Liberation Army, whose ideals stressed discipline, unity, careful attention to party policy, and restrained behavior. They rebuked classmates who modeled their behavior after peasant uprisings as "gangsters" or "hooligans." In their tabloids they began to emphasize the revolutionary tradition of the army, especially its "Three Rules of Discipline and Eight Points of Attention," which explicitly proscribed beating and cursing people and mistreating prisoners.[98] Other red guard organizations echoed these appeals by calling for emulation of the People's Liberation Army.[99]

Despite constant rhetoric about "red" heritage, the divisions over violence did not pit students from one type of family background against others. This was a division among students from "red" class background who dominated the early movement. The appeals of the Qinghua Red Guards were directed to "red class" students like themselves.[100] These splits were evident to students at the time. A mid-September essay began with an appeal to "all class brothers of five-red family origin" about the ubiquitous problem of divisions among the "red" classes. "Among these shortcomings and errors, we view one to be especially serious: the problem of unity among various red guard factions that have been formed by classmates of five-red family origins. Very recently we have done some investigating in several schools and have discovered that they all have two or even more factions formed by classmates of five-red family origin." Some divisions were due to "principled differences" over issues "like the work groups," while others were "personal contradictions" due to individual rivalry. Elections for revolutionary committees intensified the divisions.[101] Splits among "red-class" red guards at the school level were also evident citywide. In mid-August high-school red guards argued over the main goal of the movement. One side, including Beida Red Flag, wanted to curtail attacks on the Communist Youth League Central Committee and hold struggle sessions against "hooligan" students. The other side, which included the Qinghua High Red Guards, wanted to emphasize discipline and nonviolence while pursuing further attacks on the youth league.[102]

### The Maoist Shrug

The calls to curtail violence ran directly counter to the attitude of key figures on the CCRG who, on the rare occasions when they addressed the issue, appeared to view it as a necessary feature of rebellion and the suffering of victims as acceptable collateral damage. Top officials were intimately informed of the violent course of the movement. The CCRG established an intelligence network of reporters from the PLA news service and the New China News Agency that detailed school-level events in a restricted-circulation bulletin.[103] Near the end of August the Municipal Party Committee established a Red Guard Liaison Office and produced a similar bulletin based on visits to its reception center by red guards and their victims.[104]

On the eve of the movement, key CCRG leaders gave clear signals that violence against victims would not be considered a serious transgression. On July 28, in one of her first speeches to the high-school red guards, Jiang Qing had said:

> Our proletarian dictatorship is firm; we do not fear chaos. Chaos and order are inseparable. That would be like a turtle crawling along in a rut, tying you up in your own little world, unable to liberate your thinking; it is no good . . . We do not advocate beating people, but beating people is no big deal . . . You cannot beat someone's mistaken thoughts out of them, but for beatings to occur during a revolutionary outburst is not a bad thing. Chairman Mao has said, "If good people beat bad people, it serves them right; if bad people beat good people, the good people achieve glory; if good people beat good people, it is a misunderstanding; without beatings you do not get acquainted and then no longer need to beat them."[105]

On August 4 neither Jiang Qing nor Kang Sheng objected when members of Beida High Red Flag whipped the leaders of the Beida work team with belts during a denunciation meeting. To the contrary, when the whipping was over, Jiang smiled and embraced one of the students.[106] Despite this cavalier attitude, Jiang Qing initially did not object to the red guards' August 6 "Urgent Appeal." However, her attitude soon changed. She became concerned that more moderate figures on the CCRG—particularly Wang Renzhong, who was in charge of the Beijing movement and who pushed to have the appeal circulated at the Eleventh Plenum—were too enthusiastic about its message. She began to suspect that they were using the issue to limit the student rebellion. Mao also shared this view, and during one meeting when he heard a report about the August 13 mass struggle session against "hooligan" students, he reportedly turned to Wang Renzhong and said, "You and your 'urgent appeal.'"[107] Mao was in no mood to let concerns about violence derail student mobilization. Near the height of the wave of violence on August 23, at a meeting of the Politburo Standing Committee, he expressed his impatience.

> I do not think Beijing is all that chaotic. Students holding 100,000-person mass meetings, capturing assailants, getting all panicked. Beijing is too civilized, hooligans are only a minority, now is not the time to interfere . . . Rushing to make decisions, getting all worked up. Rushing to struggle

against the leftists, rushing to hold 100,000-person mass meetings, rushing to issue urgent appeals, rushing to say that to oppose the new Municipal Party Committee is to oppose the Party Center—why can you not oppose it?[108]

Xie Fuzhi, minister of public security, mirrored Mao's attitude. At the late August meeting where he directed neighborhood police stations to assist red guards in identifying "reactionary" households, Xie said, "I do not approve of the masses killing people, but the masses' bitter hatred toward bad people cannot be discouraged, and it is unavoidable."[109] As the violence intensified, Mao set the tone: the authorities should turn a blind eye to violence as an inevitable by-product of revolutionary mobilization. This was translated into official directives on August 21 and 22: local army units and bureaus of public security were strictly prohibited from taking any action against marauding red guards.[110] The targets of the red guards were left virtually defenseless.

### The Red Guard Picket Corps

Given the attitude of Mao and the CCRG, any move against red guard violence would have to be made by the students themselves.[111] Some red guards in the downtown neighborhoods shared the views of the Qinghua students. On August 25 the Western District Picket Corps announced its establishment. This was the first formal cross-campus organization, an alliance of fifty red guard groups from more than forty schools. Its members introduced themselves as "comrades in arms of the People's Liberation Army stationed in Beijing." Among their responsibilities were to "resolutely assist red guard revolutionary activities" and "resolutely suppress the counterrevolutionary activities of landlords, rich peasants, counterrevolutionaries, bad elements, and rightists and their loyal descendants." They declared that they "have the right to inspect red organizations in various schools, offices, factories, and units" and to "arrest fake red guards and hooligans."[112] Among the organization's "Six Regulations" was the responsibility to study and implement the People's Liberation Army's "Three Rules of Discipline and Eight Points of Attention," which, they claimed, included the prohibition, "It is strictly forbidden to beat and physically abuse people, it is strictly forbidden to humiliate people." Members were expected to "serve the people" and "gain their trust" and "under all circumstances remain cool headed and calm."[113]

The Western District Picket Corps dictated a set of ground rules that it intended to enforce. It prohibited red guards from invading the offices of state agencies and the homes of state officials and forbade them to eject revolutionary elders from their homes, fire their nannies, or confiscate their televisions, sofas, and cars. Foreigners and overseas Chinese must not be harassed; searching the homes of "bad elements" must be done in coordination with their work units and the local police, and anything confiscated must be turned over to public authorities. Force could be used only in self-defense.[114] Only homes of "six black elements" could be searched, and only after checking first with the local police to verify their classification. It was absolutely forbidden to search other homes; only nonviolent forms of struggle must be used. "We red guards absolutely must not arbitrarily beat people. When we use nonviolent forms of struggle, it proves that our forces are incomparably strong."[115]

The Western District Picket Corps was especially clear about violence. "In the Cultural Revolution from this point forward it is absolutely forbidden to beat people, absolutely forbidden to physically abuse them either openly or in a disguised manner; absolutely forbidden to humiliate people, absolutely forbidden to extract forced confessions"—a prohibition that applied "without exception," even to people who had already been determined to be counterrevolutionaries.[116] To avoid misunderstanding, the ground rules provided explicit detail about what constituted physical abuse: "Kneeling, lying flat, bending at the waist, carrying a heavy weight, standing for long periods, keeping hands raised for long periods, keeping heads bowed for long period, etc., all are open or disguised forms of physical abuse and are not methods of struggle that we should use." The forbidden forms of humiliation included "hanging signboards [from the neck], wearing a tall hat, being made to sing chants, shaving heads, etc." What did the rules mean by "forced confessions"? "Failing to stress investigation and research, failing to stress facts and evidence, readily believing confessions, having blind faith in confessions, using a combination of violence and threats to force a confession, and then believing the confession."[117] Counterpart organizations emerged in the Eastern and Haidian districts soon afterward.[118]

The picket corps soon found allies among the diminishing number of central leaders who actively sought to rein in violence. Given the reluctance of Mao and the CCRG to hinder mass mobilization, persuasion and voluntary self-restraint were the only politically acceptable courses. Premier Zhou Enlai worked actively behind the scenes to encourage self-policing. On August 24 he assigned Yong Wentao, vice-head of the CCP Propaganda Department, to handle liaison work with high-school red guards.[119] On August 26 Yong established a liaison office at the Cultural Palace of Laboring Peoples, a complex of buildings in an enclosed park behind the reviewing stands of Tiananmen. Late that evening Zhou Enlai spoke at the opening ceremonies.[120] In the ensuing weeks Zhou and Yong held a series of meetings with red guards to persuade them to curtail violence and exercise restraint. In the coming months Zhou attended more than forty meetings with high-school red guards organized by the liaison office, consistently arguing his case for moderation.[121]

The liaison office was quickly swamped with visits, letters, and phone calls. The contacts came from red guards seeking advice and clarification, and from citizens in the neighborhoods and leaders of schools and other government institutions who were under attack. During this period the main liaison office received up to 1,000 visitors daily. In the first month some 10,000 high-school students attended its meetings. The liaison office also provided intelligence about the social impact of the movement. The visits, phone calls, and letters were a rich source of information, and highlights were digested into a regular bulletin that was printed internally and distributed to the Party Center, the State Council, and the CCRG. The bulletins detailed the mounting violence—by September 5 the death toll had already passed the 1,000 mark—and supplemented the figures with specific examples. Members of the CCRG were unhappy about the emphasis on violence and expressed concerns about the liaison office's "incorrect standpoint."[122]

Unable to use regular police forces, Zhou Enlai turned to the picket corps as his primary instrument in this effort. When news of the Western District Picket Corps reached Zhou, he established a direct line of communication through the Office of the State Council, headed by the State Council's secretary general, Zhou Rongxin. Xu Ming, on the staff of the State Council office, handled contacts with the students. Her husband was Kong Yuan, Head of China's Central Intelligence Agency, and their son, Kong Dan, was a student at Beijing No. 4 High School and one of the founders of the Western District Picket Corps.[123] Zhou invited the group onto the rostrum during subsequent red guard rallies at Tiananmen Square. He met with its leaders and had Zhou Rongxin provide them with office space, means of transportation, and printing facilities.[124]

Zhou Enlai dispatched the picket corps to defend government offices, high officials, and other prominent citizens.[125] Under his instructions,

Zhou Rongxin and Xu Ming assigned the group's members a series of tasks: keeping order at train stations, acting as security guards at Tiananmen rallies, and rushing to halt violent home invasions of famous artists, authors, or historical figures. They handled sentry duties at international conferences and at the Beijing Hotel and other places where foreigners were received. They were dispatched to halt struggle sessions, house searches, and beatings. Eventually they were sent to ministries to protect state cadres and prevent student rebels from breaking into secure offices and opening confidential files.[126] Over the next two months the State Council office reportedly provided the Western District Picket Corps with two trucks, two jeeps, and a motorcycle, along with overcoats, shirts, army blankets, broadcasting equipment, sofas, stoves, telephones, an office, a kitchen with four cooks, and cash for expenses. Its general orders were professionally printed in large runs at the State Council's printing plant.[127]

## Collision Course

In the course of conducting these activities, the Western District Picket Corps collided with university rebels who were demonstrating at national ministries. This confrontation was not a product of the students' family origins or political allegiances before the Cultural Revolution began, nor was it even a product of different stances that they had taken under the work teams. The high-school red guards and the university minority faction had both been in the vanguard of opposition to the work teams, and the leaders of both were from revolutionary households. The minority faction attacked the ministries not because of any inherent dissatisfaction with the status quo, but because of their experiences under the work teams and their subsequent rivalry with the majority faction on their campuses. The red guard pickets, formed by students initially lionized by Mao and the mass media, were not driven by intracampus rivalries, and even if they were motivated to search for the leaders of their work teams, they would not find them in national ministries.

The picket corps' "conservatism"—if it was that—was the product of a relationship they developed with Zhou Enlai through his staff, a relationship forged by their early vocal stand against political intolerance and indiscriminate violence and by Zhou's desire to steer the red guard movement onto a less violent and disruptive path. Their dramatic confrontations with college rebels at the Ministry of Geology, the Ministry of Defense, and elsewhere in the city inadvertently crystallized a new tacit alliance with the university majority and drew them into a direct confrontation with their erstwhile sponsors on the CCRG. This confrontation soon led to the first major turning point in the conflict between red guards in the capital.

# 6

## RADICALS WITH PATRONS

### The Rise of the Rebels

In early September factional identities at the city level were still ill defined. On university campuses the majority-minority split was sharply drawn, but there was no coordinated action across campuses. Majority factions insisted that the work-team issue was settled and unimportant, and this position required little cross-campus coordination. Minority factions, on the other hand, were adamant about the errors of the work teams and sought to dislodge their campus rivals by focusing on the issue. But only a few of them, like Geology East Is Red and Aeronautics Red Flag, had dramatized the issue by attacking central government offices.

Factional identities in high schools had yet to form. The most influential groups were from "red" households, especially the offspring of officials. These early red guards, however, became embroiled in inconclusive debates about the rhyming couplet that expressed a singularly chauvinistic interpretation of the party's class line. However lively and impassioned, these debates did not signify that red guards were divided by their family origins, because at this point virtually all red guard groups were dominated by students from "red," especially "revolutionary," origins. The issue of violence and discipline was much more consequential for cross-campus alliances. The high-school movement had been remarkably brutal toward its victims, and this sharply divided the movement. This was the issue that led to the first cross-campus alliance near the end of August, the Western District Picket Corps, which was soon followed by companion organizations in the Haidian and Eastern districts. The picket corps espoused a conception of disciplined political action modeled after the People's Liberation Army and appealed to the allegedly higher political morality of students from revolutionary family heritage. With the active encouragement and material support of State Council office staff under Zhou Enlai, they set out to police the violent and chaotic movement that engulfed the city's neighborhoods.

Until early September the university and high-school movements proceeded along separate tracks. This changed after a series of skirmishes between high-school picket corps and the university minority factions that besieged national ministries. These skirmishes finally crystallized citywide factional identities and clarified the still-unformed political strategy of Mao and the CCRG. The result, after another month, was a newly minted "rebel" faction built on the foundations of the old university minority. The rebels grew with behind-the-scenes encouragement and outspoken public support of the CCRG, which publicly repudiated the old university majority and especially the high-school red guards who had been the media stars of August.

### Confrontation at the Ministries

The first confrontation at a ministry occurred on August 31, as the protest by Aeronautics Red Flag at the Ministry of Defense entered its second week. This was the first major public action of the Western District Picket Corps, established six days earlier. Defending the ministry was naturally attractive to students who idolized the traditions of the People's Liberation Army and viewed direct attacks on its headquarters as an affront to the institution that symbolized the values for which the Cultural Revolution was being waged. The Western District Picket Corps tried to forcibly dislodge the protesters, but its small force was quickly repulsed.[1]

On the next occasion it mobilized a much larger force. Geology East Is Red sent several hundred members back to the Geology Ministry on September 5 to stage a sit-in to dramatize their demand that their school's work-team head, Vice-Minister Zou Jiayou, be turned over to them. He Changgong, the ministry's party secretary and himself a revolutionary war hero, had backed Zou in his confrontation with the students in June. Now he refused to surrender him to the crowd. Instead, he requested protection from his superiors, who in turn notified the Western District Picket Corps.[2] On September 7, the third day of the siege, more than 800 members of the Western District Picket Corps surrounded the university students. They loudly accused them of counterrevolution and waded into the crowd, whipping the protesters with belts and throwing bricks. They seized several university students and held them prisoner for several days. Afterward they printed handbills denouncing attacks on the ministry.[3] It was now clear that the red guards were hopelessly split. The minority factions had to contend not only with majority opponents on their own campuses but also with a new militia of high-school students backed by the State Council.

Mao had already expressed annoyance at expressions of concern about student violence, and members of the CCRG were uneasy about the reports submitted by Yong Wentao's Liaison Office. Now the picket corps presented them with a large and unified cross-campus alliance that had no organized rival in the city, espoused a coherent political vision that was highly attractive to the student militants Mao had recently praised, and was proving capable of countering attacks on higher government officials. Under Mao's direction, the CCRG initiated a series of countermoves that reshaped and redirected the student movement.

### Citywide Alliances: The Red Guard Headquarters

If the minority faction's insurgency was to succeed, it needed a cross-campus alliance and the clear backing of the CCRG. It had both by the end of September, and by mid-October it was routing its opponents. Its alliance was called the Revolutionary Rebel Headquarters of the Capital University Red Guards, founded on September 6 and known as the Third Headquarters. Initially composed of minority-faction red guards from sixteen campuses, it adopted a new identity as the "rebel" faction. Its guiding force was Geology Institute East Is Red and one of its founders, Zhu Chengzhao.[4] Zhu and his colleagues had established contact with two members of the CCRG, Qi Benyu and Guan Feng, during their July visit to the Geology Institute to support their criticisms of the work team.[5] Later Li Na, the daughter of Mao and Jiang Qing, encouraged the group and reported regularly to her father about political developments in the school.[6] During the September siege at the Ministry of Geology, Guan Feng and other CCRG members were on the scene and provided quiet encouragement.[7] Well before the minority faction set up the Third Headquarters, Geology East Is Red had direct contacts with the CCRG and indirect contact with Mao.

As its name implies, the Third Headquarters was not the first attempt to form a citywide alliance. The first was the Capital University Red Guard Headquarters, established on August 27. The documents and speeches associated with this group show how rapidly the political environment changed. This was only two days after the Western District Picket

Corps was founded and the beginning of the Aeronautics Red Flag protest at the Ministry of Defense, and four days after Geology East Is Red's first protest at the Ministry of Geology.

Presiding at the founding meeting of the First Headquarters were a number of national officials, including Jiang Qing, acting PLA chief of staff Yang Chengwu, and officers from the Beijing Garrison Command.[8] The meeting at the Beijing Gymnasium was replete with military symbolism and claims that the "new red guards" were carrying on the glorious traditions of the "old red guards" in the "revolutionary elder generation."[9] Jiang Qing laid out a vision for the student movement that sounded very much like that of the Western District Picket Corps. She said that Yang Chengwu would serve as the "political instructor" for the red guards, and she gave them policing functions, reading out a list of government offices that they needed to protect.[10]

The most prominent school leader at this meeting was Beida's Nie Yuanzi, who led the school's red guards into this headquarters and never publicly broke from it. Nie still basked in the glory of her wall poster and Mao's extravagant praise. She was secure in her position as the leader of Beida, which was the only major campus without a majority-minority split. Nie presided at a citywide First Headquarters meeting of red guards on September 1, where Zhou Enlai and Wang Renzhong gave speeches counseling moderation and nonviolence.[11]

The First Headquarters articulated a conception of the red guard movement that was rapidly overtaken by events. The organization steadfastly ignored the majority-minority split and counseled unity and discipline. Through early October its newspaper mixed praise for the red guards with admonitions for them to emulate the PLA and observe its "three rules of discipline and eight points of attention." Its pages were filled with instructions about arrangements for Tiananmen rallies, the reception of red guards from the provinces, and international meetings with foreign students.[12] The message was remarkably similar to that of the Western District Picket Corps and was certainly congenial to campus majorities that were, like Nie herself, still securely in charge of their campuses. By ignoring the raging minority-majority conflict and blandly counseling unity and discipline, the First Headquarters became irrelevant to both campus factions, which simultaneously prepared their own breakaway headquarters.

The first to strike was the Capital University Red Guard General Headquarters, or Second Headquarters, on September 5. Most of the founders were majority factions, but some minority factions also joined, notably Aeronautics East Is Red, still engaged in its protest at the Ministry of Defense.[13] Jiang Qing greeted the group briefly, nominating Minister of Public Security Xie Fuzhi as its advisor and Liu Zhijian and Yang Chengwu as its political instructors. Liu Zhijian, vice-secretary of the PLA Political Department and the military representative on the CCRG, expressed equal support for both red guard headquarters and called for them to work together to defeat their common enemy.[14] Zhou Enlai spoke to an assembly of more than 2,000 Second Headquarters red guards on September 13 and predictably called for moderation.[15]

The majority factions that established this alliance were shifting with the political winds, altering their earlier pro-work-team position, and adopting a more militant tone in alliance with selected minority factions like Aeronautics Red Flag. This stance would help defuse the work-team issue and perhaps take the steam out of the minority faction's challenge on their home campuses. The Second Headquarters joined together disparate elements that were trying to steer a compromise course and reunite the red guard movement. During early October its newspaper praised the "revolutionary minority" and criticized the errors of the work teams but still did not demand the rehabilitation of the work teams' victims or the pursuit of the officials responsible.[16]

The Third Headquarters was established on September 6, one day after the Second Headquarters. The founders were all minority factions from sixteen different universities.[17] Once again, Liu Zhijian gave the welcoming speech, apologizing for the absence of Jiang Qing, who was ill, and Xie Fuzhi and Yang Chengwu, who had other meetings. Liu welcomed this headquarters on an equal basis to the other two and gave a version of the same speech he had given to the Second Headquarters the day before.[18] In the coming weeks the Third Headquarters presented a sharp contrast with the stances of the other two alliances. Its newspaper chronicled the persecutions inflicted by work teams on their opponents and called them "white terror." It took great pains to document the fact that the vast majority of those persecuted by work teams were from "red" households and were members of the party and youth league.[19] Unlike the other two, the Third Headquarters pushed for a confrontation with an anti-Mao line in the party.

One important component of this struggle was the refutation of Tan Lifu's now-famous speech, which had become a rallying cry for the university majority and the high-school picket corps. The speech was widely reproduced and distributed and was frequently quoted on the broadcast networks controlled by campus majorities. On September 13 Beijing Normal Jingganggshan, the minority faction led by Tan Houlan, published an open letter calling Tan Lifu's speech an "anti-Mao poisonous weed." Two days later, together with minority factions from eleven other schools, it established a cross-campus alliance to denounce Tan's speech, charging that it violated the party's verdict on the work teams and distorted the party's class line. The group held a mass meeting at Beijing Normal on September 26.[20]

### Tipping the Scales: The Maoist Intervention

The initially evenhanded treatment accorded the three red guard headquarters gave no hint of the imminent shift in the political landscape. Mao and the CCRG were moving rapidly toward wholehearted endorsement of the minority factions, and this was signaled in meetings with red guards. On September 13, for example, Minister of Public Security Xie Fuzhi met with the minority faction from the Institute of Politics and Law and said, "The general orientation of the minority faction is correct—not just in the Institute of Politics and Law, but in other schools as well . . . The truth lies with the minority faction; I support the minority."[21]

A crucial turning point was reached during meetings from September 17 to September 20 between the CCRG and the leaders of some twenty prominent minority factions. Zhu Chengzhao of Geology East Is Red helped organize the meeting and build the invitation list, which included Kuai Dafu of Qinghua, Tan Houlan of Beijing Normal, Wang Dabin of the Geology Institute, and other future red guard leaders of note. The students told of the persecutions they had suffered at the hands of work teams and complained that they had still not been cleared of the charges lodged against them. They criticized several top officials for not being sympathetic to their cause: Zhou Enlai was a "compromiser," as was Tao Zhu. The students argued that there were now two clearly opposed lines over the direction of the Cultural Revolution, and the CCRG should take a clear stand. The proceedings of the meetings were relayed directly to Mao and reinforced his growing dissatisfaction about the direction of the student movement.[22]

After the conference Mao decided to openly favor the minority camp. On September 21, the day after the meetings concluded, Chen Boda,

Guan Feng, Wang Li, and Lin Jie met with leaders of Aeronautics Red Flag and expressed support for their sit-in at the Ministry of Defense. They ordered work-team head Zhao Ruzhang to finally meet with the students. Zhao did so and was interrogated by students, and the confrontation ended on September 23 after twenty-eight days. When news of the capitulation reached the Aeronautics Institute, it shook the confidence of the majority faction, which initially refused to believe it.[23]

On September 19, while the CCRG conference was still under way, Geology East Is Red's protesters surged through the doors of the Ministry of Geology and raided the offices where the work team's files were kept. They broke open the cabinets and carted off the files compiled on the student opposition. Satisfied that they had achieved their short-term objective, they returned to the Geology Institute without work-team head Zou Jiayou.[24]

Heartened by the support now extended to them by the CCRG, Geology East Is Red moved to seize power on campus on September 23. A massive brawl over control of the campus broadcasting system left more than 100 injured. Guan Feng and Qi Benyu went to the school to relay a message from the CCRG: the skirmishes must be halted immediately, and the CCRG firmly supported East Is Red and its demand to bring Zou Jiayou back to campus.[25] Several days later Guan Feng and Qi Benyu met again with students and sharply criticized Zou for calling in the Western District Picket Corps to attack the protesters and for refusing to return to the school to apologize.[26]

On September 25 Zhou Enlai finally met with the leaders of the Third Headquarters and defended himself against criticisms of his calls for moderation: his speeches were approved by Chairman Mao, and even if he had committed errors of line, that still did not make him a counter-revolutionary. He was late in meeting with the Third Headquarters, but he supported it as well.[27] The news of CCRG support spread quickly. During the final week of September the minority factions at Qinghua, the Aeronautics Institute, and Beijing Foreign Languages Institute all seized control of their campus broadcasting systems.[28] The tide was now shifting decisively.

In light of his reputation as a compromiser, it was significant that Zhou Enlai himself delivered the definitive speech that made clear Mao's support for the minority faction. On September 26 Zhou addressed a mass rally of the Third Headquarters and stated categorically that the minority's demands for equal treatment must be respected. Claiming to speak on behalf of Mao and Lin Biao, he affirmed the minority faction's struggle and called for the rehabilitation of all those in the minority faction who had been labeled anti-party. He announced that all "black materials" collected on these individuals would be removed from their files, and that henceforth all members of the minority faction would be treated as the equals of other red guards.[29] Zhou may well have hoped that satisfying this demand would take the urgency out of the minority faction's cause and remove the primary incentive for rebel attacks on the ministries. To make sure that this message was not lost, Zhou followed up his public promise with detailed instructions about how to return or destroy materials in the files so that no incriminating materials would remain.[30] This became official policy on November 15 when the Beijing Municipal Party Committee issued a notice declaring all political labels given to the student opposition null and void and the Central Committee followed suit by ordering all materials related to these judgments removed from the party's files and destroyed.[31]

This shift in the CCRG's stance was already apparent to many in the majority coalition. Tan Lifu, who had inadvertently become a majority spokesman, immediately recognized the shifting winds when the Third Headquarters was established on September 6. His minority-faction opponent, Industrial University East Is Red, was among its founding members. That same evening Tan announced that he was disbanding his revolutionary committee and turning it into a "logistics department" for the school's many red guard organizations. Three weeks later Tan and his comrades made final speeches to their Industrial University Red Guards, who had lost control of the campus and were being disbanded. Tan accepted the responsibility for their failure: his emphasis on the class background of students from exploiting classes was "left" in form but rightist in essence and served to divide the masses.[32] In a proclamation on October 1, Tan announced to the entire school that he had already resigned from all red guard posts because of the errors he had committed, including his famous speech. Although he insisted that his motivations were honest, he admitted to virtually every error of orientation and line that the school's minority faction had charged for the past six weeks. However, he still denied that his group and the work team were counterrevolutionary. Tan then withdrew from red guard politics, left the school to the minority faction, and departed for a tour of the south.[33]

The fall of Tan Lifu coincided with the rise of Kuai Dafu, who soon emerged as China's leading student rebel. Up to this point Kuai had played only a marginal role within Qinghua's minority faction. The Qinghua minority was represented by an alliance known as the Mao Zedong Thought Red Guards. It had participated in the founding of the Third Headquarters and was strengthened by its rise. Kuai Dafu was the most famous victim of the Qinghua work team and was viewed with sympathy by the Qinghua minority. However, it considered him too reckless and mercurial to be taken seriously, and his small fighting group had little influence.[34]

Kuai's big break came when he was invited to the four-day CCRG conference with minority-faction leaders on September 17. His stubborn and outspoken stand against the Qinghua work team had attracted the attention of members of the CCRG. Apparently impressed during the conference, the CCRG decided to promote Kuai as a student leader. Zhang Chunqiao, who chaired the four-day conference, invited Kuai back for an individual session on September 23. He encouraged Kuai to start his own organization and assured him of CCRG support. The next day Kuai announced the establishment of a separate new minority organization, Qinghua Jinggangshan, and he and his group began a rapid ascent to the top of the rebel movement.[35]

Kuai was a shrewd choice to lead the Qinghua rebels. The other Qinghua minority leaders had opposed the work team and had sympathized with Kuai's stand, but Kuai had shown that he was fearless and defiant, and he had ready-made grievances against high officials who were in the CCRG's crosshairs for future purges. His harrowing campus arguments with Vice-Premier Bo Yibo were well documented, and he had also penned angry denunciations of Liu Shaoqi's wife, Wang Guangmei, who had been part of the Qinghua work team. Kuai appeared to blame his victimization by the work team on Wang Guangmei's influence, and the CCRG apparently calculated that this would make Kuai highly amenable to attacks on Wang and on Liu Shaoqi himself. He in fact issued his first demand to return Wang Guangmei to campus for self-criticism on October 9 and dramatized his demand with a march downtown for a sit-in.[36]

Less than two weeks after establishing his new rebel group, Kuai was selected to play a key role at a massive Third Headquarters rally on October 6 at Beijing Workers' Stadium. The meeting was virtually an official CCRG function, with Zhou Enlai, Chen Boda, Jiang Qing, and Zhang Chunqiao all present and addressing the crowd.[37] Kuai led the assembled students in swearing an oath of loyalty. On this day Kuai Dafu became the face of the incipient rebel movement, and his rapid ascent was assured.[38]

*The Collapse of the Majority Coalition*

The decisive shift toward support for the Third Headquarters was expressed in an authoritative *Red Flag* commentary that appeared after intensive last-minute revisions supervised by Mao.[39] This famous editorial laid out a new definition of the immediate aims of the Cultural Revolution and pronounced a new verdict on the events that had transpired during the previous four months. The work teams' errors were part of a "bourgeois reactionary line" that was manipulated from above by officials who opposed Mao and tried to obstruct the Cultural Revolution. "The two-line struggle has by no means concluded," the editorial intoned, and it followed that there were even higher officials in the state hierarchy who had masterminded the conspiracy.[40]

To ensure that officials nationwide understood the new line, Mao convened a Central Party Work Conference from October 9 to 28. One of the highlights of the conference was a report by Chen Boda—revised repeatedly by Mao beforehand—that summarized the past two months. Chen described an ongoing "two-line struggle" regarding the Cultural Revolution, and efforts on the part of both officials and red guards to blunt its impact and divert its course. Refuting arguments against red guard violence of the kind made in the "Urgent Appeals" and the directives of the Western District Picket Corps, he denied that red guards were acting "recklessly" and that among them were "opportunists joining up with careerists, thugs, brutal savages, and the like to assume the role of Cultural Revolution 'activists.'" Liu Shaoqi and Deng Xiaoping dutifully made self-criticisms about their "errors of line" regarding the work teams.[41]

One part of the offensive against the "bourgeois reactionary line" was a campaign against its student spokesman, Tan Lifu. Tan would not be permitted to quietly step down from the stage. His arguments had proven popular, so Mao and the CCRG began a nationwide campaign to clarify the "reactionary" nature of his speech. During October Tan was denounced by a long series of high party officials at red guard rallies and meetings: Xie Fuzhi, Yang Chengwu, Zhang Chunqiao, Yong Wentao, Zhou Enlai, Qi Benyu, Jiang Qing, Wang Li, Tao Zhu, Guan Feng, and others.[42] He had become a poster boy for the bourgeois reactionary line.

Chen Boda's keynote speech on October 16 began a campaign of vilification that would tie Tan to the intensifying effort to condemn Liu Shaoqi. Chen said,

Although the work teams have been withdrawn, those who do not approve of Chairman Mao's line can still use their powers of office, and use other methods in their place. For example, in some schools and government agencies there are that kind of people; they completely violate the principles of the Paris Commune contained in the instructions from the Party Center, and in advance, manipulating in secret, establish so-called Cultural Revolution preparatory committees, Cultural Revolution small groups, Cultural Revolution committees, or some other organization . . . On August 8, the Center passed a resolution regarding the Great Proletarian Cultural Revolution, but some twelve days later, at one university some "member of the Cultural Revolution Preparatory Committee" jumped out and issued a speech that opposed the sixteen-point resolution of the Party Center, distributing it widely. There are those who are not at all interested in a central party resolution personally advocated and passed by Chairman Mao, but who treat a speech that opposes a central party decision as a treasure and are terribly busy reprinting it and broadcasting it . . . Many high cadre children are good or relatively good . . . There are also those who are not so good, or who are very bad, to the point of taking the road of revisionism . . . Why must a person wield power simply because they are the child of a high cadre?

Because Tan had defended the party's class line, Chen commented on this as well: "In our revolutionary ranks, Chairman Mao and our party have always given special emphasis to class status and class origin. At the same time, they have also opposed 'class status only' . . . To fail to emphasize class status and class origin is very mistaken. Sole emphasis on class origin, and not emphasizing political performance, is also very mistaken. These mistaken viewpoints must be criticized."[43] In fact, this was exactly the position on the class line taken by Tan Lifu in his speech, but that was beside the point. Tan had used these arguments to defend his school's work team and had expressed powerful arguments against the minority's position, and by extension against the current stance of the CCRG. Moreover, Tan's defense of the party's class line had been appropriated as a rallying cry by the picket corps in their appeal to "five-red brothers" to discipline their violent excesses.[44]

As the campaign against him unfolded, Tan was still traveling in the south. In meetings with red guards in early October, Xie Fuzhi and Chen Boda suggested that Tan be escorted back to Beijing for mass criticism.[45] A delegation from Industrial University East Is Red intercepted him on November 2 in Chongqing and urged him to return to campus to debate viewpoints expressed in his departing "Proclamation" to the school.[46]

Tan returned to the school and issued a longer and more far-reaching self-criticism on November 7 in which he repeated his earlier confession of error and went further, acknowledging that his opponents were "also revolutionaries."[47] His self-criticism did not end the matter. A national campaign to denounce Tan was accelerating. East Is Red Commune compiled several editions of "criticism materials" on Tan's speech that were reprinted in thousands of copies in "liaison stations" that suddenly popped up nationwide.[48]

A final sign of the majority faction's collapse was the demise of the Second Headquarters. In the wake of the *Red Flag* editorial and the new campaign against the "bourgeois reactionary line," the Second Headquarters quickly adjusted its rhetoric and began to publish carefully worded denunciations that conformed to the proper rhetoric but still did not call for mass action against higher officials.[49] After the gigantic Third Headquarters rally to denounce the bourgeois reactionary line on October 6, the Second Headquarters decided to convene one of its own on October 9. Not a single central party leader agreed to attend. None of the minority factions within the Second Headquarters were scheduled to speak, and in response Aeronautics Red Flag disrupted the meeting, which broke up in disarray.[50] Demoralized and divided, the organization declined rapidly. On October 15 it found it necessary to refute rumors that the Second Headquarters had been dissolved.[51] On October 22 Zhou Enlai met with its leaders and called for them to repudiate and correct their errors.[52]

The end came on November 7 when Aeronautics Red Flag and a minority faction from the Light Industrial Institute seized control in an internal coup. The Third Headquarters warmly welcomed this "revolutionary" action by its Aeronautics Institute allies, who aligned the group completely with the Third Headquarters. Its newspaper gave a detailed explanation of the internal debates that had made the power seizure necessary and denounced the stance of the majority organizations that formerly had dominated the Second Headquarters.[53]

Having ignored the majority-minority split in the first place, the First Headquarters, whose most prominent member was Beida's Nie Yuanzi, survived without any apparent internal turmoil. The organization smoothly altered the contents of its newspaper to mimic the shifting Maoist line. The September 28 issue contained its standard fare of praise for the red guards and calls for military discipline. The publication of the *Red Flag* editorial denouncing the bourgeois reactionary line led to rapid backpedaling, and the October 5 issue contained only two innocuous articles on one page. The next issue carried the usual four pages, now with full-throated denunciations of the bourgeois reactionary line.[54] All three red guard headquarters coexisted, espousing the same political message, until they merged in February 1967.

The Western District Picket Corps and its counterparts, which had been established with such fanfare at the end of August and which for a few weeks had played such a prominent role in the capital, also fell into disarray. Now that their stance was clearly repudiated by the CCRG, the active support that they received from the State Council office could no longer be maintained. Their leaders were similarly demoralized and by mid-October were asking their former patrons in the Red Guard Liaison Office whether it made sense for them to continue. The picket corps ceased to exist as a coordinated citywide organization, but campus-level groups maintained their cohesion and identity for many weeks to come. The most committed among them later mounted a spirited last-ditch effort to resist the new turn in the movement, an effort that led to a daring and ill-fated confrontation with the CCRG.

## The Rebel Surge

In the wake of Zhou Enlai's September 26 speech to the Third Headquarters and the triumphant mass rally on October 6, CCRG members Qi Benyu and Guan Feng, and staff member Lin Jie, fanned out to university campuses to explain the new political line to students on both sides.[55] Buoyed by the obvious support for their position, the rebel forces surged into control of their campuses and expanded their assaults on central state organs. Aeronautics Red Flag seized its campus broadcasting station on October 4, and the next day work-team head Zhao Ruzhang finally went to the school to apologize.[56] The Agricultural Machinery Institute's minority organization, East Is Red, took over its school broadcasting station on October 8 and immediately began a campaign against its bureaucratic superiors in the Eighth Ministry of Machine Building.[57] On October 10 the minority factions at the Petroleum and Broadcasting institutes carried out similar actions.[58] Majority control of university campuses collapsed.

As minority factions took control, they focused their fire on the alleged authors of the "bourgeois reactionary line" in the agencies that had sent out their work teams. Geology East Is Red made its third and final foray into the Ministry of Geology on October 8. It held a nine-hour mass criticism session against the ministry's leaders and then took over several offices and established a "liaison station" to search the files for additional material collected by the work team and for other evidence of conspiracy to block the Cultural Revolution.[59] On October 18 it held a mass struggle session against work-team head Zou Jiayou and the ministry's party secretary, He Changgong, after which they were tied up and hauled back to the campus for additional struggle sessions.[60]

Now that this was clearly an approved course of action, a wave of new attacks on ministry-level organs followed. On October 9 Agricultural Machinery Institute East Is Red invaded the Eighth Ministry of Machine Building and subjected the minister to "four and a half hours of lively debate." In the end he was forced to sign an agreement to turn over the institute's work-team head to the students for hard labor on campus, along with all the members of the work team and the negative materials collected on students.[61] On October 10 the Red Flag Brigade of Beijing Foreign Languages Institute invaded the Foreign Ministry and proceeded to ransack its archives in search of "black materials" collected on opponents of the work team.[62] During the same period two rebel organizations from the Institute of Politics and Law marched to the Supreme People's Court, where the head of the institute's work team was a bureau chief. They forced the court's top official to announce that he was stripping the work team's head of all his posts, and the students gathered all the members of the work team together for a criticism session where they denounced the work team's leader.[63]

The targets of rebel attacks were highly predictable: the rebels went directly up the bureaucratic hierarchy to the organs that sent work teams to their schools. The pattern of attacks traced the administrative hierarchy: the Forestry Institute to the Forestry Ministry; the Geology Institute to the Geology Ministry; the Aeronautics Institute to the National Defense Scientific and Technology Commission; and so forth.[64] There was no point in crossing the lines of administrative authority; students from the Geology Institute had no grievances to address at the Forestry Ministry. In this sense, the rebel movement ran through channels defined by the national administrative hierarchy.

Only after students had met their objectives at the administrative level just above their school did they move to higher levels. One of the first cases was an October 21 attack on the State Economic Commission by a coalition of rebels from the Chemical, Post and Telecommunications,

Geology, and Forestry institutes. More than 300 red guards marched to the commission to demand an explanation from Li Renlin, who was in charge of the work teams in the cluster of ministries under the CCP Industry and Transportation Work Department. Li's immediate superior was Tao Lujia, and above the entire system was Vice-Premier Bo Yibo. All of them were in the rebels' direct line of fire. The students set up a permanent "liaison committee" in the building to investigate the industrial and transportation system.[65]

The Beijing Municipal Party Committee also had helped coordinate the work teams, and it therefore deserved its share of blame. On October 14, three leading rebel groups convened a mass meeting of 50,000 people at Beijing Normal University to denounce the committee. At the meeting Wu De congratulated the students, and Party Secretary Li Xuefeng made a self-criticism on behalf of the committee.[66] The rebels were now virtually acting at the behest of the CCRG; one week later Wu De replaced Li Xuefeng as Beijing's party secretary.[67]

### Running the Movement

The CCRG's extensive contacts with the minority faction and its public support for that faction's cause dovetailed perfectly with Mao's tactical agenda of extending purges upward into the top reaches of the state apparatus. In the course of steering the student movement, the CCRG established strong ties with campus leaders at the major universities. These individuals served as the primary means for the CCRG to steer and shape events, and the CCRG continued to rely on them until the demise of the red guards in July 1968. The CCRG was running a mass movement to subvert the established order in ways reminiscent of the underground communist movement in areas controlled by the Nationalists before 1949. The level of secrecy and risk was much lower, but the central conception of covertly steering a mass movement to challenge authorities in ways that furthered one's own somewhat different political agenda was largely the same.

The CCRG maintained intensive contacts with campus leaders throughout the Cultural Revolution. Reporters from the PLA and the New China News Agency were stationed on campuses, reported regularly on student politics, and established close relationships with key leaders who willingly used them as channels to communicate with the upper levels. The headquarters for these activities was the CCRG offices at the Diaoyutai State

Guest House on the outer edge of the Western District. This intelligence network produced regular bulletins printed in fewer than twenty copies and circulated only to Mao, members of the CCRG, and a handful of other top officials.[68] One Qinghua student leader was told by the journalist assigned to his group that any material passed to him in the morning would be delivered to the CCRG the same day and would be on Jiang Qing's desk that evening.[69]

Members of the CCRG often invited student leaders to Zhongnanhai, Diaoyutai, and the Great Hall of the People for consultations. Student leaders were granted the funds and resources they needed to conduct the movement. Soon after being designated Qinghua's primary rebel leader by the CCRG, for example, Kuai Dafu traveled around the city in a government car and had a female secretary with him at all times. Members visited campuses and attended rallies to make speeches and instruct student leaders and activists. Liaison personnel relayed CCRG instructions to favored student leaders, issued outright orders, and if necessary, backed them up with threats.[70] Throughout the movement student leaders looked to these encounters for validation of their course of action and guidance about what to do next.

The CCRG came to rely most heavily on five leaders who proved amenable to their direction from the outset. They established ties with these figures by October 1966 and maintained them until the movement was forcibly disbanded in 1968. The course and outcome of the movement ultimately depended on the relationships between these leaders and members of the CCRG, and especially on their relationships with one another. As we shall see in subsequent chapters, these relationships were often frayed, and the red guards became a source of deep frustration for the CCRG after they fell into mutual conflicts. In the fall of 1966, however, these five leaders were instrumental in turning the tide of the movement in the direction ordained by the campaign against the "bourgeois reactionary line."

The first of these leaders was something of an anomaly because she was very different by temperament, position, and experience from all the others. Nie Yuanzi, in fact, was not a student at all and had never even attended college. She was forty-five years old, thrice-married, and a middle-ranking party official—a Yan'an-era veteran with relatives and a husband in high party positions. Moreover, she and her Beida dissidents had been part of the school's work team, and she had never led or organized an insurgent movement to achieve control of her school. Nie's only claim to leadership was her signature as the first of seven authors of the wall poster instigated by Kang Sheng in late May that was subsequently hailed by Mao as the opening salvo of the Cultural Revolution. At other universities, officials like Nie were the first to be felled by red guards. Nie was viewed with suspicion and distaste by many of the student leaders—and many of her original allies at Beida—and this suspicion later proved to be an unending source of conflict.

Tan Houlan was twenty-nine years old and had worked for some years as a teacher before being sent back to college by her party superiors. A prestigious internship at the party's theoretical journal *Red Flag* put her in close contact with the figures under Chen Boda who would soon play a key role on the CCRG. She established a close working relationship with Lin Jie, an alumnus of Beijing Normal who joined the CCRG staff. Lin and his colleagues Guan Feng and Qi Benyu instructed and supported Tan during her opposition to the work team, the establishment of her minority faction Jinggangshan, and her subsequent political rise.

Kuai Dafu was a twenty-two-year-old youth league activist and student cadre before the Cultural Revolution who became the most outspoken critic and victim of the Qinghua University work team. He clashed with Wang Guangmei and Bo Yibo before he was designated as an "anti-party" rightist. He was a marginal figure in Qinghua's minority faction until he was lifted from obscurity in mid-September and groomed as a rebel leader by the CCRG. By early October he was the most visible and militant of the city's student leaders, and his actions earned him a reputation as the CCRGs "iron fist."

The final two of the "five big leaders" were the heads of Aeronautics Institute Red Flag and Geology Institute East Is Red. These two organizations distinguished themselves by being the first to lead large protests at organs of state power. Their political stance was eventually adopted as the core of the subsequent campaign against the "bourgeois reactionary line." The Geology Institute's leaders were instrumental in forming the Third Headquarters, and the Aeronautics Institute took over the Second Headquarters and aligned it with the Third. Han Aijing, the twenty-two-year-old son of a revolutionary martyr, emerged as the top leader at the Aeronautics Institute. Zhu Chengzhao, the twenty-five-year-old "cadre transfer student" and son of a bureau-level official, was groomed for this role at the Geology Institute. Zhu led the attacks on the Geology Ministry and was the driving force behind the establishment of the Third Headquarters.

## The Bureaucratic Structure of Rebellion

When Mao and the CCRG encouraged students to repudiate the "bourgeois reactionary line," they were in fact spurring them to attack directly up the lines of the national bureaucratic hierarchy. The subsequent rebel insurgency followed a distinctive bureaucratic pattern. Because the work teams were sent down to universities and institutes from their supervisory agencies in the bureaucratic system, red guards who were aggrieved after clashes with work teams followed these lines of authority upward when they sought redress. Their motives had nothing to do with their inherent stance toward the status quo or with their prior positions in it. The "rebel" factions were initially motivated to attack ministries in order to remove the possible stigma of political labels in their permanent records, and in so doing to dislodge from power the indifferent or hostile majority factions that controlled their campuses. Once they discovered powerful patrons on the CCRG, they willingly pursued further attacks on national authorities even after their initial demands were met.

The decision to use the aggrieved minority factions to renew a stalled offensive on the national leadership does not appear to have been a preordained plan. For almost a month the CCRG tried to get the students to put their differences aside. The strong grievances harbored by the minority factions at the Aeronautics and Geology institutes, which had experienced major confrontations with the work teams, provided them with another opportunity. The daring tactical innovation of these two factions (undertaken with behind-the-scenes encouragement of the CCRG) finally took the protests to the centers of national power. This political maneuver turned the tide against the dominant majority faction and the high-school pickets and redirected the student movement against nominally powerful but largely defenseless bureaucrats.

Notably absent from these autumn forays were factions from the large national-level universities under the Ministry of Higher Education—Beida, Qinghua, and Beijing Normal—whose work teams had been drawn from a collection of national agencies. Beida's work team had already been repudiated and disgraced in the most public and decisive fashion, in repeated on-campus struggle sessions overseen by CCRG officials. The head of the Beijing Normal work team was removed from power and repudiated even before the other work teams were withdrawn, and Kang Sheng himself denounced him on the campus. The head of Qinghua's work team apologized at an early August mass meeting chaired by Zhou Enlai. This removed much of the motivation of aggrieved students at these schools to protest their victimization. But even if they had still had a strong motive, they would have had to pursue the members of their work teams to a number of different commissions and ministries. The specialized ministry-run institutes, by contrast, had work teams composed entirely of personnel from one agency and directly supervised by it. Not until much later in the insurgency did a figure like Kuai Dafu pursue attacks on higher-level officials like Bo Yibo and Wang Guangmei.

These considerations provide further evidence that the motives of the rebel faction were rooted in specific political interactions during June and July, not in any lack of vested interests in the status quo. They were fighting, instead, to avoid losing what had once been a favored position and a secure future—and against the injustice that had been done to them. A movement that superficially looked chaotic and disorganized in fact developed according to a predictable bureaucratic logic. Indeed, the way in which the student movement was "run" and goaded into attacks up the lines of authority suggests that the red guard movement was not a mass movement as conventionally understood, but a form of mass participation in bureaucratic politics.

# 7

## DISSENT AND ITS SUPPRESSION

### *Challenging the Maoist Elite*

The rise and fall of red guard factions reflected their modular organization. Even within a single university, a red guard "faction" was not a single, unified organization but a collection of allied small groups, largely based on classrooms or academic departments, each with its own name, identity, and leaders. University-level factions were large coalitions of smaller units, all collected under a single banner and a collective leadership structure that represented the more dominant "fighting groups."[1] At Beijing University in mid-October 1966, there were reportedly 92 fighting groups claiming a total of around 3,000 members. At that time they were grouped into three large alliances.[2] Over the two-year course of the movement at Beida, the two factional newspapers published articles authored by 358 different fighting groups, most of which had names that linked them to specific departments and classrooms. A similar examination of the factional newspapers at Chinese People's University yielded a total of 196 separate fighting groups.[3]

The basic building block of the red guard movement was a small group of students, usually no more than ten to fifteen individuals from the same classroom, who pledged allegiance to broader factional groupings as they formed within a school. Factional coalitions grew or shrank as these small fighting groups were founded, disbanded, or renamed, and as they shifted their allegiance from one factional federation to another. The strength of a factional federation depended on its ability to mobilize small groups to write wall posters to support its position, attend rallies and meetings, or participate in protest events.

Although the vast majority of students who took part in the movement conformed to whatever line seemed to be sanctioned by Mao and the

CCRG, the loose cellular structure of student organizations made discipline and unity within factions a chronic problem. Splits and defections within rebel alliances plagued them throughout 1967 and 1968. The cellular structure had another consequence: even after the seeming defeat of a large factional alliance, small fighting groups could maintain vocal pockets of resistance, going against the tide long after the alliance's larger cause seemed to be lost. Although the university majority was defeated, some of its proponents persevered, largely through campus speeches and wall posters. And although the Western District Picket Corps and its counterparts ceased to operate by late October, many of their constituent fighting groups continued to articulate an independent point of view, and some even banded together in a last-ditch effort to turn the tide. Some of the rebel leaders in the Third Headquarters themselves began to have second thoughts about the CCRG's manipulation of the student movement and to express doubts of their own.

These dissidents never represented a serious challenge to the rebels, but they developed a daring and coherent critique of the CCRG that reflected a rare independence of mind. In wall-poster campaigns and an abortive effort to coordinate cross-campus resistance, the rebellious dissidents mounted a bold challenge—not to defenseless bureaucrats on the approved list of victims, but to CCRG officials who were manipulating the student movement toward their political ends. This small campaign briefly rattled the rebel faction and angered members of the CCRG. Alone among students at this point in Chinese history, these dissidents had a realistic view of what was actually taking place, while the "rebels" were conforming to CCRG authority and wrapping their actions in a fantasy language of conspiracy and rebellion.

The members of the CCRG welcomed criticism of officials that they wanted removed but reacted with harsh intolerance toward criticism directed at themselves. The dissidents of November and December were firmly suppressed, and their campaign was the last echo of the factional divide that split the student movement in 1966. The CCRG's response is instructive, because in addition to bringing the full weight of China's security forces down upon student rebels for the first time (violating its own earlier prohibitions), it crafted a campaign of vilification that distorted the motives and aims of these dissident students and for many decades warped our understanding of the nature of red guard factionalism.

## Challenging the Radical Bureaucrats

The challenge to the CCRG began tentatively in mid-November and climaxed during the first two weeks of December. It bore a striking resemblance to the complaints by the minority faction about its members' treatment by work teams several months before. The dissidents resented the way they were shunted aside and vilified by the CCRG in October. We have already seen that the students who supported work teams saw themselves as rebels in every sense of the word—and in the majority of schools with radical work teams there is little reason to doubt this perception. In retrospect they accepted that they had erred in supporting their work teams—even Tan Lifu acknowledged this as early as September. But they refused to accept accusations that they were "conservatives" or "revisionist red guards" who supported the "bourgeois reactionary line."

The complaints gradually escalated in an interactive process that resembled the conflict between the work teams and their opponents the previous summer. The first wall posters complaining about unfair treatment by the CCRG were denounced as attacks on the "proletarian headquarters" and attempts at "capitalist restoration." This escalated the dispute to a matter of principle: whether the CCRG was exempt from criticism, and whether it had the right to suppress a genuine mass movement sanctioned by Chairman Mao and protected by the provisions of the "Sixteen Points." As the attacks on the critics continued, the dissidents turned the tables on the CCRG and accused it of pursuing the very "bourgeois reactionary line" that it pretended to denounce. The dissidents asked why the work teams were forbidden to denounce and label student rebels who criticized them, but the bureaucrats on the CCRG were able to claim that they alone were immune from criticism and could manipulate and suppress students however they pleased. The stronger the parallels between the behavior of the CCRG and that of the reviled work teams, the more the dissidents escalated their critiques to the point where they openly accused the CCRG of unprincipled factional designs that ultimately opposed the Cultural Revolution and Chairman Mao. These were incendiary accusations, and the movement was crushed shortly after they were made.

These arguments were highly congenial to former members of the university majority and the high-school rebels associated with the picket corps. However, they were voiced by only a small number of daring individuals and fighting groups. Their wall posters and speeches were reprinted and denounced by opposing red guards throughout the city in a manner similar to the earlier attacks on Tan Lifu. It is through these denunciation materials that we have a record of their ill-fated campaign.

The first public questioning of the CCRG arose in mid-October. It originated in a school that did not figure prominently in the later dissident campaign. Issued by the Maoism Red Guards of the Beijing Broadcasting Institute—a fighting group associated with the school's "majority" faction—the wall poster was focused almost exclusively on the school's factional conflict. This group's challenge presaged the later campaign in two senses: it charged that the CCRG's interventions in its school violated the "Sixteen Points," and it demanded that members of the CCRG return to the school for criticism.[4]

The CCRG had intervened in the Broadcasting Institute's politics on July 24 when several of its members accompanied Kang Sheng to the school to denounce the work team and "liberate" its opponents.[5] What bothered the students who had supported this radical work team was not the "liberation" of the students who had opposed it but the way they were shunted aside and ignored by the CCRG. Three days after the dramatic events of July 24, the CCRG sent Guan Feng and Yao Wenyuan to the school to form a temporary Cultural Revolution committee. Guan and Yao consulted only with the work team's victims, ignored the students who had avoided conflicts with the work team, and unilaterally selected a committee composed solely of members of the minority faction. The critics explained that this violated the "Sixteen Points," which was issued two weeks later, in early August.

This sequence of events bred a minority-majority conflict that initially took an unusual form: a "minority" faction that defended its power against an excluded "majority" faction, rather than the other way around. The majority faction overthrew the minority's "temporary committee" during September, but after the CCRG openly favored the Third Headquarters, the ousted minority faction pressed its claim, accusing the majority of "violating CCRG directives." In response, the school's majority faction challenged the CCRG's initial intervention in its school. It organized a petition drive and collected 600 signatures demanding the return of the CCRG to the school for self-criticism: "The CCRG's handling of the views of the majority faction has been crude, bureaucratic, based on coercion rather than persuasion." The wall poster blamed factional divisions in the school on the CCRG, which maneuvered to put the minority faction in power. "The creation of the temporary CR committee itself is a violation of the Sixteen Points and is a manifestation of the influence of the bourgeois reactionary line."

This early challenge is significant because it presaged two major themes of the subsequent dissident campaign: it accused the CCRG of repeating the errors of the work team by implementing a "bourgeois reactionary line" that suppressed the masses and labeled opponents, and it claimed the right to criticize any leader who violated the "Sixteen Points." Like the subsequent dissidents, the challengers from the Broadcasting Institute buttressed their claims by quoting *Red Flag* editorials and policies earlier championed by the CCRG itself.

### The Dissident Campaign in the Universities

The dissident campaign began in mid-November, and its most influential authors were at the Beijing Aeronautics Institute. In a series of outspoken and influential wall posters, two fighting groups originally associated with the institute's majority red guards developed a sophisticated critique of the CCRG. The opening salvo charged the CCRG with behaving in ways associated with the work teams' "bourgeois reactionary line." The core grievance was that the majority faction was never treated as equally "revolutionary." This slight must have been felt with particular acuity at the Aeronautics Institute, where the work team, after initial hesitation, pursued a radical attack on the school's power structure.

In its first two wall posters the Aeronautics Red Guards complained that the CCRG talked only to the opposing Red Flag faction and ignored differing points of view. It likened the CCRG to big-shot bureaucrats who did not investigate for themselves but simply rode around issuing orders. Drawing parallels between its current situation and the suffering of the minority faction under the work teams, it claimed that its members were denounced as "rightists" and "conservatives," while their earlier pioneering contributions were ignored. This, the students claimed, was a "new bourgeois reactionary line." What did the majority faction do to merit the label "conservative" and be brushed aside so thoughtlessly? Militant students who mistakenly followed the work team with the best of intentions should not be reviled as conservatives. The intimidation of the former majority faction repeated what had happened under the work teams.[6]

After the minority faction lashed back at these arguments with a series of accusations, the dispute escalated to a matter of principle: was the

CCRG beyond criticism? Members of the minority faction complained that their first wall posters were met with accusations and epithets: "bastards," "sons of bitches," "small die-hard group of conservatives," "you are bombarding the proletarian headquarters," and "whoever attacks the CCRG, we will smash his dog head." The red guards continued, "It seems as if those who constantly say they want to criticize the bourgeois reactionary line still have not recognized what was reactionary about it . . . The likes of Guan Feng and Qi Benyu, full of bureaucratic airs, simply cannot represent Chairman Mao."

The criticisms became more pointed and personal, and the dissidents directed their anger at Guan Feng and Qi Benyu, the two members of the CCRG who had been stationed at the Aeronautics Institute to transfer power to the minority faction, Red Flag.

> These people see the chance to use others to attack headquarters throughout the country, ransack the homes of the masses, seize confidential files, and beat people, even to the point of attacking the Military Affairs Commission and Zhongnanhai . . . These are all the CCRG's responsibility. Moreover, Qi Benyu arbitrarily censures some of the red guards for not kneeling down before the Third Headquarters. Does this mean that which faction is leftist is determined by whatever falls from the lips of this Qi Benyu?

The red guards intensified their critique of the CCRG by accusing it of a conspiratorial and bureaucratic style of work that in fact repudiated the mass nature of the movement:

> Certain comrades on the CCRG . . . through means of factional connections, leak the new policy line to certain people who then criticize others . . . How can you possibly resolve problems of unity created by the bourgeois reactionary line by scheming to use this same mistaken line? . . . People who act like tigers whose backside you dare not touch are certainly not leftists. When the masses strongly air their objections, the CCRG instantly decides this will not do, starts plotting behind the scenes, secretly criticizes and issues directives.[7]

By the second week of December the Aeronautics Institute dissidents became more aggressive. They parried the abuse hurled at them and quoted from Red Flag editorials and speeches by Lin Biao that the essence of the Cultural Revolution was to oppose incorrect leadership that was not in accord with Mao Thought, no matter who that official might be.[8]

By far the most incendiary wall poster was one on December 12 that accused the CCRG of posing as leftists in order to engineer a palace coup:

> The special feature of class struggle today is between the bourgeoisie's "peaceful evolution" and the proletariat's struggle against "peaceful evolution," between the class enemies' "palace coup" and our struggle to suppress "palace coups." Today, the special feature of the class enemy is that they "hang up a sheep's head but sell dog meat, wave the red flag to oppose the red flag" . . . We ask the CCRG, do you intend to uphold the guiding ideology of the proletariat . . . Or do you insist on sectarian factional politics under the guidance of petty bourgeois ideology? . . . "Doubt everything" (in reality, repudiate everything) is the guiding ideology of the petty bourgeoisie. "All power to the leftists" (the majority are without power?) is the arrogant, conceited, self-important, and selfish ideology of the petty bourgeoisie. "Long Live the Red Terror" (aimed at the masses, not at the landlords and capitalists, as in the earlier stage) is the narrow-minded doctrine of revenge taking of the petty bourgeoisie and is precisely the "spirit of revolutionary rebellion" so admired by certain comrades on the CCRG.[9]

The Forestry Institute was another dissident stronghold. The primary figure was Li Hongshan, former leader of the institute's red guards. In early November Li and others formed the Red Guard Dare-to-Die Corps and held meetings with like-minded students from Qinghua and other nearby campuses.[10] On November 30 Li and one of his comrades put up a large banner at the Forestry Institute: "Kick Aside the CCRG and Make Revolution on Your Own." This slogan explicitly echoed the frequent demand to "kick aside the work team" made by minority factions in their earlier struggles. The next day Li's group explained its position: "In our view there is a phenomenon in the Great Proletarian Cultural Revolution at present that is not very good: no matter what the issue is, it is essential to seek out the CCRG. Central leaders' speeches are reprinted in large volume, sometimes with large discrepancies. Many people have several volumes consisting solely of Central leaders' speeches, and read them all day long. This is no way to truly use Mao Zedong Thought in guiding the Cultural Revolution." The authors argued that the CCRG should step back from the movement and "respect the masses' creative spirit."[11]

This presentation was restrained compared with the oral arguments Li had made on campus the day before, when he had defended his position in more vehement terms. Li argued that the CCRG had no constitutional standing; no one had ever stated that it would be exempt from criticism; and because the CCRG had not been elected according to Paris Commune principles, it violated the "Sixteen Points" and the spirit of Mao Thought. In fact, he argued, "Members of the CCRG just sit at the upper levels, acting like bureaucrats and overlords, not coming down below, not investigating, always sitting in Beijing, not going out to the provinces." Li pointed out that red guards in other cities were making revolution without interference from local CCRGs, so why should the movement in Beijing be saddled with one? "Members of the CCRG fly about like imperial envoys, spewing all kinds of verbiage, making all kinds of confused statements. Leaders' speeches are cherished like life itself, treated like precious treasures. There are already eight volumes of them . . . China can be led only by Chairman Mao. Anything else you can doubt, doubt everything. The speeches of Premier Zhou, Jiang Qing, Chen Boda, and others all must be analyzed in terms of the supreme directives. You can doubt anything."

Finally, he complained, Chen Boda labeled the majority faction "revisionist red guards," and his speech (to the October Party Work Conference) was reprinted as a pamphlet and circulated nationwide.

> They turned the spearhead of struggle against the masses, at Tan Lifu. Chen Boda said Tan Lifu's speech was a big poisonous weed. I say it was a revolutionary speech, basically in accord with the spirit of Mao Zedong Thought . . . Tan Lifu is an ordinary college student, the son of a revolutionary, a provisional party member, and the head of the Beijing Industrial University Red Guards . . . After the editorial in *Red Flag* no. 13, in every organization, every school, if they were not criticizing Tan Lifu's speech, then they were not criticizing the bourgeois reactionary line. All schools were the same—this was an organized, planned effort to turn the spearhead of struggle against the masses . . . At present the CCRG is a stumbling block at the feet of Chairman Mao, a stumbling block in the way of the Cultural Revolution . . . How can we not kick aside this kind of CCRG?[12]

This brazen challenge enraged the Forestry Institute's rebel faction, East Is Red, which attacked and ransacked the office and broadcasting station of Li's group the very same day. As was the case with other dissidents, this attempt to intimidate only led Li Hongshan to dig in his heels and intensify his criticisms. On December 2 his associates put up a wall poster at Tiananmen charging that the CCRG was carrying out "the bourgeois reactionary line."[13] The argument was essentially the same as that made by dissidents at the Aeronautics Institute: the CCRG was repeating the errors of the work teams and represented the resurgence of the bourgeois reactionary line.[14]

Li's group later heaped scorn on Chen Boda's brazen attack on an ordinary student, Tan Lifu, and his willful distortion of the content of Tan Lifu's speech. Tan had not invented the high-school "couplet" that started the debate, nor had he defended the way it was stated. He had simply defended the basic principles of the party's own class line and had certainly never argued for the idea of "natural redness." The charges against Tan Lifu were distorted and cooked up; everyone realized that the couplet was an extreme statement.[15]

Li Hongshan's notoriety drew red guards to the Forestry Institute for a series of debates. On December 5 Li, with 145 red guards from twenty-three different schools in attendance, read out his wall-poster attack on Chen Boda.[16] Among those who supported Li that day was Yi Zhenya, a red guard from nearby Qinghua University: "With regard to the question of the CCRG, we do not consider the CCRG to be the Party Center. Moreover, especially the slogans put forth by the Third Headquarters, we consider them to be reactionary, as when they say 'we will smash the dog head of anyone who opposes the CCRG' . . . Actually, the CCRG is not even a party organization, much more some kind of Party Center, and even more so is not some Chairman Mao."[17]

As Yi Zhenya's speech indicates, there were students at Qinghua who shared Li Hongshan's sentiments. One wall poster began with the declaration "The CCRG has committed errors of orientation and line and must be criticized! . . . They do not carry out Chairman Mao's Proletarian Cultural Revolution line of permitting full mobilization of the masses; they are following the 'faction boss' [toutou] line. They sit and listen to the faction bosses' reports, and give the faction bosses directives, take charge of faction bosses' headquarters, busy as all get out."[18] A subsequent "Open Letter" addressed to Mao attacked Qi Benyu and Guan Feng, the CCRG members most directly involved in engineering the Third Headquarters' victory.

Guan Feng and Qi Benyu are a work team in disguised form, they are nurse-maids, acting in accord with their bourgeois reactionary worldview . . . setting restrictions here, setting the tone there, not only unwilling to listen to the cries of the masses, but according to nonsensical notions that they take for granted, they incite the masses to struggle against one another . . . Guan

Feng styles himself as the incarnation of the proletarian revolutionary line: absolutely correct, and prepared to strike down those who criticize them. Guan Feng portrays the nation as utterly hopeless, the proletarian dictatorship as crumbling on the verge of collapse, spreading all kinds of rumors and slander, plotting to suppress the revolutionary left, and being so pleased with his own cleverness. In fact, Guan Feng and the others have committed severe errors; they are the culprits responsible for the disastrous nationwide struggles among the masses. They are scheming to incite the revolutionary teachers and students of the Third Headquarters to protect them. It is very likely that Guan Feng and Qi Benyu are careerists and conspirators.[19]

Other dissidents at Qinghua added accusations of their own. One wall poster criticized the CCRG for issuing secret directives during meetings with Third Headquarters representatives, for constantly insinuating that Premier Zhou Enlai was a "compromiser" while shamelessly inflating its own status, for violating the "Sixteen Points" through vicious attacks on Tan Lifu, an ordinary student and member of the masses, and for constantly leaking secret inner-party documents.[20] A second pointed out that the CCRG had been all in favor of wide-open criticism and rebellion until it had achieved power, and then it suddenly wanted to shut down the movement: "Now a lot of people are preparing to criticize the CCRG and debate with Guan Feng and Qi Benyu, but they now want to 'slam on the brakes.' "[21] Another wall poster returned to the familiar theme of the framing of Tan Lifu. Tan's speech certainly contained very serious errors, these authors argued, but Tan was being denounced personally with dubious claims about his reputed "backstage supporters." This was very effective for propaganda purposes, but people ignored the actual content of his speech; he had simply become a kind of label used to threaten people and shut off debate.[22]

As the wall-poster campaign at Qinghua continued, Jiang Qing came under fire for a conspiratorial relationship with Third Headquarters representatives. Dissidents cited secret meetings during which she had allegedly called for a mutual protection pact, actions that showed her fear of the masses and of a genuine mass movement. These were fundamental errors of standpoint, not strategic errors, according to the critics.[23] Another group broadened the criticism to the entire CCRG: "A lot of CCRG members (like Guan Feng, Qi Benyu, Wang Li) really like to favor certain leaders, confer on secret plans, and this unavoidably lends a sense of charisma to certain leaders (like Kuai Dafu) and divorces them from the masses, to the point of manipulating the masses." This manipulation of the movement by passing verdicts unilaterally, putting labels on people like Tan Lifu and the majority red guards, and setting limits on criticism represented a fundamental error of line and orientation.[24]

At Beida there was never a majority-minority split, but the campaign against the CCRG echoed there as well because Nie Yuanzi, under attack by rebel critics at the school, claimed CCRG support as the basis for her position. One group argued that to continue the Cultural Revolution, it was now necessary to "bombard the CCRG." "Are criticisms of the CCRG really such a serious and dangerous matter that they are met with threats? The campaign currently waged by Nie Yuanzi's Cultural Revolution Committee against critics of the CCRG is a prime example of the bourgeois reactionary line in action—not trusting masses, fearing criticism, pasting labels and intimidating people, just like the errors of the work teams. If this is not the bourgeois reactionary line, then what is?"[25]

### Resistance in the High Schools

The dissident campaign also reverberated in the high schools and largely paralleled the arguments by university students that I have already described.[26] One distinctive contribution was a wall poster written by two students at the Agricultural University High School who wrote under the pen name Yilin Dixi.[27] Their "Open Letter to Comrade Lin Biao" criticized his attitude toward Mao Thought as "mistaken" and "un-Marxist." They pointed out that his claims for Mao Thought were far in excess of what Lenin and Stalin claimed for themselves. They argued that Lin's simplistic campaign centered on the "little red book" of Mao quotations was fine to indoctrinate peasant recruits in the army, but praising Mao Thought in this fashion could not solve the problems of Chinese socialism. The authors also criticized Lin Biao's conspicuous lack of contact with the student movement. Unlike Zhou Enlai, Chen Boda, and others, he never appeared in meetings with students and never involved himself in dialogues. How could Lin become Mao's successor if he was so theoretically shallow and aloof from the student movement? "Chairman Mao has taken this road, but if Chairman Mao's successor cannot become a proletarian revolutionary commander, then the Chinese party faces the danger of becoming a fascist party."[28] For obvious reasons this wall poster became highly controversial, but in the midst of the dissident campaign the authors' point of view was enthusiastically received in some quarters.[29]

More noteworthy among high-school students was their organized resistance. The high-school picket corps were clearly in serious decline. Now considered "revisionist" red guards, they lost confidence and members in October and November and were no longer a well-organized force with a clear mission. Abandoning their original ideal of regulating the red guard movement, their remaining activists shifted to rear-guard attacks on their opponents. During November they launched sporadic acts of resistance. Around midnight on November 8 more than 100 of them burst into the Third Headquarters offices behind the Tiananmen reviewing stand, yelling hostile slogans. For the rest of the month remnants of the Western, Eastern, and Haidian pickets put up wall posters, distributed handbills, and engaged in street clashes with Third Headquarters fighting groups. On November 25 they broke into the Third Headquarters offices once again, this time tearing the place apart and injuring some of its defenders.[30]

Activists in the Haidian District held a series of discussions in late November about how to reverse their decline. On November 27 leaders of Beida High School Red Flag—the rebel students publicly favored by Mao and the CCRG only three months earlier—convened a meeting with like-minded representatives. The Red Flag leaders proposed a new organization that would unite their scattered forces and engage in coordinated resistance, and the name they settled upon was Liandong (United Action). The representatives who participated in the discussion, all from high schools in Haidian, drafted a founding declaration dated December 5, just as the dissident movement was reaching its high point.[31] Their declaration was fully in line with the campaign to criticize the CCRG.

Right after the criticism of the bourgeois reactionary line there has appeared a bourgeois reactionary line in a new guise, and this is the greatest threat facing the movement at present. It threatens the victorious accomplishments attained through the blood and sweat of the revolutionary masses. It will return the masses once again to a state of oppression under a dictatorship; it will deprive the masses of their right to educate themselves and liberate themselves; it will result in the deaths of untold numbers; it will turn back the wheel of history. It threatens us![32]

Prominent among the organizers of Liandong were the red guards from Qinghua University High School whose "Urgent Appeal" in August had been the first protest against red guard violence, and whose sentiments had originally inspired the formation of the picket corps. According to participants in these meetings, there was a common concern over the fate of their organizations, but there was little agreement about what steps to take to reverse that trend. What was most significant about this organization was that it included the shining stars of the first month of the Cultural Revolution—activists who now declared their opposition to the CCRG.[33]

### Dictatorship as Democracy: Crushing Dissent

These trends bothered the CCRG and its rebel followers. By mid-December the CCRG had heard enough, and it ordered a counterattack. The first moves came in late November. During the last three days of the month, the Third Headquarters held a large meeting of delegates from its constituent organizations to discuss strategies to combat the dissident campaign. Chen Boda and Guan Feng attended the opening session and spoke at length with the delegates.[34] The counterattack began with the publication of an editorial in the December 13 issue of *Red Flag* that charged that the dissident campaign was "an attack on the genuine left instigated by a small group of capitalist roaders." The editorial was accompanied by an article by Wang Li that extolled the importance of exercising proletarian dictatorship over enemies during the course of the Cultural Revolution.[35] Shortly after the editorial appeared, Jiang Qing met a group of rebel students who had come to the State Council to celebrate the *Red Flag* issue, and she told the assembled students, "We must resolutely overthrow the small group of capitalist roaders and reactionaries. Long live the dictatorship of the proletariat! Without the proletarian dictatorship, there can be no great democracy!"[36] The rebel faction, born as a protest movement against the dictatorial practices of the work teams, now became an enthusiastic proponent of "proletarian dictatorship."

On December 14 the CCRG met with Third Headquarters representatives who peppered its members with questions about how to handle the dissident challenge. The leaders made very clear that it would no longer be tolerated. Chen Boda explained that the students and the CCRG depended on one another for support: "You must also spur us forward, help us improve. We cannot avoid errors and shortcomings. This is quite another matter than kicking aside the CCRG or disbanding the CCRG. You want the CCRG's help, and we also want your help." Kang Sheng added, "We must carry out severe suppression of counterrevolutionaries;

this is the greatest form of democracy . . . Li Hongshan is a little counterrevolutionary ringleader," and "We must carry out dictatorship over counterrevolutionary elements . . . Only revolutionaries have freedom of speech; without proletarian dictatorship you cannot have great democracy; great democracy is a means to consolidate the dictatorship of the proletariat." After students noted that the dissidents were claiming that they were not afraid of being branded counterrevolutionaries, just as the minority faction was not afraid of the work teams, Jiang Qing responded, "They will not settle accounts with us; we will settle accounts with them," and "Do not forget that *we* are the proletarian dictatorship."[37] The students reported that the meeting strengthened their resolve.[38]

An even more dramatic demonstration of the CCRG backlash was a December 16 mass meeting of high-school activists at which Jiang Qing's speech set the tone for a campaign against the high-school pickets.

Just now some classmates spoke about the Western Pickets, Eastern Pickets, and Haidian Pickets. These so-called picket corps had a small group of little kids carrying out the bourgeois reactionary line. The spearhead of their struggle was pointed at you, and this is wrong. Today, we should engage in self-criticism. We educated them poorly; forty- and sixty-year-olds have not taught them properly. Their aristocratic arrogance, thinking that their bloodline is so noble, treating others so rudely—what nonsense!

Jiang was not making a self-criticism, however, because her next sentence contained a political bombshell: a direct attack on the leaders who had worked with Zhou Enlai to organize and supply the picket corps: "But I believe that Zhou Rongxin bears responsibility for this, Yong Wentao also is responsible, and Wang Renzhong also bears responsibility. Make them confess in front of you, how they supported this small group of bastards to behave like military policemen."

Jiang Qing then called out the apparently unsuspecting officials to stand in front of her on the stage and bow their heads to the assembled students, and continued, saying,

Now I will talk a bit about the relationship between dictatorship and democracy. Is our proletarian dictatorship firm? I think it is basically firm. But in some places, among some people, there is a small group that uses weapons to kill people, beat people. If we cringe and retreat in the face of such people, the proletarian dictatorship is weakened. Without a firm proletarian dictatorship,

how can there be great democracy? So we must resolutely oppose these cring-
ing so-called organs of dictatorship that are unwilling to intervene . . . And
we must resolutely carry out dictatorship over this small group of criminals
who murder, beat people, sabotage the revolution.[39]

Jiang made several assertions. First, the picket corps were a violent gang
of reactionary murderers, aristocrats who looked down on all other students. Second, the pickets received support behind the scenes from officials
who pursued the "bourgeois reactionary line." Third, the officials she
named worked directly under Premier Zhou Enlai, who was also sitting on
the stage and who was not aware beforehand that Jiang would spring this
accusation upon his subordinates, clearly threatening him as well.[40]

Kang Sheng spoke next, pressing the point in more specific terms, and
broadened the list of enemies to include the university students who
questioned the CCRG:

The victory of the proletarian revolutionary line represented by Chairman
Mao, and the bankruptcy of the bourgeois reactionary line, has turned a
small group of counterrevolutionary elements into cornered beasts who are
so desperate they will do anything in their last-ditch struggle. Very recently,
we have seen on the streets these kinds of slogans and wall posters, a small
group of people, some write slogans opposing Chairman Mao, especially Li
Hongshan of the Forestry Institute who put up a slogan opposing Chairman
Mao. Qinghua University's Yi Zhenya, Yi Zhenya opposed our Comrade Lin
Biao. Comrades, opposing Chairman Mao, opposing Marshall Lin, what
kind of people do this? (Crowd: counterrevolutionaries!). Right! Counterrevolutionaries, small running dogs in the employ of counterrevolutionaries! We
must unite with the vast majority, but we must struggle against this kind of
counterrevolutionary element to the end!

If Zhou Enlai was unaware of this attack beforehand, he recovered
very quickly by the time he rose to speak. He started by claiming that he
"completely agreed" with the speech by Jiang Qing. He then argued that
in a new movement like that of the red guards errors were inevitable, but
"it is right to exercise dictatorship as my two comrades have just said."
However, Zhou argued, they must recognize that these were very young
people, and they should permit them to apologize and explain why they
acted as they did.[41]

The rebels now understood what was expected, and a wave of repression followed. On December 14 the minority faction at the Forestry

Institute invaded and ransacked the headquarters of Li Hongshan's group and detained him under guard. After two days of interrogation it subjected him to a mass struggle session and handed him over to the Ministry of Public Security, where he was taken into custody. The same day members of Aeronautics Red Flag seized two Liandong members, claiming that they had stolen a motorcycle, and turned them over to the Ministry of Public Security. In the early morning hours of December 17 a team of officers led personally by a vice-minister of public security went to the Aeronautics Institute and arrested the leader of the group that had authored the series of wall posters against the CCRG.[42] On December 18 and 19 two students at Beida who had spoken in support of Yilin Dixi and Beida wall posters critical of the CCRG were captured by students and turned over to the ministry.[43] Tan Lifu was also swept up in the dragnet. He had been politically inactive since early October and had been called in for an interrogation in mid-November by Guan Feng and Qi Benyu. Tan was arrested on December 18 and charged with propagating the "reactionary bloodline theory" and with "possibly" participating in the campaign to "bombard the CCRG."[44]

That same day the CCRG and Minister of Public Security Xie Fuzhi met with rebel representatives to hear reports about the "arrest of counterrevolutionary elements." Zhang Chunqiao reported on the campaign, and Jiang Qing followed with a series of detailed instructions about how to suppress enemies. "Turn the people you have seized over to the Ministry of Public Security, not the Bureau of Public Security. The ministry is run by comrade Xie Fuzhi, and we trust him. The Western District Bureau of Public Security has serious problems; we have already sent fifty or sixty comrades over to reorganize it; the Beijing Municipal Public Security Bureau has real problems." Jiang suggested that Wang Guangmei be dragged back to the Qinghua campus for denunciation, and also Bo Yibo, "because he persecuted Kuai Dafu." "As for those who have beaten a lot of people and who have a bad attitude, you can suppress them, certainly sentence them if they are older. The younger ones you can give a provisional death sentence." Guan Feng was more emphatic: "Drag out the behind-the-scenes supporters of the Western Pickets and shoot them without mercy."

Jiang did not want the students to unilaterally hold mass struggle sessions against their targets; they needed to be properly stage-managed. She complained that students had botched a mass denunciation meeting against Wang Renzhong after they had captured him on their own. She preferred to have the captives taken directly to the Ministry of Public Security to be placed under arrest. "Zhou Rongxin, Wang Renzhong, Yong Wentao, Xu Ming, and Kong Yuan all supported the Western and Eastern Picket Corps behind the scenes. Zhou Rongxin had connections with Peng Zhen; Yong Wentao is also really bad. In the past he always carried out Wang Renzhong's mistake of trying to stall and delay the CCRG."[45] Zhou Rongxin, Wang Renzhong, Yong Wentao, and Kong Yuan were all placed under arrest. Xu Ming, assistant secretary general of Zhou Enlai's State Council office, wife of Kong Yuan, and mother of Western District Picket Corps leader Kong Dan, committed suicide on December 23.[46]

Other members of the CCRG met repeatedly with student leaders during the crackdown. On December 20 Lin Jie defended the CCRG against criticisms, calling them "slander."

> We must firmly suppress this small group of active counterrevolutionaries. We are a nation under the dictatorship of the proletariat; our great democracy is a democracy under proletarian dictatorship. Only revolutionary masses are permitted great democracy. We absolutely must not permit capitalists, American-Jiang [Kai-shek] spies, landlords, rich peasants, counterrevolutionaries, bad elements, and rightists and capitalist roaders within the party to have freedom and democracy . . . Those who oppose the proletarian dictatorship must be suppressed without mercy.[47]

The CCRG wanted the suppression campaign carried out in the most politically advantageous way, and it wanted its student followers under control and on message. In his meeting with red guards on December 22, Wang Li sought to ensure that students understood the correct line on the people who were arrested. He warned against organizing a mass struggle meeting to denounce members of the Western District Picket Corps and others seized in the wave of detentions. He argued that "these little dog legs" were beneath attention. Wang urged the students to cancel their mass meeting and instead denounce the top officials behind the bourgeois reactionary line. He pointed out that mass denunciation meetings required a period of planning and preparation. Spontaneous mass meetings might lead in the wrong direction: "The other day when they struggled against Zhou Rongxin, they asked him who gave permission. He said, 'I did.' Then they asked, 'Who gave you permission?' He said the premier [Zhou Enlai] told him to. So the spearhead was pointed in the wrong direction. Collect more material beforehand, do more investigation, prepare before the strike, and then strike with accuracy!"[48]

The dissident campaign crumbled in the face of this coordinated assault. One group, however, staged a final series of defiant gestures before its leaders, too, were arrested. The high-school students in Liandong sprang into action with their founding proclamation on December 5, shortly before the repression campaign got under way. Over the next week groups associated with them posted slogans and distributed handbills critical of the CCRG at key downtown locations. They also began to appear at rallies and debates on college campuses to refute Third Headquarters' arguments. They rarely sent more than a few dozen members, who were quickly surrounded and shouted down.[49] One confrontation took place on December 7 at a ceremony for the China-Japan Youth Friendship Association. As Chairman Liao Chengzhi began speaking, a group of Third Headquarters militants tried to shout him down and take over the meeting. Liandong members confronted them, and a heated debate ensued, with a standoff that lasted three hours. Eventually the Third Headquarters rebels left in defeat.[50]

Liandong held a mass meeting attended by several thousand students on December 26. Its leaders' original intention was to try to repair their relationship with the CCRG by offering self-criticisms for their past actions. They issued invitations to the CCRG and leaders of the Third Headquarters, but none of them attended. As the self-critical speeches droned on, the audience grew increasingly angry that the CCRG did not show up. Defiant slogans began to ring out in the hall, and several speakers surged to the rostrum to lead chants of "Overthrow the bourgeois reactionary line carried out by certain people on the CCRG." The crowd was electrified, and students threw their hats into the air and cheered loudly. When the students watched documentary footage of Mao's red guard rallies in Tiananmen Square, they cheered in approval when Mao, Zhou Enlai, and senior military officials were shown, but when CCRG members appeared on the screen, they were loudly jeered. Afterward a large contingent marched to the Forestry Institute to demonstrate at the headquarters of the rebel faction.[51]

Reports about the meeting reached the CCRG shortly thereafter. A few days later Qi Benyu called one rebel leader on the telephone to complain angrily that his faction was being too soft on Liandong.[52] Late in the evening of January 6, Liandong members engaged in an angry debate with Wang Li and Qi Benyu on the campus of Qinghua High School. Wang and Qi were defiant and unrepentant, and the argument drew a large and unruly crowd. The next day Liandong denounced Wang and Qi in a wall poster.[53] The most remarkable of Liandong's acts of defiance was a series of demonstrations at the Ministry of Public Security. As their members were imprisoned at the ministry, Liandong members repeatedly marched there to protest. Various sources claim six different confrontations at the ministry from mid-December to early January, during some of which students allegedly engaged in vandalism and physically intimidated officers in the reception area.[54]

The crackdown on Liandong began in mid-January. On January 17 Minister of Public Security Xie Fuzhi claimed that the Cultural Revolution had entered a new stage, and those currently being arrested under newly tightened public security regulations were counterrevolutionaries.[55] The same day several Liandong leaders at Beijing Industrial Institute High School were denounced on a stage, but the mass rally was interrupted by more than fifty security officers who arrested them on the spot. The captives were paraded through the city streets on the back of a truck like convicted criminals and were accompanied by some 3,000 university students from the rebel faction who chanted slogans as the procession worked its way downtown. On January 19 the top Liandong leaders at Petroleum Institute High School were arrested by agents from the Ministry of Public Security, handcuffed, and driven off in the back of open trucks. The headquarters of the organization at Beida High School was forcibly closed, and its leaders were arrested.[56]

The final suppression of Liandong was more dramatic. On the evening of January 24 the surviving members at Qinghua High School heard reports of an impending attack by rebel forces, and they reinforced their rooms and stockpiled bricks, stones, and metal shields. Early the next morning the attack began, and battles spread across campus. The leaders of the Qinghua High School Red Guards, reputed founders of the red guard movement and celebrated nationwide in August, were captured and hauled off to the Ministry of Public Security. The same day a similar operation involving thousands of rebels from nearby universities occurred at the August 1 School. The attackers vandalized the high school as they flushed out the students and dragged dozens of "Liandong elements" off to jail. Eventually more than 100 were imprisoned citywide. During repeated interrogations they were pushed to implicate Liu Shaoqi, Deng Xiaoping, and other "capitalist roaders" as leaders of a conspiracy in which they took part. Most of them were fortunate to be released near the end of April 1967.[57]

*Framing the Victims: The Campaign against the Picket Corps*

The CCRG was not content simply to suppress the dissidents; it felt compelled to build a public justification for its actions. After all, the dissidents had charged it with manipulative and repressive behavior that closely paralleled actions of the work teams and Liu Shaoqi. Its reaction—an all-out repression campaign that exceeded anything observed under the work teams and that broke the long-standing prohibition against the use of security forces against students—appeared to bear out the student critics in exaggerated form. The dissidents had charged the CCRG with carrying out a "bourgeois reactionary line," and they had crafted an ideological argument for a purge of the CCRG as traitors to the spirit of the Cultural Revolution and the directives of Chairman Mao. The CCRG responded with an extended nationwide campaign of vilification that distorted the motives of the rebels and falsified the historical record.

The denunciation campaign completely ignored the dissidents' criticisms and focused instead on the allegedly violent and reactionary nature of the picket corps and Liandong. Both were singled out as neofascist organizations that sought to defend the restoration of capitalism. They were part of an alleged conspiracy orchestrated by the State Council officials who had assisted the picket corps, and through them were linked in unspecified ways to Liu Shaoqi and Deng Xiaoping (Zhou Enlai, who actually directed these efforts, escaped untouched).

The shrillness of the campaign probably stemmed from two sources. The first was that many of the leaders of the picket corps and Liandong had once been nationally celebrated red guards. They had stood atop Tiananmen with Mao in the August rallies, had once been close to members of the CCRG, and had often resisted the work teams in their schools. To destroy the reputations of national models, one had to accuse them of major crimes. The second was that the Western District Picket Corps had actually been founded as an effort to curtail the violence of the red guards, and several top leaders of Liandong were the most outspoken public critics of violent red guards.

The portrayal of these organizations and leaders as singularly violent and reactionary served several political purposes. First, it excused the CCRG's manipulations and repressions by painting its victims as criminally violent and reactionary. Second, by pointing to the cadre parentage of many of the key leaders, it alleged political motives designed to defend a privileged "bourgeois" lifestyle. Third, it diverted attention from the

CCRG's responsibility for violence in the earlier stages of the movement by permitting it belatedly to posture as a champion of nonviolence. All of this portrayal was an elaborate cover for the primary motivation: these students had the temerity to rebel against the CCRG itself.

The campaign to portray the Western District Picket Corps as uniquely violent began with a curious November 19 visit by Chen Boda and several CCRG members to Beijing High School No. 6. Chen and his comrades were reportedly shocked and outraged to "discover" that red guards at the school had set up a private jail and interrogation center in a basement and had in the past tortured several individuals, resulting in two deaths. What is curious about Chen's "discovery" is that such actions had been endemic since August, were regularly reported to the CCRG, and had already resulted in thousands of casualties. At the time, the CCRG had downplayed reports of violence in order not to obstruct student mobilization and in fact had ordered the police and the military not to intervene. Moreover, Beijing No. 6 High School was a short walk from the leadership compound of Zhongnanhai. If the CCRG needed evidence of red guard violence, it was on its doorstep all along. Why had it taken more than three months for the CCRG to notice and act upon torture and murder by red guards?

The answer is that it was now politically expedient to do so. The perpetrators were red guards who were said to have had a connection to the Western District Picket Corps, and the victim was a student in an opposed faction and therefore counted as a follower of the CCRG. The murdered student had been killed almost two months before, on September 29.[58] The case was brought to the attention of the CCRG when students at the school sent an anonymous report on November 18. It complained that the Western District Bureau of Public Security would not do anything to bring the murderers to justice. The perpetrators were described as die-hard members of the Western District Picket Corps, and their victim, Wang Guanghua, was described as a factional opponent who wrote the first wall poster against school leaders. The anonymous report admitted that others had earlier died at the hands of the school's red guards: "At that time there were also people who were beaten to death, but most of them were little hooligans and so forth, so Wang was safe at that point in time."[59] Wang was not just a "little hooligan"—the wrong kind of person was killed.

The CCRG had displayed a cavalier attitude toward red guard violence for months, but this time it reacted immediately. The Municipal Party Committee issued an "Important Notice" forbidding private prisons the same day the letter was delivered, and within forty-eight hours the notice was transmitted nationwide as a central party document.[60] On the evening of November 19, Chen Boda, Guan Feng, Wang Li, and Qi Benyu showed up unannounced at the school. They went directly to the interrogation center and released a number of prisoners. Chen angrily ordered the facility closed and dressed down the students in charge. Chen later confronted the chief of the Beijing Municipal Bureau of Public Security to ask why he had done nothing to stop such activities, ignoring the obvious fact that the central authorities had explicitly prohibited this in late August.[61]

In the course of Chen's visit he discovered that others had suffered in the interrogation center. An old worker had been tortured to death only one week after the red guard Wang Guanghua, and several days later a teacher had been detained and tortured but had survived. Events such as these had been common in high schools since early summer, and the anonymous letter of complaint did not even bring up these cases. It was not the fact of violence that disturbed the CCRG but the identities of the victim and the perpetrators. The narrowness of the CCRG's concern is reflected in an undated dialogue between students from the school and CCRG members:

> *Students:* Wang Guanghua was on the verge of death several times, but he would wake up and shout "struggle with words, not with force!" resolutely upholding party policy. Even in his last five minutes, while being given artificial respiration, he still shouted.
>
> *Jiang Qing:* He was a hero whom you should all emulate . . .
>
> *Qi Benyu:* He put up the first wall poster opposing the party branch, he can be considered a leftist, he is considered a leftist student.
>
> *Jiang Qing:* Right, he should be considered a leftist.
>
> *Students:* How can we characterize his family origin?
>
> *Qi Benyu:* Not capitalist. Small business.
>
> *Jiang Qing:* It does not matter what his family origin is; look at his political behavior![62]

This dialogue inadvertently reveals the core of the CCRG's concern. This was a "leftist" student—the most important point. He was apparently from a capitalist household, which worried the students, but the CCRG reassured them that he was actually only "small business" (a less reactionary designation), and in any case he was on the right side politically ("leftist"). Had the student not been a "leftist," the case would not have merited attention. And had the perpetrators not been part of the Western

District Picket Corps, it would not have been politically opportune to seize on the case.

The CCRG's attention to the case did not end here. After the offending red guards closed down their interrogation center, they formed a new fighting group. During an early December confrontation with students who opposed them, one was stabbed and seriously wounded. The Municipal Bureau of Public Security—still respecting existing prohibitions—failed to arrest the offenders. When the incident was reported to the CCRG, the counterattack on the dissident red guards was already getting under way, and it was clear that the CCRG had a strategy to take advantage of the incident.

*Jiang Qing:* Was his life saved?
*Students:* He survived.
*Kang Sheng:* They tried to kill him because he was a traitor?
*Qi Benyu:* Maybe they feared he would denounce the Western Pickets.
*Jiang Qing:* They were all cadre kids, absolutely lawless.
*Students:* We could not do anything.
*Jiang Qing:* Do not worry, do not worry, we will help you. The leader of the Western Pickets is called Kong Dan, and his parents both have problems. And Zhou Rongxin cannot deny his responsibility.[63]

Jiang Qing's public denunciation of the high-school pickets and Zhou Enlai's aides followed shortly thereafter. The propaganda campaign to shape perceptions of the dissident red guards then swung into full gear, and the shrillness of the accusations far outstripped the campaign two months earlier against Tan Lifu, who had never challenged the CCRG and who had meekly stepped off the stage. The No. 6 High School case was detailed in professionally printed pamphlets that described the cruel treatment meted out to the three victims. One such pamphlet contained twelve high-resolution photographs of the interrogation center, weapons, torture instruments, and a gruesomely mutilated corpse. A drawing on the cover depicted a building in darkness that looked like a concentration camp.[64] Other high schools followed suit with descriptions of similar detention centers on their campuses, reportedly the work of "Western Picket–type" red guards.[65]

The campaign against the Western District Picket Corps for the atrocities at No. 6 High School blended seamlessly with the campaign against Liandong, and the propaganda materials made little distinction between them. The materials on No. 6 High School were included in printed pamphlets and professionally printed books that detailed the alleged crimes of Liandong, an organization that was described in similar terms. In one book, devoted to a public exhibition held at the August 1 School that displayed the "crimes of Liandong," the Western District Picket Corps was described as Liandong's "predecessor organization," and the No. 6 High School events were attributed to "Liandong elements."[66] Liandong and the Western District Picket Corps were accused of "opposing the CCRG," "trampling the Sixteen Points," "suppressing the mass movement," and engaging in violence while carrying out "white terror" in Beijing high schools. They "attacked the Third Headquarters" and even the Ministry of Public Security.[67] Locally produced pamphlets often failed to charge "Liandong elements" with the kind of murderous violence allegedly typical of the Western District Picket Corps. The denunciation of Beida High School Red Flag produced by its opponents charged it with ten "great crimes," all but one of which amounted simply to criticizing either the CCRG or the Third Headquarters. The only charge regarding violence was that it had "incited students to struggle against students."[68]

The denunciations stressed that these red guards were proponents of the reactionary "bloodline theory" of "natural redness." Proud and arrogant about their revolutionary heritage, they were said to have issued armbands that varied according to the rank of their parents in the national bureaucratic hierarchy.[69] The August 1 School was portrayed as a bastion of privilege whose students from high-ranking households led a dissolute bourgeois lifestyle, and the roots of their aristocratic privilege were traced to an elementary school for the children of privileged officials, denounced as a "cradle of revisionism."[70] The violent activities of the Western District Picket Corps were traced to the machinations of proven traitors like Yong Wentao, Zhou Rongxin, and others, who allegedly directed their violent efforts to defend the status quo from behind the scenes.[71]

The campaign tried hard to discredit the dissident red guards and tie them to a nationwide conspiracy. Accounts published after Mao's death claimed that the exhibition at the August 1 School was largely fabricated. Rebels, not "Liandong elements," had in fact caused the damage to the school when they assaulted the campus. The luxury consumer goods put on display to illustrate their privileged lifestyle were borrowed from the Ministry of Foreign Trade, and the cache of daggers and iron bars in fact was on loan from the Bureau of Public Security.[72] Some of the documents attributed to Liandong were obvious forgeries. The clearest example is the purported minutes of a secret Liandong meeting held in the central leadership compound of Zhongnanhai on October 1, two months before the organization was actually established. The document openly declared opposition to both Mao and Lin Biao. The minutes were distributed as a mock "Central Document" allegedly issued on January 1, 1967. It called for the children of party cadres to organize themselves nationwide strictly according to the rank of their parents.[73] It portrayed Liandong as plotting a political coup to subvert Mao and the Cultural Revolution. These materials left little doubt about the conclusions that readers were to draw: "In light of this it is not at all surprising that 'Liandong' elements furiously carried out the bourgeois reactionary line. 'Liandong' is now behaving crudely, like mad dogs. Whoever is revolutionary, they oppose. Whoever is reactionary, they support. They crave nothing more than chaos nationwide. Although they receive enthusiastic applause and secret overtures from clowns in Moscow and Washington, they have long ago been spurned by the broad masses."[74]

In this fashion the only red guards ever to publicly protest red guard violence and the only organization formed to prevent it were portrayed throughout China to credulous audiences as a neofascist organization that specialized in violence and torture to defend its class privileges. The officials who worked under Zhou Enlai to restrain red guard violence through the picket corps and other means—in a period when Mao and the CCRG willfully turned a blind eye—were painted as sponsors of violence in the service of a reactionary cause. These claims would distort an entire generation of research on the red guard movement abroad, and they were firmly believed by red guards in other regions of China who read these materials and repeated their claims in subsequent years.[75]

Some red guards mistakenly interpreted the attacks on Liandong as an opportunity to express ideas well outside the mainstream. The most famous example was the essay "On Class Origin," a protest by a student of capitalist class origin against the entire system of state-sponsored discrimination based on class labels. This essay did not appear until January 1967, as the attacks on Liandong reached their height.[76] The author and his supporters believed that the attacks on Liandong for its alleged "reactionary bloodline theory" gave them an opening to denounce the entire system of class labels. Unfortunately for them, they miscalculated. This was a denial of the party's class line, which none of the critics of Liandong had ever intended. The essay became highly controversial and was widely denounced by rebel organizations throughout the city. The author of the essay, Yu Luoke, was arrested at the end of 1967 and executed in March 1970.[77] There was, in fact, no debate between Yu Luoke and the already-defunct Liandong, and the viewpoint of Yu's essay, no matter how appealing it may have been in some circles, played no role in defining red guard factions in the Beijing.

### Liandong Responds: Violence and Culpability

Liandong's answer to the CCRG was not circulated in the denunciation materials, but its leaders did offer a response shortly before they disappeared into prison. On January 8 Kuang Taosheng of the Qinghua High Red Guards put up a wall poster, "To the CCRG," that was based on a draft by Luo Xiaohai, one of the group's founders.[78] These students were both members of Liandong and authored the August 1966 condemnations of red guard violence.

The authors argued that the charges of violence and murder were an obvious cover for arresting critics of the CCRG. They acknowledged that some of those arrested had indeed killed people and should be punished according to the law, but the arrests were highly selective: "Beating and killing certainly is not something done by these few individuals, and these are not the chief instigators or the primary culprits. The error of beating and killing people has been committed by many thousands of red guards." Moreover, many of those being arrested were not charged with any kind of violence, like "the young students who have spoken out to criticize or oppose the CCRG but who have not engaged in any illegal activities, like the leaders of the [Aeronautics Institute] August 1 Corps."

The authors hit on the weakest point of the CCRG's denunciation campaign by emphasizing the fact that the founders of Liandong had actually been among the first to denounce violence, and that the Western District Picket Corps had been formed to prevent it.

With regard to violence, the CCRG completely denies its own culpability and has turned Yong Wentao, Zhou Rongxin, Wang Renzhong, and certain red guards into scapegoats . . . On August 6 our red guards and the red guards from People's University and Aeronautics Institute high schools distributed an "Urgent Appeal" against violence and gave copies to all the main leaders of the CCRG, but the CCRG still did not utter a word. Because of the CCRG's error, by the end of August, when the wave of violence crested with death and injuries widespread, we were very distressed! We thought it was very strange; why did the CCRG ignore all this killing? . . . On August 20 our red guards issued "Ten Appraisals" to oppose violence, to oppose sole emphasis on class background, and to protect the "Sixteen Points" . . . But by then violence had spread throughout the country, causing great damage to the entire party. Even so, the CCRG only issued appeals in opposition to violence; it never adopted any effective measures . . . And so to this very day violence is still rampant and widespread, the CCRG finally hurries to make speeches and punish a few people. This is firing after the fact, it is already too late, the damage is already done. Why do so little in the beginning and only start to arrest people now? People cannot help but ask.

The authors pinned the responsibility on the CCRG by pointing out that its manipulations and casual attitude toward violence created a deeply factionalized and violent movement nationwide, "a wave of violence unprecedented under socialism." "The CCRG, in pushing all the responsibility down onto the lower levels, onto the masses like this, ought to be ashamed to call themselves communists."

Liandong's counterarguments were lost in the denunciation campaign as its members disappeared into prison. It is one of the many cruel ironies of the Cultural Revolution that the only students to speak out against violence from the outset of the movement were to be remembered as its most enthusiastic and arrogant practitioners. Moreover, the officials who supported the Western District Picket Corps in its attempts to restrain violence were to be charged with supporting and promoting it. Perhaps the most telling distortion of the record is the portrayal of these red guards' motivations. Eager to denounce the students as agents of a high-level conspiracy against Mao's Cultural Revolution, the CCRG portrayed them as reactionaries trying to defend their privileged positions in the status quo. In reality, the motivations of the dissidents and Liandong closely paralleled those of the minority faction before its triumph: they were trying to extricate themselves from the consequences of landing on the wrong side of an unanticipated shift in Cultural Revolution politics. Just as the members of the minority faction tried to extricate themselves from the labels given them by work teams by attacking the ministries where they worked, the dissident red guards attacked officials who had turned on them and had labeled them "revisionist red guards." The motives were rooted in political interactions during the course of the movement; they were not inherent in the position of the participants in the status quo ante.

### *Waverings in the Rebel Camp: The Purge of Zhu Chengzhao*

The crackdown on dissident red guards marked the death of the student movement as an independent political force. Further evidence is the fate of Zhu Chengzhao, leader of Geology East Is Red and founder of the Third Headquarters. By mid-December he had begun to express doubts about the overall direction of the movement. In Zhu's view, the rebels had achieved their main objectives: the rehabilitation of the students targeted by work teams, the destruction of "black materials" in their files, control of their schools, and the support of the CCRG. He called several meetings of his leading group to discuss whether there was a need to further persecute old revolutionaries. He also raised these questions in discussions with members of the CCRG. Zhu's misgivings intensified after he went to Sichuan to bring Marshall Peng Dehuai back to Beijing to turn him over to the authorities. Zhu had a series of conversations with Peng that further reinforced his qualms about the ultimate aims of the CCRG.[79]

Zhu's doubts crystallized just as the CCRG ordered the three red guard headquarters to merge into the Red Guard Congress. Arguments broke out over the election of leaders. The CCRG wanted Beida's Nie Yuanzi, who had not been part of the Third Headquarters, in the top position, but the Geology rebels were vehemently opposed. They viewed Nie as a conservative cadre who pursued policies at Beida similar to those of work teams. She had behaved in a dictatorial fashion toward red guards at her university, labeling all her critics enemies. The Geology rebels supported the large rebel movement that sought to overthrow Nie at Beida.[80]

In late January 1967 Zhu convened a series of secret meetings to discuss his misgivings. At the first meeting he and others complained that the Cultural Revolution had lost the character of a mass movement. CCRG claims were taken at face value, and anyone the CCRG criticized was seized by red guards who had no understanding of the real situation. Zhu argued that the CCRG was not mobilizing a mass movement but inciting the masses to struggle against one another, or, as he put it, the Cultural Revolution was "not a mass movement, but mass manipulation."[81] At its first meeting the group drafted resolutions that complained about the excessively harsh persecution of old revolutionaries, the manipulation of the student movement, and the extreme persecution of teenagers in Liandong. Word leaked out, and Zhu and several comrades found it necessary to write an article denying that they opposed the CCRG.[82]

At a second meeting on February 3 the group discussed whether to confront the CCRG or to ask it to send a representative for a confidential talk. Zhu argued for public confrontation, because the CCRG would be sure to react negatively no matter how the issues were raised. Someone in attendance leaked Zhu's statements to others, and later that same day one of the fighting groups issued a handbill denouncing his "reactionary speech."[83] Zhu and his comrades asked the CCRG to send a representative to talk things over. Yan Changgui came to hear them out and called their ideas "completely reactionary."[84] Zhu and his comrades were angered by this reaction and decided to display their resolutions in a public wall poster.[85]

Wang Dabin, alarmed by this move, immediately denounced his comrades to the CCRG. The leadership of East Is Red was quickly reshuffled, and Wang Dabin took over. Several months later the CCRG announced the exposure of "the crimes of the Zhu Chengzhao counterrevolutionary clique" and organized a denunciation meeting at the school.[86] Wang Dabin later headed his school's revolutionary committee, joined the standing committee of the Beijing Revolutionary Committee, and authored an essay in *Red Flag*.[87] Zhu Chengzhao, initiator of the breakthrough attack on the Geology Ministry and founder of the Third Headquarters, was described as a "counterrevolutionary rightist, a traitor to East Is Red," someone who should be "criticized until he stinks, to cleanse his lingering poison."[88] The CCRG eventually charged that his "counterrevolutionary clique" had "viciously attacked our great leader Chairman Mao, bombarded the proletarian headquarters headed by Chairman Mao, engaged in planning for a counterrevolutionary coup, betrayed the nation and gone over to the enemy, and committed unforgivable crimes." He spent more than a decade in China's labor camps.[89]

# 8

---

# FACTIONS REBORN

---

## Networks at Cross-Purposes

Soon after the CCRG and its rebel allies crushed the dissident red guards, the rebels themselves split into warring factions. Unlike the dissidents, neither rebel faction challenged the CCRG. Instead, they were quarrelsome allies whose mutual infighting was a source of enormous frustration for their elite sponsors. The rebels were not divided about the aims of the movement, nor did the CCRG openly favor one side over the other. The students resisted repeated pleas to unite and became a political liability and a distracting sideshow to the main thrust of the Cultural Revolution. In the end, Mao shut down the student movement in disgust, put China under martial law, emptied the campuses, and sent all students to be remolded through manual labor.

During the struggles of 1966 rebels largely remained within separate bureaucratic systems when they attacked officials. Rebels from other universities under the same ministry were natural allies, and their combined strength made success more likely. When they attacked the ministries in the fall, their targets were clear: the work teams and the higher officials who defended them. But after the work-team issue was settled and red guards went to government agencies to seize power, rebel groups had to choose which internal ministry faction to support. This was a much more complicated question, and they easily fell into disagreements when student rebels from different schools went to government agencies and had to decide which rebel group within the agency represented the "revolutionary cadres" who deserved to inherit the mantle of power. Different choices among student groups turned them from allies into competitors who supported different factions.

The central fulcrum of the citywide split was Beida and Qinghua, the two largest campuses with the two most prominent rebel leaders. Despite the fame of Nie Yuanzi and Kuai Dafu, rebel forces at these schools were deeply divided. The splits were not between majority and minority factions but among the rebels themselves. Because neither faction at either school was identified with the "conservative" university majority, the suppression of dissident red guards did not eliminate the rivalries. And because both sides at each school claimed the mantle of the rebel movement, the CCRG did not take sides but instead urged the two sides to unite.

### Tangled Networks: The Abortive Beijing Commune

At the end of 1966 Mao decided that the Cultural Revolution had reached a crucial phase: rebels who mobilized to rout the "bourgeois reactionary line" should now seize power in state organs. Not until February would it be clear what form the new organs of power would take, but the old leaders of state agencies would be swept aside. In the provinces, coalitions of "revolutionary" officials, student red guards, and rebel workers invaded government offices and took over key departments in regional "power seizures." The most famous case was Shanghai's January Revolution, an operation coordinated by the CCRG and its Shanghai members Zhang Chunqiao and Yao Wenyuan, where the incumbent party secretary and mayor were deposed by a coalition of rebel groups on January 6. In late January they announced the formation of the Shanghai Commune, which would replace the old Shanghai Party Committee and serve as a national model for revolutionized governments.[1]

In Beijing, Mao and the CCRG were eager to enlist their loyal student rebels to carry out this task. In mid-January Qi Benyu encouraged factions within national ministries to seize power and not wait for permission from higher levels to do so.[2] On January 17 he encouraged rebel leaders from universities and state organs to imitate Shanghai.[3] Students immediately began plans for a coalition to seize power in Beijing. Nie Yuanzi called for seizing the Beijing municipal government on January 18, and on January 27 she and Kuai Dafu announced the Beijing Commune, whose goal was to take over the city government and set up a representative assembly to rule the capital according to the principles of the Paris Commune.[4]

The effort was doomed from the beginning because the organizing committee itself was in disarray. Red guard leaders rushed off to seize power at defenseless government offices, and several competing groups arrived with the same purpose in mind. Not surprisingly, confusion reigned.[5] Worse, these uncoordinated power grabs created new conflicts among rebel organizations and soon divided the student movement once again. This new split was unrelated to the factional divide of 1966 and had different causes. Throughout 1966 students were divided about campus-level events, and the minority and majority factions had different views about the direction of the movement. The divisions of early 1967, by contrast, were based on rivalries *among* the rebel groups. The opening wedge for this new split was competition to seize power in state agencies.

During the ministry invasions of September and October 1966 students generally attacked separate agencies and were concerned only with their schools' work teams. If rebels from more than one university showed up, they were natural allies, and cooperation was advantageous. Now, however, red guard groups were no longer insulated from one another in separate bureaucratic hierarchies. Any red guard group could participate in a power seizure in any government organ. Also, a power seizure was a limited good. After the first power seizure, a second attempt to seize power instantly created conflict. The staff of virtually all state agencies had by this time mobilized into contending rebel factions, and now rebel groups from a variety of universities arrived to align themselves with one or another of these internal factions in order to seize power. This was fertile ground for rivalry and conflict.

A prime example was *Beijing Daily,* one of the most visible units in the city. In mid-January delegations from the leading rebel factions—Beida, Qinghua, Beijing Normal, and the Aeronautics and Geology institutes—set up a joint committee to seize power. On January 18 Beijing Normal Jinggangshan aligned itself with several rebel factions on the paper's staff and created a "power seizure committee." It announced a power seizure on January 21. However, Aeronautics Red Flag had already set up a separate committee with a different staff faction and was unhappy about being preempted. It promptly declared a "second power seizure" and took over the paper. The Beijing Normal faction protested, and it was supported by Geology East Is Red, which denounced the "fake power seizure," pulled out of the joint committee, and denounced Aeronautics Red Flag for a "serious error of line." The two sides fought for control until the newspaper was put under army control in March.[6]

A parallel example is the Ministry of Higher Education. Nie Yuanzi sent rebels from Beida to seize the ministry on January 19. The next day a separate ministry rebel group seized power from the first, and it had the backing of Beijing Normal Jinggangshan, headed by Tan Houlan. An argument ensued over which ministry faction to support. Nie's group charged that the leader supported by Beijing Normal had serious historical problems. Tan Houlan, however, represented the views of her *Red Flag* and CCRG sponsors, Wang Li, Guan Feng, and Qi Benyu, who had already cultivated the leader whose credentials Nie Yuanzi now questioned. Nie was pressured by aggressive phone calls from these figures, but she refused to back down. The ministry rebels aligned with Beijing Normal recruited allies to demonstrate against Nie Yuanzi at Beida from January 24 to 26.[7] The standoff at the ministry continued and culminated in an overnight battle on February 1 that injured more than 100 people. Nie yielded only after threats from Chen Boda, who forced her to withdraw her forces and apologize to Tan Houlan.[8] A similar clash occurred over the January 15 seizure of secret party archives at the CCP's United Front Work Department.[9] Yet another example was the tension between rebel factions from Agricultural University and the Forestry Institute at the Ministry of Agriculture, which culminated in armed confrontations in April and extensive destruction of the premises.[10]

In these episodes university rebels became entangled in the internal factional politics of government personnel. To seize power, an outside group had to form a pact with one of the inside factions. This immediately put it at odds with rebels in the opposed internal faction. When other university factions arrived to seize power, they could not do so unless they found internal allies. If they wanted to lead their own power seizure instead of simply signing on to the existing effort, they had to find different internal allies. The only ones available were factions that were opposed to the first power seizure. Once the outside rebels formed such an alliance, they were drawn into the factional disputes within the government agency and fell into conflict with the university rebels who supported the other side.[11]

The CCRG, aware of these problems, tried briefly to start over. It called for a "great alliance" of all factions before any attempted power seizure. In meetings during the last week of January, Chen Boda and Jiang Qing told students to combine their organizations into an allied structure to seize power from the city government, even though more than thirty organizations had already occupied its offices.[12] In response, Beijing Normal Jinggangshan sent a letter to the CCRG nominating Qi Benyu to organize the citywide power seizure.[13] Geology East Is Red later initiated a separate effort to form a joint headquarters, and other organizing committees soon appeared. By early February factions began withdrawing from one headquarters to form others, and some groups joined several simultaneously.[14] The effort fell apart.

The splits created by power seizures exacerbated existing divisions on the two largest campuses, Beida and Qinghua. Although Nie Yuanzi and Kuai Dafu aspired to seize power in Beijing, they had yet to unify their own schools' rebel forces. Both leaders were strongly supported by the CCRG, but they faced broadly based and deeply rooted opposition on their own campuses. In both schools the opposition was led by former allies of Nie and Kuai, individuals with clear rebel credentials and ties to the Third Headquarters. When cross-school rebel rivalries combined with the intraschool divisions at Beida and Qinghua, the outcome was politically explosive and split the Beijing red guards to the very end.

### Beida: Trouble at Ground Zero

Despite Mao's praise for Nie Yuanzi's wall poster, she found herself in a politically awkward position as the red guard movement took off in the late summer of 1966. Nie was a senior cadre at Beida—a general branch secretary and veteran Yan'an-era communist.[15] Moreover, she had cooperated with the university's work team and had not openly split with it until shortly before it was withdrawn. Her position at Beida was due entirely to the visits of the CCRG to the school at the end of July.[16]

In August and September, as minority factions on other campuses mobilized to protest the work teams' actions and overthrow campus majorities, Nie was firmly entrenched in power. There was no Beida minority faction. There was never an opposition movement against the Beida work team, and no more than a handful of students could claim to be victims. During the long struggle by Beijing's minority factions to unseat school Cultural Revolution committees, Nie and her comrades stood conspicuously on the sidelines.

Two separate developments converged into an anti-Nie movement in October 1966. The first was resistance to Nie's attempt to control the red guards. Nie established the Beida Red Guards on August 19, but rival organizations proliferated. By mid-October there were three large red guard alliances on campus, representing more than 3,000 student activists. During the prior two months they had conducted more than 500 house searches and untold numbers of interrogations and struggle sessions.[17] To assert her authority, Nie created a single hierarchy of departmental Cultural Revolution committees and a parallel command structure for red guards. She appointed Sun Pengyi, a political instructor, longtime Philosophy Department ally, and member of the Cultural Revolution committee, to head the Beida Red Guards.[18] Their founding declaration of September 21 ordered all red guards to obey Sun's leadership. New leaders would be chosen, and unauthorized activities across department lines must cease.[19]

This attempt to control the red guards was immediately challenged by the two large groups that rivaled the official Beida Red Guards. They objected that this "so-called unity" was imposed from above and did not represent the opinions of the majority. Sun Pengyi's red guards, they argued, should be considered only one branch of Beida's red guard movement. The separate branches should have equal status. They reserved the right to criticize Sun's red guards in wall posters and speeches.[20]

The second development was a wave of criticism from university rebels that challenged Nie's rebel credentials and criticized her dictatorial tendencies. On October 6 a wall poster criticized Nie and called for her resignation. It charged that the elections were worthless, the candidate lists were manipulated, and the leaders were unrepresentative. It accused Nie of using rebel publications to pump up her own reputation by repeatedly celebrating the famous wall poster.[21] Belittling her "rebellion," it pointed out that her wall poster appeared ten days after the Politburo decision to purge Peng Zhen and reverse the verdict on the Beida Socialist Education Movement. Finally, it charged that Nie ignored dissenting views and suppressed criticism.[22] In response, Nie's Cultural Revolution committee called for a "great debate." In the weeks that followed, one side affirmed Nie and her Cultural Revolution committee, while the other accused her of "suppressing the masses," behaving like the work team, and carrying out a "covert bourgeois reactionary line."[23]

A long critical essay by Yang Xun, an instructor in economics who had been the department's representative on the preparatory committee, expressed the frustrations of many in the school and articulated a powerful critique of Nie's actions.[24] Yang was a veteran party member who had gone south with the Eighth Route Army. Demobilized as an administrator, she was sent as a cadre-student to Chinese People's University and was assigned to Beida's Economics Department as an instructor in 1957. Yang had been an activist during Beida's Socialist Education Movement on the same side as Nie, taking a critical stand against Lu Ping.[25] Yang was elected to the Beida Preparatory Committee, but not to the Cultural Revolution committee, for reasons connected to her critique.

Yang charged Nie's Cultural Revolution committee with failing to mobilize the masses and fully expose the errors of the "right-wing work team" and with falling behind other schools in the militancy and activism of its movement. According to Yang, the leaders had become intoxicated with self-worship. They ignored criticism and attacked those with dissenting views, and the movement was becoming increasingly bureaucratized and regulated, losing its mass character. Yang raised a sensitive point: Nie had fully cooperated with the work team's "right-wing opportunist line" and had been one of its main architects. She had attacked large numbers of cadres, instructors, and party members, yet she acted as if she bore no responsibility for this. Instead, Nie had defensively warned against "people with ulterior motives" who sought to "attack genuine revolutionary leftists." Yang explained that Nie had refused to discuss her criticisms in the early days of the preparatory committee, and when she persisted, she was labeled a "fake leftist" and subjected to criticism and accusations for the next two months, sabotaging her candidacy for the Cultural Revolution committee. Yang charged that Beida's Cultural Revolution was distorted by Nie's attempts to cover up her past errors.

The publication of such criticism in *Xin Beida* showed that the critics had sympathizers on the Cultural Revolution committee—in particular, Kong Fan, standing committee member and first-ranking deputy chairman, and Yang Keming, editor of *Xin Beida*. Both had been allies of Nie in the earlier Socialist Education Movement and had been involved in the famous wall poster—Yang had actually been its initiator and primary author.[26] Kong now led critical members of the standing committee, and Yang pushed the issue on the pages of *Xin Beida*. In late October Nie forced Kong and Yang off the standing committee, appointed five of her allies in their place, and put Sun Pengyi in charge of all Cultural Revolution activities. Yang Keming was fired as editor of *Xin Beida,* and the "great debate" about Nie Yuanzi's leadership ended. The paper reverted to praise for Nie Yuanzi and her famous wall poster. Yang Xun was denounced as an "opportunist" in the November 5 issue, and several groups opposed to Nie invaded the editorial offices and halted further publication until November 21.[27]

This leadership split crystallized factional alignments. Kong Fan, Yang Keming, and their allies joined with dissident red guards, while pro-Nie forces consolidated control over the Cultural Revolution committee and Sun Pengyi's red guards. What divided the two sides was Nie's centralization of power and suppression of criticism. Two opposition groups were founded in October: New Beida Jinggangshan Red Guards and New Beida Red Rebel Army. A loyalist organization, Red Flag Corps, defended Nie.[28] Opponents accused Nie of carrying out the "bourgeois reactionary line"—suppressing mass organizations, punishing critics, and seeking to restrict the mass movement. Nie's followers accused the opposition of following the "bourgeois reactionary line" because "to oppose Nie Yuanzi is to oppose the CCRG."[29]

Although Nie faced a mounting rebellion at Beida, her ties with the CCRG strengthened. On November 16, at Mao's request, Nie led a delegation to Shanghai to assist rebels there.[30] Nie remained there for almost a month, making critical speeches about the Shanghai party leadership and encouraging the challengers with news that the CCRG supported their cause.[31] She returned to Beijing for a December 16 meeting with the CCRG to report on her efforts.[32]

Ironically, while Nie was fomenting rebellion in Shanghai, she was being attacked as a conservative at Beida. Her opponents joined the Third Headquarters, the rebel alliance of minority factions.[33] Emboldened by her CCRG ties and the crackdown on dissident red guards, Nie moved to crush her opponents. On December 12 her forces seized Yang Xun's younger brother Yang Bingzhang and Qiao Jianwu, a student in the Eastern Languages Department, as "counterrevolutionaries."[34] On December 19 Nie falsely charged that her opponents were part of the dissident campaign to oppose the CCRG and had their leaders captured and subjected to mass struggle sessions. Four days later she shut down and occupied their offices. In praising these actions, *Xin Beida* called for a "life-and-death struggle of all revolutionary teachers and students to defeat the counterattack of the bourgeois reactionary line."[35]

Nie's rebel credentials were based on her ties to the CCRG, which in turn were based on Mao's fulsome praise, and this ultimately permitted her to fend off the rebels who opposed her as a "conservative." On December 29 the Beida Cultural Revolution Committee organized a mass struggle meeting at the Beijing Workers' Stadium against the entire leadership of the old Beijing Municipal Party Committee.[36] During this period Nie met several times with Jiang Qing and Kang Sheng, who assured her of their continued support and affirmed that her critics were counterrevolutionaries.[37] On December 24 Nie spoke to a mass meeting at Beida, charged that her opponents were counterrevolutionaries, and called for "exercising proletarian dictatorship."[38] Yang Xun, her younger brother Yang Bingzhang, and Qiao Jianwu were arrested and sent to prison.[39] On

January 10 *Xin Beida* published long articles claiming that two of Nie's former allies, Kong Fan and Yang Keming, were "representatives of the bourgeois reactionary line."[40] An editorial stated that Jiang Qing had declared them followers of the "Liu-Deng reactionary line" and had called for "smashing their social base"—which included the "counterrevolutionary Yang Xun," the Jingangshan Red Guards, and the Red Rebel Army.[41] Her critics now crushed, on January 17 Nie formed a committee to formally "seize power" at Beida.[42] Nie denounced "new conspiracies" by her opponents, "proponents of the bourgeois reactionary line" who "take our party's discipline and distort it as the discipline of the bourgeoisie, as anti-party, anti–Mao Thought discipline."[43] Nie's dictatorial response to her critics—based on extreme and obviously false charges—permanently divided the rebel movement at Beida and earned her the undying enmity of rebel groups on other campuses.

### Qinghua: Objections to a Rising Star

At Qinghua the splits in the rebel camp appeared somewhat later. Like those at Beida, however, they were a reaction against a leader who rose primarily because of sponsorship by the CCRG. Qinghua's minority faction, the Mao Zedong Thought Red Guards, dominated the campus by the end of September and led the campaign against the work team and the "bourgeois reactionary line."[44] The majority red guards disbanded on September 29. Kuai Dafu was a marginal figure in the minority movement, well known for his stand against the work team and his subsequent victimization, but not influential. Kuai did not establish his own rebel organization, the Jinggangshan Red Guards, until September 24, after he was singled out by the CCRG to attend the founding meetings of the Third Headquarters, was appointed deputy head of the new organization, and held personal audiences with CCRG members.[45] His star rose after the prominent role he played at the gigantic October 6 rally, and as CCRG support for him became increasingly clear, his group attracted new adherents and became a major force at Qinghua. By early December he began efforts to unify all the existing rebel groups under his command. These efforts were blessed by the CCRG when Zhang Chunqiao came to the campus on December 18 and urged him to unite the rebel forces at Qinghua. Zhang's instructions were circulated on the campus, and the next day Kuai announced the establishment of the Jinggangshan Corps, which merged his group with the older minority faction, the Mao Zedong Thought Red Guards.[46]

Kuai's attempt to unify and lead the rebel forces quickly collapsed. Like that of Nie Yuanzi at Beida, Kuai's authority was based on his connections with higher-level political figures, not on a long grassroots struggle during which he had solidified his ties to other prominent rebels. Because he enjoyed such strong backing from above, Kuai understandably viewed himself as the voice of the CCRG at Qinghua. Once he assumed leadership of the school's rebels, he proceeded to make decisions after consultation with the CCRG, informing other prominent rebel leaders afterward. He even had his "collected works" published at the end of 1966 in an obvious effort to bolster his prestige.[47] This struck many rebels as presumptuous and arrogant. The leaders of the Mao Zedong Thought Red Guards, and even some of Kuai's allies from his Jinggangshan Red Guards, resented what they saw as Kuai's growing imperiousness.[48] Accustomed to collective leadership with wide-ranging internal debates, the other leaders openly criticized Kuai. He responded with harsh intolerance, driving many of his allies into the opposition and irrevocably splitting Qinghua's rebel movement.

The problems began near the end of December, and by mid-February 1967 the battle lines were clearly drawn. During Kuai's December 18 meeting with Zhang Chunqiao, Zhang instructed Kuai to strike directly against the author of the "bourgeois reactionary line," Liu Shaoqi. Without prior discussion with others, on December 19 and 22 Kuai's group demanded that Wang Guangmei, Wang Renzhong, and Bo Yibo return to the campus for self-criticism.[49] On December 25 Kuai organized some 5,000 Qinghua students to march downtown, chanting slogans that called for the overthrow of Liu Shaoqi and Deng Xiaoping along the route to Tiananmen Square.[50] Tang Wei, one of the original founders of Qinghua's minority faction and a prominent rebel leader, objected to attacking Liu Shaoqi and openly withdrew from Jinggangshan's leadership group. In a December 24 wall poster he cited recent statements by Zhou Enlai that Liu Shaoqi's case had not yet been decided by the Party Center. Tang formed a separate group to challenge Kuai's unilateral decisions, which he characterized as "manipulating the masses."[51]

Tang Wei's challenge unsettled Jinggangshan, and mixed signals from the national leadership exacerbated the divisions. On December 30 Jiang Qing, Wang Li, Guan Feng, and Yao Wenyuan appeared at Qinghua, praised Kuai Dafu's December 25 march, and urged further attacks against the bourgeois reactionary line.[52] But the next day Zhou Enlai told Jinggangshan leaders that their demand to bring Wang Guangmei back to Qinghua had not yet been approved by Mao, and that he disagreed with the slogan "overthrow Liu Shaoqi."[53] On January 2 Tang Wei and two other rebel leaders established the Mao Zedong Thought Column. They issued a statement explaining that they were withdrawing from Jinggangshan because Kuai was manipulating the masses and inflating his personal prestige. Tang's group called a mass criticism meeting of the entire school on January 3 that was well attended.[54]

Undeterred, on January 6 Kuai sent several dozen followers to Beijing Normal High School No. 1 to kidnap Wang Guangmei's daughter, Liu Pingping. They took her to a local hospital and placed an urgent call to her mother, pretending that she had been in a serious accident and needed her permission to perform an operation. When Wang Guangmei arrived at the hospital, she was captured and taken back to the Qinghua campus for a struggle session that lasted seven hours.[55]

Tang Wei's group opposed the struggle session. Its members argued that Kuai was going far beyond what their collective leadership had agreed to, and neither action was clearly sanctioned by Mao. Zhou Enlai was furious about the kidnapping of Wang Guangmei and criticized it bitterly in public meetings the next day. One of Kuai's loyal fighting groups, Regiment 28, argued that his followers' action was correct and responded that Kuai's critics were "spokesmen for the bourgeois reactionary line."[56] At a mass debate called by the opposition on January 7, Kuai's supporters brought slogans denouncing "the counterattack of the bourgeois reactionary line." Tang Wei's supporters countered that Kuai's group was a "new conservative faction" that failed to listen to the masses and was now attacking and manipulating them. Kuai's group attacked Tang Wei for creating splits, opposing "newborn red power," and carrying out a counterattack on behalf of the defeated majority faction.[57]

Kuai's response parroted the CCRG's reaction to the dissident red guards and occurred in the midst of the suppression campaign against Liandong. Kuai was adopting the same stance taken by Nie Yuanzi at Beida: he was supported by the CCRG; to oppose him was to oppose the CCRG, and to oppose the CCRG was an expression of the "bourgeois reactionary line." Predictably, Kuai's former rebel allies refused to accept this sophistry, and the accusation served only to deepen the split. In the days following the debate, several new "regiments" were formed through defections from Jinggangshan. Among the defectors were famous early leaders of the minority faction from the days before Kuai's ascension, including Sun Nutao, an early Kuai ally and a leader of the anti-work-team movement six months earlier.[58]

In mid-January Kuai's supporters made an important tactical blunder when they openly criticized both Zhou Enlai and Kang Sheng. They had long condemned Zhou's "compromising" attitude, especially after his stern reaction to the struggle session against Wang Guangmei. More serious, however, was a January 18 wall poster criticizing Kang Sheng. Regiment 28 targeted Kang because rebels at the Central Party School accused Kang of backing the school's president, now disgraced as a revisionist. The CCRG responded with a severity that equaled its reaction at about the same time to the Geology Institute's Zhu Chengzhao. In harshly worded notes and middle-of-the-night phone calls on January 22, both Chen Boda and Guan Feng ordered Kuai to halt the attacks on Kang Sheng.[59] Jiang Qing openly criticized him about this in an audience with red guard leaders the following evening.[60] Unlike Zhu Chengzhao at the Geology Institute, who persisted in his unorthodox notions and was ejected from the rebel movement, Kuai quickly stepped back in line.

Kuai's missteps encouraged his opponents. They now accused *him* of "bombarding the proletarian headquarters" and "opposing the CCRG." Kuai was forced to make a self-criticism in front of the CCRG.[61] His opponents mobilized several mass meetings to demand changes in Jinggangshan's leadership and criticized Kuai for opposing the CCRG and suppressing the masses—carrying out a "new bourgeois reactionary line." They turned Kuai's own inflated accusations back on him, having been handed a perfect opportunity to do so.[62]

Kuai's January 27 self-criticism was also a counterattack. He acknowledged his errors but charged that "certain people" were trying to capitalize on them to put pressure on the CCRG. His opponents, he charged, were Trotskyites and political speculators, opportunists trying to subvert the proletarian headquarters and restore the Liu-Deng bourgeois reactionary line. His followers attacked the critics, arguing that criticisms of Kuai were an attempt to reverse the verdict on Liu Shaoqi. The incendiary charge of Trotskyism incited an outraged response among the increasingly disaffected Qinghua rebels who were dismayed by Kuai's imperious behavior, which some felt verged on megalomania.[63]

To secure its loose cannon, the CCRG sent a staff member to inform Kuai that it was wrong to label his critics in this manner.[64] This further encouraged Kuai's opponents, and he was forced to admit yet another error after he was confronted at a February 7 mass meeting at Qinghua. But Kuai maintained his stance against critics, former allies whom he had alienated and unified in a remarkably short period of time. In early February six large anti-Kuai organizations issued a joint declaration that demanded a retraction of his inflated charges and new elections for school leadership bodies.[65] The rebel movement at Qinghua was irrevocably split. Kuai had permanently alienated a large bloc of Qinghua rebels.

### Forced Unity: The Capital Red Guard Congress

By the end of 1966 Mao was already disillusioned with the divided student movement and placed his hopes increasingly on the working class.[66] The exaggerated celebration of the Shanghai power seizure, in which industrial workers played the decisive role, signaled this shift. Whether it was because of the students' inept attempts at power seizures in Beijing, the political incompetence of hand-picked leaders at Beida and Qinghua who split rebel forces on their own campuses, or his concern to preserve the gains of Shanghai's January Revolution, Mao came down decisively in favor of an authoritarian solution. On February 12 Mao told Zhang Chunqiao that his new government would not be a "Shanghai Commune" of mass representatives, but instead a "Revolutionary Committee" with a strong army representation and full powers of "proletarian dictatorship."[67]

Mao also had other plans for Beijing. On February 1 Qi Benyu and Xie Fuzhi told rebels that Qi would not be in charge of Beijing's power seizure; the task required firm handling by public security forces. Xie Fuzhi, minister of public security, and Fu Chongbi, commander of the Beijing Garrison, would direct the effort.[68] The Beijing Municipal Public Security Bureau was placed under the authority of the Beijing Garrison Command, which formed a military control committee to handle public order in the capital.[69] This was a decisive shift in the capital's politics: military and security forces would now play a central role.

In early February Xie Fuzhi ordered red guards to withdraw from power seizure committees and form a preparatory committee for the Capital Red Guard Congress. The new plan was to form separate assemblies of rebels from universities, high schools, factories, and rural communes. Only after the various rebel groups were consolidated would the Beijing Revolutionary Committee be formed.[70] The process would be coordinated from above by military and security agencies. Students would not form the new power structures by themselves.[71] For this to succeed, it was still necessary to unify the student rebels. The leaders of Geology East Is Red were strongly opposed to Nie and argued vociferously against her taking the leading role in the Red Guard Congress. Their stance was unchanged by the purge of their original leader, Zhu Chengzhao.[72] One important reason for this attitude was that Nie's opponents, Beida Jinggangshan, had joined the Third Headquarters, while Nie's own organizations had stayed aloof. Qinghua's Kuai Dafu, who eventually became a firm supporter of Nie, was initially sympathetic toward her opponents.[73]

In late January the CCRG decided to squelch the wave of opposition to Nie. It acknowledged Nie's errors and repeatedly counseled her to correct them, but she remained politically indispensable as the reputed author of the famous wall poster that had launched campus rebellions. After hearing complaints about Nie from her erstwhile comrades, Kang Sheng reportedly called them together and said, "This Nie Yuanzi person is not so great. I already knew this in Yan'an. But now, even if she is a bastard and an s.o.b. [huaidan, wangbadan], we still have to support her."[74] On January 22 Jiang Qing, speaking to a large group of rebel leaders, said, "Some people have slandered Nie Yuanzi in the past, but even though she has shortcomings and has committed errors, our overall direction is the same."[75] To stabilize Nie's position, the CCRG affirmed that her opponents were indeed counterrevolutionaries, despite the fact that they were actually Third Headquarters rebels. Wang Li prepared a new *People's Daily* editorial to call for a "class analysis" of splits in the student movement, and in his comments to editors at the newspaper he lumped Nie's rebel opponents, the members of Beida Jinggangshan, together with the recently suppressed dissident red guards on the campus.[76] In response to instructions from the CCRG, Beida Jinggangshan was denounced and expelled from the Third Headquarters on January 21.[77]

Nie's aggressive response to her critics at Beida was rooted in deep insecurities about her backing from above. Her memoirs reveal that she knew that Kang Sheng's support was grudging. In fact, Kang had targeted her Henan party group during the Yan'an rectification movement of 1943, and she had barely survived the ordeal.[78] In his own memoirs, Wang Li explained that Kang Sheng detested Nie and preferred her Philosophy Department colleague Yang Keming, who had split with Nie in October 1966.[79] Nie was convinced that the strong opposition she faced from other red guard leaders was supported behind the scenes by Qi Benyu and his Red Flag colleagues on the CCRG, with whom she had clashed over the power seizure at the Ministry of Higher Education.[80] Nie was a scarred veteran of party politics going back to Yan'an, and from her painful experience during Beida's Socialist Education Movement, she knew all too well how quickly one could fall when the party line changed.[81] Her stubborn refusal to compromise with critics was rooted in a genuine feeling that her back was against the wall.

The Capital Red Guard Congress was finally inaugurated on February 22, 1967.[82] The inaugural rally included speeches by Zhou Enlai, Jiang Qing, Kang Sheng, Chen Boda, Nie Yuanzi, and officers from the Beijing Garrison Command.[83] Despite the controversy surrounding Nie Yuanzi, she was designated head of the standing committee. Kuai Dafu, Tan Houlan, and Han Aijing (Aeronautics Institute) were vice-heads.[84] Geology East Is Red did not yet supply a vice-head because of the turmoil in its leading group after Zhu Chengzhao's purge.[85] On March 8 the three red guard headquarters were dissolved.[86]

### Heaven and Earth: Rebels Divided

This forced attempt at unity was doomed from the start. The same day the Red Guard Congress was established, the Third Headquarters denounced Kuai Dafu's tabloid, *Jinggangshan,* for attacking Kuai's opponents as "Trotskyites" and for portraying them—members of the Third Headquarters—as supporters of the bourgeois reactionary line.[87] Maoist officials were keenly aware of the problem. In a March 4 meeting with the leaders of the Red Guard Congress, Xie Fuzhi and Qi Benyu pleaded with the students to cease their factional infighting; otherwise the new organization would be nothing but an "empty shell."[88]

The students ignored these pleas. Standoffs at various locations persisted and finally erupted on April 8 in a major battle at the Nationalities Museum. One faction had seized power at the museum in January, and shortly afterward a second rebel group had ousted it. The first faction, refusing to give up, allied itself with Nie Yuanzi's New Beida Commune and nineteen other rebel groups. Reinforced by its allies, it returned to the museum on April 5 to hold a mass meeting, only to have it broken up by its rivals, who mobilized allies from Geology East Is Red, Normal University Jinggangshan, and other groups. On April 8 the two sides brought in reinforcements, and in the ensuing melee hundreds of students were wounded, ten seriously.[89]

Geology East Is Red and Normal University Jinggangshan mobilized superior forces and won the skirmish. The same day the Red Guard

Congress issued a directive in the name of Nie Yuanzi and Kuai Dafu that called on both sides to withdraw and stop fighting. Because Nie's forces had been a party to the conflict, Geology East Is Red refused to accept it as a valid order and issued an editorial denouncing it.[90] Geology East Is Red's newspaper announced its victory and listed its allies in the fight.[91] On April 8 and 9 Qi Benyu, Nie, and Wu De went to the museum to mediate. The Red Guard Congress split openly into two warring factions.[92]

On April 11 Geology East Is Red took the fight to Beida. With delegations from allied organizations, it sent six broadcasting trucks to Beida to denounce New Beida Commune. Reinforcements arrived on both sides, and a large battle erupted that continued until the next morning.[93] At a mass meeting Sun Pengyi denounced the invaders as followers of the "bourgeois reactionary line."[94] Geology East Is Red and its allies issued their own denunciations of New Beida Commune.[95] The CCRG issued an "urgent notice" denouncing the campus invasion and demanded that students return to their own campuses.[96] On the evening of April 14 the CCRG met with Red Guard Congress representatives to mediate. Jiang Qing criticized Geology East Is Red for its invasion of the Beida campus, and Nie Yuanzi for wall posters calling Minister of Public Security Xie Fuzhi a "double-dealer."[97] Cross-campus alliances strengthened as similar battles broke out on other campuses in the first half of April.[98]

At first, Qinghua Jinggangshan and Aeronautics Red Flag did not openly side with Nie Yuanzi's New Beida Commune. In published proclamations about the Beida clashes they simply stated that they supported demands that the two sides disengage and solve their differences through discussions in the Red Guard Congress.[99] By mid-May, however, both of these rebel groups openly sided with Nie. The three organizations held a series of meetings along with representatives from a dozen other schools to analyze the causes of the new splits and decided that they were caused by two rebels in the Philosophy and Social Science Division of the Chinese Academy of Sciences, Pan Zinian and Wu Chuanqi. The accusation seems far-fetched, but the two had supported the other side in the infighting over power seizures at the Ministry of Higher Education and *Beijing Daily* in January. They had also openly supported the opposite side in the battles at the Nationalities Museum. Wu Chuanqi was closely associated with Guan Feng, helping draft editorials for *Red Flag,* and Guan in turn was closely tied to *Red Flag* editor Lin Jie, who was closely associated with Tan Houlan and her Normal University Jinggangshan, one of Nie's principal opponents.[100] In late May Nie Yuanzi and her allies denounced Pan Zinian as a traitor for allegedly betraying the party before 1949. These seemingly unrelated historical accusations were directly connected to the developing factional conflict and were designed to undermine the Normal University–Geology Institute alliance. In the debate over the "Pan Zinian question" the allies and opponents of Nie Yuanzi lined up on opposite sides.[101]

These disputes pulled the Red Guard Congress apart. As each side strengthened its ties with other university factions, the balance of forces within the congress became crucial. In mid-May Geology East Is Red protested the admission of a new faction from the Nationalities Institute and later countered by announcing that eighteen of its allies had been admitted as members.[102] The next day the Red Guard Congress leadership committee called the previous declaration illegal and the admission of the eighteen organizations null and void.[103] The Red Guard Congress issued a statement assessing the current stage of the rebel movement on the pages of its newspaper on May 12, and the Geology Institute's allies denounced it and issued their own alternative assessment.[104]

On August 4 there was a violent clash between the two sides during a huge rally in Tiananmen Square.[105] At first, the two factions were referred to as the Beida and Normal University factions.[106] By late summer they finally became known as the Heaven and Earth factions.[107] By this time the two sides had clear and relatively stable lists of affiliates on almost all the major campuses (see Table 8.1). The Heaven faction (*tian pai*) was led by New Beida Commune (Nie Yuanzi), Qinghua Jinggangshan (Kuai Dafu), and Aeronautics Red Flag (Han Aijing). The name "Heaven" referred to the Aeronautics Institute. The Earth faction (*di pai*) was led by Normal University Jinggangshan (Tan Houlan) and Geology East Is Red (Wang Dabin). The name "Earth" referred to the Geology Institute.

These factional divisions were unrelated to the minority-majority split of 1966. The earlier split became known, misleadingly, as a division between "conservatives" and "rebels." It originated in school-level interactions with the work teams in June and July and was sharpened by efforts of the CCRG to steer the student movement. The split between Heaven and Earth was *among* the rebels who triumphed at the end of 1966. No longer bound together in common cause to reverse the charges against them lodged by work teams, and no longer segregated from one another on separate campuses and bureaucratic hierarchies, the rebels competed to seize power in the capital. Disagreements led to clashes and alliances

*Table 8.1* University factional alignments, mid-1967

| School | Heaven faction | Earth faction |
|---|---|---|
| Beijing Aeronautics Institute | Red Flag Battle Brigade | Nil. |
| Beijing University | New Beida Commune | Jinggangshan Brigade |
| Qinghua University | Jinggangshan Brigade | April 14 Brigade |
| Beijing Geology Institute | Nil. | East Is Red Commune |
| Beijing Normal University | Rebel Regiment | Jinggangshan Commune |
| Beijing Agricultural Labor University | East Is Red Commune | — |
| Beijing Agricultural Machinery Institute | — | East Is Red Commune |
| Beijing Agricultural University | — | East Is Red Commune |
| Beijing Broadcasting Institute | Beijing Commune | Red Guard Army |
| Beijing Chemical Institute | Sixteen Points Revolutionary Rebel Brigade | East Is Red Commune; Red Flag Commune |
| Beijing Chemical Fibers Institute | Red Flag | East Is Red Commune |
| Beijing Chinese Medicine Institute | — | Red Flag Battle Regiment |
| Beijing Construction Institute | New August 1 | August 1 Red Guard Headquarters; August 1 Battle Regiment |
| Beijing Electric Power Institute | Jinggangshan | East Is Red Brigade |
| Beijing Film Academy | Jinggangshan Theater Brigade | East Is Red; Mao Zedong Communist Commune Alliance |
| Beijing Foreign Languages Institute | Red Flag Battle Brigade | Red Flag Revolutionary Rebel Regiment |
| Beijing Foreign Languages Institute No. 2 | Red Guards | Capital Red Guard Regiment |
| Beijing Forestry Institute | Lu Xun Commune | East Is Red Commune |
| Beijing Industrial Institute | Red Flag Commune | East Is Red Commune |
| Beijing Industrial University | Nil. | East Is Red Commune |
| Beijing Institute of Commerce | — | Red Rebel Army |
| Beijing Institute of Economics | — | Red Flag Commune; East Is Red Commune |
| Beijing Institute of Finance and Banking | — | Beijing Commune August 8 Battle Brigade |
| Beijing Institute of Foreign Trade | East Is Red Commune | Prairie Fire Commune |
| Beijing Institute of Irrigation and Hydropower | — | Red Guards |
| Beijing Institute of Politics and Law | Politics and Law Brigade | Politics and Law Commune |

| Institution | | |
| --- | --- | --- |
| Beijing Languages Institute | Red Flag | East Is Red Brigade |
| Beijing Light Industrial Institute | Mao Zedong Thought Red Guards; Red Eagle Brigade | July 29 Brigade |
| Beijing Machinery Institute | East Is Red Commune | Red Flag Commune; East Is Red Commune Red Alliance Battle Regiment |
| Beijing Medical College | August 18 Red Guards | Long March Red Guards; Prairie Fire Commune |
| Beijing Mining Institute | East Is Red Commune | Beijing Red Guards; East Is Red Commune Rebel-to-the-End Regiment |
| Beijing Normal Institute | — | East Is Red Commune; Jinggangshan Commune |
| Beijing Petroleum Institute | Daqing Commune | Beijing Commune; Daqing Commune Jinggangshan Column |
| Beijing Post and Telecommunications Institute | Gutian Rebel Brigade | East Is Red Commune |
| Beijing Railway Institute | Red Flag Commune | Jinggangshan Battle Regiment |
| Beijing Sports Institute | Mao Zedong Thought Commune; Sport System Revolutionary Rebel Brigade | Nil. |
| Beijing Steel Institute | — | Revolutionary Rebel Commune |
| Central Academy of Arts and Crafts | — | East Is Red Commune |
| Central Academy of Fine Arts | Red Flag Regiment | — |
| Central Academy of Music | — | Mao Zedong Thought Battle Regiment; Red Crag Regiment |
| Central Institute of Finance and Economics | August 8 Battle Regiment | Beijing Commune August 8 Battle Regiment |
| Central Nationalities Institute | Kangda Commune | East Is Red Commune |
| Chinese Academy of Music | — | Red Guard Jinggangshan Brigade |
| Chinese Medical College | Facing the Sun; To the Finish Battle Brigade | — |
| Chinese People's University | Renda Triple Red | New Renda Commune |
| Chinese University of Science and Technology | — | East Is Red Commune |
| Institute of International Relations | Maoism Red Guards | — |

*Sources:* Bu Weihua (2000), 111–112, verified and revised on the basis of the following sources: *Daqing gongshe*, 27 May 1967, 31 August 1967 (CCRM 2001, 6:2000), *Dongfanghong bao*, 11 April 1967 (CCRM 2001, 9:3266–3267); and *Dongfanghong bao*, 19 May 1967 (CCRM 2001, 9:3314–3315).

with existing intrabureaucratic factions, which in turn led each side to mobilize allies on other campuses to help them. The deep-seated splits on the largest campuses, Beida and Qinghua, provided large and powerful allies for opposing sides in these rivalries and ensured that neither side could overwhelm the other. Survival required off-campus allies, and alliances grew to create a citywide political gridlock, an interlocking puzzle of rivalries and alliances that was impervious to the pleas of the CCRG and the increasingly active military officials.

# 9

---

## ENDGAME

---

### Fighting Not to Lose

The rising involvement of military and security forces signaled that the capital's student movement had outlived its usefulness. The deepening split between the Heaven and Earth factions turned the red guards into a political liability. Despite the failure to forge unity through the Red Guard Congress, the authorities nonetheless moved ahead with plans to establish the Beijing Revolutionary Committee. When it was finally established on April 20, 1967, it had been more than four months since the first such regional government had been certified, and five provinces already had done so.[1]

Establishing a revolutionary committee signaled that the end of the mass movement was near. In order to be certified by the central government, a revolutionary committee had to have representatives of three different constituencies: army officers, civilian officials considered "revolutionary cadres," and leaders of red guard and other mass organizations.[2] Once Mao and the CCRG certified a revolutionary committee, it was free to use military and security forces against challengers. In the prior phase of the Cultural Revolution it had been open season on party officials—almost no one was off limits. Once the central authorities approved a revolutionary committee, it represented Mao's "proletarian headquarters." Opposition was counterrevolution.

This drastic shift could be very confusing outside Beijing, where local attempts to seize power created factional divisions just as deep as in Beijing. Unlike Beijing, the splits in the regions were genuine contests over political power. Local red guards had to decide whether to support a local revolutionary committee or to denounce it as a "fake power seizure." The longer the central authorities took to decide whether to sanction a power seizure, the longer the factional fighting lasted, and the deeper the divisions.[3]

This did not occur in Beijing, where there was never a serious contest for control of the capital or the central government. Mao and the CCRG were in control of the entire process. The campaign against the dissident red guards made very clear which students had CCRG support. After the initial confusion, preparations for Beijing's power seizure were given to Minister of Public Security Xie Fuzhi and the commander of the Beijing Garrison, Fu Chongbi. The CCRG told red guards repeatedly that this was Mao's plan for the capital. The splits in the student movement were not about this plan.

There could be no question of the authority of Xie Fuzhi, who was chosen to head the Beijing Revolutionary Committee. Xie, minister of public security since 1959, had worked closely with the CCRG. In August 1966 he was promoted to alternate membership in the Politburo, and in March 1967 he was added to the Standing Committee of the CCP Military Affairs Commission.[4] Fu Chongbi, commander of the Beijing Garrison, was one of four revolutionary committee vice-chairmen.[5] The capital's new government represented an impressive concentration of repressive power.

The Beijing Revolutionary Committee never faced an organized challenge. Its problems were internal: student factionalism was imported into the committee. Nie Yuanzi was one of the revolutionary committee's four vice-chairmen. Her appointment was a foregone conclusion after she became head of the Red Guard Congress in March. It was already apparent that one wing of the rebel movement strongly opposed her, and her CCRG sponsors already had doubts about her political skills. By the time the Beijing Revolutionary Committee was established, however, the situation had worsened rather than improved. Violent clashes had already occurred, and the two rival rebel alliances were almost fully formed. It was nonetheless necessary to have a "mass representative" in the municipal leadership, and Nie fit the bill. Two of Nie's red guard allies, Kuai Dafu of Qinghua and Han Aijing of the Aeronautics Institute, were among the twenty people appointed to the standing committee. Nie's most outspoken opponents, however, also had seats in the new power structure: Tan Houlan of Normal University was on the standing committee, and Wang Dabin of the Geology Institute joined her after a brief delay.[6] The infighting between the Heaven and Earth factions brought discord into the new organs of power and created frictions among its leaders and occasional challenges to Xie Fuzhi.

## Campus Revolutionary Committees

The Beijing Revolutionary Committee was intended to help unify the student movement, but in fact it had the opposite effect. This was just the first step in creating a new municipal government. Once the city's power structure was settled, parallel committees were to be created in organizations throughout the city, including universities. For red guards, this created an urgent need to push for the upper hand in school power struggles. Factional conflict intensified as each side sought to improve its position before the final political settlement. This was the primary reason that rebel factions recruited off-campus allies and formed cross-campus alliances— allies were necessary to prevent defeat at the hands of one's rivals. Signals that the movement would soon end intensified factionalism and spurred the formation of large alliances.

The central axis of contention was at Beida and Qinghua. Both Nie Yuanzi and Kuai Dafu now occupied prominent posts in the new city government, but they had both alienated a large part of their own schools' rebel movements. Their growing dispute with Earth-faction rebels strengthened their internal opponents by providing them with powerful allies. These allies, moreover, were often free to take the offensive against their opponents because they were unchallenged on their own campuses. Nie Yuanzi and Kuai Dafu were forced to play defense throughout the Cultural Revolution, but their key Earth-faction opponents were not.

The most powerful and aggressive of these opponents was Geology East Is Red. This rebel group had pioneered the attacks on central ministries in September 1966 and had coordinated the founding of the Third Headquarters. It was unchallenged on its own campus after the defeat of the majority faction in 1966. The Geology Institute was one of the first to establish a revolutionary committee—on April 3, even before the municipal government, with Wang Dabin as chairman.[7] Beijing Normal University was the third school to establish a revolutionary committee. Jinggangshan Commune, led by Tan Houlan, had dominated the school's rebel movement for months. Tan was now on the Standing Committee of the Beijing Revolutionary Committee and became the head of the Beijing Normal Revolutionary Committee on April 29.[8] Her group was free to assist Earth-faction allies on other campuses without needing to defend its home turf. Beijing Aeronautics established its revolutionary committee next, on May 20.[9] Led by Red Flag's Han Aijing, also a member of the Standing Committee of the Beijing Revolutionary Committee, it was the only one of the three leading Heaven-faction members that did not face strong intracampus opposition.

The escalating conflict between Heaven and Earth impeded the formation of revolutionary committees on campuses with divided rebel movements. When the weaker side could call on outside allies, stalemates resulted. Progress in completing campus "great alliances" was very slow. Only three more universities established revolutionary committees in late May, three in June, and two in July. By this time the split between Heaven and Earth was complete, and further progress ground to a halt. Only two more universities established revolutionary committees during 1967, and they were small institutions of marginal political importance.[10] Only fourteen universities had established a "great alliance," and some of these revolutionary committees fell apart after the Heaven-Earth split.

The most glaring failures were Beida and Qinghua. Neither Nie Yuanzi nor Kuai Dafu was ever able to establish revolutionary committees. Nie was now one of five top officials in the city, but she was constantly fending off vigorous challenges from campus opponents and their allies. Her inability to unify Beida was an embarrassment for her and the Beijing Revolutionary Committee. Kuai Dafu was similarly frustrated. Clearly China's most prominent student leader, he could not even command the undivided support of rebels in his own school. Kuai's political frustrations began in May, when he formed a preparatory group to establish Qinghua's revolutionary committee.[11] Shortly after several other institutions established revolutionary committees, Kuai pushed to complete the process at Qinghua.[12] Zhou Enlai and other central officials were invited to a rally to celebrate on May 30. The day before, however, several anti-Kuai groups formed a large new anti-Kuai alliance with a confident proclamation in a new rebel newspaper. In response, Zhou Enlai canceled his appearance at the last minute, leaving unresolved the question of the Qinghua revolutionary committee.[13]

### Rebuilding Authority: The Cadre Question

The campaign to establish revolutionary committees signaled another sudden shift—almost a U-turn—in red guard politics. To reestablish school power structures, one needed administrators certified as "revolutionary cadres." Up to this point cadres had primarily been targets of attack, but now this changed. The shift in political line was foreshadowed on March 1 by a *Red Flag* editorial that called for a more balanced evaluation of cadres' past errors and for accepting many of them back into the fold.[14] A more emphatic statement was an article and editorial in the pivotal *Red Flag* issue of March 30. An "investigation report" described how the Qinghua work team had attacked the vast majority of cadres at the school, and indeed the entire party organization, as "thoroughly rotten."[15] The "bourgeois reactionary line," formerly denounced only for suppressing student rebels, was now reinterpreted to emphasize the sufferings of cadres. At one stroke, cadres were transformed from targets of the rebels to fellow victims of the "bourgeois reactionary line."[16] This added yet another twist in the convoluted political logic of the Cultural Revolution. Rebels who resisted restoring cadres to their posts could now be accused of following the "bourgeois reactionary line."

This article marked an important shift in university politics: cadres now became potential targets for recruitment by red guard factions hoping to establish a revolutionary committee. In schools where the rebels were united—the Geology Institute, the Aeronautics Institute, and Beijing Normal University—this was not a contentious process. One faction vetted the school's cadres and judged their political reliability. But in schools where two rebel factions faced off, the process was extremely contentious in two ways. First, the two rebel groups competed to attract cadres to their side. Second, when a cadre joined one faction, he or she immediately became a target for repudiation by the other. Each side had powerful incentives to denounce the cadres pledged to the other side, and this forced each faction to defend the cadres pledged to it. The "cadre question" became part of intensified competition between opposing rebel groups. On divided campuses the attempt to ease the plight of cadres ironically intensified the attacks on them.

This shift had another important implication. For the first time since the work-team period the question of the status quo ante and individuals' positions in it came to the fore. As red guards evaluated the cadres' past behavior, they had to consider broader questions. What was the nature of the previous power structures? Were they fundamentally corrupt, riddled with unsuitable officials, or were there only a small handful of miscreants who deserved to be purged? If cadres had committed errors, how serious were they, and how thoroughly would they need to be reformed? What about their loyal followers in the past, the rank-and-file party members and student cadres who had done their bidding? Should they be vetted as well?

These issues potentially activated status-based conflicts that to this point in the Beijing movement had played at most a secondary role. The cadre question raised issues about the status quo that had clear implications for the interests of all who had formerly held favored positions within it—not just cadres but all rank-and-file party members, student cadres, and political activists. From the beginning, the minority faction and the rebel movement that grew from it were led by rank-and-file party members and student cadres who had inadvertently found themselves on the wrong side of the work teams and who had suffered severe status reversals as a result. Their outrage at the work teams and their invasions of ministry offices in search of "black materials" illustrated their overriding interest in restoring their status and preserving their future security and careers. But rebel factions were not internally uniform; they also recruited large numbers of individuals who had no favored position in the status quo ante and no real vested interests in preserving it. This raised an intriguing possibility: would rebel groups now articulate different positions on the status quo ante, with more moderate stances on the cadre question being articulated by former party members and student cadres, and more radical stances being articulated by those with weaker interests in restoring what had existed before? In the end, did the Heaven-Earth split embody underlying status conflicts?

Status-based conflicts were activated on college campuses only under certain conditions. In schools that were dominated by one unified rebel group, factions did not articulate different views on the issue. On campuses where the rebel movement was divided, however, it was more likely that status conflicts might come to the fore. At Beida these divisions never appeared. Both Nie Yuanzi and her opponents declared their firm allegiance to the new line on the cadre question and competed to attract former cadres to their side. Their positions on the former Beida power structure were indistinguishable. At Qinghua, by contrast, status-based conflicts were activated in a highly visible way. Kuai Dafu reacted very negatively to the *Red Flag* editorial that called for the rehabilitation of "revolutionary cadres." His opponents, long searching for a way to gain the upper hand, jumped at the chance to portray Kuai as out of step with the CCRG and opportunistically adopted the cadre question as their defining cause.

### Beida: Competitive Recruitment, Mutual Recrimination

Early in 1967 Nie Yuanzi began rebuilding Beida's administration in anticipation of her assumption of permanent political power. In March she held meetings where cadres were asked to declare their support for the revolution by pledging loyalty to Nie's Cultural Revolution committee. At the end of March two prominent members of the former Beida Party Standing Committee, Cui Xiongkun and Vice-President Zhou Peiyuan, pledged support.[17] In the context of the new line articulated that month in the pages of *Red Flag*, this touched off competition between Nie and her opponents to attract cadres to their side.

To understand why factional conflict over the cadre issue at Beida unfolded the way it did, we should recall that the Beida factions represented rival wings of a movement against the old party leadership that originated within the party apparatus itself. They did not offer rival programs or articulate different stances on the status quo ante. They disagreed vehemently about actions taken by Nie Yuanzi as she consolidated power over the red guards and the Cultural Revolution committee, but neither side had an interest in defining the cadre question differently. Nie was the first to offer cadres the opportunity to liberate themselves by pledging support to her side. Her opponents simply competed to recruit cadres to Jinggangshan on equally generous terms. For cadres the primary consideration was to anticipate which side had a better chance of prevailing. This choice was crucial because as soon as a cadre pledged support to one side, he or she was lauded as "revolutionary" by that side and immediately denounced as "reactionary" by the other side.

Nie charged that her opponents were "old conservatives" who were trying to "reverse verdicts,"[18] but this rhetoric was tendentious and misleading. Both sides actively courted former cadres. Nie started the process in March by encouraging "revolutionary" cadres to "take a stand" for her Cultural Revolution committee. The opposition took the upper hand in mid-1967, when Nie's position appeared to be weakening. Zhou Peiyuan switched sides and signed a public declaration of support for the opposition along with 133 other cadres.[19]

The similarity of each side's stance is seen vividly in the cases of Ge Hua and Cui Xiongkun, two members of the old Beida Party Standing Committee who sided with Nie Yuanzi in the initial controversy created by the famous wall poster. Cui Xiongkun sided with Nie in March 1967 and was put in charge of the school's campaign against the old party committee.[20] At the end of November he became vice-head of a group preparing to restore Beida's party organization.[21] Ge Hua, on the other hand, declared for the opposition and was celebrated by it as a "revolutionary cadre," as were Nie's old leftist comrades Kong Fan and Yang Keming.[22] In early October

Nie's faction issued a call to "drag out" Ge Hua and demanded that Jinggangshan surrender him for struggle sessions. On October 9 it staged a mass rally to denounce him as the "black hand" behind the opposition.[23] Nie's forces continued their accusations against Ge Hua, and on December 3 they captured him for interrogations and struggle sessions.[24] In retaliation, Jinggangshan captured Cui Xiongkun on December 30, 1967, and staged a mass struggle session against him as one of the primary architects of the old Beida. Nie's forces held another mass struggle session against Ge Hua on January 10, 1968.[25]

The two sides also adopted identical positions on the restoration of the party organization, which had lain dormant since mid-1966. In November 1967 Nie announced plans to vet the qualifications of party members and restore the Beida party organization.[26] Jinggangshan did not object but complained about its exclusion from the process. There were many prominent party members in the opposition, and by excluding them Nie had "usurped the Beida party organization."[27] In the absence of substantive differences between the two factions on the "cadre question," status politics never developed at Beida.

## Qinghua: Doctrinal Divergence

Qinghua was a different story, but not because of preexisting differences in the composition of the two factions. The doctrinal divergence between the two factions was due to yet another strategic blunder by Kuai Dafu that provided an opening for his opponents. In mid-March Kuai, still confident of victory, announced plans to rebuild department-level power structures. The opposition saw this as a continuation of his campaign against "Trotskyites" and an effort to place his own people in power. In late March 1967, when Lin Jie came to Qinghua to discuss the proposed content of the forthcoming *Red Flag* article about the Qinghua work team and the cadre question, Kuai's group opposed the interpretation, but Lin published the articles without significant changes.[28]

Kuai's group felt that the new line on cadres hurt its cause at Qinghua. Instead of embracing the new political line, as did Nie Yuanzi, his supporters openly challenged *Red Flag*. They alleged that it had not said anything about the severity of cadres' errors and had failed to praise the students' attacks on cadres. They charged that the article prepared for the restoration of capitalism at Qinghua.[29] Kuai's newspaper claimed that

Qinghua's cadres had been more deeply infected by the revisionist line under Jiang Nanxiang than cadres in other schools.[30]

Kuai's reaction handed his opponents an opportunity to embrace the new CCRG policy, show their allegiance to *Red Flag*, and attack Kuai for opposing the CCRG. The anti-Kuai forces had not previously raised the cadre question. As Shen Ruhuai, emerging leader of the growing anti-Kuai alliance, later wrote,

> Before this, the cadre question was not something that [we] had emphasized very much . . . I certainly never realized the importance of the cadre question. Our attention was focused entirely on the issue of opposition to Kuai Dafu's red guards taking power. Now, in looking back and rereading the editorials in *Red Flag* . . . I experienced a sudden realization . . . In the past we had opposed political power by Kuai Dafu's red guards, but we had never proposed an alternative solution. Now we suddenly realized that the final answer to the Qinghua problem was a three-in-one revolutionary committee under military leadership. This was best way to supplant political control by Kuai Dafu's red guards.[31]

At this point Kuai Dafu was riding high. He had finally gained Mao's approval to hold a massive struggle session at Qinghua on April 10 against Wang Guangmei.[32] Leaders of the loose anti-Kuai alliance, worried about Kuai's growing influence, concluded that they should push for a revolutionary committee that included large numbers of liberated cadres as a way to prevent a dictatorship by Kuai. "The essay by the *Red Flag* commentator had given us an excellent opportunity. We had to seize this opportunity, establish a new organization, raise high the banner of thoroughly criticizing the bourgeois reactionary line on the cadre question, and struggle to realize a revolutionary triple alliance at Qinghua."[33]

The opposition held a mass meeting on April 14 and founded the Jinggangshan Regiment April 14 Column. The group was referred to simply as "April 14," commonly rendered as "414." At its founding rally it criticized Kuai for adhering to the bourgeois reactionary line on the cadre question and exercising a dictatorship over the masses.[34] Some 700 individuals attended the founding rally, representing more than 200 small fighting groups. This was the first time that the anti-Kuai forces had stated their opposition as a matter of political principle: Kuai was a "fake leftist," and cadres urgently needed to be liberated.[35]

This strategic calculation was what led Kuai's opponents to emphasize the liberation of cadres—not an inherent interest in restoring the status quo ante. But taking this public position brought a train of consequences. First, Kuai's group felt compelled to defend its position and denounce its opponents as an "illegal organization" that was engaged in a "counterrevolutionary attempt at capitalist restoration." This led it into increasingly harsh assessments of the cadres and the party organization at Qinghua.[36] This in turn led 414 to hammer more insistently in favor of the broad "liberation" of Qinghua cadres—and adherence to current CCRG policy.[37] As it did so, cadres and party members were increasingly attracted to the more congenial opposition banner, which appeared to speak directly to their interests. Strategic calculations by the anti-Kuai alliance evolved into a form of status-group politics.

The consequences of these differing stances were soon reflected in membership profiles. On April 20, 150 cadres issued an open letter declaring their support for 414's founding declaration. Others followed suit, and the total soon reached 331.[38] Kuai's group charged that the document was a signal for Qinghua's cadres to overturn the verdicts against them.[39] Kuai's supporters conducted surveys to gauge the size and composition of the two factions' support. Their data provide a window on social status and political orientation at this stage in the factional struggle. The 414 alliance grew rapidly. Of the 8,423 individuals in the departments covered by the survey, almost half, 4,065, were members of 414. Of 1,631 party members and former student cadres surveyed, 63 percent claimed membership in 414, and only 27 percent in Kuai's Jinggangshan. Of those who had earlier affiliated with the old majority faction before its demise, 68 percent joined 414 and only 20 percent Kuai's Jinggangshan. On the other hand, 60 percent of those who had opposed former Party Secretary Jiang Nanxiang before the arrival of the work team and 66 percent of those who had opposed the work team remained in Kuai's faction (against, respectively, only 32 and 30 percent who joined 414). Party members preferred 414 to Kuai's Jinggangshan by a margin of 47 to 30 percent.[40]

Kuai's faction, which had collected the figures, used them to argue that 414 was attempting "capitalist restoration" at Qinghua. In its defense 414 did not repudiate the figures; it responded that it was simply trying to "correct the errors of the bourgeois reactionary line on the cadre question" in accord with the *Red Flag* editorial and the new emphasis of CCRG policy.[41] Of course, it was the strong contrast between the positions of the two factions on the cadre question that attracted so many cadres, party members, and student cadres to 414. These groups had borne the brunt of the work team's assault, and 414 offered to reverse the verdicts and remove the taint of guilt by association that still dogged party members and student cadres.

Kuai's group had no objection to cadres who chose to affiliate with it, however.[42] A number of them wrote wall posters repudiating 414. Most notable was a group of nine former members of the Qinghua Youth League Committee.[43] Jinggangshan appointed two high-level Qinghua cadres to an "advisory group"; one was a member of the university's party committee, and the other was general party secretary of a department. They were put in charge of vetting cadres for a new revolutionary committee.[44]

Kuai was not opposed to liberating cadres; he just wanted to control the process himself. Unfortunately, he permitted his opponents to position themselves on the cadre question in a way that was much more congenial to cadres, party members, and former student cadres. He also permitted the opposition to claim that it was now in line with CCRG policy, while Kuai was out of step. Whenever cadres or party members declared support for 414, they immediately became unacceptable to Kuai and Jinggangshan. This began a process that pushed cadres and party members toward 414 and away from Jinggangshan.

At the end of May, 414 made the split official and permanent. It changed its name from "Column" to "Headquarters," appointed leaders, and began publishing a separate newspaper, *Jinggangshan News*.[45] It was no longer merely a critic of Kuai's line on the cadre question; it was now a rival organizer of a revolutionary committee. The 414 faction flourished; by the end of June it had close to 7,000 members.[46] It eventually developed a coherent argument that expressed a more generous assessment of the prior seventeen-year history of the People's Republic and of Qinghua's party organization. With good reason scholars consider 414 a prototypical "moderate" red guard organization.[47] Its stance, however, was as much a cause as a consequence of its distinctive membership profile.

### Failed Elite Interventions

The doctrinal differences that emerged at Qinghua were not reflected in the broader Heaven-Earth split. The leaders of Qinghua 414 saw Heaven and Earth as a rivalry over leadership of the city's red guard movement, whereas their split with Kuai Dafu was over matters of doctrine and principle. They therefore did not involve themselves in off-campus activities to support the Earth faction, although they needed Earth-faction support to survive. The Earth faction did not immediately support their stance on the cadre question.[48] In its own lengthy analysis of the Heaven-Earth split, Geology East Is Red insisted that the Heaven faction had consistently taken a conservative stance throughout 1967. However, the entire analysis makes clear that the primary issue was Nie Yuanzi's effort to prevent Third Headquarters rebels from taking their rightful place in the leadership core of the Red Guard Congress. The article makes no mention of the doctrinal issues articulated with such clarity at Qinghua.[49]

After the Beijing Revolutionary Committee was founded, Xie Fuzhi and officers of the Beijing Garrison intervened repeatedly at Beida and Qinghua, as did members of the CCRG. However, the interventions usually backfired, and officials frequently expressed frustrations with stubborn rebel leaders. For their part, rebels complained about interventions unfavorable to them and openly questioned orders and the individuals who issued them. Far from the unified and disciplined instrument of proletarian dictatorship apparently intended by Mao and the CCRG, the Beijing Revolutionary Committee was consumed by factional rivalries and unending arguments.

## The Beida Troubles

The Heaven-Earth split rekindled the Beida opposition by providing it with strong external allies. In early March 1967, as Nie pushed a campaign to enforce loyalty to her organization, new splits appeared on the Beida Cultural Revolution Committee. A Philosophy Department instructor put up a wall poster criticizing Nie for her dictatorial behavior, and two standing committee members sided with him. In late May and early June four new anti-Nie alliances appeared.[50] Moreover, there were signs that CCRG support for Nie might be weakening. After new splits on the school's standing committee in late March, Chen Boda and Qi Benyu went to Beida and called for a more conciliatory approach. Chen Boda reportedly said, "You cannot just casually say that to oppose you is counterrevolution."[51] After Chen and Qi left Beida, Nie challenged them in a handbill that duplicated Chen's talk, ineptly ensuring that opponents would be encouraged by it, and she held meetings to criticize what she called a "new black line."[52]

After the violent April disturbances at Beida, Jiang Qing called for Nie Yuanzi to make a self-criticism for her role in the conflict and for resisting Xie Fuzhi's attempts to mediate.[53] Nie's clashes behind the scenes with Xie Fuzhi would continue into the next year because she was convinced that he was part of a cabal backing the attacks against her from both within Beida and without.[54] As Nie's position appeared to weaken, Chen Boda returned to the campus in early June to qualify his criticisms of Nie, and he phoned her to explain that he was not offended by her attacks on him.[55] Xie Fuzhi urged Nie to exercise diplomacy; the task was to unite rebel organizations, not to crush rivals. In response, *Xin Beida* called for correcting the errors of "certain leaders" on the Cultural Revolution committee.[56] The paper published a criticism of Nie by a group in her Philosophy Department, which charged that she had pursued factional struggles and had created deep splits. Subsequent issues welcomed criticisms from fellow leftists.[57]

Instead of accepting the olive branch, the opposition stepped up its attacks. On July 3 anti-Nie groups formed an alliance and soon established their own newspaper, *New Beida News*.[58] It carried news of a major defection of "revolutionary cadres" to their side. Zhou Peiyuan and 133 others charged Nie with errors of line and praised her opponents.[59] Too late to undo the damage, Chen Boda issued a statement on July 10 explaining that he still supported Nie. Stung by the losses, Nie went back on the attack, accusing her opponents of "creating public opinion for a plot to seize power" from her "proletarian headquarters."[60]

The elite intervention had inadvertently hardened the divisions. On August 17 anti-Nie groups formed New Beida Jinggangshan, and it was admitted to the Red Guard Congress.[61] At a mass rally to celebrate, forty-five rebel organizations proclaimed their support. Li Xingchen, a coauthor of the famous wall poster, spoke at the rally, and Nie's two most important Heaven-faction allies, Kuai Dafu and Aeronautics Red Flag, also sent their congratulations.[62]

Nie fought back against mounting odds, surviving only because of the support of Jiang Qing and ultimately Mao himself. On September 1 Jiang criticized Nie but argued that she should keep her posts and that her opponents were "bad elements." On September 16 she went further, calling Nie's opponents "old conservatives."[63] Jinggangshan countered that Nie was a reactionary who suppressed the revolutionary masses.[64] This view was validated by rebels elsewhere in the city who proclaimed that Nie's opponents were revolutionary, not counterrevolutionary, as Nie had charged. They repudiated the January decision to expel them from the Third Headquarters before its merger into the Red Guard Congress.[65] Jinggangshan threw the accusation of harboring "old conservatives" back at

Nie, reminding everyone of her role on the work team and the question-able histories of the cadres who supported her.[66]

Subsequent attempts at mediation were dogged by disputes over the terms of participation. Nie demanded that her opponents first recognize her Cultural Revolution committee as Beida's organ of power.[67] The op-position countered that the committee must first be reorganized to repre-sent both factions.[68] The Beijing Revolutionary Committee tried to break the impasse on November 23 by ruling that the Beida Cultural Revolution Committee was the official organ of power and that New Beida Commune could absorb Jinggangshan.[69] With strong backing from Earth-faction allies, Jinggangshan refused.

## Stalemate at Qinghua

Xie Fuzhi was no more successful in mediating the conflicts at Qinghua. On May 12 he went personally to the campus. He met first with Kuai and Jinggangshan and afterward with the leaders of 414. Xie was unim-pressed with 414's doctrinal arguments and asserted that 414 was wrong to target Kuai and should join an alliance under his leadership. Xie was in no mood to argue points of doctrine and quarreled loudly with Shen Ruhuai. The leaders of 414 concluded that Xie had come to Qinghua simply to help Kuai seize power. Further negotiations chaired by Xie in the Great Hall of the People were no more successful. After Kuai and his supporters made aggressive speeches against 414, its members concluded that Kuai was determined to take revenge. Shen Ruhuai recalled later, "We had no choice but to take the road of a complete split."[70]

Kuai Dafu also had critics on the CCRG. Lin Jie met with factional leaders at Qinghua on June 9 and 14 and followed up with a phone call on June 16. In these talks he pointed out that Kuai had indeed taken the wrong stand on the cadre question and the *Red Flag* editorial on the sub-ject. He pointedly criticized Kuai's response to 414—from the standpoint of trying to create unity in the rebel camp, such a response was "com-pletely mistaken." At the same time, however, Lin Jie urged 414 to join forces with Kuai, to no effect.[71] Soon afterward, on June 26, Chen Boda and Qi Benyu visited Qinghua to try to work out an agreement. During campus meetings Chen criticized Kuai's claim that 414 was attempting "bourgeois restoration." Chen and Qi urged the two sides to merge; Kuai should stop trying to crush his opponents. Whatever trust Chen Boda may have earned from 414 during these meetings was undermined when Chen accepted Kuai's claim to represent the majority of Qinghua's rebels. This led to tensions between Chen and 414, and efforts to achieve a compromise failed once again.[72]

The balance of power at Qinghua and in the city as a whole was briefly disrupted by a major CCRG crisis: the purge and arrest of Wang Li, Guan Feng, and Lin Jie in late August. These officials were made scapegoats for encouraging attacks on the army and for disrupting China's relations with foreign countries—a charge symbolized by the sacking of the British legation in Beijing on August 22.[73] The purge undermined Tan Houlan at Beijing Normal, who was closely tied to these figures, and by extension the Earth faction as a whole. Kuai Dafu immediately seized the opportunity to criticize the Earth faction for having such traitors as its "backstage bosses," and he extended the accusation to Qinghua's 414. These figures were responsible for the *Red Flag* stance on the cadre question, criticized by Kuai Dafu and championed by 414 as its central cause. The leaders of 414 were thrown into a panic.[74]

The fall of her CCRG backers almost led to the demise of Tan Houlan. A long-dormant group of rebels at her university, the Rebel Regiment, went on the offensive and pushed the criticism of Lin Jie to undermine Tan Houlan.[75] On September 7 the Rebel Regiment captured Tan Houlan and subjected her to a mass struggle session. It declared the overthrow of Tan's revolutionary committee and established a "dictatorship committee" to take over. Kuai Dafu led a march of 15,000 red guards from forty Heaven-faction organizations to the meeting and spoke in support of the power seizure.[76]

The authorities responded immediately to these events, which threatened to destabilize the Beijing Revolutionary Committee. Tan Houlan was a member of its standing committee. The CCRG sent a representative to the rally to declare its opposition to her overthrow. The CCRG, the Beijing Revolutionary Committee, and Zhou Enlai all declared their support for Tan Houlan.[77] They demanded that the "dictatorship committee" be disbanded and had some of its leaders arrested. This quelled the uproar and put an end to Kuai's plans for a parallel offensive to crush 414. In fact, Kuai was put unexpectedly on the defensive by the subsequent criticism of Wang Li and Guan Feng as "ultra-leftist," a position that obviously threatened Kuai more than his 414 opponents.[78] Kuai was surprised by this designation because he had considered their stance on the cadre question too soft. He was therefore deprived of what he saw as a perfect opportunity finally to assume control of Qinghua. The stalemate continued.

In the immediate aftermath, *People's Daily* published a new instruction from Mao calling for unity.[79] Kuai responded positively, and on September 21 the leaders of the two sides met and agreed to plan a formal alliance. Two days later they met with Nie Yuanzi, Wang Dabin, Han Aijing, and Tan Houlan and agreed on terms of unity.[80] The agreement would have established a Qinghua Revolutionary Committee, but it soon broke down over Kuai Dafu's renewed attacks on 414 leaders and cadres who were candidates for the revolutionary committee. Zhou Quanying, a member of 414's leadership group and a talented essayist, had put up a wall poster on September 17 accusing Chen Boda of being the mastermind behind the ultra-leftists, Wang Li and Guan Feng.[81] In thinly veiled language he indirectly accused the CCRG as a whole of "ultra-leftism." Zhou did this against the advice of 414's leadership collective, which argued that it was politically suicidal. When Jiang Qing heard about the wall poster, she predictably denounced Zhou Quanying in ways that threatened 414. More ominously, Zhou Enlai immediately did so as well.[82]

The leaders of 414 saw no choice but to denounce Zhou Quanying and detain him, but they insisted that his political errors did not make him a counterrevolutionary.[83] Predictably, Kuai Dafu took a less generous view, seeing a chance to weaken his new coalition partners. He pushed hard to have Zhou arrested.[84] Xie Fuzhi eventually relented and arrested Zhou and then subsequently released him into Kuai's custody for a mass struggle session on October 31, during which a fight with knives and clubs broke out that left eleven wounded.[85]

Relations broke down completely as the two factions began to vet cadres to assume leadership posts. Whenever 414 nominated prominent cadres, Jinggangshan attacked them. The first disagreement was over Tan Haoqiang, a former member of the university's Communist Youth League committee who had written a famous essay critical of Liu Shaoqi early in the Cultural Revolution. After 414 nominated Tan, Kuai's followers, who had unsuccessfully courted Tan to join their side, denounced him as unacceptable.[86] A much larger battle was touched off by the candidacy of Lu Yingzhong, formerly on the Qinghua Party Standing Committee and one of the top officials in the university. The leaders of 414 declared Lu a revolutionary cadre and permitted him to lead a mass meeting to denounce the former party secretary. Jinggangshan objected vociferously, and on November 16 it dragged him to a mass struggle session that featured him as the sole target of abuse. Members of 414 ran to the meeting to argue with Kuai's followers, and a violent confrontation ensued.[87]

Kuai responded by making Lu his main target as the alleged architect of the old Qinghua.[88] He was subjected to mass struggle sessions on December 4 and 5 at which fights broke out and several people were seriously injured. On December 7, 414's leaders demanded an apology by Jinggangshan, and the next day 287 cadres issued a declaration demanding the immediate release of Lu from detention. Kuai ignored the demands and kept Lu in detention. He was held in Jinggangshan's makeshift jail for the next eight months and was tortured repeatedly to confess to a conspiracy with 414 to undermine the Cultural Revolution at Qinghua.[89]

This case illustrates a general pattern that we have already observed at Beida: the "liberation" of cadres intensified disputes on campuses where rebels were divided. The reasons are clear: a cadre nominated by one side immediately became a threat to the other faction if he or she joined a new power structure. Increasingly the disputes took the form of capturing the cadres nominated by the other side and extracting confessions through torture.[90] By January 1968 the two sides were following the same strategy: Jinggangshan systematically targeted cadres pledged to 414 as representatives of the old Qinghua "black line," and 414 returned the favor to cadres and faculty pledged to Jinggangshan.[91] The two sides made virtually the same accusations against each other's supporters. Despite the initially different doctrinal positions of the two sides in April 1967, the factional politics surrounding the cadre question eventually took exactly the same form as they did at Beida.

Hostilities deepened further in mid-December after Kuai charged that Chen Chusan, one of 414's top leaders and a member of the alliance committee, was a counterrevolutionary. Kuai's forces captured him on December 20, beat him severely, and tortured him with burning cigarettes for fifteen hours before he was turned over to the Public Security Bureau with facial burns and broken ribs. Kuai then sent his security teams to the homes of twenty cadres who had pledged support to 414; the teams beat them and put them in detention. Kuai issued a list of forty-one cadres and leaders in 414 who were "class enemies."[92]

The leaders of 414 responded with a large protest march and mass demonstration at the offices of the Beijing Revolutionary Committee, and afterward the crowd marched to the entrances of the Public Security Bureau to demand Chen Chusan's release. A crowd estimated at 1,500 swore to stay until Chen was released. It chanted slogans criticizing Kuai Dafu and also Xie Fuzhi, who was seen as facilitating Kuai's repression. A small group broke into the building and staged its part of the sit-in indoors. This group remained there for more than fifty days, demanding that the officials who authorized Chen's arrest admit their errors.[93] Trying to defuse the conflict, Xie Fuzhi and Qi Benyu went to Qinghua. They acknowledged that Kuai's accusations against Chen Chusan were unfounded, and they stated that he would be released. During all-night meetings at the Great Hall of the People on December 27th, Xie Fuzhi, Qi Benyu, and other officials met with both sides to explain the decision.[94]

An armed clash between the factions at Qinghua on January 4, 1968, left a large number of injured. Li Zhongqi, vice-commander of the Beijing Garrison, came to negotiate. The leaders of 414 were now concerned primarily for their personal safety and demanded that the planned alliance be abandoned in favor of an army takeover of Qinghua. Kuai Dafu was strongly opposed because this would deny him political power. The military delegation left the campus on January 28 without an agreement. Two days later Kuai arrested twenty-one cadres on his list of counterrevolutionaries and had them tortured to obtain confessions; two later died in custody.[95]

### Military Mediation

The request by 414 to put Qinghua under martial law anticipated a citywide effort to use the army to hammer out agreements among warring factions. By the end of January 1968 fewer than fifteen universities had established revolutionary committees, and only three had done so since July 1967.[96] The conflicts were worsening at Beida and Qinghua, and some campuses had already descended into a state of civil war. Rebel factions at the Beijing Steel Institute and the Beijing Finance Institute had fortified buildings on their campuses, had stockpiled makeshift armaments, and were fighting over territory.[97]

To pressure factions to compromise, the army held citywide "Mao Zedong Thought Study Classes", attended by delegations of leaders from each school. The first was held on February 5, 1968, and was attended by more than 200 leaders from some twenty universities. In the following weeks the numbers expanded to some 1,400 leaders from thirty-six schools. The original plan was to hold sessions for fifteen to twenty days, but the classes stretched on for more than two months. Mao Thought Propaganda Teams staffed by military officers were also sent to some of the key campuses, including Beida and Qinghua, to try to mediate.[98]

The "study classes" had some initial success, but only at smaller schools that were not central to the Heaven-Earth split. Over a three-day period in early March, seven schools announced the formation of revolutionary committees. However, only one other school succeeded in establishing a revolutionary committee before the red guard movement was finally suppressed and all campuses were put under martial law five months later.[99] The attempt at military mediation failed for two reasons. First, important leaders from large campuses like Nie Yuanzi and Kuai Dafu, both of whom held positions on the Beijing Revolutionary Committee, were not easily pressured into agreements. So long as they resisted, their allies on other campuses could do so as well.

The second reason was more important. Shortly after the study classes convened, the participants learned that Qi Benyu had been arrested for his involvement in the Wang Li–Guan Feng–Lin Jie case.[100] This led to a renewed campaign by the Heaven faction to tie the leaders of the Earth faction to the earlier Wang Li–Guan Feng anti-party group. The first to strike was Beijing Normal's Rebel Regiment, which had attacked Tan Houlan in connection with the Wang-Guan affair the previous September. Qi Benyu had firmly supported Tan Houlan in the earlier controversy, and the Rebel Regiment now demanded that Qi's earlier position on the Tan Houlan question be retracted by the CCRG. Its demand was ignored, and the Rebel Regiment withdrew in protest from the study class on February 22. Several other members of the Heaven faction supported them.

These groups held separate meetings in mid-March at which Nie Yuanzi criticized the study classes. Before long disgruntled members of the Heaven faction were claiming that the classes were biased toward the Earth faction. Several groups openly challenged Xie Fuzhi and pointed out his close ties with Qi Benyu; some of the more extreme posters at Beida and People's University called for his overthrow and labeled him a "butcher of the revolution." Even more confusing, although Qinghua 414 was not aligned with the Heaven faction, it already had grievances against Xie Fuzhi and joined in the attacks as well.[101]

The CCRG pushed back, sending clear signals that challenges to Xie Fuzhi would not be tolerated. On March 21, 1968, Beijing Revolutionary Committee vice-chairman Wu De denounced those who used criticisms of the study classes to attack the Beijing Revolutionary Committee and Xie Fuzhi.[102] Seeing an opportunity to gain the upper hand, the Earth faction strongly defended Xie Fuzhi and his revolutionary committee and called for "dragging out" Nie Yuanzi for trying to subvert it.[103] The Heaven faction quickly backtracked, and on March 23 Nie's New Beida Commune issued a declaration of loyalty to Xie.[104] Her opponents did not relent. Beida Jinggangshan and its Earth-faction allies organized several demonstrations at Beida to "overthrow Nie Yuanzi" for opposing Xie Fuzhi. The foray ended only after Xie Fuzhi went to Beida on March 25 and gave a speech expressing support for Nie Yuanzi.[105] This halted the controversy surrounding the PLA's study classes, but they achieved little after this, and troops were finally withdrawn from all campuses on April 19.[106]

### Campus Civil War

The Earth faction's March 1968 invasion of Beida ignited the fuse that led to campus civil war. Demanding that Nie be "dragged out" for attacking Xie Fuzhi and subverting the Beijing Revolutionary Committee, Earth-faction rebels marched onto campus, loudly denouncing Nie Yuanzi. Beida Jinggangshan joined in. In response, Nie Yuanzi organized a militia to "defend with force." Three days later over 1,000 members of Agricultural University East Is Red demonstrated against Nie at Beida. Earth-faction rebels led five other organizations in a demonstration at the Municipal Revolutionary Committee offices to demand Nie's expulsion. The next day 10,000 Earth-faction rebels again demonstrated at Beida, and battles erupted across the campus. Xie Fuzhi and Wu De rushed back to Beida to broadcast demands for the withdrawal of outsiders and for the two Beida factions to unite under Nie Yuanzi. Several hundred members of Geology East Is Red, armed with clubs, nonetheless arrived the next morning, and further violence followed.[107]

On March 28 Nie ordered her forces to drive Jinggangshan out of a building. This action sparked an armed conflict that began after midnight on March 29 and continued until dawn, when Vice-Commander Li Zhongqi of the Beijing Garrison broadcast a demand for an immediate truce and negotiations. Jinggangshan refused, and as negotiations broke down, Nie Yuanzi was wounded on the hand by a knife-wielding attacker. Li Zhongqi broadcast a second demand for negotiations and this time got the two sides to sit down with Xie Fuzhi and Wen Yucheng, Beijing Garrison commander.[108] Xie demanded an immediate halt to hostilities and ordered Jinggangshan to turn over the student who had stabbed Nie.[109]

Skirmishing between the two sides continued, and mutual accusations became more bellicose and threatening. Nie's forces accused the leader of

Jinggangshan of instigating the battle and demanded that he "die a thousand deaths."[110] On April 8 *Xin Beida* called for "crushing the bourgeois headquarters" of Jinggangshan. Ominously, the statement was included in a joint declaration by the Beijing Revolutionary Committee, the Beijing Garrison Command, the Bureau of Public Security, and the Beida Cultural Revolution Committee.[111] Jinggangshan dug in behind defensive barriers. Nie Yuanzi appeared to be on the verge of complete victory. On April 24 she hosted a large rally at Beida and gave a keynote speech along with the two top commanders of the Beijing Garrison and rebel leaders from across the city.[112]

Jinggangshan tried to hold out behind its defense works, but it was no longer able to publish *New Beida News,* whose last issue appeared on March 22. Skirmishes broke out in April and June when its members tried to restore utilities and food delivery to their buildings. Nie's forces began to seize and interrogate any members of Jinggangshan whom they could capture.[113] Public struggle sessions were held against captured Jinggangshan leaders, and several captives were tortured to death.[114] Near the end of April Nie and Sun Pengyi began prosecutions of opposition leaders. They established a central prison that held 218 cadres and faculty, where inmates were regularly beaten and tortured to confess. Compromise was now out of the question; ordinary members of Jinggangshan would be treated leniently only if they turned over their leaders and surrendered.[115] By the end of June, Nie's forces claimed that 1,200 members of Jinggangshan had defected and were undergoing thought reform; Nie welcomed them in a long speech. On July 18 she held the first of a planned series of show trials of captured Jinggangshan leaders.[116]

On July 22 Nie's forces prepared for the final battle. They cut off water and electricity to the buildings still controlled by Jinggangshan, touching off a battle fought with roof tiles, spears, and bricks that spread onto adjacent streets. After Nie learned that a large force of workers and soldiers was surrounding the adjacent Qinghua campus on July 27, she called an emergency meeting to coordinate defenses and block any such force from entering Beida. Her supporters stockpiled Molotov cocktails and other weapons and posted lookouts.[117] Instead, Nie was summoned to an urgent meeting at the Great Hall of the People at 3:30 a.m. on July 28 with other red guard leaders.

This summons was a response to events that day on the Qinghua campus. The struggle between Kuai's Jinggangshan and Qinghua 414 had long since deteriorated into armed conflict. The turning point came in April as each side attacked cadres pledged to the other side. On April 14

Kuai's forces kidnapped two prominent cadres pledged to 414 and tortured them to confess to an anti-party conspiracy. After 414's demands for their release went unheeded, it retaliated by capturing a prominent cadre pledged to Jinggangshan. After Jinggangshan's angry demand for his release was ignored, it attacked a building occupied by 414, armed with rocks and spears, but was repelled. Jinggangshan concluded that it was no longer possible to negotiate, and that it would have to use force to prevail.[118]

To protest these attacks, 414 held a protest march on April 25 and ended it with a large struggle session against the captured Jinggangshan cadre. The next day 414 invaded the campus homes of teachers and workers allied with the other side, and Jinggangshan responded with an assault on one of the buildings held by 414. This touched off an exodus from the campus as residents tried to avoid hostilities. At the end of April the two sides carved up the campus into two zones; Jinggangshan seized most of the buildings.[119]

By early May the campus was a patchwork of fortified buildings and ill-defined front lines, with Jinggangshan consistently on the offensive. Initially the students were armed with clubs, spears, daggers, bricks, and stones thrown from slingshots. Injuries mounted, and the first death occurred on April 29. On May 5 members of 414 carried the corpse of their slain comrade in a protest march to Tiananmen Square and held a protest rally. A series of campus skirmishes followed that resulted in many casualties and two more deaths, with prisoners captured and brutally beaten. After one of its leaders was killed, 414 staged another protest march on May 26, carrying his corpse to Tiananmen Square in protest.[120]

A turning point was reached on May 30. In a large assault on a building controlled by 414, the two sides used spears, knives, Molotov cocktails, gas grenades, and even a makeshift tank. In the end, Jinggangshan set the building on fire and captured the 414 fighters as they tried to escape. At the end of the eleven-hour battle, three students lay dead and more than 300 were wounded.[121] In mid-June Kuai's forces obtained rifles and set up snipers outside the remaining buildings controlled by 414 and campus gates and began to pick off people who tried to leave or enter. Skirmishes continued, increasingly with grenades, firebombs, improvised explosive devices, and makeshift tanks. Desperate, 414 appealed repeatedly to the Beijing Revolutionary Committee to put the campus under martial law. On July 7 it marched to Tiananmen Square with the corpse of another slain comrade to dramatize its demand. Fighting continued, and on July 9 a large new building on campus was set on fire and virtually destroyed in a Jinggangshan attack. By the end of July twelve people had been killed, several hundred seriously wounded, and more than thirty permanently disabled. Most of the campus community had fled, and an estimated force of fewer than 400 die-hard fighters on both sides remained on campus.[122]

At the end of July the Beijing authorities finally took action.[123] On July 26 officers from the elite army unit assigned to guard national leaders began assembling thousands of workers from more than sixty nearby factories, along with a leadership core of soldiers.[124] They mobilized close to 30,000 workers to converge on Qinghua from around the city the next morning, armed only with books of Mao's quotations. This propaganda team was to surround the campus, swarm through the gates in overwhelming numbers while chanting Mao slogans, separate the two sides, and clear away barriers and fortifications. The besieged forces of 414 were relieved that help had finally arrived, and they willingly surrendered. Kuai, however, saw this as an attempt to rescue 414. He suggested that there were "black hands" in the top leadership who had sent the workers, and he ordered his followers to resist while he rushed downtown to lodge an appeal at the Beijing Revolutionary Committee.[125]

Kuai received no sympathy downtown, where he was told that the propaganda team had been sent on the orders of the Central Committee. Kuai refused to accept this and quarreled violently with Vice-Chairman Wu De. He returned to campus in the midst of a twelve-hour battle during which unarmed workers and soldiers were assaulted as they attempted to enter buildings and persuade Kuai's fighters to disarm. Eventually Jinggangshan surrendered, but not before it had killed five members of the propaganda team and wounded 731, 149 of them seriously.[126] The red guard movement had limped to an inglorious end.

### Mao's Final Solution: Martial Law

Just as the Qinghua hostilities were winding down, Kuai Dafu and four other prominent red guard leaders—Nie Yuanzi, Tan Houlan, Han Aijing, and Wang Dabin—were summoned to an urgent meeting in the Great Hall of the People. When they arrived in the early morning hours of July 28, they faced a phalanx of top officials headed by Mao himself. Marshall Lin Biao was also there—a remote figure who had had almost no contact with students during this entire period. Joining them were Zhou

Enlai, Chen Boda, Kang Sheng, Jiang Qing, Xie Fuzhi, and several others. This evidently was an unusually important event. The meeting began at 3:30 a.m. and lasted for five hours.[127]

Edited transcripts of these rambling discussions were later issued as a printed pamphlet.[128] In them, Mao is by turns solicitous, sarcastic, threatening, and angry. The urgent meeting was obviously a reaction to the Qinghua events, and Mao began the meeting by expressing strong displeasure with Kuai Dafu. Kuai was late in arriving, and Mao asked why he was not there: was it because he could not get out, or he did not want to come? Mao immediately made clear the reason for the meeting: "Kuai Dafu wants to grab the black hand, so many workers suppressing the red guards—who is the black hand? Now you cannot drag him out—the black hand is me! If he still does not come, then you grab me, come on and grab me!" The central message, despite Mao's characteristic ramblings, was clear: the red guard movement was over, and the universities were to be put under martial law.

The key points of the message were issued as a "supreme directive" from Chairman Mao and in the name of the five red guard leaders.[129] Mao was quoted as saying, "Now we have come to the point where you little generals are committing errors. Do not get swelled heads to the point where your whole body is swollen and you get edema. I do not want you split into Heaven faction and Earth faction. Form one faction and that is the end of it; what is all this about two factions?"

The key mistake, Mao made clear, was the persistence of violent factional conflict:

The Cultural Revolution has gone on for two years now! . . . Now the workers, peasants, soldiers, and residents are all unhappy, and the great majority of students are unhappy, and even some of the people who support your faction are unhappy. You have become divorced from the workers, divorced from the peasants, divorced from the army, divorced from the residents, and you are divorced from the vast majority of students.

Mao made very clear that his patience was at an end:

I say you are divorced from the masses; the masses cannot accept civil war . . . Well, now we are issuing a nationwide directive, and whoever violates it, striking at the army, sabotaging transportation, killing people, setting fires, is committing a crime. If there is a minority who will not listen to persuasion and refuses to change, then they are bandits, Guomindang. We will surround them, and if they are stubborn, we will wipe them out.

Red guards were told to return to campus and await the arrival of Mao Zedong Thought Propaganda Teams. Through August 24 the Beijing Revolutionary Committee and the Beijing Garrison Command dispatched 10,300 soldiers and 17,000 industrial workers to Beijing's universities, and propaganda teams were in place in all the universities except for nine small schools in the fine arts.[130] After these units arrived, students found that the Cultural Revolution had come full circle. These were new work teams with much greater authority and much stronger backing than the work teams of the summer of 1966. In virtually every case army officers led them, and they established their authority in no uncertain terms.

Nie Yuanzi returned to campus, and her paper published a "warm welcome" to the Mao Thought Propaganda Team. Remarkably, she continued to call for "smashing" the "counterrevolutionary" Jinggangshan organization and severe punishment of its leaders.[131] Nie obviously did not anticipate that things would change drastically when the propaganda team arrived on August 19. Her newspaper was immediately closed. All arms were turned over, and defense works were dismantled; the propaganda team took control of all broadcasting equipment; all prisoners were released. On August 21 the propaganda team met with Nie and told her to reflect on how her consistent refusal to compromise had caused armed conflicts. Her organization was disbanded on August 28, and Jinggangshan followed suit the next day.[132]

The leaders of both factions now submitted to reeducation in Mao Thought Study Classes during which they were to confess their errors. Nie Yuanzi was an unwilling student with a bad attitude. On October 15 she was criticized at a mass meeting of over 3,000 people for resisting the propaganda team's authority and persisting in factional attacks on her old enemies. On November 2 the propaganda team, still unhappy with her progress, recommended against her participation in the upcoming Municipal Party Congress. On November 21, still unbowed, she was subjected to a reeducation session attended by more than 600 people, during which she was severely criticized for her "bourgeois standpoint" and her "decadent, hypocritical ways."[133]

When Beida's revolutionary committee was finally established in September 1969, a military officer became chairman, and of the six vice-chairmen, three were soldiers and one was a worker on the propaganda team. Only two vice-chairmen were from Beida: Zhou Peiyuan and Nie Yuanzi.[134] Nie's position at Beida was completely for show, as was her subsequent elevation into the national leadership. She was isolated for reeducation for over a year and was paroled briefly only for a token appearance as a delegate to the Ninth Party Congress in April 1969 where remarkably, despite her political difficulties, she was named an alternate member of the Central Committee. In November 1969, two months after the Beida Revolutionary Committee was established, this "vice-chairman" and Central Committee member was sent to a state farm for labor reform. She remained under a political cloud until, after Mao's death, she was formally tried and imprisoned in April 1978, as the post-Mao leadership settled accounts with the "Gang of Four" and other Cultural Revolution radicals.[135]

Kuai Dafu did not fare any better. The core of the propaganda team remained on the campus. On August 10 it disarmed both factions and released their prisoners. On August 16 it established a Mao Thought Study Class for the leaders of both sides to remold their thinking. Heeding calls to return to campus, at the end of August close to 10,000 were in residence, some 65 percent of the pre–Cultural Revolution population.[136] When Qinghua's revolutionary committee was finally established in late January 1969, its chairman was the officer from 8341 Regiment who had initially led the propaganda team. Most of the vice-chairmen were soldiers and workers from the propaganda team or former Qinghua cadres.[137] Kuai Dafu lost out; in December 1968 he was transferred to work in a military factory in the remote Ningxia Muslim Autonomous Region. He was flown back to Qinghua in 1970 to be interrogated in isolation as a suspected member of an underground organization of ultra-leftists.[138] He was sent back to Ningxia and was transferred back to Beijing a few years later to work in a factory "under supervision." Like Nie Yuanzi, he was arrested in 1978 and imprisoned.[139]

Other red guard leaders suffered a similar fate. Tan Houlan was sent to perform manual labor in a military compound near Beijing in October 1968. In mid-1970 she was sent back to Beijing Normal to undergo investigation for her factional activities. After this ordeal she worked in a Beijing factory "under supervision" until she was arrested in 1978. By this time she had already contracted cancer, and she died in prison in 1982.[140] Han Aijing was similarly isolated for investigation at the end of 1968. He was sent to a factory in Hunan in late 1969 to labor "under supervision." In 1978, like the others, he was arrested and imprisoned.[141]

Wang Dabin's treatment was less severe. He was sent to a factory in Sichuan in January 1969. Arrested in 1978, he was released in 1983.[142]

Former red guard leaders were pushed aside by military officers throughout Beijing. The student chairmen of the university revolutionary committees established before martial law was imposed all lost their posts to military officers. Students were assigned to factory jobs or sent indefinitely to the countryside. Faculty and cadres were sent to remote rural regions for a year or more of hard labor. Many of Beijing's universities were hurriedly relocated to distant provinces in 1969 and 1970, after a war scare prompted by border clashes with the Soviet Union. The Geology Institute, the Machinery Institute, the Mining Institute, and the Chinese University of Science and Technology never returned.

# 10

## HIERARCHY AND REBELLION

### Reflections on the Red Guards

This book is about the social basis of politics—the relationship between social position and political orientation. I began with two competing conceptions: red guard factions were based on social categories defined by household labels, or they were based on social networks defined by shared ties to school power structures. My starting point reflected a widespread and largely unconscious assumption in much of political sociology: political orientations are derived from social position and are largely given by existing social circumstances. For several decades scholarship on the mass movements of China's Cultural Revolution, including my own, has reflected this consensus. Red guard factions, many of us were convinced, represented different social constituencies, and their political orientations were derived from their social positions. Those with favorable positions in the status quo naturally sought to defend it and adopted a conservative orientation, while those less favored in the status quo sought to change it and adopted a more radical orientation. By immobilizing a well-organized and highly repressive political system, the Cultural Revolution inadvertently provided an opportunity for these underlying interests to achieve organized expression. The struggle between these interest groups spun out of control and ultimately foiled Mao's intentions.

This is a compelling story line and a highly coherent sociological explanation, but it actually bears little relationship to the conflicts that we have examined in Beijing. One might be tempted to conclude that a social interpretation of red guard factionalism is misplaced, but this would be wrong. Instead, what I have shown is that there is much more to building a valid social interpretation than accurately characterizing the interests and identities of different groups on the eve of a major political upheaval. It is necessary to understand the political choices that individuals actually face and the organized contexts in which they face them. Their network ties or family backgrounds do not make these choices for them. It is also necessary to recognize that these contexts may change rapidly and present new, ambiguous, and difficult choices. It is especially necessary to understand the social interactions that occur as these contexts change—interactions that alter the identities and interests of individuals and create new sets of allies, new grievances, and new enemies. The process of group formation and the building of collective identities is dynamic and can take different forms under different circumstances. Ultimately a social interpretation must take into account the perceptions of actors, their interactions with authority figures, and the altered realities that these interactions create. In short, a social interpretation of politics does not end with an accurate description of social structure.

New cleavages and identities, once formed, are not fixed but continue to evolve. The rebel identity that grew out of the minority factions' struggles in late 1966 broke apart into two new factional identities, Heaven and Earth, whose mutual antagonisms surprisingly lasted much longer and became much more violent than the earlier conflict with the majority faction. The organizational context is also very important in explaining this new division, particularly the way in which the student rebellion was channeled and shaped by the capital's bureaucratic structure. The rebel assaults on national ministries and commissions in late 1966 were efforts to find and punish the leaders of a university's work team. Rebels only assaulted the ministries from which their work teams came.

Once red guards crossed into the same bureaucratic hierarchies, they turned quickly from allies into competitors. Rebel groups from different universities began to seize power back and forth from one another and engaged in violent confrontations over control of the same government agencies. These confrontations spurred alliances with rebel groups on other campuses. After the initial confrontations of January 1967, the rebel factions from the Geology Institute and Beijing Normal made common cause and were opposed by prominent rebels from Beida, Qinghua, and the Aeronautics Institute. As competitors began to invade one another's campuses, each side lined up allies on as many campuses as possible. Each side had strong backing within the CCRG.

Once these new factional identities crystallized, it is puzzling that it proved impossible for them to unite. Their elite sponsors urged them to do so throughout 1967 and 1968, and the two coalitions did not have different orientations toward the status quo or articulate different programs. Their only real difference was an unalterable opposition to each other. Why did it prove impossible to halt their conflict short of imposing martial law? The primary objective of studies of political movements is usually to explain how mobilizations become established—how collective action begins and is maintained. Here, however, the puzzle is exit from collective action—how to end conflict.

Once again, understanding the organized setting for politics is crucial at both the city and the university level. At the city level the two large coalitions achieved a rough balance of power in which neither side was able to defeat the other. The primary reason is that the two most prominent leaders on the two largest campuses—Nie Yuanzi at Beida and Kuai Dafu at Qinghua—were never able to unify the rebel forces on their own campuses. These leaders overestimated the value of strong personal backing from the CCRG. By attempting to intimidate and suppress their internal critics, they drove large sectors of their schools' rebel movements into unalterable opposition. Here the CCRG's attempts to manipulate the student movement by placing trusted subordinates in charge of the two largest campuses backfired, and both Beida and Qinghua generated large opposition movements that joined the Earth faction. Once these opponents linked up with powerful allies in the Earth faction—in particular, the aggressive rebels from the Geology Institute—the two Beijing alliances achieved a rough balance of power that prevented one side from overcoming the other.

Within each university the two sides found it impossible to achieve a lasting compromise because there was no neutral third party to enforce any agreement within the schools. In a deeply flawed policy pursued until the middle of 1968, student factions were expected to forge their own alliances and establish a revolutionary committee. By this point, however, the mutual charges each side had directed against the other made the prospect of defeat unthinkable. The mutual accusations of counterrevolution were much more severe than anything the work teams had hurled at their opponents in 1966, and there was now a well-established history of physical violence between the two sides. Peace could only be obtained if one side overwhelmed the other (unlikely so long as outside allies could be called upon), or if a neutral third party enforced an agreement (as hostile martial-law forces eventually did). Factional warfare was so hard to curtail not because the two sides represented the fundamentally opposing interests of different social constituencies, but because the die-hard activists on each side could not ensure their personal security in the event of their defeat.

I have pursued these generic questions about political movements with a single-minded focus on the red guards of Beijing. What historical generalizations should we now draw about China's Cultural Revolution? China, after all, is a vast nation of continental proportions. In the 1960s it had almost thirty province-level political units with populations larger than most nation-states, hundreds of large cities, and more than 2,000 county-level jurisdictions. What broad lessons about the mass insurgencies of these tumultuous two years can we possibly draw from a study focused on a distinctive group concentrated in three districts of Beijing?

I have argued that the divisions among Beijing's red guards and their political motives were not defined by the participants' prior social positions. We should not automatically expect to see the same pattern among other social groups in other places. This book is about the reasons why preexisting statuses and networks did not define political cleavages. The general lessons are about the processes and mechanisms that generate outcomes. There is no reason for a confident assertion about what was the most common pattern elsewhere without detailed knowledge about the contexts that generated insurgencies in other settings. Similar outcomes should have occurred only where the circumstances in Beijing's schools were replicated.

What were these circumstances? Beijing's red guard movement grew out of a school-level context that was unusual. First, the work teams intervened very early and in almost all cases removed incumbent officials. Second, the process was both harsh and unpredictable, with work teams hesitating, changing direction, and sometimes retreating before being replaced by work teams that pursued different strategies. The struggle between radical work teams and militant students over control of the purge campaign saddled many party members and student cadres with a political label. Mixed work-team strategies intentionally divided members of power structures against one another, and conservative work teams inadvertently had the same impact if they permitted free criticism for a week or two before declaring their stances. Work teams that abruptly changed strategy or were replaced by more militant successors had the same effect. In all these circumstances the specific way political institutions collapsed presented ambiguous choices to those tied to power structures in situations fraught with great personal risk.

Prior social position defined red guard factions only if power structures were not quickly immobilized by outside interventions. What would such circumstances look like? The most obvious is an organization where a work team was never sent. Outside the educational and cultural sector the power structures of organizations were largely undisturbed for many months. Initially the Cultural Revolution was not to be carried out in villages and factories, and work teams were sent to few of them. Not until late 1966, after considerable disagreements within the CCRG, were workers permitted to join in the movement.[1] In urban factories incumbent officials remained in power and continued to hold meetings and issue directives until the end of 1966. In these organizations party officials could devise strategies to ensure their survival and could mobilize their followers to engage in defensive actions.[2] In many outlying provinces officials responded to developments in Beijing by jumping on the radical bandwagon and organizing red guard units under their personal direction.[3] In such cases defensive mobilization by those tied to power structures is to be expected.[4] This occurred in many Beijing universities in the brief period before the work team arrived, but loyalist mobilization usually collapsed after work teams arrived on the scene.

A second circumstance where loyalist mobilization should occur is under a conservative work team that survived into late July, especially one that left party leaders in power to orchestrate the purge campaign. Work teams that openly tried to protect party organizations sent clear signals to all members of power structures about expected behavior and gave little reason to anticipate that incumbent leaders would fall. The major surprise of the chapters on the Beijing work teams was how extremely rare this stance was in Beijing after the first half of June.

This second circumstance may have been much more common outside the capital. Beijing's politics were distinctive, perhaps unique. Its entire municipal leadership was denounced and purged just as the Cultural Revolution began. Only several months later did similar events overtake the leaders of other cities and provinces. There were no incumbent officials in Beijing after May 1966 who could be blamed for alleged political problems in the universities. The new Beijing Municipal Party Committee had every reason to find and rectify all manner of alleged political errors in the city in order to demonstrate the proper level of loyalty to Mao's vision. In other regions, however, the choices faced by provincial, municipal, and county-level officials could be very different, and these officials generally remained in power until the end of 1966. Any alleged political problems in the schools occurred under their watch, and they could be threatened by militant student rebellions. A conservative work team could help contain the damage.

On the other hand, if student resistance was strong, regional officials might behave in ways similar to those of the ministry officials in Beijing who sent work teams into the specialized institutes for which they were responsible. In such cases the work teams would switch to a radical or mixed strategy in order to placate local rebels and contain the damage within the school itself. If this occurred, political cleavages would be generated that would be similar to those in Beijing. This clearly is not a question that can be answered without carefully examining evidence from regions outside the Chinese capital.

In short, the broader implications of my research on Beijing are not that patterns of power and privilege had little influence on the factional conflicts of the Cultural Revolution, but that they did so only when political institutions declined gradually, permitting incumbent officials to mobilize their subordinates to defend the status quo. Such circumstances were largely absent in Beijing. As a result, to portray conflict among Beijing's red guards as an expression of preexisting social and political cleavages would seriously misrepresent the origins of the factional conflict, the identity of the activists, and their political motives. Beijing shows us that short-term processes can generate severe factional conflict and strong group loyalties even in the absence of identities and interests defined by a "social base" rooted in long-standing social arrangements.

These arguments apply only to the initial formation of factions. But in Beijing and other regions the initially victorious rebels eventually split into two new factions. In Beijing, we have seen, Heaven and Earth did not articulate distinct "moderate" and "radical" points of view, although this was apparently common in many other regions. This is possibly because there was never any real conflict over political power in Beijing. The armed forces and security agencies were firmly in control and had the clear backing of Mao and the CCRG. The harsh repression campaign against dissident red guards at the end of 1966 illustrated this command. In other regions (except Shanghai) warring mass alliances united students, cadres, workers, and even peasants who fought one another for many months and in many cases challenged the armed forces who took sides. Under these circumstances mass factions often developed sharply divergent points of view, especially if military forces strongly favored social groups that previously had been strong supporters of the status quo.

What of the vigorous debate among high-school red guards about the question of class origin—a factor heavily emphasized in prior studies of red guards? Political chauvinism among students from "revolutionary" households was certainly evident in Beijing, and the controversy about the rhyming couplet was a prominent issue in the first weeks of the movement. But as a feature of factional politics, this controversy is easy to misinterpret if it is torn from its organizational and temporal context. It is clear that in the elite high schools—although not the universities—students from "revolutionary" households loudly argued that they were more qualified to lead the red guards by virtue of their parents' contributions to the revolution. Some children of high officials—an elite within the "revolutionary" group itself—were very influential in the beginning, but they were as likely to challenge the high-school work teams as they were to cooperate with them, and in the pivotal cases of Qinghua and Beida high schools the most confident and outspoken challenges to the work teams came from the offspring of national officials.

Cruelty toward members of "reactionary" households, further, was not restricted to students from revolutionary backgrounds. Handbills from the city's neighborhoods show that students from working-class households actively denounced these same families and demanded their expulsion from the city. Also, the emphasis on pure class origins in political discourse was a double-edged sword. It could excuse horrific cruelties toward members of "reactionary" households, but it could also be used as a call to conscience and a demand for discipline and conformity to nonviolent revolutionary ideals—as the "urgent appeals" about violence that emanated from elitist red guards and the subsequent formation of the picket corps illustrate. Ironically, the red guards from revolutionary origins who objected most publicly and insistently to violence were later cynically blamed for it by CCRG functionaries in a shrill denunciation campaign that has long distorted scholarship on the subject.

The debates about class origin were indeed lively, but they occurred only during a brief early period. They reflected real status distinctions and genuine cleavages in the student population, and the debate would not have occurred if the issue had not resonated strongly among students. But at the time this debate occurred—late summer and early autumn of 1966—the issue did not define factions in Beijing. Students from revolutionary and other "red" households were themselves split over the question of violence. The high-school picket corps, which strongly emphasized revolutionary heritage as a qualification for membership, sought to rein in violent students from all backgrounds, especially red guards from the same family origin as themselves. High-school factions were not clearly defined in the late summer and early fall of 1966, largely because students from "red" households were deeply split over the issue of violence. In universities, where, by contrast, factional divisions were very clearly drawn, the issue was almost never raised. It played no role in the minority-majority split that later developed into a struggle between reputed rebels and alleged conservatives.

If red guard factions did not represent the divergent interests of distinct social groups, is there any reason to view them as an independent political movement? In past writings about the red guards, both within China and abroad, there has been a clear tension between two different views. Were red guards willing agents manipulated by Maoist officials, and therefore not an independent social movement but a special form of "repressive collective action"?[5] Or did the red guards express independent social forces that spiraled out of the control of their elite sponsors? Early social interpretations of the red guard movement argued strongly for the latter: red guards did not simply carry out a suppression campaign in conformity with the directives of Maoist officials. They were not a quasi-official militia of conformists who attacked alleged enemies of the people. The split into conservative and rebel factions showed that much more was involved; underlying social forces were activated that proved impossible to control, and this is why in the end Mao was forced to impose martial law.[6]

In Chinese-language scholarship this has been a major point of contention. Some writers, consistent with the common view abroad, have distinguished between "two Cultural Revolutions": factional divisions and power struggle at the elite level and a social movement at the mass level. The movements at the mass level, according to this view, reflected real social tensions and often had very different motivations from those of their official sponsors. The "two Cultural Revolutions" proceeded along parallel but separate tracks. One version of this argument is that red guard conflicts reflected "social contradictions" within the Chinese population that were inadvertently stimulated by elite strife.[7] A more pointed version is that the rebel movement expressed independent opposition to oppressive political rule and widespread social injustice.[8] Others dispute this interpretation and deny that there is a useful distinction to be drawn between "two Cultural Revolutions." Party historians insist that there was only one Cultural Revolution. At the elite level, ultra-leftists engaged in attacks on loyal comrades and propagated erroneous theories about class struggle under socialism. At the mass level, social conflicts expressed this ideological confusion and the manipulations of elite conspirators—they were not political rebellions against oppressive institutions and certainly were not instances of class-based conflicts.[9] Others argue more directly that rebels with independent aims were actually very rare, and that the alleged alignment between social background and political orientation claimed by overseas scholars has been based on obvious conceptual confusion and the exaggeration of limited evidence.[10]

Were the red guards, then, an instance of "top-down" mobilization, a loose and disorderly militia that did the bidding of elite sponsors? Or were they an expression of "bottom-up" social forces, a mass movement that developed independent aims often at variance with those of its elite sponsors? In my portrayal of the Beijing red guards one can certainly find evidence consistent with both points of view, and it is tempting to conclude that the truth is somewhere in between. But in fact neither interpretation is satisfactory. The various movements among Beijing's red guards were not a product of top-down mobilization, even though the CCRG did manipulate and direct student militants in both obvious and less visible ways. And even though the red guards ultimately frustrated elite attempts at manipulation, their factional struggles did not express latent conflicts in Chinese society bred by its structure of social and political inequality. The evidence—at least for Beijing—points to a third and entirely different alternative.

Clearly the red guards were subject to extensive manipulation by CCRG politicians who established myriad organizational ties with student leaders, met with them constantly and advised about strategy, provided extensive resources, and maintained close surveillance of campuses through an extensive intelligence network. With rare exceptions the Beijing rebels were enthusiastic followers of the directives of their CCRG sponsors, even when this involved the draconian suppression of their student rivals on obviously trumped-up political charges. When the CCRG deemed it necessary, it did not hesitate to crush dissident red guards that directly challenged its authority.

Despite strong elite ties and extensive manipulation, the Beijing red guards nonetheless spiraled out of control. The most obvious instance is the brief but daring countermovement of the dissident red guards near the end of 1966. The dissident campaign was a full frontal assault on the

CCRG by students who had been highly active from the beginning of the Cultural Revolution, especially the high-school militants who had been celebrated by Mao himself. These students reacted against the way they were stigmatized as "revisionist red guards" by their erstwhile CCRG sponsors, and their rebellion bore a strong resemblance to the minority faction's earlier struggle against the work teams and the ministries that sheltered them.

The dissident red guards were suppressed with relative ease, but the CCRG was powerless to curb factional fighting among its loyal followers in the rebel movement after January 1967. After student rebels proved utterly incompetent in their attempts to imitate the Shanghai power seizure, they undermined efforts to stabilize new "revolutionary" organs of power in the nation's capital and became a serious political liability. Remarkably, the Beijing red guards played virtually no useful role for Mao and the CCRG after January 1967, when the main action of the Cultural Revolution moved to the provinces. The early decision to put Beijing under the joint control of the Ministry of Public Security and the Beijing Garrison Command signaled this reality. Although the rebels proved difficult to control, they were by no means attempting to take the movement in a different direction. Their battles were not with authority figures but with one another. They did periodically challenge individual leaders, occasionally taking shots at figures like Xie Fuzhi and Chen Boda, but they did not at any point challenge the authority of the CCRG or the new Beijing Revolutionary Committee. This internal squabbling led eventually to small-scale civil wars among rival followers of the CCRG. It turned the rebel movement into an irrelevant and frustrating sideshow for its elite sponsors, but it by no means constituted a political movement that had independent aims.

Beijing's red guard movement is perhaps best characterized as extensive mass participation in a tumultuous episode of bureaucratic politics. Of central importance is the fact that the factional divisions—both the 1966 split between conservatives and rebels and the later rivalry between the Heaven and Earth wings of the rebel movement—did not express conflicts of interest between groups that had different orientations toward the status quo. I have shown that the primary fault lines between the majority and minority factions in late 1966 were conflicts between diverse coalitions of students from essentially similar backgrounds. The division between the Heaven and Earth factions was a further split within the rebel movement that only occasionally—as at Qinghua University after

April 1967—spurred the articulation of different political orientations toward the status quo.[11] But even the moderate stance of Qinghua's 414 faction on the cadre question and pre–Cultural Revolution power structures originated in tactical opportunity rather than beliefs that it articulated from the beginning of the movement.

The central point in my account of Beijing's red guards is that their identities and interests were forged in a series of dramatic political interactions whose outcomes left participants on opposite sides of a new political divide. These interactions generated new cleavages and political identities and committed participants to courses of action that were highly consequential for them personally. This analysis differs from models of contentious politics that presume that the interests of participants are fixed by membership in social categories or political networks or by preexisting moral commitments or political ideologies. It also contrasts with theories of social movements that view these prior characteristics as playing out primarily through strategic responses to political opportunities or the changing availability of resources.[12] The analysis developed in this book takes context and sequences of interaction as the central mechanisms of interest in generating political cleavages and identities. It also leads to the unmistakable conclusion that red guards were not fighting either to protect vested interests or lay claim to new rights and privileges. They were, quite simply, fighting not to lose.[13] In the context of Chinese politics of that era, to end up on the losing side of a political struggle would lead at best to drastically reduced career prospects and at worst to imprisonment or physical harm.

As a form of mass participation in bureaucratic politics, the Beijing red guard movement was indelibly stamped by the features of the organized hierarchies within which it took place. The power structures of schools ensured that a minority of politically active students responded to efforts to mobilize from above. The decapitation and splintering of these power structures by work teams divided politically active students against one another. The closed nature of the political system and of educational and career ladders ensured that the stakes for students were large and the consequences of defeat potentially irreversible. The organizational structures that linked ministries with universities strictly defined lines of attack for rebel factions as they assaulted government agencies in efforts to reverse the verdicts of work teams. The rebel alliance broke apart as factions began to cross separate lines of bureaucratic authority, competed to seize power in the same state agencies, and found themselves inadvertently drawn into factional conflicts among government person-nel. The intelligence networks established by the CCRG, which reached into campuses and even into red guard factions themselves, provided ex-tensive information about the disposition of red guard groups and lines of communication to steer rebel factions in one direction or another. The Beijing red guard movement operated within a highly organized po-litical hierarchy that was temporarily in disarray but whose structures still exerted an irresistible pull on the motives and actions of the partic-ipants.

On further reflection, what is most remarkable about the Beijing red guard movement—or the variety of distinct submovements that I have described—is the extent to which the various mobilizations were ulti-mately defensive in nature, and that the conflicts and grievances they ex-pressed were generated by recent short-term processes. The minority fac-tion's rebellion against majority domination of its campuses and its attacks on ministries to "drag out" and denounce work-team leaders were attempts to nullify the potentially devastating impact of political verdicts lodged against its members in June and July 1966. The majority faction's mobilization in response to the minority faction's challenge was in turn an effort to avoid being implicated in the recent political errors of the work teams and to prevent students openly hostile to it from taking power. The daring movement by dissident red guards to challenge the CCRG as cynical manipulators was an effort to extricate themselves from the charge that they were not genuine rebels but willing tools of the "bourgeois reactionary line." In this sense, the motives of these "conser-vative" dissidents were remarkably similar to those of their "rebel" enemies.

Finally, the deep-seated and stubborn campus factionalism over the formation of school revolutionary committees and the citywide political gridlock created by the Heaven and Earth alliances resulted from the ef-fort by both sides to prevent hostile enemies from taking control of their campuses. By late 1967 factional opponents had already shown a propensity for violence that signaled a real prospect of physical harm should the other side win. Without powerful third parties to restrain the winning faction, it could act on political accusations that by the summer of 1967 had already become far more extreme than those the work teams had lodged against their opponents the previous year. In each of these in-stances, and in a variety of circumstances, the red guards were fighting not to lose. The strength of these movements and their imperviousness to persuasion and control were not due to opposing views of the status quo that expressed the conflicting interests of different status groups. These were essentially struggles to ensure that the participants would not lose their previously secure and relatively privileged positions in that status quo once the political order was rebuilt.

GLOSSARY OF NAMES

BEIJING RED GUARD CHRONOLOGY

WORK-TEAM CASE HISTORIES

NOTES

REFERENCES

INDEX

# GLOSSARY OF NAMES

**Bo Yibo** Vice-premier, alternate member of the Politburo, and chairman of the State Economic Commission and the CCP Industry and Transportation Department. Coordinated work teams sent to universities under industrial ministries.

**Cao Yi'ou** Wife of Kang Sheng, member of the Beijing University work team, and staff member of the Central Cultural Revolution Group.

**Chen Boda** Chairman of the Central Cultural Revolution Group, editor-in-chief of *Red Flag*, and deputy director of the CCP Propaganda Department.

**Cui Xiongkun** Member of the Beijing University Party Standing Committee who supported Nie Yuanzi's wall poster of May 25, 1966, immediately after it appeared, and later joined Nie's faction.

**Deng Xiaoping** General secretary of the CCP Central Committee and member of the Politburo Standing Committee. Purged in October 1966 as the party's "number two" revisionist.

**Ge Hua** Member of the Beijing University Party Standing Committee who supported Nie Yuanzi's wall poster of May 25, 1966, immediately after it appeared, but later joined the faction opposed to Nie.

**Guan Feng** Member of the Central Cultural Revolution Group and the editorial committee of *Red Flag* and vice-director of the General Political Department of the People's Liberation Army.

**Guo Yingqiu** Vice-president and party secretary of Chinese People's University. Appointed secretary for culture and education of the new Beijing Municipal Party Committee in late May 1966. Placed in charge of university work teams.

**Han Aijing** Leader of the minority Red Flag faction at Beijing Aeronautics Institute. Joined the Heaven faction in 1967.

**He Changgong** Party secretary of the Ministry of Geology who clashed with rebels from the Beijing Geology Institute.

**Hu Qili** Member of the national Secretariat of the Communist Youth League and head of the Western District Work Team in charge of high schools.

**Hu Yaobang** First party secretary of the Communist Youth League and in charge of work teams for Beijing's high schools. Denounced and purged in August 1966.

**Jiang Nanxiang** President and party secretary of Qinghua University; minister of higher education and alternate member of the Politburo.

**Jiang Qing** Wife of Mao Zedong. Vice-chairman of the Central Cultural Revolution group in May 1966. Arrested as one of the Gang of Four in 1976; committed suicide in prison in 1991.

**Kang Sheng** Chief advisor to the Central Cultural Revolution Group; member of the CCP Secretariat with responsibilities for ideology, intelligence, and security. Died in 1975.

**Kong Fan** Philosophy Department ally of Nie Yuanzi at Beijing University early in the Cultural Revolution; later split with Nie and joined the opposing faction.

**Kong Yuan** Vice-head of the External Affairs Office of the Central Party Secretariat and director of China's central intelligence agency. Father of Kong Dan, a founder of the Western District Picket Corps.

**Kuai Dafu** Minority-faction leader at Qinghua University who rose to prominence in the capital's rebel movement in late 1966; a leader of the Heaven faction in 1967.

**Li Xuefeng** Appointed first secretary of the new Beijing Municipal Party Committee in May 1966. Member of the Secretariat and the Central Committee.

**Lin Biao** Minister of defense and vice-chairman of the Central Committee; designated Mao's successor in August 1966. Died in a plane crash in 1971 after an alleged coup attempt.

**Lin Jie** Staff member of the Central Cultural Revolution Group and associate editor of *Red Flag*. Purged in September 1967.

**Liu Shaoqi** State chairman and Vice-chairman of the CCP Central Committee; China's second-ranking leader. Purged as China's leading "revisionist" in October 1966; died in prison in 1969.

**Liu Zhijian** Vice-chairman of the Central Cultural Revolution Group and chairman of the People's Liberation Army Cultural Revolution Group. Purged in December 1966 after resisting the extension of the movement into military academies.

**Lu Ping** President and first party secretary of Beijing University, criticized in the celebrated "first Marxist-Leninist wall poster" at the school and purged at the outset of the Cultural Revolution.

**Mu Xin** Member of the Central Cultural Revolution Group and editor of *Guangming ribao*. Purged in early 1967.

**Nie Yuanzi** General branch secretary of the Beijing University Philosophy Department; senior author of the "first Marxist-Leninist wall poster" of the Cultural Revolution. Aligned with the Heaven faction in 1967. Appointed chairman of the Capital Red Guard Congress in February 1967 and vice-head of the Beijing Revolutionary Committee in April 1967.

**Peng Dehuai** Minister of defense purged in 1959 for a critical letter to Mao about the Great Leap Forward. Brought back to Beijing for struggle sessions in late 1966.

**Peng Xiaomeng** Founder and leader of Beijing University High School Red Flag; initially celebrated as a model rebel but later denounced and arrested for opposition to the Central Cultural Revolution Group in late 1966.

**Peng Zhen** First party secretary and mayor of Beijing; purged in late May 1966.

**Qi Benyu** Member of the Central Cultural Revolution Group and vice-editor of *Red Flag*. Purged in February 1968.

**Shen Ruhuai** Minority-faction leader at Qinghua University; split with Kuai Dafu and led the opposing 414 faction.

**Song Shuo** Party secretary of Beijing Industrial University and vice-head of the University and Science Work Department of the Beijing Municipal Party Committee. Denounced in the "first Marxist-Leninist wall poster" at Beijing University and purged at the outset of the Cultural Revolution. Died in custody in 1968.

**Sun Pengyi** Political instructor in the Beijing University Philosophy Department and close ally of Nie Yuanzi. Second in command of Nie's rebel faction.

**Sun Youyu** Party vice-secretary of the First Machine Building Ministry and head of the Beijing Normal University work team.

**Tan Houlan** Minority-faction leader of the rebel group Beijing Normal University Jinggangshan; joined the Earth faction in 1967.

**Tan Lifu** Majority-faction leader at Beijing Industrial University whose August speech in defense of his school's second work team attained short-lived celebrity but was later denounced by the Central Cultural Revolution Group. Arrested in late 1966.

**Tao Zhu** Appointed advisor to the Central Cultural Revolution Group and head of the CCP Propaganda Department in August 1966. Purged in December 1966 after opposing the extension of the movement into industrial enterprises.

**Wang Dabin** Minority-faction leader of the rebel group Beijing Geology Institute East Is Red; joined the Earth faction in 1967.

**Wang Guangmei** Staff member of the Central Committee Secretariat and wife of Liu Shaoqi; advisor to the Qinghua University work team. Purged in late 1966.

**Wang Li** Member of the Central Cultural Revolution Group and vice-editor of *Red Flag*. Purged in September 1967.

**Wang Renzhong** Vice-chairman of the Central Cultural Revolution Group; Alternate member of the CCP Central Committee. In charge of the student movement in Beijing; purged in December 1966 for resisting the escalation of the movement.

**Wu De** First party secretary of Jilin Province; appointed second party secretary of the Beijing Municipal Party Committee in May 1966 and vice-head of its successor, the Beijing Municipal Revolutionary Committee, in April 1967.

**Xie Fuzhi** Minister of public security; appointed head of the Beijing Municipal Revolutionary Committee in April 1967.

**Xu Ming** Vice-secretary of the State Council Secretariat, mother of Kong Dan, red guard leader, and founder of the Western District Picket Corps. Purged and committed suicide in December 1966.

**Yan Changgui** Staff member of the Central Cultural Revolution Group who did liaison work with red guard factions.

**Yang Chengwu** Acting chief of staff of the People's Liberation Army. Purged in February 1968.

**Yang Keming** Philosophy Department ally of Nie Yuanzi at Beijing University during the Socialist Education Movement and the primary author of the "first Marxist-Leninist wall poster." Later split with Nie and joined the opposing faction.

**Yao Wenyuan** Member of the Central Cultural Revolution Group; vice-head of the Propaganda Department of the Shanghai Municipal Party Committee. Arrested as a member of the Gang of Four in 1976.

**Ye Lin** Vice-chairman of the State Planning Commission; headed the Qinghua University work team.

**Yong Wentao** Vice-head of the CCP Propaganda Department; handled liaison work with high-school red guards under the direction of Premier Zhou Enlai. Purged in December 1966.

**Zhang Chengxian** Head of the Beijing University work team; member of the Secretariat of the Hebei Province Party Committee. Denounced and purged in August 1966.

**Zhang Chunqiao** Vice-chairman of the Central Cultural Revolution Group; member of the Secretariat of the Shanghai Municipal Party Committee. Arrested as a member of the Gang of Four in 1976.

**Zhao Ruzhang** Headed the Beijing Aeronautics Institute work team; bureau chief in the National Defense Science and Technology Commission.

**Zhou Enlai** Prime minister and member of the Politburo Standing Committee. Survived the Cultural Revolution despite political animosities caused by his stubborn and subtle resistance to the initiatives of the Central Cultural Revolution Group. Died in January 1976.

**Zhou Rongxin** Secretary general and head of the State Council office under Zhou Enlai. Purged at the end of 1966 for his role in supporting the red guard picket corps.

**Zhu Chengzhao** Minority-faction rebel at the Beijing Geology Institute and a founder of the rebel Third Headquarters; denounced and arrested in early 1967 after expressing doubts about the aims of the Central Cultural Revolution Group.

**Zou Jiayou** Headed the Beijing Geology Institute work team; vice-minister of the Ministry of Geology.

# BEIJING RED GUARD CHRONOLOGY

## 1966

May 14   Kang Sheng sends his wife Cao Yi'ou and an "investigation group" to instigate denunciation of Beijing University's (Beida's) party secretary.

May 25   "First Marxist-Leninist wall poster" signed by Nie Yuanzi and six others at Beida denounces the party secretary.

May 28   The Central Cultural Revolution Group (CCRG) is established.

June 1   Evening radio broadcast reports the Beida wall poster with editorial praise; print media do so the next day.

June 2   Work team arrives at Beida; work teams are sent to all other Beijing schools over next two weeks.

June 8   Work teams arrive at Qinghua University and Qinghua High School; Qinghua party secretary Jiang Nanxiang is removed from all posts.

June 16   Kuai Dafu posts his first wall-poster challenge to the Qinghua University work team.

June 17   Opposition to work teams reaches high point.

June 18   Violent struggle sessions across the campus at Beida are halted by the work team, which submits report to the Central Committee denouncing the "June 18 Incident."

June 19   Kuai Dafu argues with Vice-Premier Bo Yibo on the Qinghua campus.

June 20    Tan Houlan defends the Beijing Normal University work team against its opponents in a wall poster.

June 21    "Anti-interference" campaign begins citywide counterattack against opponents of the work teams.

June 22    After consultations at *Red Flag,* Tan Houlan reverses her stand and criticizes the Beijing Normal University work team.

June 24    Criticism campaign against Kuai Dafu at Qinghua University begins.

July 4    Kuai Dafu is confined to his dormitory room and begins hunger strike.

July 13    Kang Sheng denounces the head of the Beijing Normal University work team.

July 14    The head of the work team at Beijing Foreign Languages Institute No. 2 is denounced and removed from his post.

July 16    The head of the work team at Beijing Normal University is removed from his post.

July 18    Mao Zedong returns to Beijing and criticizes the work teams.

July 19    Nie Yuanzi denounces the Beida work team.

July 21    Mao orders the withdrawal of work teams.

July 24    Jiang Qing, Kang Sheng, and Chen Boda visit the Beijing Broadcasting Institute and criticize the school's work team.

July 25–26    Jiang Qing, Kang Sheng, and other members of the CCRG lead mass rallies at Beida to criticize the work team.

July 27    Kang Sheng gives inflammatory speech at Beijing Normal University against the head of the work team.

July 28    Order to withdraw all work teams is issued; Nie Yuanzi is elected chairman of the Beijing University Preparatory Committee.

July 28    In speech to high-school red guards, Jiang Qing makes light of violence committed by students.

July 29    Mass meeting of student activists is held at the Great Hall of the People; Deng Xiaoping, Zhou Enlai, and Liu Shaoqi give self-criticisms.

July 29   Tan Lifu is appointed to the Beijing Industrial University Preparatory Committee and head of the red guards.

July 31   At the Beijing Construction Institute the first recorded factional split occurs between supporters and opponents of the work team.

August 1   Eleventh Plenum of the Eighth Central Committee is convened in Beijing and continues until August 12. Liu Shaoqi and Deng Xiaoping are demoted; Mao praises Nie Yuanzi and high-school rebels.

August 2   Dispute between red guards leads to revenge stabbing at Beijing High School No. 47.

August 3   Opponents of the work team at the Beijing Aeronautics Institute march to Central Committee offices to protest actions by the majority faction.

August 4   Kang Sheng and Jiang Qing lead a mass struggle session against the head and vice-head of the Beida work team; Zhou Enlai chairs a mass rally at Qinghua during which the work team's head gives self-criticism and the charges against Kuai Dafu and others are dropped.

August 5   The party branch secretary of Beijing Normal Girls' High School is beaten to death by students on campus, beginning a wave of red guard violence that kills more than 1,700 through September.

August 6   Jiang Qing and Kang Sheng give speeches to high-school red guards about the party's class line.

August 6   "Urgent Appeal" denouncing red guard violence is issued by red guards from Qinghua, Chinese People's University, and Aeronautics Institute high schools.

August 8   Open split erupts between two nascent factions at Qinghua University.

August 9   Decision of the CCP Central Committee on the Cultural Revolution, the "Sixteen Points," is issued.

August 10   Students from the Aeronautics Institute minority faction march to Central Committee offices to demand return of their work team's head.

August 13   High-school red guards invade and occupy the offices of the Communist Youth League Central Committee.

August 15    More than 500 minority-faction students from the Aeronautics Institute march to CCRG offices to protest a violent clash on their campus.

August 17    Beijing Geology Institute East Is Red, the minority faction, is established.

August 18    First mass rally of red guards is held at Tiananmen Square; Mao expresses his support for rebellion.

August 19    Beijing Aeronautics Institute Red Flag is established to unite the school's minority factions.

August 20    Tan Lifu gives speech in defense of the majority faction at Beijing Industrial University that is widely circulated.

August 21–22    Central Committee forbids military and security forces to interfere with the student movement.

August 22    Minority-faction Maoism Red Guards are established at Qinghua University.

August 23    Beijing Geology Institute East Is Red holds first large protest at the Ministry of Geology.

August 25    Beijing Aeronautics Red Flag begins fifty-day protest at the gates of the Ministry of Defense.

August 25    Western District Picket Corps is established and declares its intention to enforce discipline over red guard movement and curtail violence.

August 26    Red Guard Liaison Office is established by Yong Wentao under Zhou Enlai's direction and encourages self-policing of red guards to curtail violence.

August 27    Qinghua High Red Guards issue "Ten Point Assessment" of the red guard movement, denouncing its intolerance and violence.

August 27    Red guard First Headquarters is established; Jiang Qing encourages red guards to police movement and protect government offices.

August 31    Members of the Western District Picket Corps attack Aeronautics Red Flag protesters at the Ministry of Defense.

September 5    Geology Institute East Is Red sends second mass protest delegation to the Ministry of Geology and remains for two weeks.

September 5    Red guard Second Headquarters is established, dominated by majority factions.

September 6    Red guard Third Headquarters is established to unify minority factions.

September 6    Tan Lifu resigns from his leadership of red guards at Beijing Industrial University.

September 7    A large force from Western District Picket Corps attacks Geology East Is Red protesters at the Ministry of Geology.

September 13   Xie Fuzhi declares support for the minority faction at the Beijing Institute of Politics and Law.

September 15   Tan Houlan of Beijing Normal University Jinggangshan organizes a cross-campus alliance to denounce Tan Lifu's speech.

September 17   The CCRG begins a three-day conference with leaders from college minority factions.

September 19   Geology Institute East Is Red invades offices of the Ministry of Geology.

September 21   Nie Yuanzi orders Beida red guards to unify under her command.

September 21   The CCRG expresses support for Aeronautics Red Flag's protest at the Ministry of Defense.

September 23   Demands of Aeronautics Red Flag are met, and it ends its protest at the Ministry of Defense.

September 23   Zhang Chunqiao encourages Kuai Dafu to establish his own rebel organization; Kuai establishes Qinghua Jinggangshan the next day.

September 26   At a mass rally of the Third Headquarters, Zhou Enlai declares the minority faction's cause correct and orders the rehabilitation of students punished by work teams and the destruction of materials in their case files.

September 27   Red guards at Beida challenge Nie Yuanzi's attempt to consolidate control.

October 1      Tan Lifu announces his withdrawal from the red guards and leaves Beijing.

October 3      *Red Flag* editorial denounces "bourgeois reactionary line," signaling support for minority faction.

October 6    Gigantic Third Headquarters rally is held at Beijing Workers' Stadium; Kuai Dafu leads swearing-in ceremony; Jiang Qing declares CCRG support.

October 6    Wall poster at Beida challenges Nie Yuanzi and belittles her qualifications as a "rebel."

October 8    Long essay by Yang Xun criticizes Nie Yuanzi for dictatorial behavior at Beida.

October 8    Geology East Is Red leads a third protest at the Ministry of Geology, occupies offices, and establishes a permanent presence.

October 9    Central Party Work Conference begins; ends on October 28. Liu Shaoqi and Deng Xiaoping give long self-criticisms.

October 9    Agricultural Machinery Institute East Is Red invades offices of the Eighth Ministry of Machine Building.

October 9    Jinggangshan Red Guards are established as a group in opposition to Nie Yuanzi at Beida; they later join the Third Headquarters.

October 10   Beijing Foreign Languages Institute Red Flag invades the Foreign Ministry.

October 12   Majority-faction students at the Beijing Broadcasting Institute denounce CCRG interference in their school.

October 16   At the October Party Work Conference, Chen Boda denounces Tan Lifu and "revisionist" red guards in majority faction.

October 21   A coalition of rebels from the Forestry, Geology, Chemical, and Post and Telecommunications institutes invades offices of the State Economic Commission.

October 24   Nie Yuanzi expels former allies Kong Fan and Yang Keming from the leadership committee at Beida.

November 7   Beijing Aeronautics Red Flag takes over the Second Headquarters in internal coup and aligns it with the Third Headquarters.

November 16  At Mao's request, Nie Yuanzi travels to Shanghai to encourage rebellion against Shanghai party leaders; she remains there for one month.

November 19  Chen Boda and other CCRG members visit Beijing High School No. 6 and express shock at finding that red guards tortured prisoners.

November 25 Former majority red guards at the Aeronautics Institute issue a wall poster criticizing the CCRG, initiating a campaign that continues into December.

November 27 At Beijing University High School former red guard leaders critical of the CCRG meet to organize resistance.

November 27 Third Headquarters leaders begin three days of meetings with the CCRG about how to combat the dissident campaign of their opponents.

November 30 Li Hongshan, former red guard at the Forestry Institute, denounces the CCRG.

December 5 Liandong (United Action) is established as a result of the November 27 meetings at Beijing University High School.

December 5 At a Forestry Institute debate Li Hongshan criticizes Chen Boda; Qinghua student Yi Zhenya challenges the CCRG.

December 7 Members of Liandong confront Third Headquarters rebels at a conference of the China-Japan Youth Friendship Association.

December 10 Wall posters with the message "Bombard the CCRG" appear at Beida.

December 11 Wall poster by "Yilin Dixi" at Agricultural University High School criticizes Lin Biao.

December 13 *Red Flag* editorial declares the necessity to "exercise proletarian dictatorship over class enemies"; Jiang Qing extols "proletarian dictatorship" in speech to minority faction.

December 14 The CCRG meets with Third Headquarters leaders to discuss suppression of dissident red guards.

December 14 Forestry Institute East Is Red captures Li Hongshan; Aeronautics Red Flag detains two members of Liandong.

December 16 At a mass meeting Jiang Qing attacks red guard picket corps and denounces a group of officials working directly under Zhou Enlai for supporting them.

December 16 Members of Liandong invade offices of the Ministry of Public Security, demanding the release of arrested comrades; over the next month they repeat this action five times.

December 17 Agents from the Ministry of Public Security arrest critics of the CCRG at the Aeronautics Institute.

December 18   Tan Lifu is arrested; students critical of Nie Yuanzi at Beida are captured and arrested.

December 18   Zhang Chunqiao orders Kuai Dafu to unify rebel forces at Qinghua University under his command; Kuai's Jinggangshan absorbs the older minority faction the next day.

December 19   At Beida, Nie Yuanxi captures leaders of the opposition; two are arrested.

December 24   Yang Xun, prominent rebel critic of Nie Yuanzi at Beida, is arrested.

December 25   Kuai Dafu leads more than 5,000 Qinghua students in a down-town march to Tiananmen Square, calling for the overthrow of Liu Shaoqi and Deng Xiaoping.

December 26   Speakers at a mass meeting of Liandong defy the CCRG.

## 1967

January 2   Leadership of Qinghua Jinggangshan splits.

January 6   In Shanghai's January Revolution worker rebels and Zhang Chunqiao seize power from the Shanghai Party Committee.

January 15   Violent clash occurs between rival rebel factions over the seizure of confidential government files at the United Front Work Department.

January 17   Xie Fuzhi releases new public security regulations that designate dissident students as counterrevolutionaries.

January 17   Qi Benyu encourages Beijing student rebels to "seize power" in imitation of Shanghai rebels.

January 19   Liandong's leaders are arrested by agents from the Ministry of Public Security and its headquarters at Beijing University High School is closed down.

January 19   A coalition of rebels backed by Nie Yuanzi of Beida seizes power at the Ministry of Higher Education.

January 20   A second coalition of rebels backed by Tan Houlan of Beijing Normal Jinggangshan seizes power at the Ministry of Higher Education and overturns the first power seizure.

January 21   A coalition of rebels under Tan Houlan of Beijing Normal Jinggangshan seizes power at *Beijing Daily*.

January 22   A second coalition of rebels led by Beijing Aeronautics Red Flag seizes power at *Beijing Daily* and overturns the first power seizure.

January 24   The CCRG meets with rebel leaders to encourage unified rebel command before power seizures.

January 24   Battles take place at Qinghua High School and August 1st School as Liandong holdouts are attacked by opponents and arrested.

January 26   Beijing Normal Jinggangshan and their allies demonstrate on the Beida campus against Nie Yuanzi; protests continue for three days.

January 27   Nie Yuanzi and Kuai Dafu establish Beijing Commune to seize power from the Beijing Party Committee.

February 1   Clashes between rival rebels over the power seizure at the Ministry of Higher Education lead to more than 100 injuries.

February 1   Qi Benyu and Xie Fuzhi inform rebels that the Ministry of Public Security and Beijing Garrison Command will handle Beijing power seizure.

February 8   A CCRG staff member informs Geology East Is Red's Zhu Chengzhao that his views are "completely reactionary"; Zhu soon loses control of East Is Red and is replaced by Wang Dabin.

February 12   Mao informs Zhang Chunqiao that his Shanghai Commune will instead take the form of a more authoritarian revolutionary committee.

February 22   The Beijing Red Guard Congress is established with Nie Yuanzi as chairman.

March 1   *Red Flag* editorial calls for "correctly handling the cadre problem."

March 3   New splits arise on the Beida Cultural Revolution Committee, and several members are expelled after criticizing Nie Yuanzi.

March 8   Red guard First, Second, and Third Headquarters are disbanded.

March 30   *Red Flag* publishes an "investigation report" on the work team's mistreatment of cadres at Qinghua University, claiming that cadres were victims of the "bourgeois reactionary line"; Kuai Dafu challenges the editorial.

April 8    A major battle takes place at the Nationalities Museum between two rival rebel factions, one backed by Nie Yuanzi and Beida Commune, the other by Geology Institute East Is Red.

April 9    The Red Guard Congress splits over hostilities at the Nationalities Museum.

April 11    Geology East Is Red leads a large invasion of the Beida campus to demonstrate against Nie Yuanzi; battles erupt over the next three days.

April 14    A large alliance against Kuai Dafu is established at Qinghua University.

April 20    The Beijing Revolutionary Committee is established; Xie Fuzhi is chairman, and Nie Yuanzi is one of the vice-chairmen.

May 12    Xie Fuzhi orders Qinghua's 414 faction to merge back into Kuai Dafu's Jinggangshan and quarrels with 414's leaders.

May 29    Qinghua's 414 faction formalizes its opposition to Kuai Dafu's planned revolutionary committee.

June 26    Chen Boda and Qi Benyu visit Qinghua in an unsuccessful attempt to negotiate factional unity.

July 3    Several large anti–Nie Yuanzi groups at Beida form an alliance and begin publishing their own newspaper.

July 12    More than 100 cadres switch sides and declare support for Nie Yuanzi's opponents at Beida.

August 4    Violent clash erupts in Tiananmen Square between rebel groups aligned with Nie Yuanzi and Geology East Is Red; the two factions develop clear identities as the Heaven and Earth factions.

August 17    Anti–Nie Yuanzi alliance at Beida formally establishes the New Beida Jinggangshan Corps and is admitted to the Red Guard Congress.

Late August    Wang Li, Guan Feng, and Lin Jie are purged, implicating leaders of the Earth faction.

September 1    Jiang Qing tries to shore up a faltering Nie Yuanzi at Beida, criticizing her political blunders but arguing that she should keep her posts.

| September 7 | Long-dormant rebel opponents of Tan Houlan at Beijing Normal capture her and subject her to a mass struggle session; Kuai Dafu leads massive Heaven-faction march and presses attack against the 414 faction at Qinghua. |
| September 7 | The CCRG declares its support for Tan Houlan, calls for the disbanding of the opposition group, and has its leaders arrested. |
| September 17 | Zhou Quanying, member of the Qinghua 414 leadership, writes a wall poster accusing Chen Boda of being the mastermind behind the "Wang Li–Guan Feng anti-party group." |
| September 21 | Agreement to form a revolutionary committee at Qinghua breaks down after Kuai Dafu charges that Zhou Quanying is a counterrevolutionary. |
| October 19 | Repeatedly lobbied by Kuai Dafu, Xie Fuzhi has Zhou Quanying arrested. |
| October 31 | Xie Fuzhi releases Zhou Quanying from custody for struggle sessions at Qinghua, causing a battle between the two factions. |
| November 16 | Kuai Dafu's forces capture a cadre pledged to 414 and hold a struggle session against him; 414 intervenes, and a brawl ensues. |
| November 23 | Beijing Revolutionary Committee's attempt to negotiate rebel unity at Beida falls apart. |
| December 20 | Kuai Dafu's forces capture Chen Chusan, a 414 leader, charge him with counterrevolution, and torture him before turning him over to the Ministry of Public Security. |
| December 21 | The 414 faction demonstrates at Beijing Revolutionary Committee offices to protest the imprisonment of Chen Chusan. |
| December 27 | Xie Fuzhi, Qi Benyu, and others announce release of Chen Chusan. |

## 1968

| January 4 | A major clash on the Qinghua campus injures large numbers; 414 demands that the campus be put under military control. |
| January 30 | Kuai Dafu captures more than twenty cadres on his list of counterrevolutionaries and has them tortured to obtain confessions; one dies. |

February 5   Beijing Garrison Command begins Mao Zedong Thought Study Classes to resolve factional disputes; they end in failure after two months.

March 20   Geology East Is Red invades the Beida campus with a force of thousands of Earth-faction rebels from several universities; armed conflicts break out on the campus for several days; Nie Yuanzi's forces criticize Xie Fuzhi.

March 21   Wu De warns that criticisms of the Mao Thought Study Classes cannot be used as an attempt to undermine Xie Fuzhi and the Beijing Revolutionary Committee.

March 23   Nie Yuanzi and the Heaven faction declare support for Xie Fuzhi.

March 25   Xie Fuzhi visits Beida to declare support for Nie Yuanzi and orders outside groups off the campus.

March 28   Armed battle erupts between Beida factions; Nie Yuanzi is stabbed during attempts to negotiate a truce.

April 24   Nie Yuanzi receives pledges of support from commanders of the Beijing Garrison at a mass rally; Beida Jinggangshan digs in behind barriers.

April 24   At Qinghua, Jinggangshan attacks a building held by the 414 faction, which repels the attack with rocks and spears.

April 26   The 414 faction attacks cadres pledged to Jinggangshan in their on-campus homes, leading to an exodus of campus residents; Jinggangshan assaults a building held by 414.

April 27   The Qinghua campus is carved up into two zones held by the opposing factions.

May 5   The 414 faction carries the corpse of a slain comrade in a protest march to Tiananmen Square.

May 26   After further campus battles, 414 carries the corpse of another slain comrade in a march to Tiananmen Square.

May 30   A massive battle on the Qinghua campus leaves three dead and more than 300 wounded.

June 19   Nie Yuanzi welcomes defectors from Jinggangshan and claims that more than 1,200 have surrendered.

July 7   After battles at Qinghua with grenades, firebombs, improvised explosive devices, and rifles lead to further deaths, 414 stages another funeral march.

July 9   A large new building on the Qinghua campus is burned to the ground in a major battle.

July 9   The Beijing Revolutionary Committee orders the Beijing Garrison Command to separate the two factions at Qinghua.

July 22   Nie Yuanzi holds a large show trial of captured Jinggangshan leaders.

July 27   The Beijing Garrison Command assembles 30,000 unarmed workers and soldiers to swarm onto the Qinghua campus; Kuai Dafu and Jinggangshan resist, killing five and seriously wounding 149 on the peacekeeping force.

July 28   Leaders of the major red guard factions are summoned to an early morning meeting with Mao Zedong and other top officials; an angry Mao tells them that they have committed serious errors and they must return to campuses and welcome troops.

August 22   The Beijing Revolutionary Committee and the Beijing Garrison Command dispatch 10,300 soldiers and 17,000 industrial workers to the universities; campuses are put under military control.

# WORK-TEAM CASE HISTORIES

## Radical Work Teams

The work team arrived at the Beijing Broadcasting Institute on June 14, seized power, and announced that all high- and middle-level cadres would step down from their posts. Over the next three weeks all cadres and teachers were detained on campus for investigation and mass criticism. All forty-six classroom counselors were forced to step down from their posts pending investigations. The school's party secretary was held in isolation and subjected to a mass struggle session.[1]

At the Beijing Institute of Politics and Law, the work team arrived on June 4 and immediately deposed the school's party committee and announced that all officials down to the level of political instructors would step down from their posts.[2] Three days later it held a large struggle session against three of the top school officials, during which it declared that the entire party organization was revisionist: nineteen of twenty-two division-level cadres were declared followers of a revisionist "black line," as were forty out of fifty-four department-level cadres. More than 300 party and youth league branch secretaries and committee members were forced to undergo a grueling process of confession and self-examination, and 85 percent of the classroom counselors were declared followers of the school's "black line."

At Beijing Normal University the party secretary was denounced in wall posters on June 2 and was stripped of his post two days later, even before the work team arrived on June 6. The work team immediately took over the leadership of the school and conducted a radical purge of the entire power structure.[3]

The Foreign Ministry dispatched a work team to the Institute of Foreign Relations relatively late—June 17—but it acted decisively.[4] It seized power from the party committee and told all cadres to step down for investigation, from the top leaders down to the heads of teaching offices, political instructors and classroom counselors, and even ordinary members of party branch committees. The work team charged that the vast majority of cadres were "conservatives" who had suppressed the masses, and all party and youth league members were put under suspicion as well.

## Conservative Work Teams

The Beijing Institute of Irrigation and Hydropower work team solicited opinions about the party committee from cadres and students and soon found itself deluged with denunciations and complaints.[5] The Ministry of Hydropower had already purged the school's leadership during the Socialist Education Movement the year before and was unwilling to accept the charges. Pressured by its superiors in the ministry to put a lid on things, the work team argued that the party committee was "genuinely leftist." This led to a wave of criticisms of both the party committee and the work team, and the work team retaliated with a campaign against "fake leftists" and "anti-party elements" in which large percentages of cadres, faculty, and students were accused.

The work team sent to the Beijing Sports Institute was willing to conduct a thorough assault on the power structure but refused to eliminate its top officials. The State Sports Commission sent the work team, headed by Vice-Chairman Huang Zhong, on June 10.[6] The work team declared that it had come "to help the institute's party committee carry out the Cultural Revolution" and stated that the school's party leadership was "comparatively good." The work team welcomed mass criticism but refused to accept serious charges against the party secretary and his associates. Of twelve party committee members, nine were suspended from their posts, and five were put in categories 3 and 4. Purges at the lower levels of the power structure were more severe, with very high percentages classified as types 3 or 4 at the department level. Members of the party committee, general branch secretaries, and branch secretaries who denounced the party secretary or other top officials considered reliable were soon accused by others in turn, and the work team labeled them "anti-party."

## Mixed Strategies

The work team from the Ministry of Commerce arrived at the Beijing Institute of Finance and Banking on June 10 and quickly halted criticisms against certain school and ministry officials. One of the members of the school's party committee, Chen Rulong, headed the work team and directed a purge campaign that retaliated against those in the school who had written wall posters critical of him and his associates.[7]

The leaders of the Beijing Normal Institute were denounced by a number of middle-ranking cadres, including general branch secretaries, in the week before the work team's arrival on June 10. The party committee counterattacked, mobilizing its loyalists to charge that its accusers were in fact rightists and alien class elements.[8] The work team deposed the party committee and announced that all cadres, including student political instructors, would stand aside for investigation.[9] Soon it declared the party organization "completely rotten," but somehow the party secretary's own errors were not severe. The work team also decreed that three members of the party committee were genuine leftists and took them on as advisors. Out of some 200 cadres in the school, 138 were labeled "monsters and demons" and subjected to struggle sessions organized by the work team, which did not permit criticism of cadres it designated genuine leftists. All cadres, including student political instructors, were made to stand aside for investigation. From June 24 to July 14 the work team orchestrated a campaign against rebellious cadres and their student supporters, leveling political accusations against them and compiling dossiers to document the charges. After public self-criticisms, the party secretary and her close associates were restored to power.

The Chinese Academy of Sciences dispatched a work team to the Chinese University of Science and Technology on June 6.[10] The work team was organized and briefed by Yu Wen, an Academy official who had been the university's party secretary from 1958 to 1963. This was a conflict of interest that soon became apparent in the work team's conduct. The work team designated Party Secretary Liu Da as the primary target of the campaign. He was removed from all posts, and the work team took over. The work team divided school officials into an "Academy faction" and a "Liu Da faction" and declared open season on all those connected with the latter. Errors committed at the school after Liu Da took over in 1963 were vigorously exposed, but the work team refused to acknowledge that the school's political problems had begun before that date, during Yu Wen's reign. Those who criticized members of the "Academy faction" or the earlier reign of Yu Wen were attacked.

## Work Teams That Reversed Course

The Eighth Ministry of Machine Building sent its work team to the Beijing Agricultural Machinery Institute on June 4. For almost two weeks it defended the party committee against escalating attacks, and one of the vice-ministers came to the school and accused the critics of anti-party sentiments. Criticisms nonetheless escalated until the work team reversed course on June 14, took control of the school, deposed the party leadership, and made all cadres step down from their posts. The work team declared that the entire party committee was revisionist and that all but a few party members were problematic, and conducted a radical purge.[11]

The work team arrived at the Beijing Foreign Languages Institute No. 2 on June 9. The school had been established in 1964 under the State Council Commission on Foreign Cultural Relations, which assigned Zhang Yan, head of the Political Department of the State Council Office of Foreign Affairs, to lead the work team.[12] The institute's president, Li Chang, was also a vice-chairman of the Commission on Foreign Cultural Relations and head of its party group.[13] Work-team head Zhang Yan had a serious conflict of interest. His wife, Yang Chun, was a vice-chairman of the Commission on Foreign Cultural Relations and could have been directly implicated in accusations that came out of the institute.[14] Moreover, the institute's president, Li Chang, was her colleague on the commission and the head of her party organization.

Zhang initially tried to minimize accusations against the school's leaders, declaring that they had made errors but could still lead the Cultural Revolution with assistance from the work team. Criticisms of the institute's leaders directly implicated officials in the commission, including Zhang Yan's wife. As the criticisms escalated, Zhang reversed course. In a speech on June 14 he declared the school's party committee "fascist." He purged twelve of its members and seized power from the party committee. In the ensuing purge thirty-one of the sixty top leading cadres were targeted in public accusation meetings, and more than 80 percent of all the party, youth league, and political work cadres were targeted as spies and anti-party conspirators and forced to confess and name other members of their conspiracy. They were held in isolation on campus and forced to write self-criticisms. More than 30 percent of the young political instructors were criticized, along with many of the student cadres in the classrooms. In mid-July Zhang Yan was suddenly denounced by Chen Boda and Kang Sheng and removed from all posts, and this action placed his recent verdicts on school officials in doubt.[15]

The Ministry of Petroleum sent its work team to the Beijing Petroleum Institute on June 4, but left the school's party committee in power and let it conduct its own campaign for almost two weeks.[16] During this period the party committee announced plans for an investigation of cadres, but it began slowly, focusing on old professors and other instructors outside the power structure. As students accused top party officials of delaying tactics, the work team finally stepped in on June 16 and deposed the party committee. It formed a Cultural Revolution committee and divided the party leadership into "red" and "black." The party secretary and one of his vice-secretaries were designated leaders of the "red" line and helped orchestrate the purges against a "black line" allegedly headed by another vice-secretary. The ensuing campaign targeted roughly half of the school's officials: 116 cadres were designated followers of the "black line," 40 percent of the cadres in the school. The work team also beat back political challenges to the officials it protected as "red" and lodged counteraccusations against more than 240 critics, labeling 194 of them "rightists."

The Beijing Railway Institute work team abruptly changed course. After taking an initially supportive stance toward the party committee, it accused selected leaders of serious political errors. The recent history of the institute, which had merged with the Harbin Railway Institute in 1953,[17] played an important role in these developments. The Ministry of Railways sent its first work team to the institute on June 5.[18] The work team was reluctant to accept serious charges against the school's party committee. As accusations escalated, ministry officials decided to change course. The work team was reorganized, and Vice-Minister Guo Lu arrived on June 10 with a new definition of the institute's problem. Guo charged that the cadres from the old Beijing Railway Institute, long under the Beijing Municipal Party Committee, were infected by the revisionism of that body, while those who had been transferred from the old Harbin Institute were not implicated. The work team mobilized members of the institute to expose followers of the "municipal line" and to protect followers of the "ministry line." Only one of the top seven school officials was targeted for denunciation; the other six were from Harbin. Below this level, however, the search for followers of the "black line" was extensive. Ninety percent of the general branch secretaries, vice-secretaries, and youth league secretaries were made key targets of the campaign, and only one of eight general branch secretaries escaped the attacks. Almost all basic-level cadres and a significant number of political instructors and ordinary party and youth league members were accused of following the municipal faction.

## Two Work Teams

The first work team arrived at the Beijing Foreign Languages Institute on June 7 and found a campus already filled with wall posters denouncing the party committee. However, the work team's head, a member of the party committee of the Ministry of Foreign Relations, had already decided that the school's leaders had not committed serious errors. Students defied the work team with wall-poster accusations and struggle sessions against departmental party officials. The work team attempted to stop the attacks, but the students accused the work team of an anti-Mao conspiracy. On June 16 a delegation went to the Central Party offices in Zhongnanhai to denounce the work team. It returned with a signed directive stating that the first work team had committed errors and would be replaced by a new work team led by Vice-Minister Liu Xinquan, who arrived the next day. Liu immediately deposed the party committee and took control, abandoned the effort to protect the party organization, and initially won over the opponents of the first work team by permitting students freely to designate targets, make accusations, and hold struggle sessions.[19]

At the Beijing Forestry Institute the first wall posters critical of the school's party committee appeared on the evening of June 1.[20] The Ministry of Forestry's first work team arrived on June 2. Led by Lu Qing, head of the ministry's Political Department, it set up a Cultural Revolution committee led by four members of the party committee. The committee announced that the campaign would focus on only one department. Party secretaries and political instructors warned students that their names were being recorded, and prospects of party membership would be harmed if they made accusations against the party committee.

On June 13 several hundred students held a demonstration against the work team's conservative stance. Sensing that this work team was losing control, the ministry withdrew it and sent in a second one. Led by He Renyin, vice-head of the ministry's Political Department, the new work team, with 150 members, took over the institute and forced all basic-level cadres to stand down from their posts. On the afternoon of June 14, encouraged by the first work team's retreat, more than 1,000 students and teachers held a mass rally on the school's athletic field. They lodged accusations against the party committee for attempting to sabotage the school's Cultural Revolution. A group of young party members loudly denounced the leaders. They said that they were willing to risk their party membership if this was what it would take to defend the Party Center and Chairman Mao. Over the next several days students organized struggle sessions against cadres, including six members of the party standing committee. The work team initially did little to intervene, but on June 21 work-team head He Renyin showed up at a struggle session against a departmental cadre. He told the students that their actions appeared "leftist" on the surface but were actually "rightist." Angered students pursued He Renyin as he left and forced him to stand and debate. The next day the work team mobilized students for a counterattack. At mass meetings on June 23 and 25, most of the speakers criticized the opponents of the second work team and suggested that their behavior was anti-party. In early July mass struggle sessions against an "anti-party clique" expelled 1 percent of the school's party members and suspended another 10 percent. Even higher percentages of youth league activists suffered the same fate.

At the Beijing Light Industrial Institute the first work team arrived in early June. Headed by Zhang Wanhe, head of the Political Department of the First Ministry of Light Industry, it declared that all instructors should feel free to expose one another, whether they were party members or cadres.[21] However, they restricted all such criticism to faculty and lower-ranking cadres; the party committee was off limits. Any wall poster criticizing a middle- or high-ranking cadre had to be cleared in advance by the work team. Over half the faculty and lower-ranking cadres were criticized in wall posters. This policy was challenged in wall posters, and conflict escalated until the first work team was withdrawn on June 14.

The new work team removed the party committee from power and announced that all of its members would stand aside for investigation. Vice-Premier Bo Yibo accompanied the work team to the school and declared that the campaign would start with inner-party criticism and move later to "open-door" mass criticism.[22] His instructions were widely ignored by those who had led opposition to the first work team. Party members and others who refused to submit wall posters beforehand were criticized. Those who defied work-team discipline were attacked for anti-party activities, and the work team launched a campaign against them. On July 29 Jiang Qing and Chen Boda led a CCRG delegation to the school and publicly stripped the work team of its power.[23] This deepened the gulf between the activists who had served the work team and their victims.

# NOTES

In the notes I refer to a complicated array of handbills, wall-poster collections, and other unofficial publications, in addition to the usual published sources. I have tried to keep the citations as simple and clear as possible.

I use a modified version of reference-list style and have avoided complicated acronyms. All citations are in endnotes. I refer to published books and journal articles, which are listed in the References, in the standard fashion—author and date. I depart from this convention by providing full information about primary source materials in the notes. These citations are followed by a reference to a source listed in the References—usually a pamphlet, a wall-poster collection, or a published edition of source materials. The most important of these are the five reprint editions of original documents issued over two decades by the Center for Chinese Research Materials. I refer to these collections with the acronym CCRM, followed by the year that the collection was published, and volume and page numbers. Also important is the database distributed as a searchable compact disk by the Universities Service Centre for China Studies of the Chinese University of Hong Kong. I refer to original sources from this collection—usually handbills and leaders' speeches—as "Cultural Revolution Database 2002."

Wherever possible, I provide a source citation to a published collection. I am unable to do so for some documents that I cite. These materials are in my possession, usually photocopies of originals that I have made in libraries or have received from other scholars. In some cases these are documents that I have purchased in private shops in China. In these instances there is no additional reference to an item in the References.

## 1. The Beijing Red Guards

1. See Chan (1985) and the documentary film *Morning Sun*, produced and directed by Carma Hinton, Geremie Barmé, and Richard Gordon (San Francisco, 2003), which powerfully articulates this viewpoint.

2. L. White (1989).

3. See, for example, Andreas (2007), G. Yang (2000), and Zheng (2006).

4. The same point is made by Xu Youyu (1999), 127–133.

5. Andreas (2002), 467–469; Lee (1975); Lee (1978), 68–84, 129–139; Walder (1978), 39–50.

6. In recent years this consensus has been questioned, particularly by Walder (2002) and Xu Youyu (1999).

7. Lüthi (2008), 46–79; MacFarquhar (1974), 39–56; Taubman (2003), 270–289, 507–528.

8. Goldman (1967), 158–242; MacFarquhar (1960); MacFarquhar (1974), 184–252, 261–310.

9. Kung and Lin (2003); Li and Yang (2005); MacFarquhar (1997), 1–38.

10. Goldman (1969); Goldman (1981), 18–60; MacFarquhar (1997), 39–258.

11. MacFarquhar and Schoenhals (2006), 14–51.

12. During the much more modest Soviet Cultural Revolution of 1928–1931, proletarian students and party members mobilized to attack bourgeois experts and others with reactionary historical connections (Fitzpatrick 1978). Mao shared key assumptions with early Stalinist orthodoxy—most important, the idea that class struggle intensifies under socialism in the form of conspiracies within the party (Walder 1991).

13. Alternative statements of this view abound. See, for example, Andreas (2002), Lee (1975), and Tang Shaojie (1999b).

14. The earliest statements of this perspective were Oksenberg (1968); Vogel (1968); and Vogel (1969), 339–345. It was developed further by Lee (1975, 1978) and figured prominently in many subsequent studies of different social settings (Blecher and White 1979, 77–108; Chan 1982; Chan, Rosen, and Unger 1980; Hua Linshan 1996a, 1996b; Rosen 1982; Unger 1982; Walder 1978, 1996).

15. Perry and Li Xun (1997), 100–107; Walder (1978), 44–45, 69–71; L. White (1976).

16. Rosen (1981); G. White (1974); L. White (1979).

17. G. White (1980).

18. See the translation of the famous essay "On Class Origin," by Yu Luoke, and the accompanying analysis in G. White (1976).

19. Chan (1982); Chan, Rosen, and Unger (1980); Rosen (1982), 147–166; Unger (1982). These same studies found that the question of family heritage was largely absent from factional struggles on university campuses (Rosen 1982, 97).

20. Chan (1982); Kraus (1977, 1981); Rosen (1982), 11–59.

21. Shirk (1982).

22. This consensus is already reflected in standard histories of the Mao era (Barnouin and Yu Changgen 1993; Harding 1991; Meisner 1999, 316–324).

23. Barnouin and Yu Changgen (1993), 100–101.

24. Several books detail events in other cities—Shanghai (Perry and Li Xun 1997), Guangzhou (Rosen 1982), Guilin (Hua Linshan 1987), Wuhan (S. Wang 1995), and Hangzhou (Forster 1990)—although only Rosen's focuses exclusively

on students and restricts its attention to the events from 1966 to 1968. Kwong (1988) offers a concise overview of the student movement nationwide. Recent Chinese-language books on the red guards have either a national focus (Xu Youyu 1999) or concentrate on one university (Tang Shaojie 2003). Bu Weihua's (2008) account of national politics from 1966 to 1968 devotes considerable attention to Beijing.

25. See the review of new sources in Esherick, Pickowicz, and Walder (2006), 6–16.

26. Walder (1986).

27. Walder (1996).

28. Walder and Hu (2009). This figure is based on retrospective questions in a sample survey conducted in the mid-1990s.

29. Andreas (2002, 473) estimated that 7 percent of Qinghua University students were from "revolutionary" households on the eve of the Cultural Revolution.

30. I expected to see a form of network mobilization similar to that described by Gould (1991, 1996) in other historical settings.

31. Interviews with strategically placed former participants were very useful, but they could never accurately establish the timing and sequence of events or the specific claims and political language used at the time. Interviewees can recall vivid anecdotes and offer interpretations that in isolation seem highly authoritative, but I have often found that they are convincingly refuted by the documentary record, revealing inaccuracies, half-truths, and self-serving myths that would otherwise intrude directly into the analysis.

32. Barnouin and Yu Changgen (1993), 75. Similar portrayals of work teams, not always stated so clearly and emphatically, can be found in Harding (1991), 136, 142–143; Kwong (1988), 20–21; Lee (1978), 50–53; and Pepper (1991), 544–545. This portrayal was offered by prominent political actors at the time, for example, Chen Boda, who later repeated his earlier denunciation of the work teams in memoirs dictated to his son, "The emphasis of many work teams was to carry out criticisms of the so-called 'bourgeois academic authorities,' but with regard to the former school party committees and branches, they basically protected them" (Chen Xiaonong 2005, 282).

33. For example, Liu Zhijian, briefly a member of the Central Cultural Revolution Group, asserted many years later, "In general, those who originally supported the school party committees also supported the work teams who came to lead the 'Cultural Revolution'; those who originally opposed the party committees wanted to kick aside both the school party committee and the work team" (Liu Zhijian 2000, 32).

34. This is the central point of Xu Youyu's (1999, 81–83, 109–115) critique of the idea that red guard factions represented the interests of different social

constituencies. He points out that this interpretation either ignores the nationwide split in "rebel" factions or confuses it with the earlier "conservative-rebel" divide.

35. The classic early statements of this perspective are Gamson (1975), McAdam (1982), McCarthy and Zald (1977), and Tilly (1978).

36. See, for example, Benford and Snow (2000), Esherick and Wasserstrom (1990), Goodwin and Jasper (2004), Goodwin, Jasper, and Polletta (2001), and Zuo and Benford (1995).

37. See the overview and critique in Walder (2009).

38. Few, if any, of these circumstances describe the student protests in China in the spring of 1989. In that case the central puzzle is how, against a well-organized and hostile regime, the students were able to mobilize not only themselves but large numbers of ordinary citizens (Calhoun 1994; Walder 1989, 1998; D. Zhao 1998).

39. Bu Weihua (2008), 608–609; Organization Department, CCP Central Committee (2000), 10:61. MacFarquhar and Schoenhals (2006, 100) state that by 1967 it had a bureaucracy "employing hundreds, if not thousands."

40. Kang arrived at the Yan'an base area in 1937 (Byron and Pack 1992, 113–132; Zhong Kan 1982, 343–348).

41. Byron and Pack (1992), 171–184; Teiwes and Sun (1995); Zhong Kan (1982), 74–95. Kang's role in this campaign earned him many enemies, and he came under fire at the Seventh Party Congress in 1945 and lost his position as head of the intelligence and security committees. After 1949 he was shunted off to his home province of Shandong and in 1956 was demoted to alternate status on the Politburo (Byron and Pack 1992, 188–201; Organization Department, CCP Central Committee 2000, 9:36, 41; Organization Department, CCP Central Committee 2004, 290–291; Zhejiang Provincial Party Committee Party School 1984, 73–75).

42. As the movement got under way, he was elevated from alternate membership in the Politburo all the way up to the Politburo Standing Committee (Organization Department, CCP Central Committee 2000, 10:23; Organization Department, CCP Central Committee 2004, 291).

43. MacFarquhar (1997), 439–443; MacFarquhar and Schoenhals (2006), 14–19; Terrill (1999), 213–238.

44. Chen Xiaonong (2005), 305–306; MacFarquhar and Schoenhals (2006), 100–101; Organization Department, CCP Central Committee (2000), 10:61. Jiang Qing was not officially appointed to the Central Committee until the Ninth Party Congress of April 1969, when she entered the Politburo (Organization Department, CCP Central Committee 2000, 10:32).

45. Goldman (1967), 37–42; Organization Department, CCP Central Committee (2004), 35; Wylie (1980), 177–194, 213–225.

46. Like Kang Sheng, Chen Boda was elevated from alternate membership in the Politburo to the Politburo Standing Committee shortly after the Cultural

Revolution began (Organization Department, CCP Central Committee 2000, 10:23).

47. Barnouin and Yu Changgen (1993), 48–49; MacFarquhar and Schoenhals (2006), 14–20, 27–31; Walder (1978), 5–8. Zhang took over as the top leader in Shanghai in January 1967 and eventually rose near the top of the national party hierarchy, only to be arrested and vilified as a member of the Gang of Four shortly after Mao's death in 1976. Yao Wenyuan, who was Zhang's protégé before the Cultural Revolution as vice-head of the Shanghai Municipal Propaganda Bureau and editor of the Shanghai party newspaper, *Jiefang ribao* (Liberation Daily), was also a member of the CCRG but played little role in the Beijing events. Yao was arrested along with Zhang in 1976.

48. Li Yong and Wen Lequn (1994a), 71–73. Mao's previous secretary, Tian Jiaying, committed suicide on May 23 after falling in the initial wave of Cultural Revolution purges (MacFarquhar and Schoenhals 2006, 44, 472).

49. Li Yong and Wen Lequn (1994a), 55; MacFarquhar and Schoenhals (2006), 473; Organization Department, CCP Central Committee (2000), 9:65; Wang Li (2001).

50. Li Yong and Wen Lequn (1994a), 49–51.

51. Mu Xin (1994, 1997b).

52. These included Xie Fuzhi, minister of public security; Yang Chengwu, acting chief of staff of the People's Liberation Army (PLA); Ye Qun, who represented her husband, Marshall Lin Biao; Wang Dongxing, who headed Mao's security detail; and Wen Yucheng of the Beijing Garrison Command (Bu Weihua 2008, 608–609; Organization Department, CCP Central Committee 2000, 10:61).

53. According to MacFarquhar and Schoenhals (2006, 100), it began with one villa in the compound and eventually expanded to include seven buildings.

54. Liu Jinglin (2004); Shen Ruhuai (2004), 135–137.

55. This paragraph is based on figures in China Educational Yearbook (1984), 965–966, 969, 971, 1001, 1023.

56. Beijing Statistical Bureau (1990), 481, 488. The second-largest concentration of university students was in Shanghai, which had 42,346, less than half of Beijing's total (China Educational Yearbook 1984, 976–978). Guangzhou had only 22,059 (Guangzhou Statistical Bureau 1989, 543).

57. Andreas (2002, 473) estimates that 25 percent of the students at Qinghua University High School were from "revolutionary" households in 1965, and more than half were from other white-collar households.

58. China Educational Yearbook (1984), 980.

59. See Li and Walder (2001) and Walder, Li, and Treiman (2000) for survey-based estimates of the large impact of party membership on careers during this period.

## 2. The Assault on Power Structures

1. "Beijing daxue qi tongzhi yizhang dazibao jiechuan yige da yinmou" (Wall Poster by Seven Comrades at Beijing University Exposes Major Conspiracy), *Renmin ribao,* 2 June 1966, 1.

2. The Politburo Standing Committee ordered the dispatch of work teams on May 31 (Li Xuefeng 1998, 20–21; Mu Xin 1997a, 56).

3. Zhang Chengxian (1999), 17–18. Mao ordered Kang Sheng to arrange the broadcast immediately. Zhou Enlai was notified shortly beforehand, and Liu Shaoqi learned of the decision via radio (Mu Xin 2000, 170–171).

4. "Zhonggong zhongyang jueding gaizu Beijing shiwei" (Party Center Decrees Reorganization of Beijing Municipal Party Committee), *Renmin ribao,* 4 June 1966, 1.

5. "Li Xuefeng liuyue ershisan ri zai Beijing Shiwei gongzuo huiyi shang de jianghua (zhailu)" (Li Xuefeng's Speech on June 23 at the Beijing Municipal Party Committee Work Conference [Excerpts]) (Beijing University Cultural Revolution Committee 1966c, 25).

6. Beijing Aeronautics Institute Red Flag (1966b), 3.

7. Beijing University Cultural Revolution Committee (1966c), 25.

8. Chinese People's University Red Guard Headquarters (1966), 44–45.

9. "Li Xuefeng liuyue sanri zai Shiwei gongzuo huiyi shang de jianghua (zhailu)" (Li Xuefeng's Speech on June 3 at the Municipal Party Committee Work Conference [Excerpts]) (Beijing University Cultural Revolution Committee 1966c, 22–23).

10. Ibid., 25.

11. See Cheek (1997), 282–283. Deng Tuo committed suicide on May 18 (Beijing Municipal Party Committee 1987a, 11). Guo Yingqiu recalled a sense of foreboding about replacing him and tried to avoid taking up the post (Guo Yingqiu and Wang Junyi 2002, 46).

12. Guo Yingqiu and Wang Junyi (2002), 49.

13. The ministries are listed in Organization Department, CCP Central Committee (2000), 15:189.

14. Reportedly, 420 work teams were sent out to schools, research institutes, and cultural organizations; Guo Yingqiu, "Beijing shi wenjiao xitong wenhua da geming yundong huibao yaodian" (Essential Points of the Report by the Beijing Party Committee on the Cultural Revolution Movement in the Culture and Education System), 3 July 1966 (New People's University Commune 1967, 113).

15. The archives of the Beijing Municipal Party Committee cite 3,801 work-team members for fifty-one institutions; Kang Sheng cited a figure of 3,688; "Kang Sheng tongzhi yu Beijing Shida wenhua geming gongzuozu Sun Youyu deng de tanhua jiyao" (Minutes of Kang Sheng's Talk with Sun Youyu and

Others from the Beijing Normal University Cultural Revolution Work Team) (Compilation, n.d., 1–12, at 2).

16. Guo Yingqiu, "Essential Points" (New People's University Commune 1967, 114).

17. Loyalist mobilization was common in factories around the country, where work teams were rarely sent (Walder 1996). In Shanghai this generated a large worker alliance loyal to the Municipal Party Committee (Perry and Li Xun 1997).

18. The only missing school out of the largest ten is the Beijing Industrial Institute, a technical college under the National Defense Science and Technology Commission with 4,153 students (Ni Fuqing and Pan Zhitian 1995, 507). The other missing schools among the twenty-one with enrollments above 2,000 are the Beijing Chemical Institute, with 2,902 students (Zhou Wanxiang 1996, 119) and the Beijing Machinery Institute, with 2,503 (Li Xiaofeng 1992, 1043).

19. Official reports submitted at the time say that thirty-nine work teams were withdrawn after initial clashes with students (Beijing Municipal Party Committee 1987a, 21; New People's University Commune 1967, 114). In only five of the twenty-seven schools in my sample was a work team replaced. Either replacement was much more common in the many small schools not included in my sample, or many of the thirty-nine work teams "chased away" later returned.

20. Events at four smaller institutions with radical work teams—Beijing Normal University, the Beijing Institute of Politics and Law, the Beijing Broadcasting Institute, and the Institute of Foreign Relations—are documented in the Appendix, "Work-Team Case Histories."

21. Beijing University's work team was headed by a member of the Hebei Province Secretariat, and its leaders were from the CCP's Theoretical Study Group and Organization Department, the Ministry of Higher Education, the State Council Office on Culture and Education, the Communist Youth League Secretariat, and the People's Liberation Army (Wang Xuezhen et al. 1998, 644, 647–648). Qinghua's work team was led by officials from the State Economic Commission and the Ministries of Forestry and Metallurgy (Qinghua University Jinggangshan Red Guards 1966, front matter). The head of Beijing Normal University's work team was from the First Ministry of Machine Building (Compilation n.d., 1; Organization Department, CCP Central Committee 2000, 15:118). The head of the Beijing Institute of Politics and Law work team was from the Supreme People's Court (Chinese University of Politics and Law, History Editorial Group 2002, 68). None of these officials were from agencies that had supervisory jurisdiction over these schools.

22. See Beijing University Party History Office (2002); Hao (1996); and Wang Xuezhen et al. (1998), 613–628. Lu Ping was Beida's president and party secretary and was on the Beijing Municipal Party Committee (Organization Department, Beijing Municipal Party Committee 1992, 248). He was a student militant

at Beijing University during the anti-Japanese demonstrations of the late 1930s (Israel and Klein 1976, 75–76).

23. Zhao Zhengyi, one of the coauthors, was general branch vice-secretary (Mu Xin 2000, 166–167).

24. Ibid., 166. Her husband, Wu Gaizhi, was on the Standing Committee of the CCP Central Discipline Inspection Commission (Hao 1996, 79; Organization Department, CCP Central Committee 2000, 9:51–53, 10:64). Nie joined the party as a teenager in 1938 and spent the war years in Yan'an. In the 1950s she held propaganda positions in the Harbin city government and was married to Wu Hongyi, a member of the Standing Committee of the Harbin Party Committee (Organization Department, Harbin Municipality 1989a, 71–72, 82; 1989b, 88, 110). They divorced in 1959 after Wu encountered political problems and lost his posts. Nie moved to Beijing after a stint at the Central Party School in the early 1960s, joining Beida in 1963 (Cao Ying 2001, 5025–5030; Nie Yuanzi 2005, 54–82).

25. Kang Sheng initiated this through his wife, Cao Yi'ou. See He Luo and Meng Jin (2002); Lin Haoji, "Beida de yizhang dazibao shi zenyang chulong de" (How Beijing University's First Wall Poster Was Cooked Up), *Beijing ribao,* 9 January 1981; Mu Xin (2000), 167–168; and Walder (2006b).

26. "Beijing daxue wenhua da geming dashiji, 1966.5.25–1966.8.8" (Chronicle of Major Events of Beijing University's Cultural Revolution, May 25–August 8, 1966) (Beijing University Cultural Revolution Committee 1966b, 43–44; Beijing University Cultural Revolution Committee 1966e, 50–51); and Sun Yuecai, "Wo kongsu zheizhong feifa de yeman de baoxing" (I Denounce This Illegal and Brutal Atrocity), *Renmin ribao,* 5 June 1966 (see also Beijing University Cultural Revolution Preparatory Committee 1966a, 8–9).

27. Wang Xuezhen et al. (1998), 643.

28. Central Documents Research Office (1998), 62–63.

29. Zhang Chengxian (1999), 17–18.

30. Wang Xuezhen et al. (1998), 645, 647. Cao Yi'ou lobbied insistently for an appointment as vice-head of the Beijing University work team (Guo Yingqiu and Wang Junyi 2002, 49).

31. They included Liu Yangqiao, anti–Lu Ping member of the Socialist Education work team and a member of the Cao Yi'ou delegation that instigated the wall poster; Ge Hua and Cui Xiongkun, Standing Committee members who sided with Nie and her group over their wall poster; Zhang Enci, who had recently transferred out of the Philosophy Department because of his conflicts with Lu Ping; and Yang Keming and Kong Fan, philosophy instructors who had sided with Nie in earlier conflicts. See "Ping Kong Fan, Yang Keming de zichan jieji fandong lichang" (Suppress the Bourgeois Reactionary Standpoint of Kong Fan and Yang Keming), 8 January 1967 (Beijing University Cultural Revolution Committee 1967, 31–34); Wang Xuezhen et al. (1998), 647–649; and "Yao chedi geming, bu yao gailiang pai" (We Need Thorough Revolution, Not Reformists), 12 October

1966 (Beijing University Cultural Revolution Committee 1966a, 7–11). The last source and Zhang Chengxian (1999) claim that Nie Yuanzi was director of the work team's staff office, a claim that Nie denies (Nie Yuanzi 2005, 145).

32. See the detailed denunciations in Beijing University Work Team (1966a, 1966b, 1966c, 1966d).

33. Wang Xuezhen et al. (1998), 646.

34. The categories are defined in "Zhongguo gongchandang zhongyang weiyuanhui guanyu wuchan jieji wenhua da geming de jueding" (Decision of the CCP Central Committee Concerning the Great Proletarian Cultural Revolution), 8 August 1966, point 8, "On the Cadre Question" (Wang Nianyi 1988, 74–75).

35. Beijing University Cultural Revolution Committee (1967), 31–32; Wang Xuezhen et al. (1998), 648–649.

36. Mao had left Beijing the previous November, residing primarily in Hangzhou. He returned to Beijing on July 18 and expressed dissatisfaction with the work teams the same day, and after several meetings on the subject he ordered their withdrawal (Central Documents Research Office 2003, 1398–1422; Mu Xin 1997a). See Mao Zedong, "Dui che gongzuozu de zhishi" (Directive on the Withdrawal of Work Teams), 21 July 1966 (Mao Zedong 1969, 643–646).

37. See Organization Department, CCP Central Committee (2000), 15:143. Jiang was also an alternate member of the CCP Central Committee (Organization Department, CCP Central Committee 2000, 9:47). While a student at Qinghua, Jiang was an organizer of the "December 9" student movement of 1935 to protest the inaction of the Nationalist regime in the face of Japanese aggression (see Israel 1966). Jiang joined the CCP in 1933, at age twenty, and was a member of Qinghua's underground party branch (Israel and Klein 1976, 62–63). After the Japanese invasion in 1937 he retreated to various base areas and eventually made his way to Yan'an in 1941 (Fang Huijian and Zhang Sijing 2001, 2:371–372).

38. Beijing Municipal Party Committee (1987a), 16; Fang Huijian and Zhang Sijing (2001), 2:753. Tang Shaojie (2003, 1) puts their membership at 528. "Over 400" members arrived on campus on June 9. See "Qinghua daxue dashiji (6.1–6.10)" (Chronicle of Events at Qinghua University, June 1–10), *Jinggangshan,* 10 December 1966, 4 (CCRM 1999, 8:3501).

39. This account is based on " 'Daji yi dapian, baohu yi xiaocuo' shi zichan jieji fandong luxian de yige zucheng bufen" ("Attacking Many to Protect a Few" Is an Integral Part of the Bourgeois Reactionary Line), *Jinggangshan,* 1 April 1967, 2, 4 (CCRM 1999, 8:3628, 3630).

40. Accounts of similar cases at the Beijing Sports Institute and the Beijing Institute of Irrigation and Hydropower are in the Appendix, "Work-Team Case Histories."

41. This account is based on " 'Daji yi dapian, baohu yi xiaocuo' de zichan jieji fandong luxian zai wo yuan zhixing qingkuang de diaocha baogao" (Report

on an Investigation of the Implementation of the Bourgeois Reactionary Line of "Attacking Many to Protect a Few" in Our Institute), *Dongfanghong,* 25 April 1967, 1–3 (CCRM 1999, 3:983–985).

42. This account is based on "Dadao xianxing fangeming fenzi Zheng Zhongbing" (Overthrow the Active Counterrevolutionary Element Zheng Zhongbing), *Minyuan dongfanghong,* 23 January 1968, 2–3 (CCRM 1999, 10:4864–4865); and "Lin Jie fangeming jituan wei shenme ruci fengkuang fandui minyuan kangda" (Why the Lin Jie Counterrevolutionary Clique Wildly Opposed Nationalities Institute Kangda), *Kangda,* 20 September 1967, 7 (CCRM 1999, 10:4537).

43. The similar cases of the Chinese University of Science and Technology, the Beijing Normal Institute, and the Beijing Institute of Finance and Banking are described in the Appendix, "Work-Team Case Histories."

44. This account is based on " 'Daji yi dapian, baohu yi xiaocuo' zai wo xiao de fanban" (Our School's Version of "Attack Many to Protect a Few"), *Renda sanhong,* 27 April 1967, 2 (CCRM 2001, 28:10702); and "Zhongguo renmin daxue gongzuo zu zai ganbu wenti shang shi zenyang daji yi dapian, baohu yi xiaocuo de" (How the Work Team at Chinese People's University Attacked Many to Protect a Few on the Cadre Question), *Xin renda,* 27 April 1967, 1–3 (CCRM 2001, 35:13622–13624).

45. This account is based on "Chedi pipan zai ganbu wenti shang de zichan jieji fandong luxian" (Thoroughly Repudiate the Bourgeois Reactionary Line on the Cadre Question), *Xin nongda,* 1 May 1967, 3 (CCRM 2001, 34:13340); "Tan Zhenlin, Wang Guanlan 'dadao yida pian, baohu yi xiaocuo' zuize nantao" (Tan Zhenlin and Wang Guanlan Cannot Escape Responsibility for Their Crime of "Attacking Many to Protect a Few"), *Xin nongda,* 22 April 1967, 3 (CCRM 2001, 34:13328); and Wang Buzheng (1995), 366–367.

46. This account is based on "Chumu jingxin de yi mu—Yejin bu gongzuodui shi zenyang zai gangyuan shixing 'daji yi dapian, baohu yi xiao cuo' de" (A Shocking Performance—How the Ministry of Metallurgy Work Team Carried Out "Attacking Many to Protect a Few" at the Steel Institute), *Dongfanghong,* 9 April 1967, 2 (CCRM 2001, 6:2365); "Daji yi dapian shi weile baohu yi xiaocuo—Beijing gangtie xueyuan jiu dangwei he yejinbu gongzuodui zai ganbu wenti shang zhixing zichan jieji fandong luxian de chubu diaocha" (Attacking Many Was in Order to Protect a Few—Preliminary Investigation of Implementation of the Bourgeois Reactionary Line on the Cadre Question by the Old Beijing Steel Institute Party Committee and the Ministry of Metallurgy Work Team), *Xin gangyuan,* 15 April 1967, 1–4 (CCRM 2001, 33:12895–12898); and "Zichan jieji fandong luxian heqi du ye! Yejin bu gangyuan gongzuozu zai ganbu wenti shang zhixing zichan jieji fandong luxian de qingkuang diaocha" (How Cruel the Bourgeois Reactionary Line! An Investigation of the Implementation of the Bourgeois Reactionary Line at the Steel Institute by the Ministry of Metallurgy Work Team), *Dongfanghong,* 15 April 1967, 2–4 (CCRM 2001, 6:2369–2371).

47. The other four cases are described in the Appendix, "Work-Team Case Histories." At the Beijing Agricultural Machinery Institute and the Beijing Foreign Languages Institute No. 2 the work team shifted to a radical strategy. At the Beijing Petroleum Institute and the Beijing Railway Institute the work team shifted to a mixed strategy.

48. Organization Department, CCP Central Committee (2000), 17:156–157.

49. This account is based on Beijing Aeronautics Institute Red Flag (1966a, 1966b). Zhao Ruzhang was vice-head of Bureau No. 8 of the National Defense Science and Technology Commission (Beijing Aeronautics Institute Red Flag 1966a, 2).

50. The party secretary essentially resigned in a phone conversation with commission officials, calling the school ungovernable (Beijing Aeronautics Institute Red Flag 1966b, 5).

51. Li Siguang was minister of geology, but he was not a party member and played no role in this campaign. Vice-Minister He Changgong, who was the ministry's party secretary, held real power (Organization Department, CCP Central Committee 2000, 14:97, 15:128).

52. "Wo yuan wuchan jieji wenhua da geming zhong liangtiao luxian douzheng de huigu yu zhanwang" (A Retrospect and Prospect of the Struggle between the Two Lines in Our Institute's Cultural Revolution), 13 October 1966 (Beijing Geology Institute East Is Red 1966a, 4); and "Xiongguan mandao zhen ru tie, er jin maibu cong touyue—Wo yuan sige yue lai wenhua da geming zhong liangtiao luxian de douzheng" (The Impregnable Pass Is a Wall of Iron, with Firm Strides We Cross the Summit—The Struggle between the Two Lines during the Cultural Revolution in Our Institute during the Past Four Months), 30 September 1966 (Beijing Geology Institute East Is Red 1966a, 29). Mei Jianming, a political activist in the institute's Survey Department, was warned by his political instructor about the lessons of the anti-rightist movement after Mei authored wall posters critical of departmental leaders (Xiao Han and Turner 1998, 171–172).

53. Zou Jiayou was vice-minister and head of the ministry's Planning Department (Organization Department, CCP Central Committee 2000, 15:128).

54. "The Impregnable Pass" (Beijing Geology Institute East Is Red 1966a, 29–30).

55. Xu was the ministry's second-ranking party vice-secretary (Organization Department, CCP Central Committee 2000, 9:97).

56. "The Impregnable Pass" (Beijing Geology Institute East Is Red 1966a, 29–30); and "Wei you xisheng duo zhuangzhi, ganjiao riyue huan xintian" (Sacrificing Much for Lofty Goals, Daring to Show That Life Can Change) (Beijing Geology Institute East Is Red 1966a, 20).

57. The other three cases—the Beijing Forestry Institute, the Beijing Foreign Languages Institute, and the Beijing Light Industrial Institute—are described in the Appendix, "Work-Team Case Histories."

58. "Zhonggong Beijing shiwei jueding" (Decision of the Beijing Municipal Party Committee), *Renmin ribao*, 7 June 1966, 1.

59. See Walder (2004), 971.

60. This account is based on "Guanyu Beijing gongye daxue gongzuozu zai ganbu wenti shang shixing 'daji yi dapian, baohu yi xiaocuo' diaocha baogao" (Report on an Investigation of "Attacking Many to Protect a Few" on the Cadre Question by the Beijing Industrial University Work Team), *Dongfanghong*, 13 April 1967, 1–2 (CCRM 1999, 2:673–674); and Walder (2004), 971–975.

61. Wang Nianyi (2005), 68; and Wang Tongyue (1990), 408, 438. Du was assigned to the Division of Chemical Warfare.

62. This account is based on "Genzhe Mao Zhuxi zai dafeng dalang zhong qianjin" (Advancing with Chairman Mao through Great Winds and Waves), *Beiyou dongfanghong*, 3 April 1967, 2 (CCRM 2001, 3:1110); "Yijian shuangdao: Zhu Chunhe tiaodong qunzhong dou ganbu, ganbu zheng qunzhong de zui'e goudang" (Killing Two Birds with One Stone: Zhu Chunhe's Criminal Conspiracy of Inciting the Masses to Struggle against Cadres, and Cadres to Punish the Masses), *Beiyou dongfanghong*, 7 April 1967, 1 (CCRM 2001, 3:1117); "Zai wenhua da geming de zhandou zhong chengzhang" (Maturing through the Struggles of the Cultural Revolution), *Beiyou dongfanghong*, 1 January 1967, 3 (CCRM 2001, 3:1049); and "Zhu Chunhe 'daji yi dapian, baohu yi xiaocuo' er, san shi" (A Few Things about Zhu Chunhe's "Attack Many to Protect a Few"), *Beiyou dongfanghong*, 7 April 1967, 4 (CCRM 2001, 3:1120).

63. Beijing Municipal Party Committee (1966).

## 3. The Genesis of Division

1. Guo Yingqiu, "Beijing shi wenjiao xitong wenhua da geming yundong huibao yaodian" (Essential Points of the Report by the Beijing Party Committee on the Cultural Revolution Movement in the Culture and Education System), 3 July 1966 (New People's University Commune 1967, 114).

2. The other pacified campuses were the Beijing Sports Institute, the Beijing Railway Institute, the Beijing Mining Institute, the Beijing Normal Institute, and the Beijing Foreign Languages Institute No. 2.

3. Wang Xuezhen et al. (1998), 645.

4. In her memoirs Nie Yuanzi (2005, 145) denies holding an official position on the work team but does not deny that she cooperated with it.

5. Zhang Chengxian (1999), 25–28. See also "Ping Kong Fan, Yang Keming de zichan jieji fandong lichang" (Suppress the Bourgeois Reactionary Standpoint of Kong Fan and Yang Keming), 8 January 1967 (Beijing University Cultural Revolution Committee 1967, 31–34).

6. Beijing University Cultural Revolution Committee (1966b), 43–53; Beijing University Cultural Revolution Committee (1966f), 8; Wang Xuezhen et al. (1998), 645.

7. Beijing University Cultural Revolution Committee (1966b), 46–47; Wang Xuezhen et al. (1998), 645–646; Zhang Chengxian (1999), 28–30. A list of fifty-six names of the victims with their titles is provided in Qinghua University Jinggangshan 414 (1967), 2–4.

8. Zhang Chengxian (1999), 30. The work team estimated that at this stage only about 30 percent of the students were politically active in the movement and genuinely committed to it, while another 60 percent were passively going along (Beijing University Cultural Revolution Committee 1966f, 7).

9. Wang Xuezhen et al. (1998), 645–646; Zhang Chengxian (1999), 28–30.

10. Wang Xuezhen et al. (1998), 645–646; Zhang Chengxian (1999), 30. Red guards who later denounced Zhang for suppressing the movement claimed that only one person was labeled "anti-party" (Beijing University Cultural Revolution Committee 1966b, 46–47).

11. "Zhongyang zhuanfa Beijing daxue wenhua geming jianbao (di jiu hao)" (Party Center Transmits Bulletin on the Beijing University Cultural Revolution [no. 9]), 20 June 1966 (Wang Nianyi 1988, 49–50).

12. Beijing University Cultural Revolution Committee (1966f), 9. The report, titled "Report on Twenty Days of the Cultural Revolution at Beijing University," was drafted by Zhang Dehua, vice-head of the work team, with the assistance of Yang Keming (Beijing University Cultural Revolution Committee 1967, 31–34; Zhang Chengxian 1999, 31–32). Cao Yi'ou signed the copy of the report sent to the Central Committee with words of praise (Wang Xuezhen et al. 1998, 636). Zhang Chengxian (1999, 31) notes that members of the work team assumed that Cao Yi'ou represented the views of Kang Sheng.

13. The report, submitted July 3, was titled "Report on Thirty Days of the Cultural Revolution at Beijing University" (Wang Xuezhen et al. 1998, 646; Zhang Chengxian 1999, 31).

14. Wang Xuezhen et al. (1998), 646.

15. Central Documents Research Office (1996), 645–646; Central Documents Research Office (2003), 1421–1422; Mao Zedong, "Dui che gongzuozu de zhishi" (Directive on the Withdrawal of Work Teams), 21 July 1966 (Mao Zedong 1969, 643–646); Mao Zedong, "Zai jiejian daqu shuji he zhongyang wen'ge xiaozu chengyuan shi de jianghua" (Comments at a Meeting with Regional Party Secretaries and Members of the Central Cultural Revolution Group), 22 July 1966 (CCRM 1992, 1:586–587; Mao Zedong 1967, 332–334); Mu Xin (1997a), 59.

16. Beijing University Cultural Revolution Committee (1966b), 49–50; Wang Xuezhen et al. (1998), 648–649; Zhang Chengxian (1999), 33–34.

17. Wang Xuezhen et al. (1998, 649) states that Nie was informed by Kang Sheng's office about Mao's criticism of the work teams. Nie's supporters do not

claim any opposition by her before July 19 (Beijing University Cultural Revolution Committee 1966b, 50; Beijing University Cultural Revolution Committee 1967, 31–34).

18. "Jiang Qing tongzhi, Chen Boda tongzhi zai Beijing daxue de jianghua" (Talks by Comrade Jiang Qing and Comrade Chen Boda at Beijing University), 22 July 1966 (Central Comrades' Speeches 1966a, 18); "Jiang Qing tongzhi, Chen Boda tongzhi zai Beijing daxue dui bufen tongxue de jianghua jilu" (Minutes of Talks by Comrade Jiang Qing and Comrade Chen Boda with Some of the Students at Beijing University), 23 July 1966 (Central Comrades' Speeches 1966a, 18–19).

19. Wang Li, Guan Feng, Liu Zhijian, Qi Benyu, and Li Xuefeng were also present at the debate (Wang Xuezhen et al. 1998, 649; Zhang Chengxian 1999, 37). Transcripts of speeches by Jiang Qing, Kang Sheng, and Chen Boda were circulated widely at the time (Central Comrades' Speeches 1966a, 20–22).

20. This account is based on Beijing University Cultural Revolution Committee (1967, 51–52); Wang Xuezhen et al. (1998), 650; and Zhang Chengxian (1999), 39–42.

21. See "Beijing daxue wenhua geming weiyuanhui choubei wenyuanhui gonggao" (Announcement of the Preparatory Committee of the Cultural Revolution Committee of Beijing University), 28 July 1966, *Xin Beida*, 22 August 1966, 2 (CCRM 1999, 15:6913).

22. Zhang Chengxian (1999, 43) recalled that members of the work team were furious that Cao Yi'ou and Kang Sheng had evaded their own responsibility for the work team's actions.

23. The conflicts at this university are described in considerable detail in Walder (2004), on which much of this condensed account is based.

24. "Tan Lifu jianghua zhushi" (Explanatory Notes to Tan Lifu's Speech) (Beijing Industrial University East Is Red Commune 1966c, 2:23–26n21).

25. This account is based on "Chedi pipan zai ganbu wenti shang de zichan jieji fandong luxian" (Thoroughly Repudiate the Bourgeois Reactionary Line on the Cadre Question), *Xin nongda*, 1 May 1967, 3 (CCRM 2001, 34:13340); and "Tan Zhenlin, Wang Guanlan 'dadao yida pian, baohu yi xiaocuo' zuize nantao" (Tan Zhenlin and Wang Guanlan Cannot Escape Responsibility for Their Crime of "Attacking Many to Protect a Few"), *Xin nongda*, 22 April 1967, 3 (CCRM 2001, 34:13328).

26. Another example is the Beijing Light Industrial Institute.

27. Tang Shaojie (2003), 126.

28. The photo of Kuai can be found in *Renmin huabao* 11 (November 1963): 30.

29. Tang Shaojie (2003), 126.

30. Kuai Dafu, "Liuyue jiuri—sanshiri huodong qingkuang" (My Activities June 9-30), 1 July 1966 (Qinghua University Jinggangshan Red Guards 1966, 42);

"Qinghua daxue dashiji (6.1–6.10)" (Chronicle of Events at Qinghua University, June 1–10), *Jinggangshan,* 10 December 1966, 4 (CCRM 1999, 8:3502); Tang Shaojie (2003), 126–127.

31. See Kuai Dafu, "My Activities" (Qinghua University Jinggangshan Red Guards 1966, 42–43); and Kuai Dafu and Meng Jiaju, "Gongzuozu wang nali qu?" (Where Is the Work Team Heading?) (Qinghua University Jinggangshan Red Guards 1966, 1). Similar observations are recorded in "Chronicle of Events at Qinghua University" (CCRM 1999, 8:3501).

32. Kuai Dafu, "My Activities" (Qinghua University Jinggangshan Red Guards 1966, 43).

33. Kuai Dafu and Meng Jiaju, "Where Is the Work Team Heading?" (Qinghua University Jinggangshan Red Guards 1966, 1).

34. Ibid., 2.

35. Ibid., 2–3.

36. Ibid., 1. "The Nationalist's way of doing things" referred to the fact that Mao's report was penned in 1927, during the communists' early alliance with the Nationalists. The Communist Party employed struggle sessions throughout the revolutionary period (and after), but they were always organized and stage-managed by party cadres and were not the spontaneous peasant actions Mao observed in the 1920s.

37. Ibid., 1–2.

38. Kuai Dafu, "My Activities" (Qinghua University Jinggangshan Red Guards 1966, 43–44).

39. See the transcript in Qinghua University Jinggangshan Corps (1967a), 10–12; and Kuai's brief account (Qinghua University Jinggangshan Red Guards 1966, 45–46). Bo Yibo was chairman of the State Economic Commission and an alternate member of the Politburo (Organization Department, CCP Central Committee, 2000, 9:41, 15:77, 104).

40. Liu Shaoqi was ranked second in the Politburo Standing Committee, behind Mao Zedong, although he would be demoted in August and effectively purged by mid-October. Wang Guangmei was well known for her militant conduct of the 1963–1964 rural Socialist Education Movement (see MacFarquhar 1997, 399–403).

41. See the detailed account in Kuai Dafu, "Ye Lin tongzhi, zhei shi zenme yi hui shi?" (Comrade Ye Lin, What Is This All About?), 23 June 1966 (Qinghua University Jinggangshan Red Guards 1966, 4–8).

42. See Kuai Dafu, "My Activities," and the transcripts of Kuai's speeches at the debates (Qinghua University Jinggangshan Red Guards 1966, 13–22, 43, 47–48).

43. See Qinghua University Work Team (1966).

44. See "Kuai Dafu zai liuyue ershiqi ri bianlunhui shang de fayan" (Kuai Dafu's Statements at the June 27 Debate) and the four open letters of protest that

he wrote between June 28 and July 2 (Qinghua University Jinggangshan Red Guards 1966, 10–13, 22–34, 36–38).

45. See the partial transcript of Bo's statements and Kuai's brief retorts in Qinghua University Jinggangshan Corps (1967a), 12–14.

46. Kuai wrote letters to work-team head Ye Lin on July 5 and 6 reaffirming his hunger strike and demanding that he be permitted to lodge a complaint with the central party offices (Qinghua University Jinggangshan Red Guards 1966, 39–41; Tang Shaojie 2003, 126–127).

47. The visitors were Guan Feng and Wang Li (Fang Huijian and Zhang Sijing 2001, 2, 753; Tang Shaojie 2003, 3).

48. Fang Huijian and Zhang Sijing (2001), 2, 753–754.

49. Central Documents Research Office (1997), 44–46; Fang Huijian and Zhang Sijing (2001), 2, 754; Tang Shaojie (2003), 3–4; and "Zhou Enlai tongzhi zai Qinghua daxue de jianghua" (Talk by Comrade Zhou Enlai at Qinghua University), 4 August 1966 (Central Comrades' Speeches 1966a, 51–55).

50. Unless otherwise indicated, this account is based on Beijing Normal University Jinggangshan Rebel Regiment (1967), 3–6.

51. Cao Ying (2001), 5036; Li Xun (2006), 157.

52. See "Kang Sheng tongzhi yu Beijing shida wenhua geming gongzuozu Sun Youyu deng de tanhua jiyao" (Minutes of Kang Sheng's Talk with Sun Youyu and Others from the Beijing Normal University Cultural Revolution Work Team) (Compilation, n.d., 1–12, at 3–4).

53. "Fennu kongsu Sun Youyu dui women de pohai" (We Angrily Denounce Sun Youyu for Persecuting Us), *Jinggangshan,* 14 January 1967, 2 (CCRM 2001, 24:9213).

54. The outlines of the broader conflict can be inferred from statements made at the university by Wu De (quoted in the following paragraph) and Kang Sheng: "Kang Sheng zai Beijing shifan daxue de jianghua" (Kang Sheng's Speech at Beijing Normal University), 17 July 1966 (Central Comrades' Speeches 1966a, 28–30).

55. Kang was angered by Sun's charge that Lin Jie was supporting a group of rightist students with bad class backgrounds and by plans by students who supported the work team to demonstrate at the offices of *Red Flag:* "Minutes of Kang Sheng's Talk" (Compilation, n.d., 9–11). See also Li Xuefeng (1999, 649).

56. Cao Ying (2001), 5036; and "Wu De tongzhi zai Beijing shifan daxue de jianghua" (Comrade Wu De's Speech at Beijing Normal University), 10 July 1966 (the date is misprinted and should be 16 July) (Reference Materials 1966, vol. 1, sec. 7, 4–5).

57. Beijing Normal University Jinggangshan Rebel Regiment (1967), 5.

58. This account is based on "Guangrong de licheng" (Glorious Course), *Liu.yiliu zhanbao,* 16 December 1966, 4 (CCRM 2001, 26:10145); "Liu Xinquan da zheng qunzhong de qingkuang yi er" (A Bit about Liu Xinquan's Big

Rectification of the Masses), *Hongweibing,* 28 October 1966, 3 (CCRM 1999, 6:2708); and "Renjian zhengdao shi cangsang—Ping woyuan wuchan jieji wenhua da geming zhong liangtiao luxian de douzheng" (The Correct Path in the World Is Tortuous—The Struggle between the Two Lines during Our Institute's Cultural Revolution), *Hongweibing,* 19 October 1966, 1–3 (CCRM 1999, 6:2702–2704). One source of conflict was Liu's insistence that militant students not disrupt the Afro-Asian Conference that was being held at that time (Ma Jisen 2004, 29–30).

59. "Gongzuodui shi zenyang zheng qunzhong de" (How the Work Team Persecuted the Masses), *Shoudu hongweibing,* September 30, 1966, 3 (CCRM 1999, 12:5365).

60. The Beijing Forestry Institute is another case.

61. This account is based on Beijing Aeronautics Institute Red Flag (1966a, 1966b).

62. Beijing Aeronautics Institute Red Flag (1966b), 6.

63. Ibid. "Several hundred" students took part in these delegations.

64. Beijing Aeronautics Institute Red Flag (1966a), 7.

65. Unless otherwise specified, this account is based on "Xiongguan mandao zhen ru tie, er jin maibu cong touyue—Wo yuan sige yue lai wenhua da geming zhong liangtiao luxian de douzheng" (The Impregnable Pass Is a Wall of Iron, with Firm Strides We Cross the Summit—The Struggle between the Two Lines during the Cultural Revolution in Our Institute during the Past Four Months), 30 September 1966 (Beijing Geology Institute East Is Red 1966a, 29–30).

66. Beijing Geology Institute East Is Red (1967b), 49–50; "Gaoju Mao Zedong sixiang weida hongqi xiang zichan jiejie fandong luxian menglie kaohuo" (Hold High the Great Banner of Mao Zedong Thought, Open Fire on the Bourgeois Reactionary Line) (Beijing Geology Institute East Is Red 1966a, 12); and "The Impregnable Pass" (Beijing Geology Institute East Is Red 1966a, 30–31). This account of Li Gui's actions draws on Michael Schoenhals's notes on interviews with former red guard leaders from the Geology Institute.

67. In the early 1960s Li Gui had clashed with two party vice-secretaries over charges of corruption that he had brought against their favored subordinates, and for a time he lost his position on the school's party standing committee (Beijing Geology Institute East Is Red 1968, 45, 58).

68. See Israel and Klein (1976), 82; and Mei Jianming's memoir in Xiao Han and Turner (1998), 172–173.

69. See He Changgong (1987). Portions of his memoirs had already begun to appear well before the Cultural Revolution (He Changgong 1958). Students knew of his revolutionary credentials (Xiao Han and Turner 1998, 172–173).

70. Organization Department, CCP Central Committee (2000), 14:1167; Wang Jianying (1995), 1010.

71. "Hold High the Great Banner" (Beijing Geology Institute East Is Red 1966a, 12). When He Changgong returned to the campus on June 26, he reminded students that he had participated in the real thing almost forty years earlier: "[Mao's] 'Report on an Investigation of the Peasant Movement in Hunan' is already passé, it is no longer applicable today . . . Back then I was a peasant movement leader myself!" See "Wei you xisheng duo zhuangzhi, ganjiao riyue huan xintian" (Sacrificing Much for Lofty Goals, Daring to Show That Life Can Change) (Beijing Geology Institute East Is Red 1966a, 17).

72. Beijing Geology Institute East Is Red (1967b), 49–50; "Wo yuan wuchan jieji wenhua da geming zhong liangtiao luxian douzheng de huigu yu zhanwang" (A Retrospect and Prospect of the Struggle between the Two Lines in Our Institute's Cultural Revolution), 13 October 1966 (Beijing Geology Institute East Is Red 1966a, 5–6); and "Wuchan jieji wenhua da geming dashiji (yijiu liuliu nian wuyue–shiyue)" (Chronicle of Major Events during the Cultural Revolution [May–October 1966]) (Beijing Geology Institute East Is Red 1966a, 1). See "Liu yue ershier ri Bo Yibo dui dizhi xueyuan wenti de pishi" (Bo Yibo's Instructions of June 22 Regarding the Geology Institute Problem) (Qinghua University Jinggangshan Corps 1967a, 15). See also He Changgong (1987), 503–504.

73. "The Impregnable Pass" (Beijing Geology Institute East Is Red 1966a, 32).

74. "Hold High the Great Banner" (Beijing Geology Institute East Is Red 1966a, 25).

75. "Cong shengong xi 'fan ganrao' kan 'daji yi dapian, baohu yi xiaocuo'" ("Attacking Many to Protect a Few" in the Survey Department's "Anti-interference Movement"), *Dongfanghong bao,* 12 April 1967 (CCRM 2001, 9:3270).

76. Beijing Geology Institute East Is Red (1966a), 6. Figures are based on information from 68 out of 137 classes (*banji*) in the school.

77. Unless otherwise indicated, this account is based on Ministry of Post and Telecommunications Cultural Revolution Office (1966), 1–12; Revolutionary Rebel General Headquarters (1967), 2–9; "Yijian shuangdao: Zhu Chunhe tiaodong qunzhong dou ganbu, ganbu zheng qunzhong de zui'e goudang" (Killing Two Birds with One Stone: Zhu Chunhe's Criminal Conspiracy of Inciting the Masses to Struggle against Cadres, and Cadres to Punish the Masses), *Beiyou dongfanghong,* 7 April 1967, 1 (CCRM 2001, 3:1117); "Zai wenhua da geming de zhandou zhong chengzhang" (Maturing through the Struggles of the Cultural Revolution), *Beiyou dongfanghong,* 1 January 1967, 3 (CCRM 2001, 3:1049); and "Zhu Chunhe 'daji yi dapian, baohu yi xiaocuo' er, san shi" (A Few Things about Zhu Chunhe's "Attack Many to Protect a Few"), *Beiyou dongfanghong,* 7 April 1967, 4 (CCRM 2001, 3:1120).

78. Tao Lujia was Bo Yibo's deputy, head of the Political Department of the CCP Industry and Transportation Work Department, and an alternate member of the Central Committee (Organization Department, CCP Central Committee 2000, 14:1167; Wang Jianying 1995, 1010).

79. Beijing Geology Institute East Is Red (1967b), 56.

80. Unless noted otherwise, this account is based on " 'Daji yi dapian, baohu yi xiaocuo' zai wo xiao de fanban" (Our School's Version of "Attack Many to Protect a Few"), *Renda sanhong*, 27 April 1967, 2 (CCRM 2001, 28:10702); and "Zhongguo renmin daxue gongzuo zu zai ganbu wenti shang shi zenyang daji yi dapian, baohu yi xiaocuo de" (How the Work Team at Chinese People's University Attacked Many to Protect a Few on the Cadre Question), *Xin renda*, 27 April 1967, 1–3 (CCRM 2001, 35:13622–13624).

81. "Gongzuozu zai yanjiusuo shi zenyang daji geming lingdao ganbu de?" (How Did the Work Group Attack Revolutionary Leading Cadres in the Research Institute?), *Renda sanhong*, 27 April 1967, 8 (CCRM 2001, 28: 10703).

82. "Our School's Version" (CCRM 2001, 28:10702).

83. The consequences are detailed in Chinese People's University Red Guards (1966a); Chinese People's University Red Guards (1966b), 15–23; Chinese People's University Red Guards (1966c), 29–37; and Chinese People's University Red Guards (1966d), 13–23.

## 4. Divided at Birth

1. "Li Xuefeng, Deng Xiaoping, Zhou Enlai, Liu Shaoqi tongzhi zai renmin dahui tang de jianghua" (Speeches by Comrades Li Xuefeng, Deng Xiaoping, Zhou Enlai, and Liu Shaoqi at the Great Hall of the People), 29 July 1966 (Reference Materials 1966, vol. 1, sec. 7, 39).

2. Ibid., 39–41.

3. Ibid., 41–44.

4. Ibid., 44–46.

5. In his memoirs, Mao's personal physician wrote, "Listening intently, Mao said nothing until Liu Shaoqi made what he called a 'self-criticism' . . . Liu admitted to no wrongdoing, saying only that he and his associates were 'old revolutionaries facing new problems' . . . When Mao heard this, he snorted, 'What old revolutionaries? Old counterrevolutionaries is more like it' " (Li Zhisui 1994, 470). Li Xuefeng (1999, 661–664) describes Mao pacing angrily backstage, muttering sarcastic comments.

6. Li Zhisui (1994), 470. See also descriptions of this event in Beijing Municipal Party Committee (1987a), 20–21; Central Documents Research Office (1997), 43–44; and Song Bolin (2006), 104–105.

7. Their speeches were transcribed and widely circulated. Zhou Enlai appeared at Beijing Foreign Languages Institute No. 2 on July 28 and Qinghua University on August 5 (Reference Materials 1966, vol. 1, sec. 7, 25–26; sec. 8, 16–20); Deng Xiaoping spoke at Chinese People's University on August 2 and at Qinghua on August 5 (Reference Materials 1966, vol. 1, sec. 8, 4–5, 20); Liu Shaoqi went to the

Beijing Construction Institute on three successive days beginning August 2(CCRM 2001, 9:3413–3414).

8. "Chen Boda, Kang Sheng, Jiang Qing tongzhi zai guangbo xueyuan de jianghua (7.24)" (Speeches by Comrades Chen Boda, Kang Sheng, and Jiang Qing at the Beijing Broadcasting Institute [24 July]) (Cultural Revolution Database 2002).

9. Ibid.

10. "Kang Sheng tongzhi yu Bei shida de jianghua" (Comrade Kang Sheng's Speech at Beijing Normal University), 27 July 1966 (Special Compilation 1997, vol. 1, 149–151).

11. "Jiang Qing, Zhu De, Kang Sheng tongzhi zai Beida pipan Zhang Chengxian dahui shang de jianghua (ba yue siri)" (Speeches by Comrades Jiang Qing, Zhu De, and Kang Sheng at the Mass Rally to Criticize Zhang Chengxian [August 4]) (Cultural Revolution Database 2002). Zhang Dehua, vice-head of the work team, authored the report. Kang Sheng's wife, Cao Yi'ou, penned her strong approval of this "counterrevolutionary" report on the copy that she forwarded to the CCP Secretariat. See Zhang Chengxian (1999), 42–43, and the account in Chapter 3.

12. "Speeches by Comrades Jiang Qing, Zhu De and Kang Sheng."

13. Zhang Chengxian (1999), 43.

14. The account in this paragraph is based on Wang Nianyi (2005), 41–51.

15. Mao Zedong, "Paoda silingbu—Wode yizhang dazibao" (Bombard the Headquarters—My Wall Poster), 5 August 1966 (Wang Nianyi 1988, 70). The "wall poster" read: "The nation's first Marxist-Leninist wall poster and the *People's Daily* commentary—how well written they are! Comrades, please reread both of them. It is too bad that over a fifty-day period so many leading comrades from the Center to the localities have acted in violation of their principles. Taking the standpoint of the bourgeoisie, carrying out bourgeois dictatorship, beating back the tumult of our proletarian Cultural Revolution, confusing right and wrong, black and white, surrounding revolutionaries and suppressing different opinions, carrying out white terror, so proud of oneself, propping up the prestige of the bourgeoisie, destroying the aspirations of the proletariat, how despicable! On the heels of the 1962 rightist trend and the 1964 'left' in form but right in essence, is not this cause for deep concern?"

16. Wang Nianyi (2005), 45–46; see also Liu Zhijian (2000), 33–34.

17. "Zhongguo gongchandang zhongyang weiyuanhui guanyu wuchan jieji wenhua da geming de jueding (yijiu liuliu nian bayue bari tongguo)" (Decision of the CCP Central Committee Concerning the Great Proletarian Cultural Revolution [Passed August 8, 1966]), *Hongqi* 10 (10 August 1966), 10–13 (see also Wang Nianyi 1988, 72–77).

18. Beijing Geology Institute East Is Red (1967b), 79–80.

19. On August 4 he met with members of the work team in Zhongnanhai (Central Documents Research Office 1996, 647–648). See "Liu Shaoqi zai

Beijing jiangong xueyuan de sici heihua" (Liu Shaoqi's Four Black Speeches at the Beijing Construction Institute), *Bayi zhanbao Dongfanghong bao (lianhe ban)*, 3 August 1967, 3–4 (CCRM 2001, 9:3413–3414).

20. See the account in Chapter 2.

21. Shen Ruhuai (2004), 19, 25.

22. "Zhou Enlai tongzhi zai Qinghua daxue de jianghua" (Comrade Zhou En-lai's Speech at Qinghua University), 4 August 1966 (Central Comrades' Speeches 1966a, 51–55).

23. Shen Ruhuai (2004), 20–21. The term *chuanlian hui,* which I translate here as "alliance," is more commonly translated as "liaison," but the term literally means "association of links" or "ties."

24. Ibid., 21.

25. Ibid., 5–11.

26. Ibid., 8–10.

27. Ibid., 17.

28. Ibid., 27; see also Zheng (2006).

29. Shen Ruhuai (2004), 22, 28.

30. Ibid., 28–31. The current gate is a reconstructed replica.

31. See Xiao Han and Turner (1998), 10.

32. Ibid., 171–173.

33. Ibid., 173.

34. Beijing Geology Institute East Is Red (1967b, 93); "Beijing dizhi xueyuan dongfanghong gongshe xuanyan" (Proclamation of Beijing Geology Institute East Is Red Commune) [August 17, 1966] *Dongfanghong bao,* 17 February 1967, 2 (CCRM 2001, 9:3218); Xiao Han and Turner (1998), 173. Longer accounts are in Beijing Geology Institute East Is Red (1966b).

35. Michael Schoenhals, unpublished paper on Zhu Chengzhao and the Geology Institute East Is Red faction, based on interviews with Zhu Chengzhao conducted by Niu Xiaohan before Zhu's untimely death in 1999. Niu also conducted the interviews with Mei Jianming that I draw upon elsewhere in this section (Xiao Han and Turner 1998, 171–176). See also Song Yongyi, "Zhu Chengzhao—Yige hongweibing shi shang bu yingdang wangque de mingzi" (Zhu Chengzhao—A Name in the History of the Red Guards That Should Not Be Forgotten), unpublished paper posted on several Chinese-language Web sites (e.g., zyzg.us/archiver/tid-62553.html).

36. "Beijing dizhi xueyuan hongweibing xuanyan (cao'an)" (Proclamation of the Beijing Geology Institute Red Guards [draft]), *Hongweibing,* 21 September 1966 (CCRM 2001, 20:7668).

37. See the account in Chapter 3 and Xiao Han and Turner (1998), 175.

38. The account in this section is based on Beijing Aeronautics Institute Red Flag (1966b), 9–13.

39. Wang Xuezhen et al. (1998), 650.

40. The first such issue reprinted the same type of denunciations of the former party committee that were common under the work team (Beijing University Cultural Revolution Preparatory Committee 1966a).

41. See Beijing University Cultural Revolution Preparatory Committee (1966b, 1966c, 1966d).

42. See Beijing University Cultural Revolution Preparatory Committee (1966f, 1966g).

43. "Zenyang dahao renmin zhanzheng (shitiao jianyi)" (How to Successfully Wage People's War [Ten Suggestions]) 7 September 1966 (Beijing University Cultural Revolution Committee 1966b, 28–31).

44. Wang Xuezhen et al. (1998), 651–652.

45. Ibid., 651; "Xin Beida hongweibing xuanyuan (cao'an)" (Proclamation of the New Beida Red Guards [Draft]), 22 August 1966 (Beijing University Cultural Revolution Committee 1966b, 40–41).

46. The other Philosophy Department delegates were Yang Keming and Zhao Zhengyi, veterans of the earlier battles, and two newcomers, Sun Pengyi and Wei Quangui. "Beijing daxue wenhua geming daibiao dahui gongbao" (Communique of the Beijing University Cultural Revolution Congress), *Xin Beida,* 13 September 1966, 2 (CCRM 1999, 15:6930). Deng Xiaoping's son, Deng Pufang, was elected as a student from the Applied Physics Department.

47. According to Nie's opponents, of the forty-four members of the Cultural Revolution committee, twelve had been members of the work team, eighteen were heads of departments appointed by the work team, and twenty-nine were people whom the work team had certified as reliable, and of the fourteen people on the standing committee, ten had actively supported the work team; "Nie Yuanzi daodi yikao shei, tuanjie shei, dadao shei?" (Who Did Nie Yuanzi Actually Rely upon, Unite with, and Overthrow?), *Xin Beida bao,* 5 November 1967, 3 (CCRM 1999, 16:7823).

48. These paragraphs are based on "Renjian zhengdao shi cangsang: Ping woyuan wuchan jieji wenhua da geming zhong liangtiao luxian de douzheng" (Following the Correct Path Can Change the World: An Assessment of the Struggle between the Two Lines in Our Institute's Cultural Revolution), *Hongweibing,* 19 October 1966, 1–3 (CCRM 1999, 6:2702–2704).

49. See Kraus (1981), 122–124; and Lee (1978), 91–92.

50. For a longer treatment of this case that elaborates this argument, see Walder (2004).

51. Organization Department, Beijing Municipal Party Committee (1992), 242, 482; Organization Department, CCP Central Committee (2000), 15:42, 69.

52. See Tan Bin, "Fasheng zai dangnian de yichang bianlun" (A Debate That Occurred Back in Those Days), *Sanyue feng* 5 (1986) (reprinted in Tan Bin 1996, 382–391).

53. "Tan Lifu 9 yue 7 ri zai nongji xueyuan de jianghua" (Tan Lifu's September 7 Speech at the Agricultural Machinery Institute) (Beijing Industrial University East Is Red Commune 1966c, 2:27).

54. "Tan Lifu jianghua zhushi" (Explanatory Notes to Tan Lifu's Speech) (Beijing Industrial University East Is Red Commune 1966c, 2:23–26, n. 25); see also "Beijing gongye daxue diaocha baogao" (Investigation Report on Beijing Industrial University) (Qinghua University Jinggangshan 1966, 20).

55. Du Wanrong, the head of the second work team, transferred to a new post as vice-chairman of the Cultural Revolution Office of the Beijing Municipal Party Committee (Beijing Geology Institute East Is Red 1967b, 90).

56. See Walder (2004), 980–981, and the discussion later in this section.

57. See Tan Lifu and Liu Jing, "Cong duilian tanqi" (Regarding the Couplet), August 12, 1966 (Beijing Industrial University East Is Red Commune 1966c, 1:24–25). This is the same charge that Nie Yuanzi made against the party committee at Beijing University during the Socialist Education Movement and at the beginning of the Cultural Revolution.

58. See "Bianlun hui Tan Lifu fayan jilu" (Transcript of Tan Lifu's Speech at the Debate), August 20, 1966 (Beijing Industrial University East Is Red Commune 1966c, 1:26–32, at 28).

59. See the Beida wall posters that chronicle Lu Ping's alleged failure to follow the party's class line at Beida in terms almost identical to Tan Lifu (Beijing University Cultural Revolution Preparatory Committee 1966e).

60. "Transcript of Tan Lifu's Speech" (Beijing Industrial University East Is Red Commune 1966c, 1:31).

61. Ibid., 28.

62. Ibid., 29.

63. Ibid., 29-30.

64. Ibid., 28.

65. Ibid., 27, 31.

66. Ibid., 29.

67. "Guanyu Bejing gongye daxue gongzuozu zai ganbu wenti shang shixing 'daji yi dapian, baohu yi xiaocuo' diaocha baogao" (Report on an Investigation of the Implementation of 'Attacking Many to Protect a Few' on the Cadre Question by the Beijing Industrial University Work Team), *Dongfanghong*, 13 April 1967, 2 (CCRM 1999, 2:674).

68. "Explanatory Notes to Tan Lifu's Speech" (Beijing Industrial University East Is Red Commune 1966c, 2:23–24nn2, 10).

69. "Xiao wen'ge fangxiang de luxian de cuowu—Chu ping Tan Lifu fayan" (Errors of Orientation and Line of the School Cultural Revolution Committee— An Initial Criticism of Tan Lifu's Speech), 24 August 1966 (Beijing Industrial University East Is Red Commune 1966c, 1:5–7, at 7).

70. "Tan Lifu de jianghua" (Tan Lifu's Speech), August 29, 1966, at a meeting of the leaders of Beijing Industrial University Red Guards (Beijing Industrial University East Is Red Commune 1966a, 22–23).

71. "Tan Lifu's September 7 Speech," in Beijing Industrial University East Is Red Commune (1966c), 2:28.

72. "Transcript of Tan Lifu's Speech" (Beijing Industrial University East Is Red Commune 1966c, 1:31).

73. McAdam (1983) shows how a series of tactical innovations—boycotts, sit-ins, freedom rides, and urban riots—provided political breakthroughs that temporarily served to quicken the pace of insurgency in the U.S. civil rights movement.

74. Beijing Aeronautics Institute Red Flag (1966b), 13–14; see also the brief account in Zhou Junlun (1999), 1026–1027.

75. Beijing Aeronautics Institute Red Flag (1966b), 14–15.

76. Ibid., 15–16.

77. Beijing Geology Institute East Is Red (1967b), 93.

78. Ibid., 98–99, and Xiao Han and Turner (1998), 176.

79. Another early demonstration at a national ministry was by Beijing Machinery Institute East Is Red at the No. 1 Ministry of Machine Building on August 26, where it demanded and received a public self-criticism by the head of its school's work team. "Zai baofengyu zhong duanlian chengzhang" (Tempering and Growing in the Midst of Storms), *Dongfanghong*, 23 August 1967, 2 (CCRM 2001, 7:2672).

80. As described earlier in this chapter, by Zhou Enlai at Qinghua on August 4 and Kang Sheng at Beijing Normal on July 27.

## 5. Class and Violence

1. By "high school" I refer to the three-year upper division of middle schools. The data in this paragraph are based on Beijing Education Annals Editorial Committee (1992), 499, 604; Beijing Statistical Bureau (1990), 488; and Xu Wenqi and Yu Dali (1998), 157, 366–386.

2. See Rosen (1982) and Unger (1982), who document a similar phenomenon in Guangzhou.

3. Walder and Hu (2009).

4. Andreas (2002), 473.

5. This account is based on a five-hour interview in October 1996.

6. Hu Qili was an alternate member of the CCP National Communist Youth League Secretariat (Organization Department, CCP Central Committee 2004, 220). As a member of the Politburo Standing Committee in 1989, he voted against martial law during the student demonstrations and lost his position as a result (Baum 1994, 269–270, 295).

7. The "jet plane" was a mild form of physical abuse in which the victim of a struggle session was forced to bend forward with arms stretched upward behind the back for long periods of time.

8. These regulations were passed at a Politburo Standing Committee meeting chaired by Liu Shaoqi on June 3. They prohibited large-scale struggle sessions, home invasions, and "beating and humiliating" people (Central Documents Research Office 1996, 640).

9. The deaths at this school have been documented independently (Wang Youqin 2004).

10. See "Bo Yibo zai 'Gongjiao ge bu wenhua da geming dongtai (di 113 qi)' shang de pishi" (Bo Yibo's Instructions on "Industrial and Transportation Ministries Cultural Revolution Situation Report, No. 113"), 27 June 1966 (Special Compilation 1997, vol. 1, 87).

11. This account is based on Wang Youqin (2004), 2–24; and Ye (2006).

12. He was soon promoted to alternate membership in the Politburo (Organization Department, CCP Central Committee 2004, 650).

13. "Deng Xiaoping dui Beijing shida nü fuzhong gongzuozu de tanhua" (Deng Xiaoping's Talk with the Bejing Normal Girls' High Work Group), 5 July 1966 (Cultural Revolution Database 2002).

14. One of the founders of the organization recalled the date as May 31 or June 1. Shen Ning was a department chief in the Ministry of Construction (my interview with a former leader of Beida High School Red Flag, April 1992).

15. Unless otherwise indicated, this account is based on Niu Wanping, Peng Xiaomeng, and Gong Xiaoji, "Zhe jiu shi shishi" (These Are the Facts), 21 July 1966 (Beijing University Cultural Revolution Preparatory Committee 1966f, 40–49).

16. Gong Xiaoji's father, a revolutionary cadre, was vice-head of the PLA logistics department in the 1950s. Niu Wanping's was a revolutionary cadre who taught in the PLA Military Sciences Institute (my interviews with a former leader of Beida High School Red Flag in April 1992 and December 1998). Peng Xiaomeng's father, Peng Yan, was secretary general of the Chinese Red Cross and had joined the party in 1937. See his obituary in *Renmin ribao*, 31 May 1991, 4.

17. Beijing University Cultural Revolution Committee (1966b), 48.

18. Ibid., 48–49; Zhang Chengxian (1999), 39.

19. Beijing University Cultural Revolution Committee (1966b), 49.

20. "Beijing daxue wenhua geming weiyuanhui choubei weiyuanhui gonggao" (Proclamation of the Beijing University Cultural Revolution Committee Preparatory Committee), *Xin Beida xiaokan*, 15 August 1966, 4.

21. Zhang Chengxian (1999), 43.

22. Bu Weihua (1999), 96–97. Among the leaders were Wang Ming, whose father was Luo Ruiqing's political secretary and former party secretary of Qinghai Province; Bu Dahua, whose father was a revolutionary cadre in the No. 7 Machine Building Ministry; Luo Xiaohai, whose father was a revolutionary cadre; Kuang

Taosheng, an exception, whose father apparently was not a party member (notes from a Qinghua High School student's diary, copied from wall posters, in November 1967). Song Bolin's father was a major general in the PLA and party secretary of the Hainan Military District before his 1965 transfer to Beijing to become vice-president of the PLA Political Academy (Song Bolin 2006, 4).

23. Bu Weihua (1999), 97–98. Bu Weihua was a third-year student in Qinghua High School's lower division in 1966, and his older brother, Bu Dahua, was one of the founders and leaders of the school's red guards.

24. "He Mao Yuanxin de tanhua" (Talk with Mao Yuanxin), March 1964 (Mao Zedong 1969, 465–471).

25. "He Wang Hairong tongzhi de tanhua" (Talk with Comrade Wang Hairong), 24 June 1964 (Mao Zedong 1969, 526–531); Kong Dongmei (2006), 15, 35–36. Red guard tabloids at the time commonly identified Wang Hairong as a student at the Beijing Foreign Languages Institute; the latter source, authored by her cousin (Mao's granddaughter), corrects the record.

26. Bu Weihua (1999), 98–100; Luo Xiaohai, "Zaofan jingshen wansui" (Long Live the Spirit of Rebellion), 28 October 1965 (Red Guard Combat School Red Guards 1966, 17–18); Luo Xiaohai's "Preface" to Song Bolin's diary and Song's own account (Song Bolin 2006, 15–18, 36–82).

27. Bu Weihua (1999), 100–101.

28. "Zui jiji, zui zijue de canjia zheichang jianrui de jieji douzheng" (Actively and Conscientiously Take Part in This Severe Episode of Class Struggle), 16 May 1966 (Red Guard Combat School Red Guards 1966, 19–20). One detailed account of the students' frictions with the school authorities during May is in "Wei you xisheng duo zhuangzhi" (Only through Sacrifice Are Lofty Ideals Attained), June 1966 (Red Guard Combat School Red Guards 1966, 35–40).

29. Bu Weihua (1999), 102–103.

30. Luo Xiaohai and Song Bolin's diary date the formation of the red guards on June 3 and report that the original name was not *hongweibing* but *hongweishi* (Song Bolin 2006, 19, 75). The term previously used to refer to "red guard" in historical writings was *chiweidui*, a term often adopted by worker organizations during the Cultural Revolution and usually translated as "scarlet guard" (see Perry 2006, 262–263). The new term was reportedly invented by one of the students, Zhang Chengzhi, in an earlier wall poster (Bu Weihua 1999, 103–105).

31. Bu Weihua (1999), 105–107.

32. "Jianjue ba wuchan jieji wenhua da geming jinxing daodi" (Resolutely Carry Out the Great Proletarian Cultural Revolution to the End), 5 June 1966; "Jiechuan yige da pianju" (Expose a Major Fraud), 5 June 1966; "Peiyang shenme yang de jieban ren?" (Train What Kind of Successors?), 4 June 1966; "Shisi baowei wuchan jieji zhuanzheng! Shisi baowei Mao Zedong sixiang!" (Pledge Your Life to Protect the Proletarian Dictatorship! Pledge Your Life to Protect Mao Zedong Thought!), 2 June 1966; and "Yiqie yao gemingde tongzhi zhanqilai!"

(All Comrades Who Want Revolution, Stand Up!), 6 June 1966 (all in Red Guard Combat School Red Guards 1966, 21–25, 28–30).

33. Bu Weihua (1999), 108–112.

34. Ibid., 113. See also Luo Xiaohai's account and the entries in the diary of Song Bolin (2006), 19–20, 78–79. One of the wall posters left by the visiting delegations was signed by two sons of Vice-Premier Bo Yibo (Bo Xiyong and Bo Xicheng); see Red Guard Combat School Red Guards (1966), 26–27.

35. Bu Weihua (1999), 113–115.

36. Ibid., 116. Bu cites internal work-team reports from the period. See also Luo Xiaohai in Song Bolin (2006), 20–22.

37. "Bixu chuji linghun" (You Have to Touch the Soul), 25 June 1966; and "Zhongguo qingnian bao shelun 'zuopai xuesheng de guangrong zeren' yinggai chedi pipan!" (The *China Youth News* Editorial "Glorious Responsibilities of Leftist Students" Must Be Thoroughly Repudiated), 24 June 1966 (both in Red Guard Combat School Red Guards 1966, 41–42, 49–50).

38. "Wuchan jieji de geming zaofan jingshen wansui" (Long Live the Proletarian Spirit of Revolutionary Rebellion), 24 June 1966; and "Zai lun wuchan jieji de geming zaofan jingshen wansui" (More on Long Live the Proletarian Spirit of Revolutionary Rebellion), 4 July 1966 (both in Red Guard Combat School Red Guards 1966, 6–9).

39. Bu Weihua (1999), 121–122.

40. Ibid., 122–123; Song Bolin (2006), 100–104; "Xiang Qinghua fuzhong gongzuozu de cuowu yanxing menglie kaihuo" (Fiercely Open Fire on the Erroneous Words and Deeds of the Qinghua High School Work Team), 27 July 1966 (Red Guard Combat School Red Guards 1966, 52–53).

41. Bu Weihua (1999), 124.

42. At the Eleventh Plenum, Mao had the Beida wall poster reprinted and circulated to all delegates (Wang Nianyi 2005, 42). On August 18 he met with Nie Yuanzi and provided his calligraphy for the masthead of her new campus newspaper, *Xin Beida* (Beijing Geology Institute East Is Red 1967b, 92).

43. "Mao Zhuxi tong Beida geming shisheng zai yiqi" (Chairman Mao Together with the Revolutionary Teachers and Students of Beida), *Renmin ribao*, 19 August 1966, 3.

44. Wang Nianyi (2005), 42.

45. "Mao Zedong gei Qinghua daxue fushu zhongxue hongweibing de xin" (Mao Zedong's Letter to the Red Guards of Qinghua University High School), 1 August 1966 (Bu Weihua 1999, 124–125; Wang Nianyi 1988, 62).

46. Bu Weihua (1999), 124–125; Wang Nianyi (1988), 63–65; Wang Nianyi (2005), 42. Song Bolin (2006, 107–108) heard of the letter before the meeting with Wang Renzhong when he was visiting another high school.

47. Bu Weihua (1999), 126–127; Luo Xiaohai in Song Bolin (2006), 26; and Song Bolin's diary (2006), 217–222. Also, "Mao Zhuxi jiejianle women

'hongweibing' " (Chairman Mao Receives Our "Red Guards") (Red Guard Combat School Red Guards 1966, 85–87), an article originally published in *Renmin ribao,* 21 August 1966; and "Mao Zhuxi tong hongweibing zai Tiananmen" (Chairman Mao with Red Guards at Tiananmen), *Renmin ribao,* 19 August 1966, 3.

48. Jiang Qing began her speech by saying, "Revolutionary comrades! . . . In fact, everything I had planned to say has already been said by Peng Xiaomeng. I wanted to express the CCRG's attitude toward you. We resolutely support your spirit of rebellion against the capitalists." "Jiang Qing tongzhi dui Beijing shi Haidian qu zhongxuesheng de jianghua (yi jiu liu liu nian qiyue ershiba ri zai Beijing zhanlanguan)" (Comrade Jiang Qing's Speech to the Beijing High School Red Guards from the Haidian District [July 28, 1966, at the Beijing Exhibition Hall]) (Reference Materials 1966, vol. 1, sec. 7, 28).

49. "Comrade Peng Xiaomeng's denunciation of Zhang Chengxian at Beida, I think, was completely correct and reasonable. You comrades who rose up in revolution at People's University High School and the red guards at other schools who advocated reorganizing the youth league, I think this demand is correct." "Kang Sheng, Jiang Qing tongzhi ba yue liuri zai tianqiao juchang dui zhongxue hongweibing de jianghua" (Talks by Comrades Kang Sheng and Jiang Qing at the Tianqiao Theater on August 6 with High School Red Guards) (State Science Commission Red Guards 1966, 26).

50. Mao Zedong, "Di yici jiejian hongweibing shi zai Tiananmen shang tong Peng Xiaomeng de jianghua" (Conversation with Peng Xiaomeng atop Tiananmen at the First Red Guard Rally), 18 August 1966 (Cultural Revolution Database 2002).

51. Three wall posters by the Qinghua High School Red Guards and one by red guards at Beijing No. 1 Girls' High School were reprinted in *Red Flag* 11 (21 August 1966): 22–30. See also the various essays reprinted in *Renmin ribao,* 19 August 1966, 3; *Beijing ribao,* 24 August 1966, 2; and *Beijing ribao,* 27 August 1966, 2.

52. Zhang Liqun et al. (2005), 393. Zhang Wenshou was head of Xuanwu District Work Team (Beijing Normal University No. 1 High School 1967, 36).

53. "Guan Feng tongzhi dui bufen tongxue de jianghua" (Comrade Guan Feng's Talk with a Group of Students), 2 August 1966 (Central Comrades' Speeches 1966a, 44–47).

54. Zhang Liqun et al. (2005), 396.

55. Beijing Geology Institute East Is Red (1967b), 88.

56. All four youth league vice-secretaries were detained and subjected to struggle sessions along with Hu Yaobang: Hu Keshi, Wang Wei, Wang Zhaohua, and Hu Qili (Zhang Liqun et al. 2005, 397–399). Hu Yaobang survived to become CCP general secretary in 1980 and China's leading political reformer. He lost his post in 1987 for alleged sympathy with student pro-democracy protests. His

April 1989 death sparked massive student demonstrations (Baum 1994, 206–208, 242–251).

57. "Li Fuchun tongzhi dui tuan zhongyang jiguan quanti gongzuo renyuan he shoudu bufen qingnian shisheng de jianghua" (Comrade Li Fuchun's Speech to the Entire Staff of the Youth League Central Committee Offices and to Young Teachers and Students from the Capital), 15 August 1966, Reference Materials (1966), vol. 1, sec. 8, 34–37; Zhang Liqun et al. (2005), 393.

58. Members of the Aeronautics Institute High School Red Guards themselves claimed credit only for certain additions to the core rhyme, which they said were the work of students at other schools. See Beida fuzhong geweihui, hongweibing, "Guanyu duilian de huida" (A Response Regarding the Couplet), 14 August 1966 (Cultural Revolution Database 2002).

59. Kraus (1977, 1981).

60. See Rosen (1982) and Unger (1982).

61. "A Response Regarding the Couplet" (Cultural Revolution Database 2002).

62. Mu Xin (1994), 335.

63. "Kang Sheng, Jiang Qing tongzhi ba yue liuri zai tianqiao juchang dui zhongxue hongweibing de jianghua" (Speeches by Comrades Kang Sheng and Jiang Qing on August 6 at the Tianqiao Theater with High School Red Guards) (State Science Commission Red Guards 1966, 24–25).

64. Ibid., 25–26.

65. Wu Qingtong (2002), 52. In memoirs edited by his son, Chen Boda confirms that he was alarmed by red guard attacks on him at the time and for a period feared that he would be purged (Chen Xiaonong 2005, 297).

66. "Chen Boda tongzhi zai Beijing daxue de jianghua (yijiuliuliu nian ba yue ershisi ri)" (Comrade Chen Boda's Talk at Beijing University [24 August 1966]) (Reference Materials 1966, vol. 1, sec. 8, 75).

67. Bu Weihua (1999), 114.

68. "Jiaqiang hongweibing de sixiang zuzhi jianshe, jiang geming jinxing dao di!" (Strengthen Red Guard Consciousness and Organization, Carry Out the Revolution to the End!), 10 August 1966 (Red Guard Combat School Red Guards 1966, 61).

69. "Guanyu hongweibing zuzhi de qige wenda" (Answers to Seven Questions about Red Guard Organizations), 13 September 1966 (in Red Guard Combat School Red Guards 1966, 63–66, at 64).

70. Estimated by Andreas (2002), 473.

71. "Wuchan jieji de jieji luxian wansui (xiugai gao)" (Long Live the Proletarian Class Line [Revised]), 20 July 1966 (Red Guard Combat School Red Guards 1966, 44–46).

72. Ibid., 43.

73. Ibid., 44, 46.

74. Ibid., 43.

75. Beijing No. 1 High School Red Flag Combat Team (1967), 3.

76. See the entries for Beijing during this period in Wang Youqin (2004).

77. Wang Youqin (2004) describes twenty such cases during this period in Beijing.

78. Beijing Municipal Party Committee (1987a), 24.

79. Ibid., 24–25; Fan Jin, Zhang Dazhong, and Xu Huaicheng (1989), 167. Lao She was the author of the novel *Luotuo Xiangzi,* which was translated into English as *Rickshaw Boy* in 1945 and became a Book-of-the-Month Club selection in the United States. See also Li Yong and Wen Lequn (1994b), 28–34; and Shu Yi (1987), 54–86.

80. "Zuihou tongdie" (Final Ultimatum), Kangda fuzhong (donghuamen) hongweibing, handbill, 22 August 1966 (CCRM 1975, 19:6074). A similar handbill demanded that "property-owning landlord exploiters" immediately surrender spare rooms for occupants from worker and peasant households: "Geming de huyushu" (Revolutionary declaration), 21 August 1966 (CCRM 1975, 19:6088).

81. "Tongling—Guanyu quzhu silei fenzi de wuxiang mingling" (General Order: Five Directives on the Expulsion of Four Type Elements), Beijing sizhong geming shisheng, 24 August 1966 (CCRM 1975, 19:6069).

82. "Jinji huyu" (Urgent Declaration), Dongfanghong erzhong hongweibing, 26 August 1966 (CCRM 1975, 19:6091).

83. "Jinji tongdie" (Urgent Ultimatum), Beijing sanshi zhong hongweibing, 22 August 1966 (CCRM 1975, 19:6075).

84. "Zalan jiyou heihuo" (Destroy Contraband Stamp Collecting), Beijing bashiliu zhong chusan yiban dongfeng zhandou xiaozu, handbill, 24 August 1966.

85. "Beijing erzhong 'hongweibing' zuihou tongdie" (Final Ultimatum of No. 2 High School "Red Guards"), Beijing erzhong "hongweibing," handbill, 18 August 1966.

86. Fan Jin, Zhang Dazhong, and Xu Huaicheng (1989), 167. Local police stations held the household registers in which class origins were recorded.

87. Cao Zixi and Yu Guangdu (1994), 68–73; Fan Jin, Zhang Dazhong, and Xu Huaicheng (1989), 167–168.

88. Beijing Municipal Party Committee (1987a), 24; Fan Jin, Zhang Dazhong, and Xu Huaicheng (1989), 168.

89. Beijing Municipal Party Committee (1987a), 26; Fan Jin, Zhang Dazhong, and Xu Huaicheng (1989), 168; and Wang Youqin (2004), 224, quoting internal government bulletins.

90. "Hongweibing jinji huyu shu" (Urgent Appeal to Red Guards), 6 August 1966 (Red Guard Combat School Red Guards 1966, 69–70); Wang Nianyi (1988), 71–72.

91. At the time, Kang Sheng publicly expressed his admiration of this appeal, which was read out at a mass meeting of Haidian District red guards on August 6 (State Science Commission Red Guards 1966, 26).

92. "Jiaqiang hongweibing de sixiang zuzhi jianshe, jiang geming jinxing dao di!" (Strengthen Red Guard Consciousness and Organization, Carry Out the Revolution to the End!), 10 August 1966 (Red Guard Combat School Red Guards 1966, 58–62).

93. Mu Xin (1994), 338.

94. Beijing Geology Institute East Is Red (1967b), 88; Beijing Municipal Party Committee (1987a), 23; Li Xuefeng (1966), 11; Mu Xin (1994), 335–336.

95. "Hongweibing zhanxiao (qian Qinghua fuzhong) hongweibing dui muqian xingshi de shidian guji"(Ten-Point Assessment of the Current Situation by the Red Guards of Red Guard Combat School [Formerly Qinghua High School]), 27 August 1966 (Red Guard Combat School Red Guards 1966, 71–72). The "five red" classes were workers, poor and lower-middle-class peasants, revolutionary soldiers, revolutionary martyrs, and revolutionary cadres.

96. Ibid., 74–76.

97. Mao Zedong, "Report on the Peasant Movement in Hunan," February 1927 (Schram 1994, 429–464).

98. The three rules of discipline were "Obey orders in all actions. Do not take even a needle or thread from the masses. All things confiscated must be turned over to the public." The eight points of attention were "Speak politely. Deal fairly with people. Return what you borrow. Compensate people for damages. Do not beat or curse people. Do not damage crops. Do not molest women. Do not mistreat prisoners." See Zhongguo renmin jiefangjun zongbu guanyu chongxing banbu sanda jilu baxiang zhuyi de xunling (Directive of the People's Liberation Army Political Department on the Reissue of the Three Rules of Discipline and Eight Points of Attention), 10 October 1947.

99. For example, "Mao Zedong zhuyi hongweibing xuanyan (cao'an)" (Proclamation of the Maoism Red Guards [Draft]), Beijing changzheng zhongxue, 31 August 1966; and "Beijing changzheng zhongxue Mao Zedong zhuyi hongweibing ba.yiba hongweibing xuanyan" (Proclamation of the Maoism August 18 Red Guards of Long March High School), 1 September 1966.

100. "The people we were trying to control were also 'old red guards'; they were people from the same kind of background as us" (interview with leader of Beida High School Red Flag, December 1998).

101. "Tuanjie douzheng yizhi duidi (buchong shidian guji di wu tiao)" (Unite in Struggle against the Enemy [Fifth Supplementary Point to the Ten-Point Assessment]), Beijing erqi geming yizhong Mao Zedong sixiang xuanchuan dui fanyin, 12 September 1966.

102. See Luo Xiaohai's account of the August 13 mass meeting (Song Bolin 2006, 22–24).

103. Liu Jinglin (2004). The author, a reporter in the network, recounts several harrowing stories of high-school-level violence that he witnessed and reported on during the month of August.

104. Yong Wentao (1995).

105. "Jiang Qing tongzhi dui Beijing shi Haidian qu zhongxuesheng de jianghua" (Comrade Jiang Qing's Speech to the High-School Students of the Haidian District), 28 July 1966 (Reference Materials 1966, vol. 1, sec. 7, 28).

106. Zhang Chengxian (1999), 43.

107. Mu Xin (1994), 338–341, 339.

108. Ibid., 341.

109. Fan Jin, Zhang Dazhong, and Xu Huaicheng (1989), 167; Wang Nianyi (2005), 60–61.

110. "Zong canmou bu, zong zhengzhi bu guanyu juedui bu xu dongyong budui wuzhuang zhenya geming xuesheng yundong de guiding" (Orders of the General Staff Headquarters and General Political Department Concerning the Absolute Prohibition against Deploying Armed Force to Suppress the Revolutionary Student Movement), 21 August 1966; and "Zhongyang tongyi gong'an bu guanyu yanjin chudong jingcha zhenya geming xuesheng yundong de guiding" (Party Center Approves of Ministry of Public Security Orders Strictly Prohibiting the Dispatch of Police Forces to Suppress the Revolutionary Student Movement), 22 August 1966 (both in Wang Nianyi 1988, 90–91).

111. Luo Xiaohai reports that members of his group met with Wang Renzhong at the Diaoyutai State Guest House to consult with him about their critical assessment of the red guard movement several days before it was issued on August 27, and they received encouragement (Song Bolin 2006, 24–25).

112. "Shoudu hongweibing jiuchadui (xicheng fendui) xuangao chengli" (Founding Proclamation of the Capital Red Guard Picket Corps [Western District Branch]), 25 August 1966 (Capital Red Guard Picket Corps 1966, 1–5).

113. "Liuxiang shouze" (Six Regulations) (Capital Red Guard Picket Corps 1966, 6–7).

114. "Di san hao tongming" (General Order no. 3), 27 August 1966 (Capital Red Guard Picket Corps 1966, 11–13).

115. "Di si hao tongming" (General Order no. 4), 29 August 1966 (Capital Red Guard Picket Corps 1966, 14–20).

116. "Di wu hao tongming" (General Order no. 5), 3 September 1966 (Capital Red Guard Picket Corps 1966, 21–22).

117. "Di liu hao tongming" (General Order no. 6), 9 September 1966 (Capital Red Guard Picket Corps 1966, 23–26). General Orders 7 and 8 placed restrictions on the expulsion of "bad-class" households from Beijing.

118. "Shoudu hongweibing jiucha dui dongcheng fendui diyi hao tongming" (General Order no. 1 of the Capital Red Guard Picket Corps, Eastern District), *Hongweibing zhanbao*, 10 September 1966, 2 (CCRM 2001, 22:8381).

119. Yong was transferred from the Guangzhou Municipal Party Committee to Beijing in June 1966 at the same time as Tao Zhu. He was also head of the High School Cultural Revolution Committee of the new Beijing Municipal Party Committee (Yong Wentao 1995, 4).

120. Ibid., 5; Central Documents Research Office (1997), 52; "Zhou Enlai tongzhi zai shoudu hongweibing daibiao huiyi shang de jianghua" (Comrade Zhou Enlai's Speech at the Meeting of Representatives of the Capital Red Guards), 27 August 1966, early morning hours (Central Comrades' Speeches 1966a, 82–83).

121. Yong Wentao (1995), 5–7. See the transcripts of speeches by Zhou Enlai to mass assemblies of red guards on September 1, September 10, and September 13 in Central Comrades' Speeches (1966a), 95–98 and 124–133.

122. Yong Wentao (1995), 5–6, 8.

123. Wu Qingtong (2002), 49–50, 61. Kong Yuan was the head of the CCP's Intelligence Department and an alternate member of the Central Committee. He had previously been vice-director of the State Council Foreign Affairs Office under Zhou Enlai (Shen Xueming and Zheng Jianying 2001, 111–112).

124. Wu Qingtong (2002), 59–60.

125. Gao Wenqian (2003), 137–138.

126. Wu Qingtong (2002), 59–60.

127. State Council (1967a), 39–40.


## 6. Radicals with Patrons

1. Beijing Aeronautics Institute Red Flag (1966b), 15.

2. He Changgong (1987), 504.

3. Beijing Geology Institute East Is Red (1967b), 103–104; He Changgong (1987), 504–505; "Women jiu shi yao dang geming de 'baotu'" (Indeed We Do Want to Be the "Thugs" of Revolution), Shoudu hongweibing (Capital Red Guards), 21 September 1966 (CCRM 1999, 12:5362).

4. MacFarquhar and Schoenhals (2006), 134. The official Chinese name for the Third Headquarters was Shoudu dazhuan yuanxiao hongweibing geming zaofan silingbu.

5. He Changgong (1987), 504.

6. Mei Jianming in Xiao Han and Turner (1998), 175. See also MacFarquhar and Schoenhals (2006), 133–134.

7. He Changgong (1987), 505.

8. See the entire issue of Hongweibing, 1 September 1966 (CCRM 2001, 20:7765–7768), which describes the founding meeting and carries the group's proclamation and charter. The official Chinese name for the First Headquarters was Shoudu dazhuan yuanxiao hongweibing silingbu.

9. See, in particular, "Geming de dahui, tuanjie de dahui" (A Revolutionary Rally, a Rally of Unity), Xin Beida, 2 September 1966, 1 (CCRM 1999, 15:6921);

and "Yongyuan zuo Mao Zhuxi de hongse xiaobing" (Forever Be Chairman Mao's Little Red Soldiers), *Hongweibing* (Red Guard), 1 September 1966, 1 (CCRM 2001, 20:7766).

10. "Jiang Qing, Yang Chengwu tongzhi zai shoudu dazhuan yuanxiao hongweibing silingbu chengli dahui de jianghua" (Speeches by Comrades Jiang Qing and Yang Chengwu at the Mass Meeting to Commemorate the Founding of the Capital University Red Guard Headquarters) (Reference Materials 1966, vol. 1, sec. 8, 86); Wang Xuezhen et al. (1998), 651.

11. Central Documents Research Office (1997), 55–56; "Zhou Enlai, Wang Renzhong dui Beijing shi hongweibing daibiao de jianghua" (Speeches by Zhou Enlai and Wang Renzhong to Representatives of Beijing Red Guards), 1 September 1966 (Cultural Revolution Database 2002).

12. See the issues of the First Headquarters' tabloid *Hongweibing*, 11, 22, and 28 September 1966 (CCRM 2001, 20:7769–7780).

13. Beijing Geology Institute East Is Red (1967b), 102–103. The official Chinese name for the Second Headquarters was *Shoudu dazhuan yuanxiao hongweibing zongbu*.

14. "Jiang Qing Liu Zhijian zai shoudu dazhuan yuanxiao hongweibing zongbu chengli dahui shang de jianghua" (Speeches by Jiang Qing and Liu Zhijian at the Inaugural Mass Meeting of the Capital University Red Guard General Headquarters), 5 September 1966 (Cultural Revolution Database 2002). Liu Zhijian was also the president of the PLA Academy of Arts and at the time was vice-chairman of the CCRG (Organization Department, CCP Central Committee 2004, 477; Party History Research Office Department No. 1 2004, 581).

15. Central Documents Research Office (1997), 63; "Zhou Enlai, Chen Yi zai shoudu dazhuan yuanxiao hongweibing zongbu hongweibing dahui shang de jianghua" (Speeches by Zhou Enlai and Chen Yi at the Mass Meeting of Red Guards from the Capital University Red Guard General Headquarters), 13 September 1966 (Cultural Revolution Database 2002).

16. See the issues of the Second Headquarters tabloid *Dongfanghong*, 6, 13, and 20 October 1966 (CCRM 2001, 8:2824–2835).

17. Beijing Geology Institute East Is Red (1967b), 103–104.

18. "Liu Zhijian tongzhi zai shoudu dazhuan yuanxiao hongweibing geming zaofan silingbu chengli dahui shang de jianghua" (Comrade Liu Zhijian's Speech at the Inaugural Meeting of the Revolutionary Rebel Headquarters of the Capital University Red Guards), 6 September 1966 (Reference Materials 1966, vol. 2, sec. 9, 6–7). The inaugural issue of the Third Headquarters' tabloid details the proceedings and the group's founding declarations: *Shoudu hongweibing*, 13 September 1966 (CCRM 1999, 12:5357).

19. *Shoudu hongweibing*, 30 September 1966 (CCRM 1999, 12:5362–5366).

20. Beijing Geology Institute East Is Red (1967b), 106–108, 111.

21. Ibid., 106; and "Xie Fuzhi fuzongli jianghua" (Speech by Vice-Chairman Xie Fuzhi), 13 September 1966 (Reference Materials 1966, vol. 2, sec. 9, 33–35).

22. Beijing Geology Institute East Is Red (1967b), 109; Gao Wenqian (2003), 149; MacFarquhar and Schoenhals (2006), 134–135; Wang Li (2001), 625–626.

23. Beijing Aeronautics Institute Red Flag (1966b), 18–19.

24. Beijing Geology Institute East Is Red (1967b), 104; Xiao Han and Turner (1998), 176.

25. "Guan Feng, Qi Benyu dui Beijing dizhi xueyuan hongweibing daibiao deng de jianghua" (Talks by Guan Feng and Qi Benyu with Representatives of the Geology Institute Red Guards and Others), 23 September 1966; "Guan Feng, Qi Benyu zai Beijing dizhi xueyuan de jianghua" (Speeches by Guan Feng and Qi Benyu at Beijing Geology Institute), 24 September 1966 (both in Cultural Revolution Database 2002); also Reference Materials (1966), vol. 2, sec. 9, 74–76).

26. "Guan Feng tongzhi zai Beijing dizhi xueyuan tongxue zuotanhui shang de jianghua" (Comrade Guan Feng's Speech at the Discussion Meeting with Students from Beijing Geology Institute), 28 September 1966; and "Guan Feng, Qi Benyu tongzhi dui Beijing diyuan hongweibing daibiao ji shisheng de jianghua jiyao" (Summary of Speeches by Comrades Guan Feng and Qi Benyu with Red Guard Representatives and Teachers and Students at the Beijing Geology Institute), 31 September 1966 (Reference Materials 1966, vol. 2, sec. 9, 94–98).

27. Central Documents Research Office (1997), 68–69; "Zhou Zongli zai jiejian shoudu dazhuan yuanxiao hongweibing geming zaofan silingbu zhuyao fuze ren shi de jianghua" (Premier Zhou's Speech at a Reception with Top Leaders of the Revolutionary Rebel Headquarters of the Capital University Red Guards), 25 September 1966 (Reference Materials 1966, vol. 2, sec. 9, 78–83).

28. Beijing Geology Institute East Is Red (1967b), 109.

29. Ibid., 111; "Zhou Enlai zai shoudu dazhuan yuanxiao hongweibing geming zaofan zong silingbu de jianghua" (Zhou Enlai's Speech at the Mass Meeting Convened by the Revolutionary Rebel Headquarters of the Capital University Red Guards), 26 September 1966 (Cultural Revolution Database 2002).

30. "Zhou Enlai guanyu geren dang'an cailiao chuli de yijian" (Zhou Enlai's Suggestions about the Disposal of Materials in Individual Dossiers), 25 October 1966 (Cultural Revolution Database 2002).

31. "Zhonggong Beijing shiwei guanyu gei geming qunzhong pingfan de jinji tongzhi" (Urgent Notice of the Beijing Municipal Party Committee on the Rehabilitation of Revolutionary Masses), 15 November 1966 (Beijing Municipal Party Committee 1987a, 29); "Zhonggong Zhongyang guanyu chuli wuchan jieji wenhua da geming zhong dang'an cailiao wenti de buchong guiding" (Supplementary Regulations of the CCP Central Committee on the Handling of Materials Placed in Files during the Great Proletarian Cultural Revolution), 16 November 1966 (Wang Nianyi 1988, 162–163).

32. "Tan Lifu de jianghua" (Tan Lifu's Talk), 27 September 1966 (Beijing Industrial University East Is Red Commune 1966a, 24).

33. "Gao quanxiao geming tongzhi shu" (Announcement to Revolutionary Comrades of the Entire School), 1 October 1966 (Beijing Industrial University East Is Red Commune 1966c, 2:32–34).

34. See the account in Chapter 4; Shen Ruhuai (2004), 23–24; and Zheng (2006), 44–47.

35. Shen Ruhuai (2004), 32.

36. Ibid., 33; Beijing Geology Institute East Is Red (1967b), 117. Zhou Enlai took responsibility for negotiating with Kuai's group and attempted to parry its demands (Central Documents Research Office 1997, 76); "Zhou Zongli, Zhang Chunqiao tongzhi jiejian Qinghua daxue bage zuzhi de wuge daibiao zuotan jiyao" (Minutes of the Meeting between Premier Zhou, Comrade Zhang Chunqiao, and Five Representatives of Eight Qinghua University Organizations), 9 October 1966 (Reference Materials 1966, vol. 2, sec. 10, 22–24). Zhou refused to turn over Wang Guangmei to the students but instead produced her written self-criticism the next day: "Wang Guangmei gei Qinghua daxue geming shisheng yuangong de shumian jiancha" (Wang Guangmei's Self-Examination Written for the Teachers, Students, Staff, and Workers of Qinghua University), 10 October 1966 (Cultural Revolution Database 2002).

37. "Zhou Enlai, Chen Boda, Jiang Qing, Zhang Chunqiao deng siwei tongzhi zai zai jing geming shisheng xiang zichan jieji fandong luxian menglie kaihuo shishi dahui shangde jianghua" (Speeches by Comrades Zhou Enlai, Chen Boda, Jiang Qing, and Zhang Chunqiao at the Mass Oath-Taking Rally of Revolutionary Teachers and Students in Beijing to Fiercely Open Fire on the Bourgeois Reactionary Line), 6 October 1966 (Reference Materials 1966, vol. 2, sec. 10, 19–21).

38. Beijing Geology Institute East Is Red (1967b), 114–115; Shen Ruhuai (2004), 33; Zheng (2006), 49.

39. MacFarquhar and Schoenhals (2006), 135.

40. "Zai Mao Zedong sixiang da lu shang qianjin" (Advance on the Great Road of Mao Zedong Thought), *Hongqi* 13 (1 October 1966): 4–6.

41. MacFarquhar and Schoenhals (2006), 137; Wang Nianyi (2005), 88–90.

42. For a representative sampling of excerpts, see Beijing Industrial University East Is Red Commune (1966b), 4–6; "Kang Sheng, Xie Fuzhi, Yang Chengwu yu Beijing hangkong xueyuan 'hongqi' daibiao tanhua" (Talks by Kang Sheng, Xie Fuzhi, and Yang Chengwu with Representatives of Beijing Aeronautics "Red Flag"), 6 October 1966 (Cultural Revolution Database 2002); "Yan Changgui jiejian Beijing hangkong xueyuan ji Beijing dizhi xueyuan daibiao de jianghua" (Yan Changgui's Talk with Representatives from the Beijing Aeronautics Institute and Beijing Geology Institute), 12 October 1966 (Cultural Revolution Database

2002); and "Yong Wentao zai Qinghua daxue de jianghua" (Yong Wentao's Speech at Qinghua University), 5 October 1966 (Cultural Revolution Database 2002).

43. "Chen Boda zai zhongyang gongzuo huiyi shang de jianghua" (Chen Boda's Speech at the Central Party Work Conference), 16 October 1966 (Cultural Revolution Database 2002).

44. Tan had also referred to "comrade Liu Shaoqi" and had ridiculed the practice of "simplifying Mao's quotations down into horseshit," sentiments that were perhaps even more inexcusable in this political context than the alleged errors for which he was pilloried.

45. "Chen Boda, Qi Benyu, Guan Feng jiejian shoudu hongweibing disan si-lingbu tongxue de jianghua" (Talks by Chen Boda, Qi Benyu, and Guan Feng in a Meeting with Students from the Red Guard Third Headquarters), 25 October 1966 (Cultural Revolution Database 2002).

46. "Zoufang Tan Lifu zhuiji" (Notes on an Interview with Tan Lifu), 2 November 1966 (Beijing Industrial University East Is Red Commune 1966d, 19–20).

47. Tan Lifu, "Hui dao Mao Zedong sixiang de dadao shang lai—Wo de jian-cha" (Returning to the Great Road of Mao Zedong Thought—My Self-Criticism), 7 November 1966 (Beijing Industrial University East Is Red Commune 1966d, 2–7).

48. In addition to several editions published by various organizations in Beijing, reprints issued in Wuhan, Fuzhou, Guangzhou, Chongqing, Harbin, and Shanghai have made their way into overseas collections (Walder 2004, 968).

49. See, for example, its denunciations of the "bourgeois reactionary line" in *Dongfanghong*, 6, 13, and 20 October 1966 (CCRM 2001, 8:2824–2835).

50. Beijing Geology Institute East Is Red (1967b), 117.

51. The organization was renamed the Rebel Liaison Station of the Capital University Red Guard General Headquarters. "Shoudu dazhuan yuanxiao hong-weibing di yi hao shengming" (General Headquarters of the Capital University Red Guards, Announcement no. 1), *Dongfanghong*, 20 October 1966 (CCRM 2001, 8:2835).

52. Central Documents Research Office (1997), 81.

53. Beijing Geology Institute East Is Red (1967b), 127; the issues of *Dong-fanghong*, 16 and 27 November and 9 December (CCRM 2001, 8:2840–2851) contain detailed accounts of the internal disagreements within the organization in the form of critical histories of the majority factions' positions.

54. *Hongweibing*, 28 September and 5 and 11 October 1966 (CCRM 2001, 20:7777–7785).

55. "Lin Jie jiejian Beijing hangkong xueyuan he Beijing dizhi xueyuan bufen tongzhi de jianghua" (Lin Jie's Speech at a Meeting with Comrades from Beijing Aeronautics and Beijing Geology), 3 October 1966 (Cultural Revolution Database

2002); "Lin Jie dui Qinghua daxue hongweibing de jianghua" (Lin Jie's Talk with Qinghua University Red Guards), 4 October 1966 (Cultural Revolution Database 2002); "Qi Benyu Guan Feng dui Beihang gongren chiweidui he diyuan hongweibing de jianghua" (Speeches by Qi Benyu and Guan Feng to the Beijing Aeronautics Workers Scarlet Guards and Geology Institute Red Guards), 12 October 1966 (Cultural Revolution Database 2002); "Wang Li, Guan Feng, Qi Benyu zai quanguo shaoshu pai tongxue huiyi shang de jianghua" (Speeches by Wang Li, Guan Feng, and Qi Benyu at the All-China Meeting of Minority Faction Students), 17 October 1966 (Cultural Revolution Database 2002).

56. Beijing Geology Institute East Is Red (1967b), 114.

57. Ibid., 116.

58. Beijing Geology Institute East Is Red (1967b), 116; "Zaofan zhankuang" (Rebel Battle Report), *Shoudu hongweibing,* 15 October 1966, 4 (CCRM 1999, 12:5378).

59. He Changgong (1987), 505. Li Fuchun ordered the ministry to provide the students with an office and open up its files for their investigation, and he ordered the five top officials of the ministry, including Zou Jiayou, to submit to a struggle session; "Li Fuchun dui Beijing dizhi xueyuan 'dongfanghong' gongshe wu tongxue de jianghua" (Li Fuchun's Talk with Five Students from Beijing Geology "East Is Red" Commune), 9 October 1966 (Cultural Revolution Database 2002). See also "Zhou Rongxin zai Beijing dizhi xueyuan shisheng yuangong dahui shang de jianghua" (Zhou Rongxin's Speech at the Mass Meeting of Teachers, Students, Staff, and Workers at Beijing Geology Institute) (Cultural Revolution Database 2002). The rebels later published denunciations of ministry officials based on their examination of these and other files (Beijing Geology Institute East Is Red 1967a).

60. Mei Jianming, in Xiao Han and Turner (1998), 176. He Changgong had a tense conversation with Kang Sheng at the October Party Work Conference that confirmed his suspicion that the CCRG was behind the attacks on the ministry (He Changgong 1987, 505–506).

61. "Zaofan zhankuang" (Rebel Battle Report), *Shoudu hongweibing,* 15 October 1966, 4 (CCRM 1999, 12:5378).

62. Beijing Geology Institute East Is Red (1967b), 116. Zhou Enlai was still trying to negotiate their evacuation from the ministry's offices in mid-December (Central Documents Research Office 1997, 84–85). According to Ma Jisen (2004, 39), the students carted off eight burlap bags of documents.

63. "Zaofan zhankuang" (Rebel Battle Report), *Shoudu hongweibing,* 15 October 1966, 4 (CCRM 1999, 12:5378).

64. Rebels from institutes outside Beijing also occasionally took part. The minority faction from the Harbin Military Engineering College invaded the offices of the National Defense Science and Technology Commission on October 21 in search of "black materials" collected by its school's work team (Zhou Junlun 1999, 1033).

65. Beijing Geology Institute East Is Red (1967b), 122. On October 23 Zhou Enlai chaired an emergency State Council meeting to discuss with his besieged subordinates how to respond to these escalating demands (Central Documents Research Office 1997, 81).

66. Beijing Geology Institute East Is Red (1967b), 119; Li Xuefeng (1966); "Wu De zai Beijing shifan daxue pipan yi Li Xuefeng wei daibiao de fandong luxian dahui shang de jianghua" (Wu De's Speech at the Mass Meeting to Criticize the Reactionary Line Represented by Li Xuefeng), 14 October 1966 (Cultural Revolution Database 2002).

67. Beijing Municipal Party Committee (1987a), 28.

68. These arrangements are detailed by Liu Jinglin (2004), who was an army reporter who worked in this network from the time it was first organized in August 1966.

69. Shen Ruhuai (2004), 135–137; thereafter Shen's group invited the reporter to attend all its rallies and leadership meetings.

70. Liu Jinglin (2004), 67. Liu recounts one instance where Kuai Dafu was threatened with military force if he persisted in a plan to storm Tiananmen Gate during a mass rally.

## 7. Dissent and Its Suppression

1. This pattern is described clearly in the memoirs of former red guards from Qinghua University (Shen Ruhuai 2004), the Geology Institute (Xiao Han and Turner 1998, 171–189), and Beijing University (Chen Huanren 2006).

2. Wang Xuezhen et al. (1998), 652; "Guanyu dangqian yundong de liudian jianyi" (Six Suggestions on the Movement at Present), Xin Beida, 13 September 1966, 3 (CCRM 1999, 15:6931).

3. The counts were based on the issues of Xin Beida, Xin Beida bao, Xin Renda, and Renda sanhong reprinted in CCRM (1999) 15: 6912–7406, 16: 7407–7863; and CCRM (2001) 28: 10693–10914, 35: 13568–13864. I thank Weiwei Shen and Dongtao Qi for creating the databases of factional names that formed the basis for these counts.

4. "Zhongyang wen'ge xiaozu bixu lai wo yuan jiancha" (The CCRG Must Come to Our Institute to Make a Self-Criticism), Beijing guangbo xueyuan Mao Zedong zhuyi hongweibing xianfeng, 12 October 1966, Beijing pinglun 2 (December 1966): 19–21.

5. See the account in Chapter 4. The delegation included Chen Boda, Jiang Qing, Guan Feng, Qi Benyu, Zhang Chunqiao, Yao Wenyuan, and others. See also the account in Rittenberg and Bennett (1993), 309–310.

6. "Yi wen zhongyang wen'ge xiaozu" (A Question for the CCRG), 25 November 1966; "Er wen zhongyang wen'ge xiaozu" (A Second Question for the CCRG), 29 November 1966; and "San wen zhongyang wen'ge xiaozu" (A Third

Question for the CCRG), 2 December 1966, Beihang hongweibing ba yi zongdui (Qinghua University 1966, 15–20).

7. "Ye wen zhongyang wen'ge xiaozu" (More Questions for the CCRG), Beijing hangkong xueyuan hongweibing ba yi yezhan bingtuan, 2 December 1966 (Qinghua University 1966, 20–23).

8. "Piping he jiandu zhongyang wen'ge de dianxing yiyi" (The Significance of the Model of Criticizing and Monitoring the CCRG), Beihang hongweibing zongdui, 9 December 1966 (Cultural Revolution Database 2002).

9. "Ye wen zhongyangg wen'ge (er)—Wuchan jieji da minzhu wansui" (More Questions for the CCRG (2)—Long Live Great Proletarian Democracy), Beihang hongweibing ba yi yezhan bingtuan, 12 December 1966 (Cultural Revolution Database 2002).

10. Beijing Geology Institute East Is Red (1967b), 130; "Beijing kuangye xueyuan shoudu hongweibing zongbu ji qi hongse youji dui yu Beijing Linxueyuan fangeming fenzi Li Hongshan huxiang goujie jinxing fangeming huodong de zuizheng (sige fujian)" (Criminal Evidence of the Collaboration between the Beijing Mining Institute Capital Red Guards and Its Red Guerilla Brigade and the Counterrevolutionary Element Li Hongshan of the Beijing Forestry Institute in Carrying Out Counterrevolutionary Activities [four attachments]), printed broadsheet, Beijing kuangye xueyuan dongfanghong gongshe, 20 December 1966.

11. "Gei zhongyang wen'ge xiaozu de yifeng gongkai xin" (An Open Letter to the CCRG), Beijing linxueyuan hongweibing changzheng zhandoudui, 1 December 1966 (Cultural Revolution Database 2002).

12. "Waidi geming shisheng tong Li Hongshan bianlun zhengli de huiyi jilu" (Edited Minutes of the Debate between Revolutionary Teachers and Students from the Provinces and Li Hongshan), 1 December 1966 (Cultural Revolution Database 2002). A shorter version was issued the next day: "Tikai zhongyang wen'ge xiaozu, jin gen Mao zhuxi nao geming" (Kick Aside the CCRG, Make Revolution Closely alongside Chairman Mao), Beijing linxueyuan hongwei zhandou bingtuan, hongweibing, 2 December 1966, in the Beijing University publication *Wenhua geming tongxun* 4 (January 1967): 22–23.

13. Beijing Geology Institute East Is Red (1967b), 135; Qinghua Jinggangshan (1966), 3.

14. "Kan, zhongyang wen'ge xiaozu zai wuchan jieji wenhua da geming zhong zhixingle yitiao shenme luxian?" (Look, What Line Is the CCRG Carrying Out in the Cultural Revolution?), Beijing linxueyuan hongweibing zhandou bingtuan yier.jiu zhandoudui, yong xiang dang zhandoudui, yong xiang dong zhandoudui deng, 2 December 1966 (Cultural Revolution Database 2002).

15. "Esha wuchan jieji wenhua da geming de da ducao—Ping Chen Boda tongzhi liangge yue yundong de zongjie" (Exterminate the Big Poisonous Weed of the Cultural Revolution—On Chen Boda's Assessment of the Movement's First

Two Months), Beijing linxueyuan hongweibing zhandou bingtuan yier.jiu, yong xiang dang zhandoudui deng, 5 December 1966 (Cultural Revolution Database 2002).

16. Beijing Geology Institute East Is Red (1967b), 139; Qinghua Jinggangshan (1966), 3–4.

17. Yi Zhenya and Wan Huiqin, "Shi'er yue wuri wan zai linxueyuan bianlunhui shang de fayan" (Speech at the Debate on the Evening of December 5 at the Forestry Institute), 5 December 1966 (Cultural Revolution Database 2002).

18. "Zhongyang wen'ge xiaozu de luxianxing cuowu bixu pipan" (The CCRG's Errors of Line Must Be Criticized), Qinghua daxue hongweibing honglei zhandoudui, 4 December 1966, in Qinghua daxue, *Dongtai bao, haowai* 5 December 1966 (Cultural Revolution Database 2002). Similar sentiments appeared at Qinghua (Qinghua Jinggangshan 1966).

19. "Gei Mao zhuxi de yifeng gongkai xin" (An Open Letter to Chairman Mao), Qinghua daxue hongweibing zhanshi Yan Xiaodong, 9 December 1966 (Cultural Revolution Database 2002).

20. "Zhongyang wen'ge xiaozu xiang hechu qu?" (Where Is the CCRG Headed?), Qinghua daxue "Hanwei shiliu tiao zhanshi," 9 December 1966, *Fanmian cailiao* (mimeographed), 14 December 1966 (Cultural Revolution Database 2002).

21. "Yu zhongyang wen'ge xiaozu shangque zhier—Yao jishache, jizhuanwan ma? Qieman!" (Second Discussion with the CCRG—Slam on the Brakes and Make a Fast U-Turn? Not So Fast!), Qinghua daxue hongweibing sijun zhandoudui, 10 December 1966 (Cultural Revolution Database 2002).

22. "Yu zhongyang wen'ge xiaozu shangque zhisan—Shi pipan Tan Lifu jianghua de cuowu haishi tuixing Tan Lifu jianghua de cuowu?" (Third Discussion with the CCRG—Criticizing the Errors of Tan Lifu's Speech or Committing the Errors of Tan Lifu's Speech?), Qinghua daxue hongweibing sijun zhandoudui, 10 December 1966, in *Ducao ji* (mimeographed), December 1966 (Cultural Revolution Database 2002).

23. "Yong Mao Zedong sixiang jiancha yiqie!" (Use Mao Zedong Thought to Analyze Everything!), Qinghua daxue hongweibing "Xuelian" zhandoudui, 11 December 1966, in *Ducao ji* (mimeographed), December 1966 (Cultural Revolution Database 2002).

24. "Zhongyang wen'ge xiaozu de cuowu jiushi bixu pipan" (The CCRG's Errors Indeed Must Be Criticized), Qinghua daxue hongweibing qishou zhandoudui, 14 December 1966, in *Ducao ji* (mimeographed), December 1966 (Cultural Revolution Database 2002).

25. "Di yi ba huo" (First Assault), Beijing daxue hushanxing zhandoudui, 10 December 1966 (Cultural Revolution Database 2002); and "Mao Zhuxi de da minzhu wansui!" (Long Live Chairman Mao's Great Democracy!), Beijing daxue hushanxing zhandoudui, 10 December 1966, in *Dazibao xuan,* Beijing

daxue wenhua geming weiyuanhui, 25 December 1966, 39 (Cultural Revolution Database 2002).

26. See, for example, the Railway Institute High School wall poster that echoed the arguments of the university dissidents: "Zhongxuesheng wen zhongyang wenge—Jiu zhongxue liangtiao luxian wenti" (High School Students Ask the CCRG—Regarding the Question of the Two-Line Struggle in the High Schools), Beijing tiedao xueyuan fuzhong hong houdai tiexue zongdui, November 1966 (Cultural Revolution Database 2002).

27. "Yilin" was the pen name of a student whose father had been a military officer under the Nationalists and had fled to Taiwan; "Dixi" was from a working-class household. Both had reportedly expressed doubts about the worship of Mao from the outset of the Cultural Revolution. See *Wenhua geming tongxun* 4 (January 1967): 16.

28. "Gei Lin Biao tongzhi yifeng gongkai xin" (An Open Letter to Comrade Lin Biao), Beinongda fuzhong Yilin Dixi, 15 November 1966, in Beijing daxue, *Wenhua geming tongxun* 4 (January 1967), 17–19.

29. "Lin Biao fu tongshuai ye shi keyi piping de" (Vice–Commander in Chief Lin Biao Can Also Be Criticized), Qinghua daxue wuli xi Liu Zhonghuan, Yang Chuanzhao, 11 December 1966 (Cultural Revolution Database 2002).

30. Beijing Geology Institute East Is Red (1967b), 130–134; Qinghua Jinggangshan (1966), 1–2.

31. Beijing University High School (1967), 15; Bu Weihua (2001), 130; Qiao Yi and Xu Yaya, " 'Liandong' shijian shimo" (The Story behind the "Liandong" Incident), *Zhuiqiu* 5 (1986) (Wang Nianyi 1988, 167–174); and my interview with a former leader of Beijing University High School Red Flag, April 1992.

32. "Shoudu hongweibing lianhe xingdong weiyuanhui xuanyan" (Proclamation of the Capital Red Guard United Action Committee), 5 December 1966 (Cultural Revolution Database 2002).

33. Bu Weihua (2001), 130–131; my interview with a former leader of Beijing University High School Red Flag, April 1992. Niu Wanping and Gong Xiaoji, two founders of Beida High School Red Flag, were instrumental in founding Liandong. Peng Xiaomeng, the third founding leader, refused to join, reportedly saying, "I am not joining Liandong, but not because I do not oppose the CCRG. What Liandong opposes is beside the point; all they know how to do is attack. You have to sit down and calmly prepare your materials, and only then will it really count" (Beijing University High School 1967, 6–7). Other members included Bu Dahua and other founders of the Qinghua High School Red Guards (Qiao Yi and Xu Yaya, "Liandong," in Wang Nianyi 1988, 168–169).

34. Beijing Geology Institute East Is Red (1967b), 136; "Chen Boda, Guan Feng tongzhi jiejian shoudu dazhuan yuanxiao hongweibing geming zaofan zong silingbu quanti renyuan he Beihang 'hongqi' deng tongzhi shi de jianghua" (Speeches by Comrades Chen Boda and Guan Feng in a Meeting with All Members

of the Capital University Red Guard Revolutionary Rebel General Headquarters and Beijing Aeronautics "Red Flag" and Other Comrades), 27 November 1966 (Central Comrades' Speeches 1966b, 160–167).

35. "Duoqu xin de shengli" (Seize a New Victory), and Wang Li, Gu Yixue, and Li Xin, "Wuchan jieji zhuanzheng he wuchan jieji wenhua da geming" (Proletarian Dictatorship and the Great Proletarian Cultural Revolution), *Hongqi* 15 (13 December 1966): 14–24.

36. Beijing Geology Institute East Is Red (1967b), 142; "Jiang Qing tongzhi jiejian xiang 'Hongqi' zazhi hexi qunzhong de jianghua" (Comrade Jiang Qing's Speech When Receiving the Masses Who Have Come to Celebrate at *Red Flag* Magazine), late evening 12 December, early morning 13 December, at the State Council North Gate (Reference Materials 1966, vol. 4, sec. 12, 71).

37. "Chen Boda, Kang Sheng, Jiang Qing deng tongzhi shier yue shisi ri xiang yisi, sansi, Beihang hongqi, kuangyuan dongfanghong deng danwei de jianghua" (Speeches by Chen Boda, Kang Sheng, Jiang Qing, and Other Comrades with the First Headquarters, Third Headquarters, Aeronautics Red Flag, Machinery Institute East Is Red, and Other Units on December 14) (Special Compilation 1997, vol. 4, 107).

38. Beijing Geology Institute East Is Red (1967b), 142.

39. "Zhongyang lingdao tongzhi zai 'Beijing shi zhongxue pipan zichan jieji fandong luxian dahui' shang de jianghua" (Speeches by Leading Comrades from the Party Center at the Beijing Municipal High School Mass Meeting to Denounce the Bourgeois Reactionary Line), 16 December 1966 (Reference Materials 1966, vol. 4, sec. 12, 87–89).

40. Wu Qingtong (2002, 61–62), who was the head of the State Council Secretary General's Office directly under Zhou Rongxin, states that neither Zhou Rongxin nor Zhou Enlai was aware of this attack beforehand, and he sees Jiang's attack on Zhou's subordinates as an attack on Zhou Enlai himself, as does Gao Wenqian (2003, 147–149). Wang Li (2001, 646) characterizes Jiang's speech as an attack on Zhou that put him in "an extremely defensive posture." See also Schoenhals (1994), 20–21.

41. "Speeches by Leading Comrades," 16 December 1966 (Reference Materials 1966, vol. 4, sec. 12, 87–89). Jiang and Chen repeated the charges at a mass meeting of university rebels at Beijing Workers' Stadium the next day, and Zhou Enlai once again stated that he "completely agreed" and moreover announced the arrest of violent picket corps leaders. "Jiang Qing, Chen Boda, Zhou Enlai tongzhi zai 'quanguo zai jing geming zaofanpai xiang zichan jieji fandong luxian menglie kaihuo shishi dahui' shang de jianghua" (Speeches by Comrades Jiang Qing, Chen Boda, and Zhou Enlai at the "Mass Rally of Revolutionary Rebels from throughout the Nation to Fiercely Open Fire on the Bourgeois Reactionary Line"), 17 December 1966 (Reference Materials 1966, vol. 4, sec. 12, 93–95).

42. Beijing Geology Institute East Is Red (1967b), 143–144.

43. They were Qiao Jianwu, a student in the Eastern Languages Department who wrote an "Open Letter to Comrade Lin Biao" that approved of Yilin Dixi's arguments, and Yang Bingzhang, campus resident and younger brother of one of Nie Yuanzi's vocal opponents, who spoke out in support of a local wall poster critical of the CCRG; ibid., 144–145; and Yang Bingzhang (1998), 166–169.

44. Tan Bin (1996), 387. He was held in solitary confinement on short rations until the spring of 1967 and was interrogated repeatedly about his connections to Liu Shaoqi, Deng Xiaoping, and other "black backstage supporters."

45. "Jiang Qing, Zhang Chunqiao deng tongzhi zai renmin dahui tang tong yisi, ersi zaofan lianluozhan, sansi deng daibiao de zuotan jiyao" (Minutes of the Discussion between Jiang Qing, Zhang Chunqiao, and Other Comrades in the Great Hall of the People with Representatives of the First Headquarters, Second Headquarters Rebel Liaison Station, Third Headquarters, and Others), 18 December 1966 (Central Comrades' Speeches 1966b, 251–252).

46. Central Documents Research Office (1997), 103.

47. "'Hongqi' zazhi fu zongbian Lin Jie tongzhi tanhua jiyao" (Minutes of the Talk by *Red Flag* Assistant Editor Lin Jie), at the CCP Propaganda Department, 20 December 1966 (Reference Materials 1966, vol. 4, sec. 12, 122–123).

48. "Wang Li deng yu bufen Beijing dazhuan yuanxiao hongweibing zuotan jiyao" (Minutes of the Meeting of Wang Li and Others with Red Guards from Beijing Colleges), 22 December 1966 (Cultural Revolution Database 2002). Denunciation materials later prepared against Zhou Rongxin expressed outrage that he claimed that everything he had done was on the direct orders of Zhou Enlai (State Council 1967b, 1).

49. Qinghua Jinggangshan (1966), 4–5; Qiao Yi and Xu Yaya, "Liandong," in Wang Nianyi (1988), 169.

50. Beijing University High School (1967), 15; Qiao Yi and Xu Yaya, "Liandong," in Wang Nianyi (1988), 169–170.

51. Beijing University High School (1967), 16; Bu Weihua (2001), 136; Qiao Yi and Xu Yaya, "Liandong," in Wang Nianyi (1988), 169–170.

52. Qiao Yi and Xu Yaya, "Liandong," in Wang Nianyi (1988), 170–171.

53. Bu Weihua (2001), 137.

54. One source describes demonstrations on December 16, 28, and 31 and January 6, 9, and 11 (Shanghai Red Guard Headquarters 1967, 12–14). See also Beijing Geology Institute East Is Red (1967b), 147–148; Beijing University High School (1967), 17.

55. "Xie Fuzhi tongzhi zai zhongyang zhengfa ganxiao dui lai jing zhengfa ganbu de jianghua" (Comrade Xie Fuzhi's Speech to Legal and Public Security Cadres at the Central Legal and Public Security Cadre School), 17 January 1967 (Central Comrades' Speeches 1967, 155–156). This was the "Six Articles on Public Security," drafted at the urging of the CCRG, which defined a whole range of actions as "counterrevolutionary" and included a prohibition against

"using great democracy and other means to distribute reactionary opinions" (Wang Nianyi 2005, 161–163).

56. Qiao Yi and Xu Yaya, "Liandong," in Wang Nianyi (1988), 172.

57. Bu Weihua (2001), 145–146; Qiao Yi and Xu Yaya, "Liandong," in Wang Nianyi (1988), 172; Tan Bin (1996), 387–390.

58. The details were gruesome. Wang Guanghua was captured at a bus stop on September 27 and was beaten so severely in the interrogation center that he died two days later (Beijing No. 6 High School Beijing Commune, n.d., 7–8). This document is reprinted in Shanghai Red Guard Headquarters (1967), 36–72. A parallel account is in Beijing No. 6 High School Red Rebel Brigade (1966).

59. Beijing No. 6 High School Beijing Commune (n.d.), 9–10.

60. Beijing Municipal Party Committee (1987a), 29. The notice stated, "All factories, mines, schools, offices, and other units are not permitted to set up private jails, courts, and to seize and torture people," and "Anyone who directs such activities openly or from behind the scenes must receive punishment according to state law and party discipline."

61. Beijing No. 6 High School Beijing Commune (n.d.), 16–18.

62. Ibid., 8.

63. Ibid., 18.

64. Ibid., 21–22 and cover.

65. For example, descriptions of a "labor reform bureau" at the Beijing No. 1 High School contained no accounts of either torture or murder but attributed to old red guards a dictatorial approach to governing the school (Beijing No. 1 High School Red Flag Combat Team 1967; Capital Red Army Corps 1967).

66. Shanghai Red Guard Headquarters (1967), 50–67. See also Capital High School Red Guard Congress (1967) and Capital University Red Guard Congress (1967).

67. Shanghai Red Guard Headquarters (1967), 12–13.

68. Beijing University High School (1967), 2.

69. Shanghai Red Guard Headquarters (1967), 105–109.

70. Ibid., 78–95. See also Beijing University High School (1967), 32–34.

71. Shanghai Red Guard Headquarters (1967), 22–35.

72. Qiao Yi and Xu Yaya, " 'Liandong," in Wang Nianyi (1988), 167–174.

73. "Zhongyang, Beijing dang zheng jun ganbu zidi (nü) lianhe xingdong weiyuanhui tonggao" (Notice of the United Action Committee of the Sons [Daughters] of Party, Government, and Military Cadres of the Center and Beijing), 1 January 1967 (Shanghai Red Guard Headquarters 1967, 124–127).

74. Shanghai Red Guard Headquarters (1967), 109.

75. The portrayal of the Western District Picket Corps and Liandong in scholarly publications sometimes uncritically reproduces the charges against them (Barnouin and Yu Changgen 1993, 96–99, 103–105; Yan Jiaqi and Gao Gao 1996, 81–83, 106–111). This portrayal was highly influential among rebels in

other regions who put themselves forward years later as expert observers and critics. See, for example, the account by the Guangzhou red guard who emerged as a democracy activist in the late 1970s and wrote an underground history of the Cultural Revolution (Liu Guokai [1980] 1987).

76. "Chushen lun" (On Class Origin), *Zhongxue wen'ge bao,* 18 January 1967, 1–2 (CCRM 1999, 17:8351–8352).

77. Li Yong and Wen Lequn (1994b), 233–246. See the translation and interpretive essay in G. White (1976). The case became a cause célèbre in the immediate post-Mao era. Yu Luoke was memorialized in a popular fictionalized account by his sister (Yu Luojin 1986) and a memoir by his brother (Yu Luowen 2000).

78. Bu Weihua (2001, 139–144) reproduces the entire text of the wall poster.

79. This narrative is based on the account of Mei Jianming, one of Zhu's lieutenants, as recorded in the interview transcripts published in Xiao Han and Turner (1998), 182–187, and on the transcript of Zhu's "confession," which was circulated in the school in August 1967 (Zhu Chengzhao 1967, 3–4, 6–7).

80. Mei Jianming, in Xiao Han and Turner (1998), 183–184; see Walder (2006b) for an account of the opposition to Nie Yuanzi at Beijing University.

81. This is my translation of "bu shi qunzhong yundong, shi yundong qunzhong." Mei Jianming, in Xiao Han and Turner (1998), 189–190. The term *yundong qunzhong* is repeated in Zhu's "confession" (Zhu Chengzhao 1967, 5).

82. Xiao Han and Turner (1998), 190–191; Zhu Chengzhao, Jiang Liangpu, and Yang Yuzhong, "Guanyu dizhi xueyuan dongfanghong gongshe muqian xingshi de jidian shengming" (Declarations Regarding Current Trends in Geology Institute East Is Red Commune), *Dongfanghong bao,* 31 January 1967, 4 (CCRM 2001, 9:3208).

83. Xiao Han and Turner (1998), 191–192. Mei Jianming recalled, "The CCRG had us under their control from the beginning. They had spies in our midst, and when we were first engaged in our rebellion these spies encouraged us and supervised us; but when we began to stop listening to them, they turned around and informed on us." Zhu reported that Chen Boda sent him a hostile note at this time questioning his loyalty, and that Qi Benyu had already criticized him severely in late December for his doubts (Zhu Chengzhao 1967, 4, 7).

84. "Yan Changgui tongzhi yu dizhi xueyuan bufen shisheng zuotan jiyao" (Minutes of Comrade Yan Changgui's Discussion with Some Teachers and Students from the Geology Institute), 8 February 1967 (Central Leaders' Speeches 1967b, 69–73).

85. Mei Jianming, in Xiao Han and Turner (1998), 192–193. Zhu Chengzhao (1967, 5) reported that he was earlier angered by Chen Boda's hostile note.

86. Mei Jianming, in Xiao Han and Turner (1998), 192–194; Zhu Chengzhao (1967), 9–10.

87. Wang Dabin, " 'Tongzhi' zhimingle douzheng de dafangxiang" (The "Notice" Points Clearly to the General Direction of the Struggle), *Hongqi* 7 (20 May 1967): 20–21.

88. Zhu Chengzhao (1967), cover page. Later denunciations painted Zhu as a "reactionary anarchist"; "Zhu Chengzhao shi fandong de wuzhengfu zhuyizhe" (Zhu Chengzhao Is a Reactionary Anarchist), *Dongfanghong bao,* 1 September 1967 (CCRM 2001, 9:3460).

89. "Beijing dizhi xueyuan geming weiyuanhui tongming" (Order of the Beijing Geology Institute Revolutionary Committee), *Dongfanghong bao,* 19 January 1968, 2 (CCRM 2001, 10:3627); Mei Jianming, in Xiao Han and Turner (1998), 218–221; and Schoenhals, unpublished paper cited in Chapter 4, note 35.

# 8. Factions Reborn

1. MacFarquhar and Schoenhals (2006), 165–167; Walder (1978), 51–64; Wang Nianyi (2005), 138–154.

2. "Qi Benyu tongzhi jiejian guojia kewei shaoshu pai tongzhi de jianghua" (Speech by Comrade Qi Benyu to Minority Faction Comrades in the State Science and Technology Commission), 12 January 1967 (Central Leaders' Speeches 1967a, 101–103); Wang Nianyi (2005), 159. See also Wang Li in Schoenhals (1994), 35.

3. "Qi Benyu tongzhi yu Beihang hongqi, dizhi dongfanghong deng tongzhi de jianghua" (Comrade Qi Benyu's Talk with Aeronautics Red Flag, Geology East Is Red, and Other Comrades), 17 January 1967 (Central Leaders' Speeches 1967a, 142); Wang Nianyi (2005), 160.

4. "Beijing geming zaofan gongshe changyi shu" (Proclamation of the Beijing Revolutionary Rebel Commune), *Xin Beida,* 28 January 1967, 2 (CCRM 1999, 15:7044); Wang Li in Schoenhals (1994), 38; Wang Xuezhen et al. (1998), 656–657.

5. Nie Yuanzi later recalled, "At the time, seizing power was a matter of who ran the fastest; power went to whoever got there first and captured the official seal. So Kuai Dafu's people all ran off without telling us" (Nie Yuanzi 2005, 196).

6. Bu Weihua (2000), 101.

7. "Fencui 'fan Xin Beida' niliu" (Smash the "Oppose New Beida" Countercurrent), *Xin Beida,* 31 January 1967, 2 (CCRM 1999, 15:7048); Wang Xuezhen et al. (1998), 657.

8. Bu Weihua (2000), 102; Nie Yuanzi (2005), 199–202.

9. Nie Yuanzi (2005), 202–204. See the competing accounts of this incident in "Jianguo yilai zui da de guojia mimi dang'an qiangjie an zhenxiang" (The Real Story behind the Biggest Plunder of Secret State Archives since the Founding of the People's Republic), *Kangda,* 25 October 1967, 2; and "Yichang gou yao gou

de chouju—ping '1.15' dang'an shijian de zheng, hong zhi zheng" (An Absurd Story of Dog Bites Dog—Assessing the Argument over the "January 15" Archives Incident between Zheng and Hong), *Minyuan dongfanghong*, 5 December 1967, 4 (CCRM 1999, 10:4552, 4854).

10. "Hongdaihui Beijing linxueyuan dongfanghong gongshe yanzheng shengming" (Solemn Declaration of the Red Guard Congress Beijing Forestry Institute East Is Red Commune), 21 April 1967 (CCRM 1975, 19:6085).

11. See the overview of factional strife in thirty-four government ministries in "Zhongyang ge bu duoquan qingkuang baodao" (Report on Power Seizure Situation at Various Central Ministries), *Xianfeng*, 31 January 1967, 3 (CCRM 2001, 32:12698).

12. "Chen Boda, Jiang Qing, Kang Sheng, Wang Li, Qi Benyu deng tongzhi zai renmin dahuitang yu shoudu da, zhong zhuan yuanxiao geming zaofanpai xuesheng daibiao zuotan jiyao" (Minutes of the Discussion at the Great Hall of the People between Chen Boda, Jiang Qing, Kang Sheng, Wang Li, Qi Benyu, and Other Comrades with Representatives of Revolutionary Rebel Students of the Capital's Universities and High Schools), 26 January 1967 (Central Comrades' Speeches 1967, 238–242); "Zhongyang wen'ge zhaoji de bufen xuexiao zaofanpai zuzhi zuotanhui" (CCRG Meeting Convened with Rebel Factions from Some of the Schools), late evening 23 January–early morning 24 January (Central Leaders' Speeches 1967a, 212–217).

13. Bu Weihua (2000), 102–104.

14. By mid-February there were three large power seizure committees in Beijing; "Beijing shi da lianhe choubei gongzuo jianjie" (An Introduction to the Preparations for Great Alliances in Beijing), *Jinggangshan*, 20 February 1967, 3 (CCRM 1999, 8:3582).

15. Nie's first marriage was to Hu Jingyi, described by Nie's opponents as a "traitor," perhaps a victim of the 1943 Yan'an rectification movement during which Nie herself was attacked. See "Nie shi fangeming jiazu jianjie" (Introduction to the Counterrevolutionary Nie Clan), in "Nieshi jiazu fumie he Nie Yuanzi de qiantu" (The Destruction of the Nie Clan and the Future of Nie Yuanzi), Hongdai hui xin Beida jinggangshan bingtuan piao hongqi zhandoudui, n.d., four-page pamphlet, at 4.

16. Wang Renzhong orchestrated the formation of the Beida Cultural Revolution Committee behind the scenes, working out of the CCRG offices at the Diaoyutai State Guest House, where Nie visited frequently (Nie Yuanzi 2005, 155–158).

17. Wang Xuezhen et al. (1998), 652–653. The three largest were the official Beida Red Guards, the Beida Maoism Red Guards, and the New Beida Mao Thought Red Guard General Headquarters. In early September there were already more than eighty red guard organizations with close to 3,000 members; "Guanyu dangqian yundong de liudian jianyi" (Six Suggestions on the

Movement at Present), *Xin Beida,* 13 September 1966, 3 (CCRM 1999, 15:6931). One-third of Beida undergraduates were considered active red guards at this point.

18. Sun, an army veteran from a poor peasant and revolutionary martyr household, had been criticized along with Nie Yuanzi during the Socialist Education Movement. Chen Huanren (2006), 309; Nie Yuanzi (2005), 88, 169; "Guanyu Sun Pengyi tongzhi wenti de yanzheng shengming" (Solemn Declaration Regarding the Question of Comrade Sun Pengyi), *Xin Beida,* 26 March 1968, 4 (CCRM 1999, 16:7578).

19. "Beijing daxue hongweibing tongyi gongzuo weiyuanhui diyi ci quanti huiyi gongbao" (Communique of the First Plenary Session of the Beijing University Red Guard Unification Work Committee), *Xin Beida,* 27 September 1966, 1 (CCRM 1999, 15:6953).

20. "Guanyu hongweibing tongyi wenti de lianhe shengming" (A United Declaration on the Question of Red Guard Unification), *Xin Beida,* 27 September 1966, 1 (CCRM 1999, 15:6953).

21. The wall-poster collections published by the Cultural Revolution committee, even in late September, still reprinted the May 25 wall poster with articles praising its historical significance. See Beijing University Cultural Revolution Committee (1966a).

22. Lu Yuan and Zhou Chuang, "Bankai Nie Yuanzi, Beida cai neng luan" (Remove Nie Yuanzi, Beida Will Only Then Be in Upheaval), *Xin Beida,* 8 October 1966, 2 (CCRM 1999, 15:6972).

23. Wang Xuezhen et al. (1998), 652. The debate was inaugurated in *Xin Beida,* 8 October 1966. A collection of wall posters on both sides of the Nie issue is in Beijing University Cultural Revolution Committee (1966d).

24. Yang Xun, "Beida wenhua geming you chu zai guanjian shike" (Beida's Cultural Revolution Is Again at a Crucial Turning Point), *Xin Beida,* 8 October 1966, 3 (CCRM 1999, 15:6973).

25. Yang Xun (2004), introduction and 134.

26. Mu Xin (2000), 168–170, states that Yang wrote the final draft and that Nie Yuanzi was uninvolved in the drafting process and only affixed her name at the end.

27. "Lun jihui zhuyi de zhen mianxiang" (On the True Face of Opportunism), *Xin Beida,* 5 November 1966, 4 (CCRM 1999, 15:6994). The two sides presented their opposed positions on the closure of the newspaper in *Xin Beida,* 21 November 1966, 2 (CCRM 1999, 15:6996). The last article critical of Nie to appear in the pages of *Xin Beida* was in the 12 December 1966 issue.

28. The opposition groups joined the rebel Third Headquarters in November (Wang Xuezhen et al. 1998, 652–653).

29. See the exchange in *Xin Beida,* 12 December 1966, 5–7 (CCRM 1999, 15:7003–7005).

30. The request was delivered by Li Na, the daughter of Mao and Jiang Qing and a 1965 Beida graduate, who was Mao's confidential liaison with Nie during this period (Nie Yuanzi 2005, 172–190; Wang Li 2001, 758–764).

31. Nie also established links with dissident members of the Shanghai Municipal Party Committee, called for its overthrow at a mass meeting in People's Square on November 25, and informed students who challenged the municipal leadership that they had the backing of the CCRG (Chen Pixian 2005, 99–108).

32. Wang Xuezhen et al. (1998), 654–655.

33. Nie Yuanzi (2005, 208–209) states that her people did not join any of the red guard headquarters, although she did attend the First Headquarters inaugural meeting.

34. "Douzheng fangeming fenzi Yang Bingzhang, Qiao Jianwu, pipan 'hushanxing' de fangeming yanlun" (Struggle against Counterrevolutionary Elements Yang Bingzhang and Qiao Jianwu, Repudiate the Counterrevolutionary Viewpoints of "Hushanxing"), *Xin Beida*, 24 December 1966, 2 (CCRM 1999, 15:7008). The lead article in the same issue celebrated the *Red Flag* editorial calling for the suppression of critics of the CCRG. Qiao Jianwu put up a wall poster in August calling for the abolition of the party and youth league and the creation of revolutionary committees and in December put up a wall poster challenging Lin Biao; "Qingdian yixia 'chenhuo' " (Clearing Out Some "Shopworn Goods"), *Xin Beida*, 12 December 1966, 7 (CCRM 1999, 15:7005); and "Beida jinggangshan—fangeming fenzi de da benying" (Beida Jinggangshan—Big Base Camp for Counterrevolutionary Elements), *Xin Beida*, 23 May 1968, 4 (CCRM 1999, 16:7646). Yang Bingzhang, a campus resident but not a student, wrote a series of letters privately to Chairman Mao, many of which criticized Jiang Qing's behavior (Yang Bingzhang 1998, 136–152). For public consumption, Yang was labeled an "active counterrevolutionary" for saying that the Cultural Revolution was simply a factional struggle stirred up by members of the CCRG; "Women yao wei renmin zhengquan duoyin—tongsu Yang Bingzhang de fangeming zuixing" (We Must Seize Power on Behalf of the People—A Bitter Account of Yang Bingzhang's Counterrevolutionary Crimes), *Xin Beida*, 1 January 1967, 3 (CCRM 1999, 15:7013).

35. Wang Xuezhen et al. (1998), 655; *Xin Beida*, 24 December 1966, 2 (CCRM 1999, 15:7008).

36. Nie could not have staged this massive display without the active cooperation of the Central Case Examination Group, which controlled access to these political suspects (Schoenhals 1996).

37. Wang Xuezhen et al. (1998), 655. Jiang and Kang named several critics and personally branded them counterrevolutionaries, including Yang Xun and her brother Yang Bingzhang. See "Zhongyang wen'ge xiaozu jiejian Beijing daxue daibiao tanhua jiyao" (Minutes of CCRG Reception with Beijing University Representatives), 3 January 1967 (Central Leaders' Speeches 1967a, 1). See also "Kang Sheng tongzhi dui Beida jishu wuli xi Cui Ziming deng ren liangfen

fandong xinjian de pibo" (Comrade Kang Sheng's Refutation of Two Reactionary Letters by Cui Ziming and Others from the Beida Applied Physics Department), 3 January (Central Leaders' Speeches 1967a, 19–20).

38. "Nie Yuanzi tongzhi dui geming shisheng yuangong he hongweibing zhanshi de jianghua" (Comrade Nie Yuanzi's Speech to Revolutionary Teachers, Students, Staff, and Workers, and Red Guard Comrades in Arms), *Xin Beida*, 1 January 1967, 2 (CCRM 1999, 15:7012).

39. Wang Xuezhen et al. (1998), 656; Yang Bingzhang (1998), 166–170; Yang Xun (2004), 159–167.

40. "Kong Fan, Yang Keming tongzhi shi zichan jieji fandong luxian zai Beida de daibiao" (Comrades Kong Fan and Yang Keming Are Representatives of the Bourgeois Reactionary Line at Beida), and "Kong Fan, Yang Keming zai xiaokan ganle shenme?" (What Did Kong Fan and Yang Keming Do on the School Newspaper?), *Xin Beida*, 10 January 1967, 5–7 (CCRM 1999, 15:7019–7021).

41. See Jiang's statement and the references to Kong and Yang having fled from campus in the minutes of the 3 January reception with the CCRG (Central Leaders' Speeches 1967a, 17–18).

42. Wang Xuezhen et al. (1998), 655. Sun Pengyi and Xu Yunpu (a student in the Russian Department), both vice-chairmen of the Cultural Revolution committee, were put in charge.

43. See the transcript of her 19 January speech in *Xin Beida*, 20 January 1967, 1 (CCRM 1999, 15:7031).

44. The minority-faction wall-poster collections throughout this period were issued in its name. See Qinghua University Mao Zedong Thought Red Guards (1966a, 1966b, 1966c, 1966d); also Zheng (2006), 48.

45. See "Jinggangshan hongweibing choubei jianli weiyuanhui di yi hao jueyi—Guanyu zuzhi yuanze" (First Resolution of the Preparatory Committee to Establish the Jinggangshan Red Guards—On Organizational Principles), 23 September 1966; and "Jinggangshan hongweibing xuanyan (cao'an)" (Proclamation of the Jinggangshan Red Guards [Draft]), 23 September 1966 (Cultural Revolution Database 2002).

46. Zheng (2006), 48–50, 62. See the announcement in *Jinggangshan*, 22 December 1966, 1 (CCRM 1999, 8:3509).

47. Qinghua University Jinggangshan Red Guards (1966).

48. Shen Ruhuai (2004), 50–52.

49. Ibid., 48. See "Wang Renzhong bixu hui Qinghua jiancha" (Wang Renzhong Must Return to Qinghua to Confess), *Jinggangshan*, 19 December 1966, 2 (CCRM 1999, 8:3506); Kuai Dafu's speech dated 19 December in *Jinggangshan*, 22 December 1966, 2 (CCRM 1999, 8:3510); and "Wang Guangmei, Bo Yibo, Wang Renzhong bixu hui Qinghua jiancha jiaodai" (Wang Guangmei, Bo Yibo, and Wang Renzhong Must Return to Qinghua to Confess Their Errors), *Jinggangshan*, 25 December 1966, 1 (CCRM 1999, 8:3513). Jiang Qing approved

these demands the day before; "Jiang Qing, Xie Fuzhi, Zhang Chunqiao deng tongzhi jiejian yi, er, sansi ji bufen yuanxiao geming pai daibiao shi de zuotan jiyao" (Minutes of the Discussion between Jiang Qing, Xie Fuzhi, Zhang Chunqiao, and Other Comrades with Representatives of Revolutionary Factions from the First, Second, and Third Headquarters and Other Schools), 18 December 1966 (Reference Materials 1966, vol. 4, sec. 12, 107).

50. Shen Ruhuai (2004), 49; Zheng (2006), 50. See also "Xiang Liu Deng fandong luxian menglie kaihuo—ji Jinggangshan bingtuan shier yue ershiwu ri da xingdong" (Fiercely Open Fire on the Liu-Deng Reactionary Line—Commemorating Jinggangshan Regiment's December 25 Great Action), *Jinggangshan*, 1 January 1967, 5 (CCRM 1999, 8:3528).

51. Shen Ruhuai (2004), 49–50; Zheng (2006), 50–51. Tang also could have cited Jiang Qing, who explicitly told rebel students on December 18 that it was "not yet strategic" to target Liu Shaoqi and Deng Xiaoping openly—this was an internal party matter yet to be decided (Reference Materials 1966, vol. 4, sec. 12, 107). She evidently reversed this stand within days.

52. Shen Ruhuai (2004), 50. See "Jiang Qing tongzhi lai Qinghua jian geming shisheng yuangong" (Jiang Qing Comes to Qinghua to See Revolutionary Teachers, Students, Staff, and Workers), *Jinggangshan*, 31 December 1966, 1; and the transcripts of the brief speeches by Jiang, Wang Li, and Yao Wenyuan in the same issue (CCRM 1999, 8:3522–3523).

53. Shen Ruhuai (2004), 50–51. See "Zhou zongli yu Qinghua daxue tongxue zuotan jiyao" (Minutes of the Discussion between Premier Zhou and Classmates from Qinghua University), 31 December 1966 (Reference Materials 1966, vol. 4, sec. 12, 191–192).

54. Shen Ruhuai (2004), 51.

55. Ibid., 52.

56. Ibid., 51–53; "Zhou zongli tan '1.6' xingdong" (Premier Zhou Talks about the 'January 6' Action), 7 January 1967 (Central Leaders' Speeches 1967a, 38–39).

57. See three articles that express different points of view in *Jinggangshan*, 1 February 1967, 1 (CCRM 1999, 8:3560); and Shen Ruhuai (2004), 53–54.

58. Shen Ruhuai (2004), 55–57; Zheng (2006), 51.

59. "Chen Boda tongzhi yu Kuai Dafu tongzhi tong dianhua jilu" (A Record of Comrade Chen Boda's Phone Conversation with Comrade Kuai Dafu), 22 January 1967, 2:50 a.m. (Central Leaders' Speeches 1967a, 193–194); "Chen Boda tongzhi gei Kuai Dafu tongzhi xie de zitiao" (Comrade Chen Boda's Note to Kuai Dafu), 22 January 1967 (Central Comrades' Speeches 1967, 198). Shen Ruhuai (2004, 58–62) notes that only later did they call back to warn against criticisms of Zhou Enlai.

60. "Jiang Qing tongzhi deng jiejian geming shisheng zuotan jiyao" (Minutes of the Discussions among Comrade Jiang Qing and Others with Revolutionary

Teachers and Students), 22 January 1967 (Central Leaders' Speeches 1967a, 197–198).

61. See the transcript of a meeting in which Kuai engaged in a groveling self-criticism in front of Jiang Qing and other CCRG leaders: "Chen Boda, Jiang Qing, Kang Sheng, Wang Li, Qi Benyu tongzhi yu shoudu dazhongzhuan yuan-xiao geming zaofanpai xuesheng daibiao zuotan jilu" (Transcript of the Meeting between Comrades Chen Boda, Jiang Qing, Kang Sheng, Wang Li, Qi Benyu, and Representatives of Revolutionary Rebel Student Factions from the Capital's Universities and High Schools), 26 January 1967 (Central Leaders' Speeches 1967c, 236–240).

62. Shen Ruhuai (2004), 67–68.

63. Ibid., 69–71. See "Qingchu tuo pai" (Expel the Trotskyites), *Jinggang-shan*, 1 February 1967, 4 (CCRM 1999, 8:3563).

64. "Yan Changgui tongzhi gei Qinghua jinggangshan zongbu de dianhua jilu" (A Record of Comrade Yan Changgui's Telephone Call to Qinghua Jing-gangshan General Headquarters), 5 February 1967 (Central Leaders' Speeches 1967b, 54). Yan was also the staff member assigned to straighten out Zhu Chengzhao and the leaders of Geology East Is Red during the same week.

65. Shen Ruhuai (2004), 71–73.

66. Wang Nianyi (2005), 162–165.

67. "Dui Shanghai wenhua da geming de zhishi" (Directive Regarding the Cultural Revolution in Shanghai), 12 February 1967 (Mao Zedong 1969, 667–672). See also MacFarquhar and Schoenhals (2006), 168; and "Talks at Three Meetings with Comrades Chang Ch'un-ch'iao and Yao Wen-yuan," February 1967 (Schram 1974, 277–279); and Xu Jingxian (2004), 84–86. Mao said, "Communes are too weak when it comes to suppressing counter-revolution" (Schram 1974, 278).

68. Bu Weihua (2000), 104; "Xie fu zongli, Qi Benyu tongzhi jiejian Beijing zhengfa xueyuan 'zhengfa gongshe', kuangyuan 'dongfanghong' he Beijing shi gong'an ganbu shi de jianghua" (Speeches by Vice-Premier Xie and Comrade Qi Benyu While Meeting with Beijing Institute of Politics and Law "Politics and Law Commune," Mining Institute "East Is Red," and Cadres from the Beijing Bureau of Public Security), 1 February 1967 (Central Leaders' Speeches 1967b, 11–14).

69. "Zhonghua renmin gongheguo gong'an bu, zhongguo renmin jiefang jun Beijing weishu qu silingbu bugao" (Notice of the Ministry of Public Security of the People's Republic of China and the Beijing Garrison Command of the People's Liberation Army), 11 February 1967 (Wang Nianyi 1988, 291).

70. See the sequence of events described in Bu Weihua (2000), 104–105; "Shoudu dazhuan yuanxiao geming zaofan hongweibing daibiao dahui chengli jiankuang" (Brief Introduction to the Establishment of the Capital University Revolutionary Rebel Red Guard Congress), *Jinggangshan*, 20 February 1967, 3 (CCRM 1999, 8:3582); "Xie Fuzhi fu zongli jiejian sange silingbu ji qita

renyuan de tanhua" (Vice-Premier Xie Fuzhi's Speech in a Meeting with the Three Headquarters and Other Personnel), 6 February 1967 (Central Leaders' Speeches 1967b, 57–58); and "Xie Fuzhi fu zongli yu sansi deng geming zuzhi zuotan jiyao" (Minutes of Vice-Premier Xie Fuzhi's Discussion with the Third Headquarters and Other Revolutionary Organizations), 10 February 1967 (Central Leaders' Speeches 1967b, 80–82).

71. The new procedures were to apply to all rebel groups, students and non-students alike: "Xie Fuzhi fu zongli zai renmin dahui tang jianghua zhaiyao" (Transcript of Vice-Premier Xie Fuzhi's Talk at the Great Hall of the People), 9 February 1967 (Central Leaders' Speeches 1967b, 73–74).

72. Mei Jianming, in Xiao Han and Turner (1998), 183.

73. Note the tension between the two in the transcript of the January 26 meeting with CCRG officials cited earlier, in which Jiang Qing insists on self-criticisms from both Nie and Kuai, who initially seem more eager to criticize one another (Central Leaders' Speeches 1967c, 236–240).

74. Beijing University Party History Office (2001), 36.

75. "Jiang Qing tongzhi jiejian geming shisheng zuotan jiyao" (Minutes of Comrade Jiang Qing's Discussion with Revolutionary Teachers and Students), 22 January 1967 (Central Leaders' Speeches 1967a, 197–198).

76. "Wang Li tongzhi dui renmin ribao she de dianhua zhishi" (Comrade Wang Li's Telephone Instructions to *People's Daily*), 22 January 1967 (Central Leaders' Speeches 1967a, 194–195).

77. Bu Weihua (2001), 106; "Silingbu tonggao" (Announcements from Headquarters), *Shoudu hongweibing,* 25 January 1967, 4 (CCRM 1999, 12:5456).

78. Nie Yuanzi (2005), 54–55.

79. Wang Li (2001), 603, 721–722.

80. Nie Yuanzi (2005), 216–218.

81. Ibid., 82–88.

82. "Shoudu dazhuan yuanxiao hongweibing daibiao dahui (hongdaihui) xuanyan" (Proclamation of the Representative Assembly of University Red Guards of the Capital [Red Guard Congress]), *Shoudu hongweibing,* 3 March 1967, 2 (CCRM 1999, 12:5482).

83. See the transcripts of more than a dozen speeches and telegrams of congratulations with added commentary in *Shoudu hongweibing,* 3 March 1967, 3–4 (CCRM 1999, 12:5483–5484).

84. "Xie Fuzhi fu zongli, Qi Benyu tongzhi jiejian hongdaihui hexin chengyuan ji bufen gongzuo renyuan de jianghua" (Speeches by Vice-Premier Xie Fuzhi and Comrade Qi Benyu While Meeting with Core Members and Some of the Working Personnel of the Red Guard Congress), 4 March 1967 (Central Leaders' Speeches 1967c, 43).

85. See the detailed discussion between Qi Benyu and various East Is Red leaders about how to reconstitute their leadership: "Qi Benyu tongzhi jiejian

diyuan dongfanghong bufen tongxue jianghua" (Comrade Qi Benyu's Talk with Some Students from Geology East Is Red), 5 March 1967 (Central Leaders' Speeches 1967c, 44–47). Wang Dabin emerged as the top leader in March. See "Dongfanghong gongshe zhaokai quanyuan shisheng yuangong dahui" (East Is Red Commune Convenes All-School Assembly of Teachers, Students, Staff, and Workers), *Dongfanghong bao*, 25 March 1967, 1 (CCRM 2001, 9:3245).

86. "Shoudu hongdaihui zhongyao tongzhi" (Important Notice of the Capital Red Guard Congress), *Shoudu hongweibing*, 15 March 1967, 4 (CCRM 1999, 12:5492).

87. "Qinghua 'Jinggangshan' bao zai lianhe zhong banyanle shenme jiaose" (The Role Played by *Jinggangshan* in the Great Alliance), *Shoudu hongweibing*, 22 February 1967, and two similar articles on the same page (CCRM 1999, 12:5480).

88. Central Leaders' Speeches (1967c), 43.

89. Beijing Geology Institute East Is Red (1967b), 212–213; Bu Weihua (2001), 107; Nie Yuanzi (2005), 206–208.

90. The exchange was reprinted in *Xin Beida*, 13 April 1967, 6–7 (CCRM 1999, 15:7176–7177).

91. "'Minzu gongzuo zhanlan' shi yizhu fan Mao Zedong sixiang de da ducao" (The "Nationalities Work Exhibition" Is a Huge Anti–Mao Zedong Thought Poisonous Weed), *Dongfanghong bao*, 11 April 1967, 2–3 (CCRM 2001, 9:3266–3267).

92. Bu Weihua (2000), 108.

93. See the detailed account of the events of April 8 and 11 in Bu Weihua (2000), 109; Chen Huanren (2006), 304–306; and "Yige xumou yijiu de fangeming shijian—Hong Tao, diyuan dongfanghong deng yi xiaocuo suo zhizao de 'si.ba' he 'si.yiyi' shijian zhenxiang" (A Long-Premeditated Counterrevolutionary Incident: The Truth about the "April 8" and "April 11" Incidents Created by Hong Tao, Geology East Is Red, and Others), *Xin Beida*, 13 April 1967, 6–8 (CCRM 1999, 15:7176–7178).

94. "Sun Pengyi tongzhi daibiao xiao wen'ge, Xin Beida gongshe, Xin Beida gongshe hongweibing zongbu zai wo xiao wanren shishi dahui shang de jianghua" (Comrade Sun Pengyi's Speech Representing the School Cultural Revolution Committee, New Beida Commune, and New Beida Commune Red Guard Headquarters at the Mass Oath-Taking Meeting at Our School), *Xin Beida*, 13 April 1967, 1–3 (CCRM 1999, 15:7171–7173).

95. See "Xin Beida yi xiaocuo ren tiaoqi wudou, wo dongfanghong gongshe fabiao yanzheng shengming" (A Handful of People in New Beida Instigate Violent Conflict, Our East Is Red Commune Issues Solemn Declaration), *Beiyou dongfanghong*, 15 April 1967, 1 (CCRM 2001, 3:1125).

96. "Zhongyang wen'ge jinji tongzhi" (Urgent CCRG Notice), 12 April, 7 p.m., *Xin Beida*, 13 April 1967, 2 (CCRM 1999, 15:7172).

97. "Chen Boda, Kang Sheng, Xie Fuzhi, Jiang Qing deng zhongyang wen'ge xiaozu chengyuan jiejian hongdaihui ge yuanxiao daibiao de jianghua" (Speeches by Chen Boda, Kang Sheng, Xie Fuzhi, Jiang Qing, and Other CCRG Members in a Meeting with Red Guard Congress Representatives from Various Universities), in the Great Hall of the People, 14 April 1967 (Central Leaders' Speeches 1967d, 116–122). Nie Yuanzi (2005, 206–208) believed that Xie was trying to unseat her and told her supporters, who in turn called openly for "dragging out" Xie Fuzhi as the backstage supporter of Nie's opponents.

98. Bu Weihua (2000, 111) lists seven instances from April 4 to April 19 at the Petroleum, Railway, Chemical Fibers, and Foreign Languages institutes and the Central Institute of Finance and Economics and No. 2 Medical School.

99. Ibid., 112. Beijing Normal University Jinggangshan took a similar stand; "Shoudu hongdaihui Beijing shida Jinggangshan gongshe yanzheng shengming" (Solemn Declaration of Capital Red Guard Congress Beijing Normal University Jinggangshan Commune), *Jinggangshan,* 13 April 1967, 1 (CCRM 2001, 24:9254).

100. See Nie Yuanzi's detailed retrospective account of her rationale for these attacks (Nie Yuanzi 2005, 216–224); and Bu Weihua (2000), 114–115.

101. Bu Weihua (2000), 115. See the series of articles in the joint special issue published by Aeronautics Red Flag, Qinghua Jinggangshan, and its allies from the Mining and Sports institutes on 3 June (CCRM 1999, 8:3752–3755), especially the article on p. 2, which lists sixteen rebel groups that supported the accusations; and *Xin Beida,* 20 May 1967, 1–3 (CCRM 1999, 15:7225–7227). Chen Boda and Xie Fuzhi tried to mediate these quarrels about the tangled relationships between the Academy of Science radicals and the CCRG in early June; "Chen Boda, Xie Fuzhi deng tongzhi jiejian shoudu dazhuan yuanxiao hongdaihui hexinzu he gongzuo renyuan shi de jianghua" (Talks by Chen Boda, Xie Fuzhi, and Other Comrades in a Meeting with Core Leaders and Staff of the Capital Red Guard Congress), 5 June 1967, in *Wuchan jieji wenhua da geming ziliao* 6 (Materials on the Great Proletarian Cultural Revolution, 6), September 1967: 167–176.

102. "Shoudu hongdaihui bufen dazhuan yuanxiao lianhe yanzheng shengming" (Joint Solemn Declaration of Some Schools in the Capital Red Guard Congress), 14 May 1967, *Dongfanghong bao,* 19 May 1967, 4 (CCRM 2001, 9:3315); "Shoudu dazhuan yuanxiao hongweibing daibiao dahui gonggao" (Proclamation of the Capital University Red Guard Congress), 4 June 1967, *Shoudu hongweibing,* 6 June 1967, 3 (CCRM 1999, 12:5575); "Relie zhuhe shiba ge xiongdi zuzhi guangrong jiaru hongdaihui" (Enthusiastically Congratulate Eighteen Brother Organizations' Glorious Entry into Red Guard Congress), *Dongfanghong bao,* 6 June 1967, 1 (CCRM 2001, 9:3332).

103. "Shoudu dazhuan yuanxiao hongweibing daibiao dahui weiyuanhui yanzheng shengming" (Solemn Declaration of the Capital University Red Guard

Congress Committee), 6 June 1967, *Shoudu hongweibing,* 7 June 1967, 1 (CCRM 1999, 12:5579).

104. See "Dui shoudu dazhuan yuanxiao muqian xingshi de jidian yijian" (A Few Opinions on the Current Situation in the Capital's Universities), 10 May 1967, *Shoudu hongweibing,* 12 May 1967 (CCRM 1999, 12:5545); and "Shoudu bufen dazhuan yuanxiao wuchan jieji geming pai guanyu muqian xing-shi zuotan jiyao" (Minutes of the Discussion of Some of the Proletarian Revolutionary Factions in the Capital's Universities Regarding the Current Situation), 15 May 1967, *Dongfanghong bao,* 19 May 1967, 3 (CCRM 2001, 9:3314). The latter was signed by rebel organizations from twenty-eight universities.

105. Bu Weihua (2000), 115–116.

106. Ibid., 114; Nie Yuanzi (2005), 209.

107. The labels are freely used in the long discussion of the split by Jiang Qing, Zhou Enlai, Kang Sheng, and Chen Boda in "Zhongyang shouzhang fenbie jiejian dazhuan yuanxiao daibiao de jianghua" (Central Leaders' Speeches during Separate Meetings with University Representatives), 16 September 1967 (Cultural Revolution Database 2002).

## 9. Endgame

1. The five were Heilongjiang (January 31), Shandong (February 3), Shanghai (commune, February 5; revolutionary committee, February 23), Guizhou (February 14), and Shanxi (March 19) (Bu Weihua 2008, 731–733; Xi Xuan and Jin Chunming 2006, 167–169).

2. MacFarquhar and Schoenhals (2006), 170–183.

3. Shanghai, where CCRG members Zhang Chunqiao and Yao Wenyuan took over in January 1967, was an exception (Perry and Li Xun 1997; Walder 1978; Xu Youyu 1999, 56–63).

4. Organization Department, CCP Central Committee (2004), 871–872.

5. "Beijing shi geming weiyuanhui xuangao chengli" (Proclamation of the Founding of the Beijing Municipal Revolutionary Committee), 20 April 1967, *Renmin ribao,* 21 April 1967, 1. The other three were Wu De, also first party secretary of the Beijing Garrison; Zheng Weishan; and Nie Yuanzi (Organization Department, Beijing Municipal Party Committee 1992, 580).

6. "Beijing shi geming weiyuanhui xuangao chengli" (Proclamation of the Founding of the Beijing Municipal Revolutionary Committee), 20 April 1967, *Renmin ribao,* 21 April 1967, 1; Cao Ying (2001), 5039.

7. See *Dongfanghong bao,* 4 April 1967 (CCRM 2001, 9:3257). The Beijing Sports Institute established the first university revolutionary committee on March 26; See the list of university revolutionary committees and their dates of establishment published in *Shoudu hongweibing,* 18 August 1968, 2 (CCRM 1999, 12:5675).

8. "Beijing shifan daxue geming weiyuanhui tonggao" (Proclamation of the Beijing Normal University Revolutionary Committee), *Jinggangshan*, 30 April 1967 (CCRM 2001, 24:9279).

9. "Beijing hangkong xueyuan geming weiyuanhui xuangao chengli" (Beijing Aeronautics Institute Revolutionary Committee Founding Declaration), *Hongqi*, 21 May 1967, 1 (CCRM 2001, 16:6045).

10. These were the Beijing Institute of Water Conservation and Hydropower and the Beijing No. 2 Medical School. See the list in *Shoudu hongweibing*, 18 August 1968, 2 (CCRM 1999, 12:5675).

11. "Qinghua yuan de xin shuguang—Relie huanhu geweihui choubei xiaozu de chengli" (A New Dawn on the Qinghua Campus—Warmly Hail the Establishment of the Revolutionary Committee Preparatory Group), *Jinggangshan*, 8 May 1967, 2 (CCRM 1999, 8:3709).

12. "Liji jianli geming weiyuanhui!" (Immediately Establish the Revolutionary Committee!), *Jinggangshan*, 25 May 1967, 1 (CCRM 1999, 8:3736).

13. Fang Huijian and Zhang Sijing (2001), 2, 756–757; Shen Ruhuai (2004), 158–159.

14. "Bixu zhengque duidai ganbu" (We Must Treat Cadres Correctly), *Hongqi* 4 (1 March 1967): 5–11.

15. " 'Daji yi da pian, baohu yi xiaocuo' shi zichan jieji fandong luxian de yige zucheng bufen" ("Attack Many to Protect a Few" Is an Integral Part of the Bourgeois Reactionary Line), *Hongqi* 5 (30 March 1967): 26–30.

16. "Zai ganbu wenti shang de zichan jieji fandong luxian bixu pipan" (We Must Criticize the Bourgeois Reactionary Line on the Cadre Question), *Hongqi* 5 (30 March 1967): 24–25.

17. Chen Huanren (2006), 296–299. Cui had supported Nie's wall poster after it first appeared. Zhou earned a Ph.D. in theoretical physics after studying at the University of Chicago and the California Institute of Technology before 1949 and later become Beida's president.

18. See, for example, "Shi 'huan wo xin Beida', haishi fubi jiu Beida?" ("Return to New Beida" or Restore the Old Beida?), *Xin Beida*, 10 September 1967, 7 (CCRM 1999, 15:7381).

19. "Zhou Peiyuan, Guo Jinghai deng yibai sanshisi ming ganbu zhi geming he yao geming de ganbu de gongkai xin" (Open Letter by 134 Cadres Such as Zhou Peiyuan and Guo Jinghai to All Revolutionary Cadres and All Cadres Who Want Revolution), *Xin Beida bao*, 12 July 1967, 3 (CCRM 1999, 15:7750).

20. Wang Xuezhen et al. (1998), 661, 664–665.

21. "Zhonggong Xin Beida lingdao xiaozu zhengshi jianli" (New Beida Communist Party Leading Group Established), *Xin Beida*, 2 December 1967, 1 (CCRM 1999, 16:7479).

22. "Chedi jiefang geming ganbu Kong Fan, Yang Keming" (Thoroughly Liberate Revolutionary Cadres Kong Fan and Yang Keming), *Xin Beida bao*, 30

November 1967, 1–2 (CCRM 1999, 16:7833–7834); Wang Xuezhen et al. (1998), 665.

23. "Chedi qingsuan sanfan fenzi Ge Hua de fangeming zuixing" (Thoroughly Expose and Criticize the Counterrevolutionary Crimes of Three-Anti Element Ge Hua), *Xin Beida*, 7 October 1967, 5–8 (CCRM 1999, 16:7411–7414); Wang Xuezhen et al. (1998), 664.

24. "Ping Kong Yang shangtai hou jinggangshan bingtuan de xin dongxiang" (New Trends in Jinggangshan Regiment after Kong and Yang Take Office), *Xin Beida*, 9 December 1967, 2–3 (CCRM 1999, 16:7489); "Chuochuan Beida jinggangshan hei gaocan Ge Hua fangeming liangmian pai de zuilian" (Expose the Counterrevolutionary Double-Dealing Features of Beida Jinggangshan's Black Mentor Ge Hua), *Xin Beida*, 14 December 1967, 4 (CCRM 1999, 16:7494); Wang Xuezhen et al. (1998), 666.

25. "Jianjue dadao Cui Xiongkun, hen wa heixian shiqinian" (Resolutely Overthrow Cui Xiongkun, Ruthlessly Dig Out the Seventeen-Year Black Line), *Xin Beida bao*, 6 January 1968, 3–4 (CCRM 1999, 16:7750–7751); "Cui Xiongkun jiushi Liu Deng hei silingbu de fa zougou" (Cui Xiongkun Is the Tired Old Running Dog of the Liu-Deng Black Headquarters), *Xin Beida bao*, 15 January 1968, 1–3 (CCRM 1999, 16:7852–7854); Wang Xuezhen et al. (1998), 667.

26. "Zhonggong Xin Beida lingdao xiaozu zhengshi jianli" (New Beida Communist Party Leading Group Established), *Xin Beida*, 2 December 1967, 1 (CCRM 1999, 16:7479).

27. "Geming de gongchandang yuan xingdong qilai, shisi hanwei Mao zhuxi de jiandang luxian" (Revolutionary Party Members Swing into Action, Swear to Defend Chairman Mao's Line on Party Building to the Death), *Xin Beida bao*, 22 December 1967, 2 (CCRM 1999, 16:7842).

28. Shen Ruhuai (2004), 88, 95.

29. "Hongqi zazhi bianjibu diaochayuan qipian Mao zhuxi zuize nantao" (Red Flag Editorial Board's Investigator Cannot Escape Responsibility for Deceiving Chairman Mao), April 1967 (Qinghua University Jinggangshan United General Headquarters 1967b, 42–46); "Zai ping Hongqi pinglunyuan, diaochayuan wenzhang" (A Reevaluation of the Articles by the *Red Flag* Commentator and Investigator), 12 April 1967 (Qinghua University Jinggangshan 414 Headquarters 1967, 16–20); "Geming de qunzhong yundong wansui! Ping liuyue zhongxun de 'youjie yundong'" (Long Live the Revolutionary Mass Movement! Assessing the "Parading [Cadres] Movement" of Mid-June), 19 April 1967 (Qinghua University 414 1967, 20–22).

30. "Chedi pipan ganbu wenti shang de zichan jieji fandong luxian" (Thoroughly Criticize the Bourgeois Reactionary Line on the Cadre Question), Qinghua University Jinggangshan Corps (1967b), 4–12; "Ganbu liangxiang bixu yibian dao" (When Cadres Take a Stand, They Must Lean to One Side) and "Tantan

Qinghua ganbu de tedian" (About the Special Features of Qinghua's Cadres), *Jinggangshan,* 18 April 1967, 1–2 (CCRM 1999, 8:3670–3671).

31. Shen Ruhuai (2004), 98–99.

32. "Ju you weida lishi yiyi de zhanyi: Wo jinggangshan bingtuan he geming qunzhong jishiwan ren hendou Wang Guangmei" (A Battle of Great Historic Significance: Our Jinggangshan Regiment and Several Tens of Thousands of Revolutionary Masses Severely Struggle against Wang Guangmei), *Jinggangshan,* 11 April 1967, 1 (CCRM 1999, 8:3655); Shen Ruhuai (2004), 100–101.

33. Shen Ruhuai (2004), 101.

34. See, for example, "Qinghua jinggangshan 414 geming chuanlianhui guanyu baohu geming ganbu de yanzheng shengming" (Solemn Declaration by Qinghua Jinggangshan 414 Revolutionary Column on the Protection of Revolutionary Cadres), 16 April 1967 (Qinghua University Jinggangshan United General Headquarters 1967b, 22); and the lengthy statement of 414's views in "Muqian cunzai de yuanze fenqi jiujing shi shenme?" (What in Fact Are the Present Differences in Principle?), 7 May 1967 (Qinghua University Jinggangshan 414 Headquarters 1967, 25–29).

35. Fang Huijian and Zhang Sijing (2001), 2, 756. Shen Ruhuai (2004, 102–105), lists the leadership group of this new alliance; all were old minority-faction rebels.

36. For example, "Quanxin quanli wei renmin fuwu haishi ti faxisi maili—Ye tan dui Qinghua ganbu de guji" (Serving the People with All One's Heart or Working Hard on Behalf of Fascists—More on the Assessment of Qinghua's Cadres), 19 May 1967 (Qinghua University Jinggangshan United General Headquarters 1967b, 37–40).

37. A systematic overview of the 414 position was presented in Sun Nutao and Ji Peng, "Lun liangtiao luxian douzheng de xin jieduan" (On the New Stage in the Struggle between the Two Lines) (Qinghua University Jinggangshan United General Headquarters 1967b, 16–21); and Shen Ruhuai (2004), 111–112.

38. "Qinghua daxue yibai wushi ming zhong ji ceng ganbu zhi guangda ganbu de yifeng gongkai xin" (Open Letter to All Cadres by 150 Qinghua University Middle- and Basic-Level Cadres), 20 April 1967 (Qinghua University Jinggangshan United General Headquarters 1967b, 28–30); "Zai da pipan zhong chedi jiefang ganbu: Ping wo xiao sanbaiyu ming geming ganbu lianming fabiao gongkaixin" (Thoroughly Liberate Cadres in the Midst of the Great Criticism: An Assessment of the Open Letter Issued Jointly by More than 300 Revolutionary Cadres in Our School), *Jinggangshan bao,* 18 July 1967, 3 (CCRM 1999, 9:4280). See also the accounts of Qinghua party vice-secretary Liu Bing (1998), 111–121; and Shen Ruhuai (2004), 126–129.

39. Shen Ruhuai (2004), 128–129.

40. Ibid., 115–117. Shen's source for these figures is an internal bulletin produced by Kuai's faction for reporting to the CCRG: *Neibu cankao,* no. 20, 26 April 1967; and no. 22, 9 May 1967.

41. Shen Ruhuai (2004), 119–120.

42. Biographies of several "revolutionary cadres" who pledged support to Kuai were published in *Jinggangshan,* 29 April and 30 April 1967 (CCRM 1999, 8:3687–3693).

43. Shen Ruhuai (2004), 129–130. Shen observed that lower-ranking cadres tended to side with 414, while Jinggangshan recruited a large majority of the higher-level cadres to its side. He speculated that they calculated that Kuai would eventually win and be better able to protect them.

44. Ibid., 138. See also the article by Han Yinshan, described as a revolutionary cadre and vice-head of the Revolutionary Committee Preparatory Group, "Ganbu yao zuo dalianhe de cujin pai" (Cadres Must Be Promoters of the Great Alliance), *Jinggangshan,* 17 June 1967, 3 (CCRM 1999, 8:3770).

45. See 414's programmatic statement, "Qinghua daxue jinggangshan 414 geming chuanlianhui hexinzu guanyu shixian wo xiao geming 'sanjiehe' de jianyi (cao'an)" (Qinghua University Jinggangshan Corps 414 Revolutionary Column Core Leading Group's Recommendations on the Attainment of a Revolutionary "Triple Combination" in Our School), 17 May 1967 (Qinghua University Jinggangshan 414 Headquarters 1967, 1–5); and Shen Ruhuai (2004), 152–155.

46. Shen Ruhuai (2004), 170–173. The membership of 414 must have approached parity with that of Kuai's Jinggangshan at that time; there were 16,300 students, faculty, and staff at Qinghua.

47. See Andreas (2002) and Tang Shaojie (1999a, 1999b). Zheng (2006, 57–58) presents a brief and clear overview of the fully evolved positions of the two sides, emphasizing the essay by the Qinghua 414 writer Zhou Quanying, "Si.yisi sichao bisheng!" (The 414 Trend of Thought Must Win!), 3 August 1967 (Cultural Revolution Database 2002).

48. Shen Ruhuai (2004), 167.

49. "Wo diyuan dongfanghong de duiwai luxian burong zhongshang" (The External Line of Geology Institute East Is Red Is Unassailable), *Dongfanghong bao,* 25 August 1967, 2–3 (CCRM 2001, 9:3447–3448).

50. Chen Huanren (2006), 280–285; Nie Yuanzi (2005), 88; Wang Xuezhen et al. (1998), 658, 660–661. The critic, Guo Luoji, had stood with Nie since the Socialist Education Movement.

51. Central Leaders' Speeches (1967c), 272.

52. Wang Xuezhen et al. (1998), 658.

53. Central Leaders' Speeches (1967d), 116–122. Sun Pengyi challenged Xie Fuzhi's leftist credentials at a mass meeting on April 12 and called him a "double-dealer" who took political credit for others' contributions (Chen Huanren 2006, 306).

54. Nie Yuanzi (2005), 206–210, 216–224. Nie was convinced that the Earth faction acted on behalf of Qi Benyu and with the acquiescence of Xie Fuzhi.

55. Chen Huanren (2006), 344–347.

56. "Zai zhandou zhong zhengfeng" (Rectification amid Struggle), *Xin Beida*, 10 June 1967, 1 (CCRM 1999, 15:7249).

57. See "Xiao wen'ge zhidao sixiang shang de cuowu bixu pipan" (Errors in the Guiding Thought of the School's Cultural Revolution Committee Must Be Criticized), *Xin Beida*, 14 June 1967, 2 (CCRM 1999, 15:7254); and similar articles in *Xin Beida*, 17 and 21 June 1967 (CCRM 1999, 15, 7257–7258, 7261–7263. Sun Pengyi made a self-criticism in a mass meeting on 29 June that was loudly ridiculed by the opposition; Nie gave her self-criticism on 4 July; Chen Huanren (2006), 363–365.

58. The first issue carried an article detailing the degeneration of the movement under the Nie faction: "Huanhu Xin Beida bao de dansheng" (Hail the Birth of *New Beida News*), *Xin Beida bao*, 12 July 1967, 2 (CCRM 1999, 15:7749).

59. "Zhou Peiyuan, Guo Jinghai deng yibai sanshisi ming ganbu zhi geming he yao geming de ganbu de gongkai xin" (Open Letter by 134 Cadres Such as Zhou Peiyuan and Guo Jinghai to All Revolutionary Cadres and All Cadres Who Want Revolution), *Xin Beida bao*, 12 July 1967, 3 (CCRM 1999, 15:7750).

60. Wang Xuezhen et al. (1998), 662.

61. Ibid., 663; "Xin Beida jinggangshan bingtuan guangrong dansheng bing jiaru shoudu hongdaihui" (New Beida Jinggangshan Corps Born in Glory and Enters Capital Red Guard Congress), *Xin Beida bao*, 25 August 1967, 1 (CCRM 1999, 16:7778).

62. "Shoudu geming zaofanpai xinlianxin" (Capital's Revolutionary Rebels Linked Heart to Heart), *Xin Beida bao*, 25 August 1967, 2 (CCRM 1999, 16:7779); Wang Xuezhen et al. (1998), 663. Kuai Dafu called Beida Jingangshan the true rebel faction. At the time, Beida students heard that Kuai secretly supported one of the anti-Nie groups, and Nie's supporters openly praised Qinghua 414 on several occasions (Chen Huanren 2006, 326–327).

63. Wang Xuezhen et al. (1998), 664; "Zhongyang shouzhang fenbie jiejian dazhuan yuanxiao daibiao de jianghua" (Central Leaders' Speeches during Separate Meetings with University Representatives), 16 September 1967 (Cultural Revolution Database 2002).

64. "Fencui eryue fubi niliu, huifu 'jing', 'hong' benlai mianmu" (Smash the February Restorationist Countercurrent, Restore the Honor of "Jinggangshan" and "Red Allied Army"), *Xin Beida bao*, 7 September 1967, 5–8 (CCRM 1999, 16:7794–7797).

65. "Relie huanhu shoudu sansi wei 'yuan' xin Beida jinggangshan chedi fan'an" (Enthusiastically Hail the Capital Third Headquarters thorough Rehabilitation of the "Former" Beida Jinggangshan), *Xin Beida bao*, 16

September 1967, 1 (CCRM 1999, 16:7798); also see the discussion in the previous chapter.

66. See, for example, "Nie Yuanzi daodi yikao shei, tuanjie shei, daji shei?" (Whom, After All, Has Nie Yuanzi Relied upon, United with, and Attacked?), *Xin Beida bao*, 5 November 1967, 3 (CCRM 1999, 16:7823); "Nie Yuanzi zongrong Beida de laobao fantian" (Nie Yuanzi Connives with the Rebellion of Old Conservatives), *Xin Beida bao*, 7 November 1967, 4 (CCRM 1999, 16:7828); "Ba Nie Yuanzi baobi de huairen tongtong jiuchulai!" (Drag Out All the Evil Characters Shielded by Nie Yuanzi!), *Xin Beida bao*, 22 December 1967, 3 (CCRM 1999, 16:7843); "Ba Nie shi da hongsan xia de wangba tongtong jiuchulai" (Drag Out All the Bastards under the Red Umbrella of the Nie Clan), *Xin Beida bao*, 6 January 1968, 4 (CCRM 1999, 16:7851).

67. "Shoudu hongdaihui xin Beida gongshe zongbu guanyu da lianhe de shengming" (Capital Red Guard Congress New Beida Commune Headquarters Proclamation Regarding the Great Alliance), *Xin Beida*, 23 September 1967, 2 (CCRM 1999, 15:7396); "Shoudu dazhuan yuanxiao hongdaihui weiyuanhui jueyi" (Decision of the Capital University Red Guard Congress), *Xin Beida*, 19 October 1967, 1 (CCRM 1999, 16:7423); "Guanyu shixian an xitong, banji de geming da lianhe de yanzheng shengming" (Solemn Declaration Regarding the Attainment of Revolutionary Great Alliances in Systems and Classrooms), *Xin Beida*, 22 October 1967, 2 (CCRM 1999, 16:7428).

68. "Guanyu chedi gaizu xiao wen'ge, an xitong, an banji shixing geming da lianhe de yanzheng shengming" (Solemn Declaration on Thoroughly Reorganizing the School Cultural Revolution Committee and Implementing the Revolutionary Great Alliances in Systems and Classrooms), *Xin Beida bao*, 23 October 1967, 1 (CCRM 1999, 16:7817); and the accompanying articles and editorials in that issue.

69. Wang Xuezhen et al. (1998), 665.

70. Shen Ruhuai (2004), 141–142, 151–152.

71. Ibid., 167–169.

72. "Chen Boda, Qi Benyu tongzhi guanxin wo xiao wenhua da geming" (Comrades Chen Boda and Qi Benyu Are Concerned about Our School's Cultural Revolution), *Jinggangshan*, 27 June 1967, 1 (CCRM 1999, 8:3792); "Zhongyang wen'ge xiaozu guanxin wo xiao wenhua da geming" (Members of CCRG Are Concerned about Our School's Cultural Revolution), *Jinggangshan bao*, 28 June 1967, 1 (CCRM 1999, 9:4266); Shen Ruhuai (2004), 178–183.

73. Bu Weihua (2003); MacFarquhar and Schoenhals (2006), 224–233; Schoenhals (2005), 294–298.

74. Shen Ruhuai (2004), 233–237.

75. Bu Weihua (2000), 116. See the group's wall poster, "Lin Jie, geming renmin dui ni de shenpan kaishile" (Lin Jie, Your Trial before the Revolutionary People Has Begun), *Jinggangshan*, 6 September 1967, 4 (CCRM 1999, 8:3925);

and the more detailed account of Tan Houlan's connections with Lin Jie in Beijing Normal University Jinggangshan Rebel Regiment (1967).

76. Bu Weihua (2000), 117; Shen Ruhuai (2004), 234–235.

77. See Bu Weihua (2000), 117; and the collected testimonials dated September 17 through 24 and published by Beijing Normal Jinggangshan in "Fencui 'jiu.qi' fangeming shijian" (Smash the Counterrevolutionary Incident of September 7), *Jinggangshan tongxun* 14 (25 October 1967): 19–21.

78. Bu Weihua (2000), 117; Shen Ruhuai (2004), 235–237. Qinghua 414 warmly embraced the accusation of "ultra-leftism" and made no mention of Lin Jie's connection to Tan Houlan at Beijing Normal: "Lin Jie he ji 'zuo' sichao" (Lin Jie and the Ultra-"Left" Trend of Thought), *Jinggangshan bao,* 14 September 1967, 4 (CCRM 1999, 9:4325). See the defensive editorial in Kuai's newspaper, which challenged the criticism of Lin Jie and the others as "ultra-left": "Ping shenme 'jizuo sichao'?!" (Criticize What "Ultra-left Trend of Thought"?!), *Jinggangshan,* 16 September 1967, 1 (CCRM 1999, 8:3942).

79. "Mao Zhuxi zui xin zhishi de huihuang shengli—huanhu Shanghai geming da lianhe de xin gaochao" (Glorious Victory of Chairman Mao's Latest Instruction—Hailing the New High Tide in Shanghai's Revolutionary Great Alliance), *Renmin ribao,* 18 September 1967, 1.

80. See Shen Ruhuai (2004), 245–247; and "Xueping shantou, dadao sizi, shixian geming dalianhe" (Subdue Mountaintops, Overthrow Selfishness, Complete the Revolutionary Great Alliance), *Jinggangshan,* 23 September 1967, 1 (CCRM 1999, 8:3958).

81. Zhou Quanying and Yang Jifei, "Paoda cuanduo wenhua da geming chengguo de Yuan Shikai" (Bombard the Yuan Shikai Who Has Usurped the Fruits of the Cultural Revolution), 17 September 1967 (Cultural Revolution Database 2002).

82. Shen Ruhuai (2004, 237–242) reports that Zhou Enlai struck first. In a meeting with red guards on the same day Zhou Quanying's poster appeared, Zhou referred to him by name as "a thief who deceives honest people"; "Zhongyang shouzhang fenbie jiejian dazhuan yuanxiao daibiao de jianghua" (Central Leaders' Talks in Separate Meetings with Representatives from the Universities), 17 September 1967 (Cultural Revolution Database 2002). Jiang Qing's denunciation came much later. See "Jiang Qing, Chen Boda zai zhongyang zhishu wenyi xitong zuotanhui shang de jianghua" (Talks by Jiang Qing and Chen Boda at the Conference of the Central Committee Cultural System), 12 November 1967 (Cultural Revolution Database 2002).

83. Shen Ruhuai (2004), 242–244. See also "Guangda si yi si zhanyou tongsu Zhou Quanying zhiliu" (Broad Masses of 414 Severely Reprimand Zhou Quanying and His Ilk), *Jinggangshan,* 23 September 1967, 4 (CCRM 1999, 8:3961).

84. Kuai's faction insisted on the counterrevolutionary label from the outset. See "Zhou Quanying de duoluo ji qi yanzhong jiaoxun" (The Degeneration of

Zhou Quanying and Its Serious Lessons), *Jinggangshan,* 23 September 1967, 4 (CCRM 1999, 8:3961).

85. See the news of Zhou's arrest in "Kan! Fangeming xiaoniu de xiachang" (Look! The Downfall of a Counterrevolutionary Thief), and "Jiuzhu xiaoniu Zhou Quanying, hengsao yiqie hairen chong" (Seize the Thief Zhou Quanying, Sweep Away All Vermin), *Jinggangshan,* 21 October 1967, 4 (CCRM 1999, 8:3981); and the report of the mass denunciation meeting in "Pichou da ducao 'bisheng,' doulan fangeming xiaoniu Zhou Quanying, dashu teshu weida Mao Zedong sixiang de juedui quanwei" (Criticize the Big Poisonous Weed "Must Win" Until It Stinks, Struggle the Counterrevolutionary Thief Zhou Quanying to a Pulp, Fully Establish the Absolute Authority of the Great Mao Zedong Thought), *Jinggangshan,* 9 November 1967, 1 (CCRM 1999, 8:3994). Also see Fang Huijian and Zhang Sijing (2001), 2, 757; Shen Ruhuai (2004), 248–250.

86. Hinton (1972), 142–143; Shen Ruhuai (2004), 250–251.

87. See Fang Huijian and Zhang Sijing (2001), 2, 757, 809; "Pichou Lu Yingzhong daolu, zalan jiu shiyanhua gongchang" (Criticize the Lu Yingzhong Road Until It Stinks, Smash the Old Experimental Factory), *Jinggangshan,* 24 November 1967, 1 (CCRM 1999, 8:4006); and Shen Ruhuai (2004), 252–254.

88. See "Lu Yingzhong daolu tongxiang hefang" (Where the Lu Yingzhong Road Was Headed), *Jinggangshan,* 7 December 1967, 2–3 (CCRM 1999, 9:4019–4020); and "Ping louwang da youpai Lu Yingzhong" (Criticize Lu Yingzhong, Big Rightist Who Slipped through the Net), *Jinggangshan,* 7 December 1967, 1–2 (CCRM 1999, 9:4022–4023).

89. Fang Huijian and Zhang Sijing (2001), 2, 757; Shen Ruhuai (2004), 255–256.

90. Fang Huijian and Zhang Sijing (2001), 2, 758; Hinton (1972), 150–151; Shen Ruhuai (2004), 254.

91. Shen Ruhuai (2004), 301–304. Liu Bing (1998, 121–138), Qinghua's first-ranking party vice-secretary, describes this process and his prison experiences after October 1967.

92. Hinton (1972), 145–150; Shen Ruhuai (2004), 258–261.

93. Shen Ruhuai (2004), 265–267, 279–280.

94. Ibid., 268–274. See also "Kuai Dafu xianhai Chen Chusan de yinmou bixu jiechuan" (Kuai Dafu's Plot to Frame Chen Chusan Must Be Exposed), *Jinggangshan bao,* 12 January 1968, 3 (CCRM 1999, 9:4368).

95. Fang Huijian and Zhang Sijing (2001), 2, 758; Hinton (1972), 150–151; Shen Ruhuai (2004), 304–306.

96. *Shoudu hongweibing,* 18 August 1968, 2 (CCRM 1999, 12: 5675).

97. Shen Ruhuai (2004), 307–310.

98. Bu Weihua (2000), 118; Fang Huijian and Zhang Sijing (2001), 2, 758; Shen Ruhuai (2004), 308–310.

99. Bu Weihua (2000), 119; *Shoudu hongweibing*, 18 August 1968, 2 (CCRM 1999, 12: 5675).

100. The arrest occurred sometime in February but was initially kept secret (MacFarquhar and Schoenhals 2006, 236).

101. Bu Weihua (2000), 119–121; Shen Ruhuai (2004), 322–326.

102. "Zheng Weishan, Wu De zai Beijing shi geming weiyuanhui huiyi shang de jianghua" (Speeches by Zheng Weishan and Wu De at a Meeting of the Beijing Revolutionary Committee), 21 March 1968 (Cultural Revolution Database 2002).

103. See "Beijing dizhi xueyuan 'dongfanghong' gongshe zongbu guanyu muqian xingshi de zaici yanzheng shengming" (Another Solemn Declaration on the Current Situation by Beijing Geology Institute "East Is Red" Commune), *Dongfanghong bao,* 25 March 1968, 1 (CCRM 2001, 10:3678); "Dianfu geming weiyuanhui de xuanyan shu" (A Proclamation to Overthrow the Revolutionary Committee), *Dongfanghong bao,* 27 March 1968, 4 (CCRM 2001, 10:3682).

104. "Beijing daxue wenhua geming weiyuanhui guanyu muqian xingshi de yanzheng shengming" (Solemn Declaration of the Beijing University Cultural Revolution Committee on the Current Situation), *Xin Beida,* 23 March 1967, 1 (CCRM 1999, 16:7571).

105. "Xie fu zongli qinlin wo xiao zuo zhongyao zhishi" (Vice-Premier Xie Personally Visits Our School and Gives Important Instructions), *Xin Beida,* 26 March 1968, 1 (CCRM 1999, 16:7575). Wu De, Ding Guoyu, and Nie Yuanzi all made speeches on this occasion, and the transcripts were reprinted in this issue of Nie's newspaper.

106. Bu Weihua (2000), 122–125.

107. Wang Xuezhen et al. (1998), 668–669. Transcripts of the speeches by Xie Fuzhi and Wu De were printed in *Xin Beida,* 26 March 1968, 1–2 (CCRM 1999, 16:7575–7576).

108. Wen Yucheng had just been appointed to this position to replace Fu Chongbi, who had been purged under murky circumstances and accused of an anti-party conspiracy in March (MacFarquhar and Schoenhals 2006, 246; Organization Department, Beijing Municipal Party Committee 1992, 780).

109. Wang Xuezhen et al. (1998), 669. A transcript of the statements by Xie Fuzhi and Li Zhongqi was published in *Xin Beida,* 30 March 1968, 1 (CCRM 1999, 16:7587).

110. "Niu Huilin zhiliu taoqi wudou pohuai Mao zhuxi weida zhanlüe bushu zui gai wansi" (Niu Huilin and His Ilk Deserve to Die a Thousand Deaths for the Crime of Inciting Armed Struggles to Sabotage Chairman Mao's Great Strategic Deployment), *Xin Beida,* 30 March 1968, 2 (CCRM 1999, 16:7588).

111. "Chedi cuihui zichan jieji silingbu she zai Beida de qiaotoubao, jianjue jiuchu jinggangshan bingtuan zhong fandui zhongyang wen'ge de fandong xiao jituan" (Thoroughly Smash the Bridgehead Established by the Bourgeois

Headquarters at Beida, Resolutely Drag Out the Reactionary Clique Opposed to the CCRG within the Jinggangshan Regiment), *Xin Beida,* 8 April 1968, 4 (CCRM 1999, 16:7592); "Guanyu jiuchu fangeming xiongshaba jiqi houtai de guangbo dongyuan" (Broadcast Mobilization on Dragging Out Counterrevolutionary Assassins and Their Backstage Supporters), *Xin Beida,* 18 April 1968, 3 (CCRM 1999, 16:7601).

112. The entire issue of *Xin Beida,* 29 April 1968, was devoted to the rally and transcripts of the delegates' speeches (CCRM 1999, 16, 7607–7614).

113. Excerpts from the confessions of several captive leaders were published in *Xin Beida,* 17 July 1968 (CCRM 1999, 16, 7703–7706).

114. In late May Deng Xiaoping's son, Deng Pufang, and his daughter, Deng Nan, were arrested and imprisoned on campus and tortured to confess to plotting an attack on Jiang Qing. It was during this imprisonment that Deng Pufang was forced to jump from the upper story of a campus building, causing injuries that made him a paraplegic (Wang Xuezhen et al. 1998, 670–671).

115. Ibid., 671–672. See "Gei zai xiaowai de jinggangshan bingtuan geming tongzhi he qita geming tongzhi de xin" (Letter to Revolutionary Comrades from Jinggangshan Who Are off Campus and Other Revolutionary Comrades), *Xin Beida,* 13 May 1968, 1 (CCRM 1999, 16:7631).

116. See the report of Nie's speech in *Xin Beida,* 20 June 1966, 1–2 (CCRM 1999, 16:7675–7676). The number of defectors reached 1,400 by mid-July; *Xin Beida,* 17 July 1968, 4 (CCRM 1999, 16:7706). Transcripts of the show trials were published in "Wo xiao shouci gongshen caozong Beida de xianxing fangeming jituan zhongyao chengyuan Niu Huisheng, Wang Zhonglin, Xu Yunpu" (Our School's First Public Trial of Niu Huisheng, Wang Zhonglin, and Xu Yunpu, Important Members of Beida's Active Counterrevolutionary Clique), *Xin Beida,* 23 July 1968, 3–4 (CCRM 1999, 16:7713–7714).

117. Wang Xuezhen et al. (1998), 672.

118. Fang Huijian and Zhang Sijing (2001), 2:758; Hinton (1972), 151–153; Tang Shaojie (2003), 14–15.

119. Fang Huijian and Zhang Sijing (2001), 2:758; Tang Shaojie (2003), 15–16.

120. Tang Shaojie (2003), 17–18.

121. Fang Huijian and Zhang Sijing (2001), 2:758; Hinton (1972), 156–161; Tang Shaojie (2003), 18–20.

122. Fang Huijian and Zhang Sijing (2001), 2:758; Hinton (1972), 164–168; Tang Shaojie (2003), 21–26.

123. The Beijing Revolutionary Committee ordered the Beijing Garrison Command to disarm the two sides on July 9 (Beijing Municipal Party Committee 1987b, 11).

124. This unit was known as 8341 Regiment. It was assigned to protect central party and military officials and the leadership compound of Zhongnanhai

but was used during this period for a range of politically sensitive tasks (Shambaugh 2002, 120).

125. Fang Huijian and Zhang Sijing (2001), 2:758; Hinton (1972), 188–195; Tang Shaojie (2003), 26–27.

126. Beijing Municipal Party Committee (1987b), 13; Fang Huijian and Zhang Sijing (2001), 2:758–759; Hinton (1972), 188, 195–212; Tang Shaojie (2003), 27–30. Additional sources for the events at Qinghua during this period are the detailed memoirs of Shen Ruhuai (2004), 349–415; and Tang Shaojie (2000).

127. MacFarquhar and Schoenhals (2006), 250–251; "Mao Zhuxi Lin fuzhuxi wuxian guanhuai hongweibing xiaojiang qinqie jiejian shoudu hongdaihui hexin fuze tongzhi" (Chairman Mao and Vice-Chairman Lin Show Boundless Concern for Red Guards, Kindly Grant an Audience to Comrades in Leadership Core of Red Guard Congress), Xin Beida, 28 August 1968, 1 (CCRM 1999, 16:7726); Nie Yuanzi (2005), 282–315.

128. The original pamphlet is cited in Zheng (2006), 299, n. 149. See Mao Zedong, "Zhaojian shoudu hongdaihui 'wu da lingxiu' shi de tanhua" (Speech upon Summoning the "Five Great Leaders" of the Capital Red Guard Congress), 28 July 1968 (Cultural Revolution Database 2002).

129. "Mao Zhuxi guanyu zhizhi wudou wenti de zhishi" (Chairman Mao's Directive Concerning the Problem of Preventing Armed Struggles), Xin Beida, 30 July 1968, 1 (CCRM 1999, 16:7730).

130. Beijing Municipal Party Committee (1987b), 15.

131. See "Pichou xianxing fangeming fenzi Niu Huilin de fanjun jiaoxiao" (Criticize the Anti-Army Outcry of Counterrevolutionary Element Niu Huilin until He Stinks), Xin Beida, 3 August 1968, 4 (CCRM 1999, 16, 7735), and the articles devoted to welcoming the work teams and celebrating Mao's directive in Xin Beida, 30 July 1968, 1–2; Xin Beida, tekan, 30 July 1968, 2; and Xin Beida, 3 August 1968, 1 (CCRM 1999, 16:7727–7732).

132. Wang Xuezhen et al. (1998), 674–675.

133. Ibid., 675–676.

134. Ibid., 679, 684.

135. Cao Ying (2001), 5030; Nie Yuanzi (2005), 319–369. Nie was formally dropped from the Beijing Revolutionary Committee in January 1971 (Organization Department, Beijing Municipal Party Committee 1992, 580) and was formally dropped from the Central Committee at the Tenth Party Congress in 1973. Nie's labor reform continued after she was transferred to a Beijing factory in 1972. After eight years in prison she was released in 1986.

136. Fang Huijian and Zhang Sijing (2001), 2:759.

137. Ibid., 760. The propaganda team ruled Qinghua for much of the next decade (Andreas 2006).

138. Cao Ying (2001), 5035; Hinton (1972), 275–286. Kuai was caught up in the "Anti–May 16 Elements Campaign."

139. Kuai was released in 1987 and returned to Ningxia (Cao Ying 2001, 5035–5036).

140. Ibid., 5038.

141. Han was released in 1991 (ibid., 5038–5039).

142. Ibid., 5039, 5041.

## 10. Hierarchy and Rebellion

1. MacFarquhar and Schoenhals (2006), 140–144. Among those who initially resisted were Zhou Enlai, Chen Boda, Tao Zhu, and Wang Renzhong, and the latter two were ejected from the CCRG and purged in large part for their opposition.

2. Walder (1996).

3. Xu Youyu (1999), 68–69.

4. In his critique of social interpretations of red guard factionalism, Xu Youyu (1999, 68–100) has emphasized in considerable detail the differences between factional divisions in Beijing and in most outlying provinces. My analysis reinforces his argument by providing a possible explanation for those differences.

5. This interpretation is emphasized by Gong (2003).

6. This interpretation is either implied or explicitly argued in a wide range of publications: Chan, Rosen, and Unger (1980); Lee (1975, 1978); Oksenberg (1968); Perry and Li Xun (1997); Rosen (1982); Unger (1982); Vogel (1968, 1969); and Walder (1978, 1996).

7. Tang Shaojie (1999b); Yin Hongbiao (1996, 1997, 1999).

8. Hua Linshan (1996a, 1996b). Xu Youyu (1999) cites similar arguments in essays in émigré journals by former rebels like Wang Xizhe and Yang Xiguang.

9. Jin Chunming (2002), 399–426.

10. Xu Youyu (1996a, 1996b).

11. According to Xu Youyu (1999, 109–121) and Tang Shaojie (1999b), the mass factions that fought for real political power in the provinces (except Shanghai) in 1967 and 1968 developed clearly distinguishable moderate and radical orientations toward the status quo ante that were similar to the doctrinal divisions at Qinghua. The reasons that these cleavages developed elsewhere, but not in Beijing, are a major subject for future research. Xu Youyu (1999, 56–63) attributes Beijing's distinctiveness to the intimate involvement of the CCRG, the lack of active involvement by organized workers and peasants, and the relatively muted involvement of the armed forces.

12. Although Charles Tilly pioneered this perspective on contentious politics, his earlier analysis of the counterrevolutionary uprising in western France in 1793 in fact described a local interactive process under ambiguous circumstances that split members of the same social groups into two opposing camps (Tilly 1964, 227–304). See the discussion in Walder (2006a, 737–738).

13. Xu Youyu (1999, 180) has already observed that as the movement progressed throughout China, each faction appeared increasingly motivated primarily to avoid having the other side take revenge on it if it were defeated: "To say that they were pursuing group interests is less accurate than saying that their behavior was defensive in nature."

## Work-Team Case Histories

1. " 'Daji yi da pian, baohu yi xiaocuo' de youyi tiezheng" (More Ironclad Evidence of "Attacking Many to Protect a Few"), *Zhandou bao*, 30 April 1967, 1–3 (CCRM 2001, 38:15049–15051).

2. This account is based on "Chedi pipan wo yuan gongzuozu zai ganbu wenti shang zhixing de zichan jieji fandong luxian" (Thoroughly Criticize the Bourgeois Reactionary Line on the Cadre Question Carried Out by Our School's Work Team), *Zhengfa gongshe*, 16 April 1967, 2 (CCRM 2001, 39:15460); and Chinese University of Politics and Law, History Editorial Group (2002), 68–69.

3. Details are provided in "Zichan jieji fandong luxian heqi duye—Waiyu xi gongzuozu zai ganbu wenti shang zhixing zichan jieji fandong luxian de diaocha baogao" (How Cruel the Bourgeois Reactionary Line—Report on an Investigation of the Foreign Language Department Work Team's Implementation of the Bourgeois Reactionary Line on the Cadre Question), *Jinggangshan*, 25 April 1967, 2 (CCRM 2001, 24:9275).

4. This account is based on "Zheng Weizhi gongzuozu shi zenyang zai ganbu wenti shang shixing 'daji yi dapian, baohu yi xiaocuo' de" (How Zheng Weizhi's Work Team Carried Out "Attack Many to Protect a Few" on the Cadre Question), *Hongwei zhanbao*, 1 May 1967, 2 (CCRM 2001, 22:8468).

5. " 'Daji yi dapian, baohu yi xiaocuo' de zichan jieji fandong luxian zai woyuan de zhongzhong biaoxian" (The Various Manifestations of the Bourgeois Reactionary Line of "Attack Many to Protect a Few" in Our Institute), *Shuidian hongweibing*, 30 April 1967, 5, 8 (CCRM 2001, 29:11241, 11244).

6. This account is based on "Xiuxiang ba 'dadao yiqie' de zuiming qiangjia zai geming pai toushang" (Do Not Imagine That You Can Force the Accusation of "Overthrowing Everything" onto the Heads of the Revolutionary Faction), *Tiyu zhanbao*, 8 April 1967, 3 (CCRM 1999, 13:5890); and "Chumu jingxin de 'daji yi dapian, baohu yi xiaocuo" (The Shocking Reality of "Attacking Many to Protect a Few"), *Tiyu zhanbao*, 6 May 1967, 1–2 (CCRM 1999, 13:5919–5920). The commission's leaders are listed in Organization Department, CCP Central Committee (2000), 15:145.

7. This account is based on "Fennu kongsu Liu Deng zichan jieji fandong luxian dui wo de duhai he pohai" (Angry Denunciation of the Poison and Persecution Directed at Me by the Liu-Deng Bourgeois Reactionary Line), *Beijing gongshe*, 30 April 1967, 2 (CCRM 1999, 1:350). This source does not explain what hap-

pened to the party secretary or the rest of the party committee. If the Party Secretary remained in his post, this case would be classified as conservative.

8. This account of the period before the work team's arrival is based on Li Yanjie, "Kongsu Liu Deng zichan jieji fandong luxian dui wo de pohai" (I Denounce the Liu-Deng Bourgeois Reactionary Line for the Persecution I Suffered), *Jinggangshan*, 4 May 1967, 3–4 (CCRM 2001, 24:9157–9158).

9. "Yijiuliuliu nian liuqiyuefen Beijing shifan xueyuan gongzuozu zai ganbu wenti shang suo zhixing de zichan jieji fandong luxian qingkuang de chubu diaocha baogao" (Preliminary Report on an Investigation into the Work Team's Implementation of the Bourgeois Reactionary Line on the Cadre Question at Beijing Normal Institute during June and July 1966), *Jinggangshan*, 4 May 1967, 4 (CCRM 2001, 24:9158).

10. This account is based on "Chedi pipan keda gongzuozu zai ganbu wenti shang de zichan jieji fandong luxian" (Thoroughly Criticize the UST Work Team's Bourgeois Reactionary Line on the Cadre Question), *Dongfanghong*, 26 April 1967, 2–4 (CCRM 2001, 8:3035–3037); and Xi Fuyun et al. (1998), 73–74.

11. This account is based on "Chu jie ganbu wenti shang de zichan jieji fandong luxian" (Preliminary Exposure of the Bourgeois Reactionary Line on the Cadre Question), *Dongfanghong zhanbao*, 7 April 1967, 3–4 (CCRM 2001, 10:3900–3901); and "Tiezheng ru shan, zuize nantao—Kan wo yuan gongzuozu shi ruhe 'daji yi dapian, baohu yi xiaocuo' de" (Irrefutable Evidence, Undeniable Crime—See How Our Institute's Work Team "Attacked Many to Protect a Few"), *Dongfanghong zhanbao*, 19 April 1967, 2–3 (CCRM 2001, 10:3908–3909).

12. This account is based on "Zai ganbu wenti shang de Liu Deng zichan jieji fandong luxian zai wo yuan de taotian zuixing" (The Monstrous Crimes of the Liu-Deng Bourgeois Reactionary Line on the Cadre Question in Our Institute), *Hongwei bao*, 12 April 1967, 5–8 (CCRM 2001, 20:7566–7567); and "Zhang Yan shi zhenya duiwai wenwei wenhua da geming de guizishou" (Zhang Yan Is the Executioner Who Suppressed the Cultural Revolution in the Commission on Foreign Cultural Relations), *Hongwei bao*, 24 June 1967, 6 (CCRM 2001, 20:7614).

13. Organization Department, CCP Central Committee (2000), 9:106, 15:146. Li Chang was a prominent leader of the militant student movement at Qinghua University in the 1930s (Israel 1966, 166–72; Israel and Klein 1976, 54–55).

14. Organization Department, CCP Central Committee (2000), 15:146.

15. Chen and Kang denounced Zhang on July 14 for allegedly trying to shield his wife from critics in the Foreign Languages Institute by attacking those who denounced her, and for persisting even after a direct warning from Kang Sheng. See "Chen Boda, Kang Sheng tongzhi zai duiwai wenwei de jianghua" (Speeches by Comrades Chen Boda and Kang Sheng at the Commission on Foreign Cultural Relations), July 14, 1966 (Reference Materials 1966), vol. 1, sec. 7: 5–7. In

heated Politburo sessions in mid-July Chen Boda denounced Zhang Yan's work team as "the worst work team in the whole country" (Liu Shufa 1995, 1157).

16. This account is based on Wang Chunli (2003), 57; Yu Shicheng (2003), 90–91; "Yinxian, jiaohua, heqi duye! Shiyou bu, yuan dangwei zai wo yuan tuixing 'daji yi dapian, baohu yi xiaocuo' de zichan jieji fandong luxian de zuixing diaocha" (How Sinister, Crafty, and Cruel! An Investigation into the Crimes of the Ministry of Petroleum and the Institute Party Committee in Carrying Out the Bourgeois Reactionary Line of "Attacking Many to Protect a Few" in Our Institute), *Changzheng*, 1 June 1967, 2–4 (CCRM 2001, 5:1657–1659); and " 'Daji yi dapian, baohu yi xiaocuo' de Liu Deng zichan jieji fandong luxian zai wo yuan de biaoxian" (The Manifestation of the Liu-Deng Bourgeois Reactionary Line of "Attacking Many to Protect a Few" in Our Institute), *Daqing gongshe*, 15 April 1967, 1, 3–4 (CCRM 2001, 5:1996, 1998–1999).

17. Northern Transportation University Annals Editorial Committee (2001), 11.

18. This account is based on " 'Daji yi dapian, baohu yi xiaocuo' de zichan jieji fandong luxian zai wo yuan de zuixing" (Crimes of the Bourgeois Reactionary Line of "Attacking Many to Protect a Few" in Our Institute), *Tiedao hongqi*, 21 May 1967, 1–3 (CCRM 1999, 14:6337–6339); Northern Transportation University Annals Editorial Committee (1996), 275–277; and Northern Transportation University Annals Editorial Committee (2001), 46.

19. This school was referred to as "Yi wai" (Foreign Languages One) after the establishment of Foreign Languages Institute No. 2 in 1964. This account is based on "Guangrong de licheng" (Glorious Course) *Liu.yiliu zhanbao*, 19 November 1966, 4 (CCRM 2001, 26:10141).

20. This account is based on "Kan linye bu wenhua da geming zhong liangtiao luxian de douzheng" (See the Struggle between the Two Lines during the Cultural Revolution in the Ministry of Forestry), *Bei Lin Dongfanghong*, 16 February 1967, 1–2 (CCRM 2001, 3:928–929); "Wo yuan gongzuozu zai ganbu wenti shang de Liushi luxian" (The Liuist Line of Our Institute's Work Team on the Cadre Question) and "Chedi pipan Liu Deng fangeming xiuzheng zhuyi de ganbu luxian" (Thoroughly Criticize the Counterrevolutionary Revisionist Liu-Deng Cadre Line), *Bei Lin Dongfanghong*, 6 April 1967 (CCRM 2001, 3:958); and "Linye bu, gongzuozu, yuan dangwei zhong zou ziben zhuyi daolu dangquan pai ji qi bangxiong hemou pohuai wo yuan wenhua da geming zhenxiang" (The True Story of How Capitalist Roaders in the Forestry Ministry, the Work Team, and the Institute Party Committee along with Their Accomplices and Coconspirators Sabotaged the Cultural Revolution in Our Institute), 25 August 1966 (Beijing Forestry Institute East Is Red 1966a, 2–25). Related wall posters recounting the events of the period are in Beijing Forestry East Is Red (1966b, 1966c, 1966d). Names and dates have been checked against Fan Jizhou and Sun Licheng (1992), 187–190; and Zhu Jinzhao (2002), 48–50.

21. This account is based on "Wo yuan ganbu wenti shang 'daji yi dapian, baohu yi xiaocuo' de zichanjieji fandong luxian bixu chedi pipan" (Our Institute's Bourgeois Reactionary Line on the Cadre Question of "Attacking Many to Protect a Few" Must Be Thoroughly Repudiated), *Hong ying,* 6 May 1967, 2–3 (CCRM 1999, 7:3164–65).

22. The second work team was led by Deng Dongzhe, vice-head of the Political Department of the Industrial-Transportation Department of the CCP Secretariat (Organization Department, CCP Central Committee 2000, 14:1167; Wang Jianying 1995, 1010).

23. "Jiang Qing, Chen Boda tongzhi zai chexiao qinggong xueyuan gongzuodui dahui shang de jianghua" (Speeches by Comrades Jiang Qing and Chen Boda at the Mass Meeting to Revoke the Light Industrial Institute Work Team), 29 July 1966 (Reference Materials 1966), vol. 1, sec. 7:30–32.

# REFERENCES

Andreas, Joel. 2002. "Battling over Political and Cultural Power during the Chinese Cultural Revolution." *Theory and Society* 31 (August): 463–519.
———. 2006. "Institutionalized Rebellion: Governing Tsinghua University during the Late Years of the Chinese Cultural Revolution." *China Journal* 55 (January): 1–28.
———. 2007. "The Structure of Charismatic Mobilization: A Case Study of Rebellion during the Chinese Cultural Revolution." *American Sociological Review* 72 (June): 434–458.
Barnouin, Barbara, and Yu Changgen. 1993. *Ten Years of Turbulence: The Chinese Cultural Revolution.* London: Kegan Paul International.
Baum, Richard. 1994. *Burying Mao: Chinese Politics in the Age of Deng Xiaoping.* Princeton, N.J.: Princeton University Press.
Beijing Aeronautics Institute Red Flag. 1966a. "Beijing hangkong xueyuan wuchan jieji wenhua da geming de 120 tian" (The 120 Days of the Cultural Revolution at Beijing Aeronautics Institute), 26 September. Printed pamphlet.
———. 1966b. "Beijing hangkong xueyuan wuchan jieji wenhua da geming liangtiao luxian douzheng dashiji" (Chronicle of Major Events in the Struggle between the Two Lines during the Cultural Revolution at Beijing Aeronautics Institute), 22 October. Printed pamphlet.
———. 1967. *Beijing hangkong xueyuan dazibao xuanbian, di 5 ji* (Selected Wall Posters of Beijing Aeronautics Institute, No. 5), May. Beijing: Hongqi yuan dazibao bianweihui.
Beijing Education Annals Editorial Committee. 1992. *Beijing shi putong jiaoyu nianjian, 1949–1991* (Beijing Basic Education Yearbook, 1949–1991). Beijing: Beijing chubanshe.
Beijing Forestry Institute East Is Red. 1966a. *Wuchan jieji wenhua da geming dazibao xuanbian (di yi qi)* (Selected Wall Posters of the Great Proletarian Cultural Revolution [issue 1]), 25 October. Beijing: Beijing linxueyuan dongfanghong gongshe dazibao zu bian.

———. 1966b. *Wuchan jieji wenhua da geming dazibao xuanbian (di er qi)* (Selected Wall Posters of the Great Proletarian Cultural Revolution [issue 2]), 28 October. Beijing: Beijing linxueyuan dongfanghong gongshe dazibao zu bian.

———. 1966c. *Wuchan jieji wenhua da geming dazibao xuanbian (di san qi)* (Selected Wall Posters of the Great Proletarian Cultural Revolution [issue 3]), 3 November. Beijing: Beijing linxueyuan dongfanghong gongshe dazibao zu bian.

———. 1966d. *Wuchan jieji wenhua da geming dazibao xuanbian (di si qi)* (Selected Wall Posters of the Great Proletarian Cultural Revolution [issue 4]), 3 November. Beijing: Beijing linxueyuan dongfanghong gongshe dazibao zu bian.

Beijing Geology Institute East Is Red. 1966a. *Beijing dizhi xueyuan liangtiao luxian de douzheng* (The Struggle between the Two Lines at Beijing Geology Institute), undated, probably December. Beijing: Beijing dizhi xueyuan dongfanghong gongshe, Mao Zedong sixiang hongjiaolian, Mao Zedong sixiang hongganlian, Mao Zedong sixiang chiweidui.

———. 1966b. *Dazibao xuanbian (liangtiao luxian douzheng de zhuanji)* (Selected Wall Posters [Special Edition on the Struggle between the Two Lines]), 21 October. Beijing: Beijing dizhi xueyuan dongfanghong gongshe dazibao bianweihui.

———. 1967a. "Beijing dizhi xueyuan 'Dongfanghong gongshe' geming weiyuanhui zhu dizhibu lianluo zhan dui dizhi bu jiguan wenhua da geming qingkuang de diaocha baogao" (Investigation Report by the Geology Ministry Liaison Station of Beijing Geology Institute "East Is Red" Revolutionary Committee on the State of the Cultural Revolution within the Geology Ministry), 12 August. Mimeo.

———. 1967b. *Tianfan difu kaierkang—Wuchan jieji wenhua da geming dashiji (1963.9–1967.10)* (Deep Outrage That Moved Heaven and Earth—Chronicle of Major Cultural Revolution Events [September 1963–October 1967]). Beijing: Beijing dizhi xueyuan "dongfanghong" bianji bu.

———. 1968. *Dongfanghong 2–3* (East Is Red 2–3), February–March. Beijing: Beijing dizhi xueyuan dongfanghong zazhi bianji bu.

Beijing Industrial University East Is Red Commune. 1966a. *Dongfanghong (chedi pipan Tan Lifu fayan di san ji)* (East Is Red [Thoroughly Criticize Tan Lifu's Speech, no. 3]), October. Beijing: Beijing gongye daxue "dongfanghong" gongshe bianjibu.

———. 1966b. *Tongda loushui gou (you guan Tan Lifu jianghua cailiao zhuanji)* (Beat the Dog in the Water [Special Collection of Materials on the Criticism of Tan Lifu's Speech]), 20 November. Beijing: Beijing gongye daxue "dongfanghong gongshe" bianji bu.

———. 1966c. *Xiang zichan jieji fandong luxian menglie kaihuo (chedi pipan Tan Lifu jianghua zhuanji)* (Violently Open Fire on the Bourgeois Reactionary Line [Special Edition on the Thorough Criticism of Tan Lifu's Speech]), vols. 1 and 2, November. Wuhan: Beijing gongye daxue "dongfanghong gongshe" Wuhan lianluo zhan.

———. 1966d. *Xiang zichan jieji fandong luxian menglie kaihuo (pipan Tan Lifu jianghua cailiao di si ji)* (Violently Open Fire on the Bourgeois Reactionary Line [Tan Lifu Criticism Materials, no. 4]), 17 December. Beijing: Shoudu hongweibing nanxia geming zaofan jun.

Beijing Municipal Party Committee. 1966. "Ti: Gaodeng yuanxiao he zhongxue zhidao yundong zhong zhuyi de jige wenti" (Topic: Some Problems of Note in Guiding the Movement in Colleges and High Schools). *Meiri kuaibao* 36 (19 July). Zhonggong Beijing shiwei bangongting.

———. 1987a. "Beijing shi 'wenhua da geming' dashiji" (Chronicle of Events during the "Cultural Revolution" in Beijing). *Beijing dangshi ziliao tongxun, zengkan* 17 (May). Beijing: Zhonggong Beijing shiwei dangshi ziliao zhengji weiyuanhui.

———. 1987b. "Beijing shi 'wenhua da geming' dashiji" (Chronicle of Events during the "Cultural Revolution" in Beijing). *Beijing dangshi ziliao tongxun, zengkan* 18 (June). Beijing: Zhonggong Beijing shiwei dangshi ziliao zhengji weiyuanhui.

Beijing No. 1 High School Red Flag Combat Team. 1967. *Liu Deng zichan jieji fandong luxian zai yizhong de xuexing chanwu—Xuesheng "laogai dui"* (The Blood-Stained Product of the Liu-Deng Bourgeois Reactionary Line at No. 1 High School—The Student "Labor Reform Brigade"), February. Beijing: Beijing yi zhong hongqi zhandoudui.

Beijing No. 6 High School Beijing Commune. N.d. *Liu Deng luxian zai liu zhong de taotian zuixing* (The Monstrous Crimes of the Liu Deng Line at No. 6 High School). Beijing: Beijing liu zhong Beijing gongshe.

Beijing No. 6 High School Red Rebel Brigade. 1966. *Jiekai Beijing liu zhong laogaisuo de neimu* (Expose the Inside Story behind the Labor Reform Office of Beijing No. 6 High School), 28 December. Beijing: Beijing liu zhong hongse zaofan bingtuan.

Beijing Normal University History Editorial Group. 1982. *Beijing shifan daxue xiaoshi* (History of Beijing Normal University). Beijing: Beijing shifan daxue chubanshe.

Beijing Normal University Jinggangshan Rebel Regiment. 1967. *Beijing shifan daxue wuchan jieji wenhua da geming liangtiao luxian douzheng gaikuang—Fangeming liangmian pai Lin Jie zhiliu pohuai shida wenhua geming zuixing lu* (Survey of the Struggle between the Two Lines during the Cultural Revolution at Beijing Normal University—The Crimes of Counterrevolutionary Double-Dealer Lin Jie and His Ilk in Sabotaging

Normal University's Cultural Revolution), September. Beijing: Bei shida jinggangshan zaofan bingtuan.

Beijing Normal University No. 1 High School. 1967. *Fennu kongsu Liu Shaoqi zhenya Beijing shida yi fuzhong wuchan jieji wenhua da geming taotian zuixing* (Angrily Denounce the Monstrous Crimes of Liu Shaoqi in Suppressing the Cultural Revolution at Beijing Normal University No. 1 High School), January. Beijing: Beijing shida yi fuzhong liu.erling.

Beijing Statistical Bureau. 1990. *Beijing sishi nian: Shehui jingji tongji ziliao* (Beijing's Forty Years: Social and Economic Statistics). Beijing: Zhongguo tongji chubanshe.

Beijing University Cultural Revolution Committee. 1966a. *Dazibao xuan, zengkan (ershi) zhiyi* (Selected Wall Posters, Supplement [12], part 1), 28 November. Beijing: Beijing daxue wenhua geming weiyuanhui dazibaozu bian.

———. 1966b. *Wuchan jieji wenhua da geming dazibao xuan (yi)* (Selected Wall Posters of the Great Proletarian Cultural Revolution, [1]), 20 September. Beijing: Wenhua geming weiyuanhui dazibaozu bian.

———. 1966c. *Wuchan jieji wenhua da geming dazibao xuan (er): Chedi pipan Beijing shi yi Li Xuefeng tongzhi wei daibiao de zichan jieji fandong luxian zhuanji* (Selected Wall Posters of the Great Proletarian Cultural Revolution [2]: Special issue of Thorough Criticism of the Bourgeois Reactionary Line Represented by Comrade Li Xuefeng of Beijing Municipality), November. Beijing: Beijing daxue wenhua geming weiyuanhui chuanlianzu bian.

———. 1966d. *Wuchan jieji wenhua da geming dazibao xuan (san)* (Selected Wall Posters of the Great Proletarian Cultural Revolution, [3]), November. Beijing: Wenhua geming weiyuanhui geming chuanlianzu bian.

———. 1966e. *Wuchan jieji wenhua da geming dazibao xuanbian* (Selected Wall Posters of the Great Proletarian Cultural Revolution), 3 September. Beijing: Beijing daxue wenhua geming weiyuanhui bangongshi bian.

———. 1966f. *Xuexi cailiao, di er ji* (Study Materials, Issue no. 2), 20 October. Beijing: Beijing daxue wenhua geming weiyuanhui xuanchuanzu.

———. 1967. *Wuchan jieji wenhua da geming dazibao xuan (si)* (Selected Wall Posters of the Great Proletarian Cultural Revolution, 4), 1 March. Beijing: Wenhua geming weiyuanhui dazibaozu bian.

Beijing University Cultural Revolution Preparatory Committee. 1966a. *Dazibao xuan (shier)* (Selected Wall Posters, 12), 28 July. Beijing: Beijing daxue wenhua geming weiyuanhui (chouwei hui) bangongshi bian.

———. 1966b. *Dazibao xuan (shisan)* (Selected Wall Posters, 13), 18 July. Beijing: Beijing daxue wenhua geming weiyuanhui (chouwei hui) bangongshi bian.

———. 1966c. *Dazibao xuan (shisi)* (Selected Wall Posters, 14), 12 July. Beijing: Beijing daxue wenhua geming weiyuanhui (chouwei hui) bangongshi bian.

———. 1966d. *Dazibao xuan (shiwu)* (Selected Wall Posters, 15), 16 July. Beijing: Beijing daxue wenhua geming weiyuanhui (chouwei hui) bangongshi bian.

———. 1966e. *Dazibao xuan (ershi)* (Selected Wall Posters, 20), 14 August. Beijing: Beijing daxue wenhua geming weiyuanhui (chouwei hui) bangongshi bian.

———. 1966f. *Dazibao xuan zengkan (er)* (Selected Wall Posters, Supplementary Issue, 2), 1 August. Beijing: Beijing daxue wenhua geming weiyuanhui (chouwei hui) bangongshi bian.

———. 1966g. *Dazibao xuan zengkan (san)* (Selected Wall Posters, Supplementary Issue, 3), 28 July. Beijing: Beijing daxue wenhua geming weiyuanhui (chouwei hui) bangongshi bian.

Beijing University High School. 1967. *Dazibao xuan* (Selected Wall Posters), April. Beijing: Hongdaihui xin Beida fuzhong jinggangshan bingtuan zongbu.

Beijing University of Science and Technology Archives Office. 2006. *Beijing keji daxue xiaoshi, 1952–2002* (History of Beijing University of Science and Technology, 1952–2002). Beijing: Beijing keji daxue dang'anguan.

Beijing University Party History Office. 2001. "Kang Sheng, Cao Yi'ou yu 'diyi zhang dazibao'" (Kang Sheng, Cao Yi'ou, and the "First Wall Poster"). *Bainian chao* 9: 32–38.

———. 2002. "Beida shejiao yundong de shishi jingguo" (The Course of the Socialist Education Movement at Beijing University). *Zhonggong dangshi ziliao* 81 (March): 90–99.

Beijing University Work Team. 1966a. *Dazibao xuan (liu)* (Selected Wall Posters, 6), 1 July. Beijing: Beijing daxue gongzuozu bangongshi bian.

———. 1966b. *Dazibao xuan (ba)* (Selected Wall Posters, 8), 2 July. Beijing: Beijing daxue gongzuozu bangongshi bian.

———. 1966c. *Dazibao xuan (shi)* (Selected Wall Posters, 10), 10 July. Beijing: Beijing daxue gongzuozu bangongshi bian.

———. 1966d. *Dazibao xuan (shiyi)* (Selected Wall Posters, 11), 15 July. Beijing: Beijing daxue gongzuozu bangongshi bian.

Benford, Robert D., and David A. Snow. 2000. "Framing Processes and Social Movements: An Overview and Assessment." *Annual Review of Sociology* 26: 611–639.

Blecher, Marc J., and Gordon White. 1979. *Micropolitics in Contemporary China: A Technical Unit during and after the Cultural Revolution.* White Plains, N.Y.: M.E. Sharpe.

Bu Weihua. 1999. "Qinghua fuzhong hongweibing chengli shimo" (The Story behind the Founding of the Qinghua High School Red Guards). *Zhonggong dangshi ziliao* 70 (June): 96–127.

———. 2000. "Guanyu 'wen'ge' zhong Beijing de 'tianpai' he 'dipai' " (On the "Heaven" and "Earth" Factions during Beijing's "Cultural Revolution"). *Zhonggong dangshi ziliao* 73 (March): 100–126.

———. 2001. "Qinghua fuzhong hongweibing chengli hou de yixie qingkuang" (Some Circumstances after the Establishment of the Qinghua University Red Guards). *Zhonggong dangshi ziliao* 80 (December): 126–146.

———. 2003. " 'Huoshao Yingguo daibanchu' shimo" (The Story behind "Torching the British Diplomatic Offices"). *Zhonggong dangshi ziliao* 86 (June): 135–140.

———. 2008. *Zalan jiu shijie: Wenhua da geming de dongluan yu haojie* (Smashing the Old World: The Catastrophic Turmoil of the Cultural Revolution). Hong Kong: Zhongwen daxue chubanshe.

Byron, John, and Robert Pack. 1992. *The Claws of the Dragon.* New York: Simon and Schuster.

Calhoun, Craig. 1994. *Neither Gods nor Emperors: Students and the Struggle for Democracy in China.* Berkeley: University of California Press.

Cao Ying, ed. 2001. *Zhongguo gongchandang shi quanjian (di ba juan)* (Comprehensive Reference on Chinese Communist Party History, vol. 8). Beijing: Zhongguo wenshi chubanshe.

Cao Zixi and Yu Guangdu, eds. 1994. *Beijing tongshi, di shi juan* (Comprehensive History of Beijing, vol. 10). Beijing: Zhongguo shuju.

Capital High School Red Guard Congress. 1967. *Zalan "liandong"* (Smash "Liandong" to a Pulp). Beijing: Shoudu zhongxue hongdaihui hong bayue geming zaofan lianluozhan.

Capital Red Army Corps. 1967. *Bixu chedi suqing Liu Deng luxian zai wo xiao de liudu (yi)* (Thoroughly Eliminate the Lingering Poison of the Liu Deng Line from Our School [1]). Beijing: Shoudu hongjun bingtuan (Beijing yi zhong fentuan).

Capital Red Guard Picket Corps. 1966. *Tongling ji (1–10)* (Collected General Orders 1–10), September. Printed pamphlet. Beijing: Shoudu hongweibing jiucha dui xicheng zhihui bu.

Capital University Red Guard Congress. 1967. *Cuihui fangeming zuzhi "liandong" zhanlanhui ziliao xuanbian* (Destroy the Counterrevolutionary Organization "Liandong": Selected Exhibition Materials), July. Beijing: Shoudu dazhuan yuanxiao hongdai hui cuihui fangeming zuzhi "liandong" zhanlanhui [CCRM 1980, 7:3291–3350].

CCRM (Center for Chinese Research Materials). 1975. *Red Guard Publications.* 20 vols. Washington, D.C.: Center for Chinese Research Materials, Association of Research Libraries.

———. 1980. *Red Guard Publications, Supplement I.* 8 vols. Washington, D.C.: Center for Chinese Research Materials.

———. 1992. *Red Guard Publications, Supplement II.* 8 vols. Oakton, Va.: Center for Chinese Research Materials.

———. 1999. *A New Collection of Red Guard Publications.* Yuan Zhou, ed. 20 vols. Oakton, Va.: Center for Chinese Research Materials.

———. 2001. *A New Collection of Red Guard Publications, Part II: Special Compilation of Newspapers from the Beijing Area.* Yongyi Song, ed. 40 vols. Oakton, Va.: Center for Chinese Research Materials.

Central Comrades' Speeches. 1966a. *Zai wuchan jieji wenhua dageming zhong zhongyang fuze tongzhi jianghua chaolu (di yi ji)* (Transcripts of Speeches during the Great Proletarian Cultural Revolution by Responsible Comrades of the Party Center [no. 1]), October. Typeset volume, no publisher named.

———. 1966b. *Zai wuchan jieji wenhua dageming zhong zhongyang fuze tongzhi jianghua chaolu (di er ji)* (Transcripts of Speeches during the Great Proletarian Cultural Revolution by Responsible Comrades of the Party Center [no. 2]), December. Typeset volume, no publisher named.

———. 1967. *Zai wuchan jieji wenhua dageming zhong zhongyang fuze tongzhi jianghua chaolu (di san ji)* (Transcripts of Speeches during the Great Proletarian Cultural Revolution by Responsible Comrades of the Party Center [no. 3]), January. Typeset volume, no publisher named.

Central Documents Research Office, ed. 1996. *Liu Shaoqi nianpu, xia juan* (Liu Shaoqi Chronology, vol. 2). Beijing: Zhongyang wenxian chubanshe.

———. 1997. *Zhou Enlai nianpu, xia juan* (Zhou Enlai Chronology, vol. 3). Beijing: Zhongyang wenxian chubanshe.

———. 1998. *Jianguo yilai Mao Zedong wengao, di shi'er ce* (Mao Zedong's Post-1949 Manuscripts, vol. 12). Beijing: Zhongyang wenxian chubanshe.

———. 2003. *Mao Zedong zhuan, 1949–1976 (xia)* (Biography of Mao Zedong, 1949–1976 [vol. 2]). Beijing: Zhongyang wenxian chubanshe.

Central Leaders' Speeches. 1967a. *Zhongyang shouzhang jianghua 1* (Central Leaders' Speeches, 1), March. Beijing: Beijing boli zongchang hongweibing lianluozhan.

———. 1967b. *Zhongyang shouzhang jianghua 2* (Central Leaders' Speeches, 2), March. Beijing: Beijing boli zongchang hongweibing lianluozhan.

———. 1967c. *Zhongyang shouzhang jianghua 3* (Central Leaders' Speeches, 3), April. Beijing: Beijing boli zongchang hongweibing lianluozhan.

———. 1967d. *Zhongyang shouzhang jianghua 4* (Central Leaders' Speeches, 4), May. Beijing: Beijing boli zongchang hongweibing lianluozhan.

Chan, Anita. 1982. "Images of China's Social Structure: The Changing Perspectives of Canton Students." *World Politics* 34 (January): 295–323.

———. 1985. *Children of Mao: Personality Development and Political Activism in the Red Guard Generation.* Seattle: University of Washington Press.

Chan, Anita, Stanley Rosen, and Jonathan Unger. 1980. "Students and Class Warfare: The Social Roots of the Red Guard Conflict in Guangzhou (Canton)." *China Quarterly* 83 (September): 397–446.

Chang Dianyuan, ed. 1994. *Beijing di'er waiguoyu xueyuan zhi (Zhongguo lüyou xueyuan)* (Beijing Foreign Languages Institute No. 2 Annals [China Tourism Institute]). Beijing: Lüyou jiaoyu chubanshe.

Cheek, Timothy. 1997. *Propaganda and Culture in Mao's China: Deng Tuo and the Intelligentsia*. Oxford: Clarendon Press.

Chen Huanren. 2006. *Hongweibing riji* (Red Guard Diary). Hong Kong: Zhongwen daxue chubanshe.

Chen Pixian. 2005. *Chen Pixian huiyilu: Zai "yiyue fengbao" de zhongxin* (Chen Pixian's Memoirs: At the Center of the "January Storm"). Shanghai: Shanghai renmin chubanshe.

Chen Xiaonong. 2005. *Chen Boda zuihou koushu huiyi* (Chen Boda's Final Oral Reminiscences). Hong Kong: Yangguang huanqiu chuban Xianggang youxian gongsi.

China Educational Yearbook. 1984. *Zhongguo jiaoyu nianjian, 1949–1981* (China Educational Yearbook, 1949–1981). Beijing: Zhongguo dabaike quanshu chubanshe.

Chinese People's University. 1992. *Zhongguo renmin daxue dashiji, 1937 nian 7 yue–1992 nian 2 yue* (Chinese People's University Chronicle of Events, July 1937–February 1992). Beijing: Zhongguo renmin daxue gaodeng jiaoyu yanjiu shi, xiaoshi bianxie xiaozu.

Chinese People's University Red Guard Headquarters. 1966. *Guo Yingqiu fan dang fan shehui zhuyi fan Mao Zedong sixiang de yanlun* (Guo Yingqiu's Anti-party, Anti-socialist, Anti–Mao Thought Statements), 16 September. Printed pamphlet. Beijing: Zhongguo renmin daxue hongweibing zongbu bianyin.

Chinese People's University Red Guards. 1966a. *Dazibao xuanbian (yi)* (Selected Wall Posters [1]), 20 October. Beijing: Zhongguo renmin daxue hongweibing, hongweidui, hongweijun.

———. 1966b. *Dazibao xuanbian (er)* (Selected Wall Posters [2]), 16 October. Beijing: Zhongguo renmin daxue hongweibing, hongweidui, hongweijun bian.

———. 1966c. *Dazibao xuanbian (san)* (Selected Wall Posters [3]), 22 October. Beijing: Zhongguo renmin daxue hongweibing, hongweidui, hongweijun bian.

———. 1966d. *Dazibao xuanbian (si)* (Selected Wall Posters [4]), 24 October. Beijing: Zhongguo renmin daxue hongweibing, hongweidui, hongweijun bian.

Chinese University of Politics and Law, History Editorial Group. 2002. *Zhongguo zhengfa daxue xiaoshi* (History of Chinese University of Politics and Law). Beijing: Zhongguo zhengfa daxue chubanshe.

Compilation. n.d. "Wuchan jieji wenhua da geming zonghe cailiao (yi) 1966 nian" (Compilation of Materials on the Great Proletarian Cultural Revolution, 1, 1966). Unpublished. Stanford, Calif.: Hoover Institution Library.

Cultural Revolution Database. 2002. *The Chinese Cultural Revolution Database* (CD-ROM). Song Yongyi, ed. Hong Kong: Universities Service Centre for China Studies, Chinese University of Hong Kong.

Esherick, Joseph W., Paul G. Pickowicz, and Andrew G. Walder. 2006. "The Chinese Cultural Revolution as History: An Introduction." Pp. 1–28 in *The Chinese Cultural Revolution as History,* edited by Joseph W. Esherick, Paul G. Pickowicz, and Andrew G. Walder. Stanford, Calif.: Stanford University Press.

Esherick, Joseph W., and Jeffrey N. Wasserstrom. 1990. "Acting Out Democracy: Political Theater in Modern China." *Journal of Asian Studies* 49 (November): 835–856.

Fan Jin, Zhang Dazhong, and Xu Huaicheng, eds. 1989. *Dangdai Zhongguo de Beijing (shang)* (Contemporary China: Beijing, vol. 1). Beijing: Zhongguo shehui kexue chubanshe.

Fan Jizhou and Sun Licheng, eds. 1992. *Beijing linye daxue xiaoshi, 1952–1992* (History of Beijing Forestry University, 1952–1992). Beijing: Zhongguo linye chubanshe.

Fang Huijian and Zhang Sijing, eds. 2001. *Qinghua daxue zhi* (Annals of Qinghua University). 2 vols. Beijing: Qinghua daxue chubanshe.

Fitzpatrick, Sheila. 1978. "Cultural Revolution as Class War." Pp. 8–40 in *Cultural Revolution in Russia, 1928–1931,* edited by Sheila Fitzpatrick. Bloomington: Indiana University Press.

Forster, Keith. 1990. *Rebellion and Factionalism in a Chinese Province: Zhejiang, 1966–1976.* Armonk, N.Y.: M. E. Sharpe.

Gamson, William. 1975. *The Strategy of Social Protest.* Homewood, Ill.: Dorsey.

Gao Wenqian. 2003. *Wannian Zhou Enlai* (Zhou Enlai's Later Years). Hong Kong: Mirror Books.

Gao Yi, ed. 1982. *Zhongguo gaodeng xuexiao jianjie* (Introduction to China's Institutions of Higher Education). Beijing: Jiaoyu kexue chubanshe.

Goldman, Merle. 1967. *Literary Dissent in Communist China.* Cambridge, Mass.: Harvard University Press.

———. 1969. "The Unique 'Blooming and Contending' of 1961–62." *China Quarterly* 37 (January): 54–83.

———. 1981. *China's Intellectuals: Advise and Dissent.* Cambridge, Mass.: Harvard University Press.

Gong, Xiaoxia. 2003. "The Logic of Repressive Collective Action: A Case Study of Violence in the Cultural Revolution." Pp. 113–132 in *The Chinese Cultural Revolution Reconsidered,* edited by Kam-yee Lau. London: Palgrave Macmillan.

Goodwin, Jeff, and James M. Jasper, eds. 2004. *Rethinking Social Movements: Structure, Meaning, and Emotion.* Lanham, Md.: Rowman and Littlefield.

Goodwin, Jeff, James M. Jasper, and Francesca Polletta. 2001. *Passionate Politics: Emotions and Social Movements.* Chicago: University of Chicago Press.

Gould, Roger V. 1991. "Multiple Networks and Mobilization in the Paris Commune, 1871." *American Sociological Review* 56 (December): 716–729.

———. 1993. "Trade Cohesion, Class Unity, and Urban Insurrection: Artisanal Activism in the Paris Commune." *American Journal of Sociology* 98 (January): 721–754.

———. 1996. "Patron-Client Ties, State Centralization, and the Whiskey Rebellion." *American Journal of Sociology* 102 (September): 400–429.

Guangzhou Statistical Bureau. 1989. *Guangzhou sishinian, 1949–1989* (Guangzhou's Forty Years, 1949–1989). Guangzhou: Guangzhou tongji chubanshe.

Guo Yingqiu with Wang Junyi. 2002. "Guo Yingqiu linzhong koushu: 'Wen'ge' qinliji" (Guo Yingqiu's Deathbed Testimony: A Personal Account of the "Cultural Revolution"). *Yanhuang chunqiu* 128 (November): 44–53.

Hao, Ping. 1996. "Reassessing the Starting Point of the Cultural Revolution." *China Review International* 3 (April): 66–86.

Harding, Harry. 1991. "The Chinese State in Crisis." Pp. 107–217 in *The Cambridge History of China,* vol. 15, edited by Roderick MacFarquhar and John K. Fairbank. Cambridge: Cambridge University Press.

He Changgong. 1958. *Qingong jianxue shenghuo huiyi* (Recollections of Life in the Work-Study Program). Beijing: Gongren chubanshe.

———. 1987. *He Changgong huiyilu* (He Changgong's Memoirs). Beijing: Jiefangjun chubanshe.

He Luo and Meng Jin. 2002. "Quanguo 'di yi zhang dazibao' chulong zhenxiang" (The Real Story behind the Nation's "First Wall Poster"). *Zhonggong dangshi ziliao* 83 (September): 113–127.

Hinton, William. 1972. *Hundred Day War: The Cultural Revolution at Tsinghua University.* New York: Monthly Review Press.

Hua Linshan. 1987. *Les années rouges.* Translated by Henri Leuwen and Isabelle Thireau. Paris: Éditions du Seuil.

———.1996a. "Wen'ge qijian qunzhongxing paixi chengyin" (Causes of Mass Factionalism in the Cultural Revolution). Pp. 191–208 in *Wenhua da geming: Shishi yu yanjiu* (The Cultural Revolution: Evidence and Analysis), edited by Liu Qingfeng. Hong Kong: Zhongwen daxue chubanshe.

———. 1996b. "Zhengzhi pohuai yu zaofan yundong" (Political Oppression and the Rebel Movement). Pp. 219–230 in *Wenhua da geming: Shishi yu yanjiu* (The Cultural Revolution: Evidence and Analysis), edited by Liu Qingfeng. Hong Kong: Zhongwen daxue chubanshe.

Institute History Editorial Group. 2001. *Huabei shuili shuidian xueyuan zhi* (North China Institute of Irrigation and Hydropower). Xi'an: Shaanxi renmin chubanshe.

Israel, John. 1966. *Student Nationalism in China, 1927–1937*. Stanford, Calif.: Stanford University Press.

Israel, John, and Donald W. Klein. 1976. *Rebels and Bureaucrats: China's December 9ers*. Berkeley: University of California Press.

Jin Chunming. 2002. *Jin Chunming zixuan wenji* (Jin Chunming's Selected Essays). Chengdu: Sichuan renmin chubanshe.

Jin Jichun, ed. 1994. *Beijing tiyu xueyuan xiaozhi* (Annals of Beijing Sports Institute). Beijing: Beijing tiyu xueyuan xiaozhi bianzuan weiyuanhui.

Kong Dongmei. 2006. *Gaibian shijie de rizi: Yu Wang Hairong tan Mao Zedong waijiao wangshi* (Days That Changed the World: Talks with Wang Hairong about Mao Zedong and Foreign Affairs). Beijing: Zhongyang wenxian chubanshe.

Kraus, Richard Curt. 1977. "Class Conflict and the Vocabulary of Social Analysis in China." *China Quarterly* 69 (March): 54–74.

———. 1981. *Class Conflict in Chinese Socialism*. New York: Columbia University Press.

Kung, James Kai-sing, and Justin Yifu Lin. 2003. "The Causes of China's Great Leap Famine, 1959–1961." *Economic Development and Cultural Change* 52 (October): 51–73.

Kwong, Julia. 1988. *Cultural Revolution in China's Schools, May 1966–April 1969*. Stanford, Calif.: Hoover Institution Press.

Lee, Hong Yung. 1975. "The Radical Students in Kwangtung during the Cultural Revolution." *China Quarterly* 64 (December): 645–683.

———. 1978. *The Politics of the Chinese Cultural Revolution: A Case Study*. Berkeley: University of California Press.

Li, Bobai, and Andrew G. Walder. 2001. "Career Advancement as Party Patronage: Sponsored Mobility into the Chinese Administrative Elite, 1949–1996." *American Journal of Sociology* 106 (March): 1371–1408.

Li Rongfa, ed. 2000. *Beijing gongye daxue zhi, 1960–1998* (Beijing Polytechnic University Annals, 1960–1998). Beijing: Beijing gongye daxue chubanshe.

Li, Wei, and Dennis Tao Yang. 2005. "The Great Leap Forward: Anatomy of a Central Planning Disaster." *Journal of Political Economy* 113 (August): 840–877.

Li Xiaofeng, ed. 1992. *Zhongguo gaodeng xuexiao bianqian* (The Evolution of China's Institutions of Higher Education). Shanghai: Huadong shifan daxue chubanshe.

Li Xuefeng. 1966. "Li Xuefeng tongzhi daibiao Zhonggong Beijing shiwei guanyu zai wenhua da geming zhong suo fan fangxiangxing de, luxianxing de cuowu jiancha tigang" (Comrade Li Xuefeng's Self-Criticism on Behalf of the Beijing Municipal Party Committee Regarding the Errors of Orientation and Line It Committed during the Cultural Revolution), 7 December. Mimeo. [CCRM 1992, 4:2213–2220].

———. 1998. "Wo suo zhidao de 'wen'ge' fadong neiqing" (What I Know about the Inside Story behind the Launching of the "Cultural Revolution"). *Bainian chao* 4: 14–21.

———. 1999. "Huiyi 'wenhua da geming' chuqi de 'wushi tian luxian cuowu': Cong '6.18' shijian dao '7.29' dahui" (Recalling the "Fifty-Day Erroneous Line" of the Early "Cultural Revolution": From the Incident of "June 18" to the "July 29" Mass Meeting). Pp. 641–664 in *Huishou "wen'ge": Zhongguo shinian "wen'ge" fenxi yu fansi* (The "Cultural Revolution" in Retrospect: Analysis and Reflections on China's Ten-Year "Cultural Revolution"), edited by Zhang Hua and Su Caiqing, 2 vols. Beijing: Zhonggong dangshi chubanshe.

Li Xun. 2006. *Wenhua da geming tudian* (Illustrated Dictionary of the Cultural Revolution). Hong Kong: Riyue chuban gongsi.

Li Yong and Wen Lequn. 1994a. *Wenhua da geming zhong de mingren zhi sheng* (Notable Figures Who Ascended during the "Cultural Revolution"). Beijing: Zhongyang minzu xueyuan chubanshe.

———. 1994b. *Wenhua da geming zhong de mingren zhi si* (Notable Figures Who Died during the "Cultural Revolution"). Beijing: Zhongyang minzu xueyuan chubanshe.

Li Zhisui. 1994. *The Private Life of Chairman Mao.* New York: Random House.

Liu Bing. 1998. *Fengyu suiyue: Qinghua daxue "wenhua da geming" yishi* (Stormy Times: A Memoir of the "Cultural Revolution" at Qinghua University). Beijing: Qinghua daxue chubanshe.

Liu Guokai. [1980] 1987. *A Brief Analysis of the Cultural Revolution.* Armonk, N.Y.: M. E. Sharpe.

Liu Jinglin. 2004. "Wen'ge chuqi wo gei Zhou Enlai zongli dang lianluoyuan" (I Served as Liaison Officer for Zhou Enlai in the Early Phase of the Cultural Revolution). *Yanhuang chunqiu* 12: 65–69.

Liu Shufa, ed. 1995. *Chen Yi nianpu, xia juan* (Chen Yi Chronology, vol. 2). Beijing: Renmin chubanshe.

Liu Zhijian. 2000. "Dongluan zhichu de jingli he zaoyu" (My Experiences and Misfortunes at the Beginning of the Turmoil). *Zhonggong dangshi ziliao* 74 (June): 23–59.

Lüthi, Lorenz M. 2008. *The Sino-Soviet Split: Cold War in the Communist World.* Princeton, N.J.: Princeton University Press.

Ma Jisen. 2004. *The Cultural Revolution in the Foreign Ministry of China.* Hong Kong: Chinese University of Hong Kong Press.

MacFarquhar, Roderick. 1960. *The Hundred Flowers and the Chinese Intellectuals*. New York: Praeger.

———. 1974. *The Origins of the Cultural Revolution 1: Contradictions among the People, 1956–1957*. New York: Columbia University Press.

———. 1983. *The Origins of the Cultural Revolution 2: The Great Leap Forward, 1958–1960*. New York: Columbia University Press.

———. 1997. *The Origins of the Cultural Revolution 3: The Coming of the Cataclysm, 1961–1966*. New York: Columbia University Press.

MacFarquhar, Roderick, and Michael Schoenhals. 2006. *Mao's Last Revolution*. Cambridge, Mass.: Harvard University Press.

Mao Zedong. 1967. *Mao Zedong sixiang wansui* (Long Live Mao Zedong Thought), February. No publisher named.

———. 1969. *Mao Zedong sixiang wansui* (Long Live Mao Zedong Thought), August. No publisher named.

McAdam, Doug. 1982. *Political Process and the Development of Black Insurgency, 1930–1970*. Chicago: University of Chicago Press.

———. 1983. "Tactical Innovation and the Pace of Insurgency." *American Sociological Review* 48 (December): 735–754.

McCarthy, John D., and Mayer N. Zald. 1977. "Resource Mobilization and Social Movements: A Partial Theory." *American Journal of Sociology* 82 (May): 1212–1241.

Meisner, Maurice. 1999. *Mao's China and After: A History of the People's Republic*. 3rd ed. New York: Free Press.

Ministry of Post and Telecommunications Cultural Revolution Office. 1966. *Youdian bu wenhua geming dashiji* (Chronology of the Cultural Revolution in the Ministry of Post and Telecommunications), October. Beijing: Youdian bu wenhua geming bangongshi.

Mu Xin. 1994. *Ban "Guangming ribao" shinian zishu (1957–1967)* (An Account of My Ten Years in Charge of *Guangming Daily*, 1957–1967). Beijing: Zhonggong dangshi chubanshe.

———. 1997a. "Guanyu gongzuozu cun fei wenti" (On the Question of Whether to Withdraw the Work Teams). *Dangdai Zhongguo shi yanjiu* 2: 55–64.

———. 1997b. *Jiehou changyi: Shinian dongluan jishi* (Memories of Turmoil—An Account of Ten Years of Chaos). Hong Kong: Xintian chubanshe.

———. 2000. " 'Quanguo diyizhang dazibao' chulong jingguo" (How the "Nation's First Wall Poster" Was Cooked Up). *Zhonggong dangshi ziliao* 75 (September): 166–173.

New People's University Commune. 1967. *Fangeming xiuzheng zhuyi fenzi Guo Yingqiu fandang fan shehuizhuyi fan Mao Zedong sixiang de zuixing (yi)* (The Anti-party, Anti-socialist, Anti–Mao Zedong Thought Crimes of the Counterrevolutionary Revisionist Guo Yingqiu, 1). Beijing: Shoudu dazhuan yuanxiao hongdaihui, Zhongguo renmin daxue xin renda gongshe, Mao Zedong sixiang hongweibing.

Ni Fuqing and Pan Zhitian, eds. 1995. *Beijing ligong daxue zhi* (Annals of Beijing College of Science and Engineering). Beijing: Beijing ligong daxue chubanshe.

Nie Yuanzi. 2005. *Nie Yuanzi huiyi lu* (Memoirs of Nie Yuanzi). Hong Kong: Shidai guoji chuban youxian gongsi.

Northern Transportation University Annals Editorial Committee. 1996. *Beifang jiaotong daxue dashiji (1909–1995)* (Chronology of Major Events at Northern Transportation University, 1909–1995). Beijing: Beifang jiaotong daxue.

———. 2001. *Beifang jiaotong daxue zhi* (Annals of Northern Transportation University). Beijing: Zhongguo tiedao chubanshe.

Oksenberg, Michel. 1968. "Occupational Groups in Chinese Society and the Cultural Revolution." Pp. 1–44 in *The Cultural Revolution: 1967 in Review*. Michigan Papers in Chinese Studies no. 2. Ann Arbor: Center for Chinese Studies, University of Michigan.

Organization Department, Beijing Municipal Party Committee. 1992. *Zhongguo gongchandang Beijing shi zuzhi shi ziliao, 1921–1987* (Materials on the Organizational History of the Chinese Communist Party in Beijing, 1921–1987). Beijing: Renmin chubanshe.

Organization Department, CCP Central Committee. 2000. *Zhongguo gongchandang zuzhishi ziliao, 1921–1997* (Materials on the Organizational History of the Chinese Communist Party, 1921–1997). 19 vols. Beijing: Zhonggong dangshi chubanshe.

———. 2004. *Zhongguo gongchandang lijie zhongyang weiyuan da cidian, 1921–2003* (Dictionary of Central Committee Members, 1921–2003). Beijing: Zhonggong dangshi chubanshe.

Organization Department, Harbin Municipality. 1989a. *Heilongjiang sheng Haerbin shi zheng jun tong qun xitong zuzhishi ziliao, 1945–1987* (Materials on the Organizational History of Government, Military, United Front, and Mass Organizations of Harbin Municipality, Heilongjiang Province, 1945–1987). Harbin: Zhonggong Haerbin shiwei zuzhibu, zhonggong Haerbin shiwei dangshi gongzuo weiyuanhui, Haerbin shi dang'an ju.

———. 1989b. *Zhongguo gongchandang Heilongjiang sheng Haerbin shi zuzhishi ziliao, 1923–1987* (Materials on the Organizational History of the Chinese Communist Party in Harbin Municipality, Heilongjiang Province, 1923–1987). Harbin: Zhonggong Haerbin shiwei zuzhibu, zhonggong Haerbin shiwei dangshi gongzuo weiyuanhui, Haerbin shi dang'an ju.

Party History Research Office Department No. 1, CCP Central Committee. 2004. *Zhongguo gongchandang di qi ci quanguo daibiao dahui daibiao minglu* (Delegates to the Seventh Party Congress of the Chinese Communist Party). Beijing: Zhonggong dangshi chubanshe.

Pepper, Suzanne. 1991. "Education." Pp. 540–593 in *The Cambridge History of China*, vol. 15, edited by Roderick MacFarquhar and John K. Fairbank. Cambridge: Cambridge University Press.

Perry, Elizabeth J. 2006. *Patrolling the Revolution: Worker Militias, Citizenship, and the Modern Chinese State.* Lanham, Md.: Rowman and Littlefield.

Perry, Elizabeth J., and Li Xun. 1997. *Proletarian Power: Shanghai in the Cultural Revolution.* Boulder, Colo.: Westview Press.

Qinghua Jinggangshan. 1966. *Kan! Shier yue hei feng* (Look! The December Black Wind), 19 December. Handwritten stencil. 7 pp. Beijing: Qinghua jinggangshan bingtuan 8.18.

Qinghua University. 1966. *Dazibao xuanbian (1)* (Selected big-character posters, 1), 19 December. Beijing: Qinghua daxue dazibao bianweihui.

Qinghua University Jinggangshan. 1966. *Pipan Tan Lifu fayan zhuanji—Pipan zichan jieji fandong luxian* (Special Collection on the Criticism of Tan Lifu's Speech—Criticize the Bourgeois Reactionary Line). Beijing: Qinghua daxue Jinggangshan hongweibing zongbu, Mao Zedong sixiang hongweibing linshi zongbu, Mao Zedong sixiang hongweibing ba ba zongbu lianhe zhu ban "Jinggangshan" bao.

Qinghua University Jinggangshan Corps. 1967a. *Dadao fangeming xiuzheng zhuyi fenzi Bo Yibo (yi)* (Overthrow the Counterrevolutionary Revisionist Bo Yibo [1]), January. Beijing: Qinghua daxue jinggangshan bingtuan dazibao bianweihui. [CCRM 1992, 8:4291–4314].

———. 1967b. *Jinggangshan* (Jinggang Mountain) 4 (22 April). Beijing: Hongdaihui Qinghua daxue jinggangshan bingtuan.

Qinghua University Jinggangshan 414. 1967. *Dazibao xuanbian (er)* (Selected Wall Posters [2]), May. Beijing: Hongdaihui Qinghua jinggangshan 414 geming chuanlianhui bian.

Qinghua University Jinggangshan 414 Headquarters. 1967. *Dazibao xuanbian (si)* (Selected Wall Posters [4]). Beijing: Hongdaihui Qinghua jinggangshan bingtuan 414 zongbu dazibao bianweihui.

Qinghua University Jinggangshan Red Guards. 1966. *Qinghua daxue dazibao xuan (Kuai Dafu tongzhi de dazibao)* (Qinghua University Selected Wall Posters [Wall Posters by Comrade Kuai Dafu]), undated, probably December 1966. Printed pamphlet. Beijing: Qinghua daxue jinggangshan hongweibing xuanchuandui bian.

Qinghua University Jinggangshan United General Headquarters. 1967a. *Dazibao xuanbian—Pipan ganbu wenti shang zichan jieji fandong luxian zhuanji, di yi ji* (Selected Wall Posters—Special Compilation of Criticism of the Bourgeois Reactionary Line on the Cadre Question, no. 1), October.

Beijing: Hongdaihui Qinghua jinggangshan lianhe zongbu (yuan 414 ganbu bangongshi).

———. 1967b. *Dazibao xuanbian—Pipan ganbu wenti shang zichan jieji fandong luxian zhuanji, di er ji* (Selected Wall Posters—Special Compilation of Criticism of the Bourgeois Reactionary Line on the Cadre Question, no. 2), October. Beijing: Hongdaihui Qinghua jinggangshan lianhe zongbu, yuan 414 ganbu bangongshi.

Qinghua University Mao Zedong Thought Red Guards. 1966a. *"Ba.ba" tongxun—Pipan zichan jijie fandong luxian zhuanji* ("August 8" Bulletin—Special Collection of Materials on the Criticism of the Bourgeois Reactionary Line), 23 October. Beijing: Qinghua daxue Mao Zedong sixiang hongweibing, dongfanghong gongshe "ba.ba" zongbu.

———. 1966b. *Qinghua daxue dazibao xuanbian* (Qinghua University Selected Wall Posters), 7 October. Beijing: Qinghua daxue Mao Zedong sixiang hongweibing, dongfanghong gongshe.

———. 1966c. *Qinghua daxue dazibao xuanbian—Pipan gongzuozu cuowu luxian zhuanji* (Qinghua University Selected Wall Posters—Special Edition of Criticisms of the Work Team's Erroneous Line), 27 September. Beijing: Qinghua daxue Mao Zedong sixiang hongweibing, dongfanghong gongshe.

———. 1966d. *Xiang zichan jieji fandong luxian menglie kaohuo* (Fiercely Open Fire on the Bourgeois Reactionary Line), October. Beijing: Qinghua daxue dongfanghong gongshe, Mao Zedong sixiang hongweibing xuanchuan zu.

Qinghua University Work Team. 1966. *Qinghua daxue dazibao xuanbian (shi)* (Qinghua University Selected Wall Posters [10]), 6 July. Beijing: Zhonggong Beijing xin shiwei gongzuo zu ziliaozu bian.

Red Guard Combat School Red Guards. 1966. *Wen canmang dadi, shei zhu chenfu? (Hongweibing dazibao xuanbian)* (Ask the Boundless Land, Who Are Masters of Their Fortune? [Selected Red Guard Wall Posters]), September. Beijing: Hongweibing zhanxiao hongweibing.

Reference Materials. 1966. *Wuchan jieji wenhua da geming cankao ziliao* (Reference Materials on the Great Proletarian Cultural Revolution). 4 vols. Beijing: Beijing jingji xueyuan wuchanjieji geming zaofan tuan, Beijing huagong xueyuan hongse xuanchuanyuan zhandouzu, Beijing shi dongfanghong yinshua chang geming zaofan lianluo chu, Huagong bu huaxue gongye chubanshe yinshuachang.

Revolutionary Rebel General Headquarters. 1967. *Youdian bu jiguan wenhua da geming yundong shiliao* (Materials on the History of the Cultural Revolution Movement in the Ministry of Post and Telecommunications), August 1. Beijing: Geming zaofan zongbu zhenli zhandoudui.

Rittenberg, Sidney, and Amanda Bennett. 1993. *The Man Who Stayed Behind.* New York: Simon and Schuster.

Rong Shixing, ed. 2001. *Zhongyang minzu daxue wushi nian* (The Fifty Years of Central Nationalities University). Beijing: Zhongyang minzu daxue chubanshe.

Rosen, Stanley. 1981. *The Role of Sent-Down Youth in the Chinese Cultural Revolution: The Case of Guangzhou.* Berkeley: Institute of East Asian Studies, University of California.

———. 1982. *Red Guard Factionalism and the Cultural Revolution in Guangzhou (Canton).* Boulder, Colo.: Westview Press.

Schoenhals, Michael, ed. 1994. *"An Insider's Account of the Cultural Revolution: Wang Li's Memoirs." Chinese Law and Government* 27(6): 3–89.

———. 1996. "The Central Case Examination Group, 1966–79." *China Quarterly* 145 (March): 87–111.

———. 2005. " 'Why Don't We Arm the Left?' Mao's Culpability in the 'Great Chaos' of 1967." *China Quarterly* 182 (June): 277–300.

Schram, Stuart, ed. 1974. *Chairman Mao Talks to the People: Talks and Letters, 1956–1971.* New York: Pantheon.

———, ed. 1994. *Mao's Road to Power: Revolutionary Writings, 1912–1949,* vol. 2. Armonk, N.Y.: M. E. Sharpe.

Shambaugh, David. 2002. *Modernizing China's Military: Progress, Problems, and Prospects.* Berkeley: University of California Press.

Shanghai Red Guard Headquarters. 1967. *Zalan "Liandong"* (Smash "United Action" to a Pulp), May. Shanghai: Hongweibing Shanghai silingbu.

Shen Ruhuai. 2004. *Qinghua daxue wen'ge jishi—Yige hongweibing lingdao de zishu* (An Account of the Cultural Revolution at Qinghua University—The Personal Account of a Red Guard Leader). Hong Kong: Shidai yishu chubanshe.

Shen Shituan, ed. 2000. *Beijing hangkong hangtian daxue xiaozhi, 1952–1992* (Annals of Beijing University of Aeronautics and Aerospace, 1952–1992). Beijing: Beijing hangkong hangtian daxue chubanshe.

Shen Xueming and Zheng Jianying, eds. 2001. *Zhonggong diyi jie zhi shiwu jie zhongyang weiyuan* (Members of the First through Fifteenth Central Committees of the Chinese Communist Party). Beijing: Zhongyang wenxian chubanshe.

Shirk, Susan L. 1982. *Competitive Comrades: Career Incentives and Student Strategies in China.* Berkeley: University of California Press.

Shu Yi. 1987. *Lao She zhi si* (The Death of Lao She). Beijing: Guoji wenhua chuban gongsi.

Song Bolin. 2006. *Hongweibing xingshuai lu: Qinghua fuzhong lao hongweibing shouji* (The Rise and Decline of the Red Guards: The Diary of an Old Red Guard from Qinghua High School). Hong Kong: Desai youxian chuban gongsi.

Special Compilation. 1997. *"Wenhua da geming" chuqi zhonggong zhongyao renwu yanlun huibian zhuanji* (Special Compilation of Speeches by Important

Party Leaders in the Early "Cultural Revolution" Period). Los Angeles: Service Center for Chinese Publications.

State Council. 1967a. *Fangeming xiuzheng zhuyi fenzi Zhou Rongxin bixu chedi dadao: Zhou Rongxin cailiao zhi shiyi* (Counterrevolutionary Revisionist Element Zhou Rongxin Must Be Thoroughly Overthrown: Zhou Rongxin Materials, no. 11), 20 June. Printed pamphlet. Beijing: Guowuyuan jiguan diaocha Zhou Rongxin zuixing xiaozu.

———. 1967b. *Zhou Rongxin zai zhengzhi shang zhichi he caozong xijiu de tiezheng: Zhou Rongxin cailiao zhi qi* (Ironclad Evidence That Zhou Rongxin Politically Supported and Manipulated the Western District Picket Corps: Zhou Rongxin Materials, no. 7), 3 June. Beijing: Printed pamphlet. Guowuyuan jiguan diaocha Zhou Rongxin zuixing xiaozu.

State Science Commission Red Guards. 1966. *Zhongyang fuze tongzhi jianghua huibian* (Collection of Speeches by Responsible Comrades of the Party Center), October. Beijing: Guojia kewei xitong hongweibing lianluozhan.

Tan Bin (Tan Lifu). 1996. *Chizi baihua* (Empty Talk of an Innocent). Beijing: Beijing tushuguan chubanshe.

Tang Shaojie. 1999a. "Cong Qinghua daxue de liangpai tan 'wenhua da geming' qunzhong zuzhi jiegou, gongneng" (Structure and Function of "Cultural Revolution" Mass Organizations: The Case of the Two Factions at Qinghua University). *Zhonggong dangshi ziliao* 72 (September): 66–81.

———. 1999b. "Qinghua daxue liangpai kan 'wenhua da geming' zhong qunzhong zuzhi de duili he fenqi" (Antagonisms and Splits among Mass Organizations during the "Cultural Revolution": The Case of the Two Factions at Qinghua University). Pp. 774–788 in *Huishou "wen'ge": Zhongguo shinian "wen'ge" fenxi yu fansi* (The "Cultural Revolution" in Retrospect: Analysis and Reflections on China's Ten-Year "Cultural Revolution"), edited by Zhang Hua and Su Caiqing, 2 vols. Beijing: Zhonggong dangshi chubanshe.

———. 2000. "Qinghua wudou yu xuanchuan dui jinzhu" (Armed Struggle at Qinghua and the Entry of the Propaganda Team). *Bainian chao* 9: 63–69.

———. 2003. *Yiye zhiqiu: Qinghua daxue 1968nian "Bairi da wudou"* (An Episode in the Cultural Revolution: The 1968 Hundred-Day War at Qinghua University). Hong Kong: Zhongwen daxue chubanshe.

Taubman, William. 2003. *Khrushchev: The Man and His Era*. New York: Norton.

Teiwes, Frederick C., and Warren Sun. 1995. "From a Leninist to a Charismatic Party: The CCP's Changing Leadership, 1937–1945." Pp. 339–387 in *New Perspectives on the Chinese Communist Revolution*, edited by Tony Saich and Hans van de Ven. Armonk, N.Y.: M. E. Sharpe.

Terrill, Ross. 1999. *Madame Mao: The White-Boned Demon*. Rev. ed. Stanford, Calif.: Stanford University Press.

Tilly, Charles. 1964. *The Vendée*. Cambridge, Mass.: Harvard University Press.

————. 1978. *From Mobilization to Revolution*. Reading, Mass.: Addison-Wesley.

Unger, Jonathan. 1982. *Education under Mao: Class and Competition in Canton Schools, 1960–1980*. New York: Columbia University Press.

Vogel, Ezra F. 1968. "The Structure of Conflict: China in 1967." Pp. 97–123 in *The Cultural Revolution: 1967 in Review*. Michigan Papers in Chinese Studies no. 2. Ann Arbor: Center for Chinese Studies, University of Michigan.

————. 1969. *Canton under Communism: Programs and Politics in a Provincial Capital, 1949–1968*. Cambridge, Mass.: Harvard University Press.

Walder, Andrew G. 1978. *Chang Ch'un-ch'iao and Shanghai's January Revolution*. Michigan Papers in Chinese Studies no. 32. Ann Arbor: Center for Chinese Studies, University of Michigan.

————. 1986. *Communist Neo-Traditionalism: Work and Authority in Chinese Industry*. Berkeley: University of California Press.

————. 1989. "The Political Sociology of the Beijing Upheaval of 1989." *Problems of Communism* 38 (September–October): 30–40.

————. 1991. "Cultural Revolution Radicalism: Variations on a Stalinist Theme." Pp. 41–61 in *New Perspectives on the Cultural Revolution,* edited by William A. Joseph, Christine P. W. Wong, and David Zweig. Cambridge, Mass.: Harvard University Press.

————. 1996. "The Chinese Cultural Revolution in the Factories: Party-State Structures and Patterns of Conflict." Pp. 167–198 in *Putting Class in Its Place: Worker Identities in East Asia,* edited by Elizabeth Perry. Berkeley: Institute of East Asian Studies, University of California.

————. 1998. "Collective Protest and the Waning of the Communist State in China." Pp. 54–72 in *Challenging Authority: The Historical Study of Contentious Politics,* edited by Michael Hanagan, Leslie Page Moch, and Wayne te Brake. Minneapolis: University of Minnesota Press.

————. 2002. "Beijing Red Guard Factionalism: Social Interpretations Reconsidered." *Journal of Asian Studies* 61 (May): 437–471.

————. 2004. "Tan Lifu: A 'Reactionary' Red Guard in Historical Perspective." *China Quarterly* 180 (December): 965–988.

————. 2006a. "Ambiguity and Choice in Political Movements: The Origins of Beijing Red Guard Factionalism." *American Journal of Sociology* 112 (November): 710–750.

————. 2006b. "Factional Conflict at Beijing University, 1966–1968." *China Quarterly* 188 (December): 1023–1047.

————. 2009. "Political Sociology and Social Movements." *Annual Review of Sociology* 35: 393–412.

Walder, Andrew G., and Songhua Hu. 2009. "Revolution, Reform, and Status Inheritance: Urban China, 1949–1996." *American Journal of Sociology* 114 (March): 1395–1427.

Walder, Andrew G., Bobai Li, and Donald J. Treiman. 2000. "Politics and Life Chances in a State Socialist Regime: Dual Career Paths into the Urban Chinese Elite, 1949–1996." *American Sociological Review* 65 (April): 191–209.

Wang Buzheng. 1995. *Beijing nongye daxue xiaoshi (1949–1987)* (History of Beijing Agricultural University [1949–1987]). Beijing: Beijing nongye daxue chubanshe.

Wang Chunli. 2003. *Shiyou daxue nianpu* (Chronology of Petroleum University). Beijing: Shiyou daxue chubanshe.

Wang Dechong and Lin Jintong, eds. 2005. *Beijing youdian daxue xiaoshi (1955–2005)* (History of Beijing Post and Telecommunications University [1955–2005]). Beijing: Beijing youdian daxue chubanshe.

Wang Jianying, ed. 1995. *Zhongguo gongchandang zuzhishi ziliao huibian: Lingdao jigou yange chengyuan minglu (zengding ben)* (Materials on the Organizational History of the Chinese Communist Party: Registry of Officeholders and Changes in Leadership Structures [rev. and enlarged ed.]). Beijing: Zhonggong zhongyang dangxiao chubanshe.

Wang Li. 2001. *Wang Li fansi lu* (Wang Li's Reflections). Hong Kong: Xianggang beixing chubanshe.

Wang Nianyi, ed. 1988. "*Wenhua da geming*" *yanjiu ziliao* ("Cultural Revolution" Research Materials), vol. 1. Beijing: Zhongguo renmin jiefangjun guofang daxue dangshi dangjian zhenggong jiaoyanshi.

———. 2005. *Da dongluan de niandai* (Turbulent Decade). Zhengzhou: Henan renmin chubanshe.

Wang, Shaoguang. 1995. *Failure of Charisma: The Cultural Revolution in Wuhan*. Oxford: Oxford University Press.

Wang Tongyue, ed. 1990. *Zhongguo renmin jiefang jun zuzhi yange he geji lingdao chengyuan minglu (xiuding ben)* (Organizational Changes and Leaders at Various Levels of the Chinese People's Liberation Army [rev. ed.]). Beijing: Junshi kexue chubanshe.

Wang Xuezhen, Wang Xiaoting, Huang Wenyi, and Guo Jianrong, eds. 1998. *Beijing daxue jishi (yibajiuba–yijiujiuqi)* (Beijing University Chronology [1898–1997]). 2 vols. Beijing: Beijing daxue chubanshe.

Wang Youqin. 2001. "Student Attacks against Teachers: The Revolution of 1966." *Issues and Studies* 37(1): 29–79.

———, ed. 2004. *Wen'ge shounanzhe: Guanyu pohai, jianjin yu shalu de xunfang shilu* (Victims of the Cultural Revolution: An Investigative Account of Persecution, Imprisonment, and Massacres). Hong Kong: Kaifang zazhishe.

White, Gordon. 1974. "The Politics of *Hsia-hsiang* Youth." *China Quarterly* 59 (July/September): 491–517.

———. 1976. *The Politics of Class and Class Origin: The Case of the Cultural Revolution*. Contemporary China Papers 9. Canberra: Contemporary China Centre, Australian National University.

———. 1980. "The Politics of Demobilized Soldiers from Liberation to Cultural Revolution." *China Quarterly* 82 (June): 187–213.

White, Lynn T., III. 1976. "Workers' Politics in Shanghai." *Journal of Asian Studies* 36 (November): 99–116.

———. 1979. "The Road to Urumqi: Approved Institutions in Search of Attainable Goals during Pre-1968 Rustication from Shanghai." *China Quarterly* 79 (September): 481–510.

———. 1989. *Policies of Chaos: The Organizational Causes of Violence in China's Cultural Revolution.* Princeton, N.J.: Princeton University Press.

Wu Peixu, Wu Shoujun, Shi Yujun, Wang Congshi, and Ma Shaocheng, eds. 1992. *Zhongguo kuangye daxue zhi* (Chinese Mining University Annals). Xuzhou: Zhongguo kuangye daxue chubanshe.

Wu Qingtong. 2002. *Zhou Enlai zai "wenhua da geming" zhong* (Zhou Enlai in the "Cultural Revolution"). Exp. ed. Beijing: Zhonggong dangshi chubanshe.

Wylie, Raymond F. 1980. *The Emergence of Maoism: Mao Tse-tung, Ch'en Po-ta, and the Search for Chinese Theory, 1935–1945.* Stanford, Calif.: Stanford University Press.

Xi Fuyun, Wang Qiaoshan, Feng Miaolin, Liu Jie, and Yang Chuanxia. 1998. *Zhongguo kexue jishu daxue dashiji: 1958–1987* (Chronicle of Events at Chinese University of Science and Technology: 1958–1987). Hefei: Zhongguo kexue jishu daxue.

Xi Xuan and Jin Chunming. 2006. *"Wenhua da geming" jianshi* (Brief History of the "Cultural Revolution"). Rev. and exp. ed. Beijing: Zhonggong dangshi chubanshe.

Xiao Han and Mia Turner, eds. 1998. *789 jizhong ying: Zhongguo gaogan zinü zhong yige teshu qunti de gushi* (Concentration Camp 789: The Story of a Special Group of Sons and Daughters of Chinese High Officials). Ontario, Canada: Mirror Books.

Xu Jingxian. 2004. *Shinian yi meng: Qian Shanghai shiwei shuji Xu Jingxian wen'ge huiyi lu* (Ten-Year Dream: Cultural Revolution Memoirs of Former Shanghai Municipal Party Secretary Xu Jingxian). Hong Kong: Shidai guoji chuban youxian gongsi.

Xu Wenqi and Yu Dali, eds. 1998. *Dongcheng qu putong jiaoyu zhi* (Eastern District Basic Education Annals). Beijing: Beijing chubanshe.

Xu Youyu. 1996a. "Wen'ge zhong hongweibing de paibie douzheng" (Factional Struggle among Red Guards during the Cultural Revolution). *Zhongguo yanjiu* 2: 23–35.

———. 1996b. "Zai shuo wen'ge zhong de zaofan pai—Yu Hua Linshan shangque" (More on the Rebel Faction in the Cultural Revolution—A Discussion with Hua Linshan). Pp. 209–218 in *Wenhua da geming: Shishi yu yanjiu* (The Cultural Revolution: Evidence and Analysis), edited by Liu Qingfeng. Hong Kong: Zhongwen daxue chubanshe.

———. 1999. *Xingxing sese de zaofan: Hongweibing jingshen suzhi de xingcheng ji yanbian* (Rebellion of All Hues: The Formation and Evolution of Red Guard Mentalities). Hong Kong: Zhongwen daxue chubanshe.

Yan Jiaqi and Gao Gao. 1996. *Turbulent Decade: A History of the Cultural Revolution.* Translated and edited by D. W. Y. Kwok. Honolulu: University of Hawaii Press.

Yang Bingzhang. 1998. *Cong Beida dao Hafo: Xian gei Zhongguo zhishi fenzi* (From Beida to Harvard: For China's Intellectuals). Beijing: Zuojia chubanshe.

Yang, Guobin. 2000. "The Liminal Effects of Social Movements: Red Guards and the Transformation of Identity." *Sociological Forum* 15 (September): 379–406.

Yang Xun. 2004. *Xinlu: Liangzhi de mingyun* (Ways of the Heart: The Fate of a Conscience). Beijing: Xinhua chubanshe.

Ye, Weili. 2006. "The Death of Bian Zhongyun." *Chinese Historical Review* 13 (Fall): 203–240.

Yin Hongbiao. 1996. "Hongweibing yundong de liangda chaoliu" (The Two Major Streams of the Red Guard Movement). Pp. 179–190 in *Wenhua da geming: Shishi yu yanjiu* (The Cultural Revolution: Evidence and Analysis), edited by Liu Qingfeng. Hong Kong: Zhongwen daxue chubanshe.

———. 1997. " 'Wenhua da geming' zhong de shehuixing maodun" (Social Contradictions in the "Cultural Revolution"). *Zhonggong dangshi yanjiu* 2: 77–82.

———. 1999. "Hongweibing yundong shuping" (An Overview of the Red Guard Movement). Pp. 688–723 in *Huishou "wen'ge": Zhongguo shinian "wen'ge" fenxi yu fansi* (The "Cultural Revolution" in Retrospect: Analysis and Reflections on China's Ten-Year "Cultural Revolution"), edited by Zhang Hua and Su Caiqing, 2 vols. Beijing: Zhonggong dangshi chubanshe.

Yong Wentao. 1995. "Zai 'hongweibing yundong' zhong" (Amid the "Red Guard Movement"). Pp. 4–14 in *Zhou Enlai de zuihou suiyue, 1966–1976* (Zhou Enlai's Final Years, 1966–1976), edited by An Jianshe. Beijing: Zhongyang wenxian chubanshe.

Yu Luojin. 1986. *A Chinese Winter's Tale.* Translated by Rachel May and Zhu Zhiyu. Hong Kong: Renditions.

Yu Luowen. 2000. *Wo jia* (My Family). Beijing: Zhongguo shehui kexue chubanshe.

Yu Shicheng, ed. 2003. *Shiyou daxue xiaoshi* (History of Petroleum University). Beijing: Shiyou daxue chubanshe.

Zhang Chengxian. 1999. " 'Wenhua da geming' chuqi de Beida gongzuozu" (Beijing University's Work Team in the Early Stages of the "Cultural Revolution"). *Zhonggong dangshi ziliao* 70 (June): 16–44.

Zhang Liqun, Zhang Ding, Yan Ruping, Tang Fei, and Li Gongtian. 2005. *Hu Yaobang zhuan, di yi juan (1915–1976)* (Biography of Hu Yaobang, vol. 1 [1915–1976]). Beijing: Renmin chubanshe, zhonggong dangshi chubanshe.

Zhao, Dingxin. 1998. "Ecologies of Social Movements: Student Mobilization during the 1989 Prodemocracy Movement in Beijing." *American Journal of Sociology* 103 (May): 1493–1529.

Zhao Pengda, ed. 2002. *Lijing tuzhi wushiqiu—Zhongguo dizhi daxue jianshi* (Fifty Years of Effort on Behalf of National Prosperity—A Brief History of the Chinese University of Geology). Wuhan: Zhongguo dizhi daxue chubanshe.

Zhejiang Provincial Party Committee Party School. 1984. "*Wenhua dageming*" *shiqi ziliao xuanji* (Selected Materials on the "Cultural Revolution" Period), December. Hangzhou: Zhonggong Zhejiang shengwei dangxiao dangshi jiaoyanshi.

Zheng, Xiaowei. 2006. "Passion, Reflection, and Survival: Political Choices of Red Guards at Qinghua University, June 1966–July 1968." Pp. 29–63 in *The Chinese Cultural Revolution as History,* edited by Joseph W. Esherick, Paul G. Pickowicz, and Andrew G. Walder. Stanford, Calif.: Stanford University Press.

Zhong Kan. 1982. *Kang Sheng pingzhuan* (Critical Biography of Kang Sheng). Beijing: Hongqi chubanshe.

Zhou Junlun, ed. 1999. *Nie Rongzhen nianpu* (Nie Rongzhen Chronology). Beijing: Renmin chubanshe.

Zhou Wanxiang, ed. 1996. *Beijing huagong xueyuan zhi (Beijing huagong daxue), 1958–1992* (Beijing Chemical Institute Annals [Beijing Chemical University], 1958–1992). Beijing: Huaxue gongye chubanshe.

Zhu Chengzhao. 1967. "Wode jiancha yu jiaodai" (My Self-Criticism and Confession), 15 August. Dongfanghong gongshe da pipan lianluozhan. Mimeographed.

Zhu Jinzhao, ed. 2002. *Beijing linye daxue xiaoshi, 1952–2002* (History of Beijing Forestry University, 1952–2002). Beijing: Zhongguo linye chubanshe.

Zuo, Jiping, and Robert D. Benford. 1995. "Mobilization Processes and the 1989 Chinese Democracy Movement." *Sociological Quarterly* 36 (Winter): 131–156.

# INDEX

*Note:* Page numbers followed by *t* indicate tables.

Printed in the USA
CPSIA information can be obtained
at www.ICGtesting.com
CBHW010444041223
2266CB00002B/50

9 780674 064133